T0303332

BEST-KEPT SECRETS OF

ALASKA

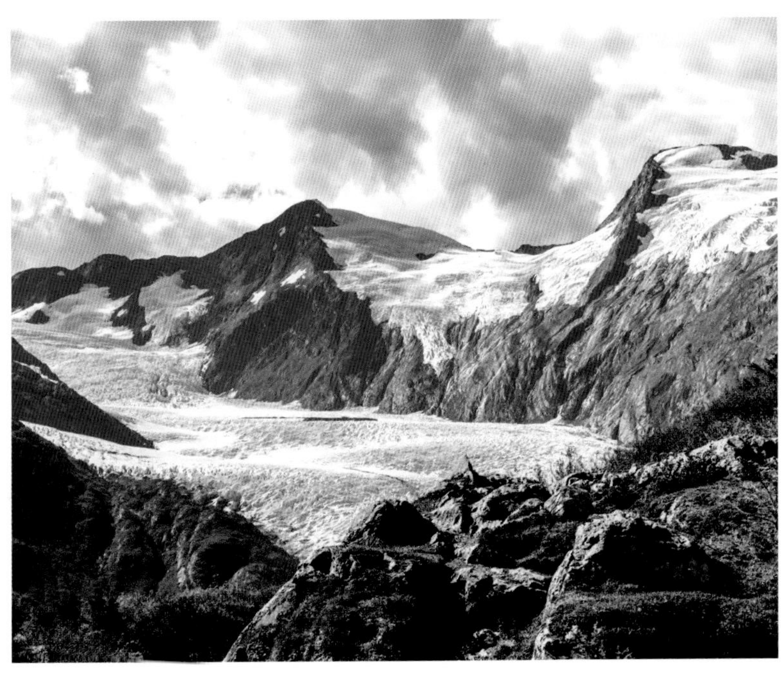

Publisher and Creative Director: Nick Wells
Commissioning Editor: Polly Prior
Art Director: Mike Spender
Layout Design: Jane Ashley
Copy Editor: Claire Rogers

Special thanks to: Catherine Taylor, Taylor Bentley, Dawn Laker, Helen Snaith.

FLAME TREE PUBLISHING
6 Melbray Mews
London SW6 3NS
United Kingdom

www.flametreepublishing.com

First published 2019

19 21 23 22 20
1 3 5 7 9 10 8 6 4 2

A CIP record for this book is available from the British Library upon request.

Courtesy of and © **SuperStock**/Sunny Awazuhara-Reed/Alaska Stock-Design Pics: 47. Courtesy of **Shutterstock.com** and © the following contributors: 12, 13, 65, 101, 108, 145, 156 Michelle Holihan; 14, 18, 26, 27 Reimar; 15 chris_dagorne; 17 Anita Warren-Hampson; 19 Dhanachote Vongprasert; 21, 39 Troutnut; 22 375Ultramag; 23 R. Vickers; 25, 80 FloridaStock; 28, 33 Bob Pool; 29 Danita Delmont; 30 T.M. Urban; 32 Lloyd Wallin Photography; 35 Nickolas warner; 36 Steven Randel; 37 Digital Producto Media; 40 Kyle Waters; 41 Olga Khrustaleva; 44, 121 Ovidiu Hrubaru; 45, 48, 71, 98 Uwe Bergwitz; 46, 58, 60, 61, 64, 96 Pecold; 50 Ethan Helgager; 51 youli zhao; 52, 86 EQRoy; 53, 54, 56 Gary Whitton; 55 Leeweh; 57 travellife18; 62, 143 Jef Wodniack; 63 Ralf Broskvar; 66, 85 Tracey Mendenhall Porreca; 68, 138 Richard Seeley; 69 Emma Rogers; 70 Jonathan A. Mauer; 73 Amine Abassir; 74 Terry W Ryder; 75, 82 Joseph Sohm; 76 Dara J; 77 gary yim; 83 Rob Crandall; 88 Fitawoman; 89 norikko; 90 Jacob Player; 91 Ludmila Ruzickova; 92, 118 Tomasz Wozniak; 95 Frank Fichtmueller; 97, 115 Menno Schaefer; 99, 154 Robert Szymanski; 100, 131 Rocky Grimes; 103 Susan R. Serna; 104 A.Hornung; 105 Flaxphotos; 106 Victoria Ditkovsky; 107, 159 Andrea Izzotti; 109 vagabond54; 110 akphotoc; 111 Amanda Wayne; 112 Iuliia Sheliepova; 114, 124, 175 CSNafzger; 116 Pete Niesen; 117, 136, 137, 153 M. Cornelius; 120 Mhgstan; 122, 123 Jay Yuan; 125 Jesse Hasup; 129 Todamo; 130 Snafzger; 132 Benny Marty; 133 inEthos Design; 134 Jiri Kulisek; 139 Jo Crebbin; 140 aarbois; 141 Gillian Santink; 142, 161 emperorcosar; 144 takmat71; 147 MH Anderson Photography; 148 NancyS; 149 Chad Zubar; 150 Maridav; 152 Lee Prince; 155 Steve Faber; 157 Ramunas Bruzas; 158 Salparadis; 160 Chuckyboy31; 164 Jorge Moro; 165 Hal Brindley; 166 Alaska Wanderer; 167 liveyourlife; 168 Lori Ellis; 169, 183 Photovolcania.com; 170, 187 Terence Mendoza; 171 Melissamn; 172 Gudkov Andrey; 174, 176 Warren Metcalf; 177 kojich; 178, 179 Nick Pecker; 180 sirtravelalot; 182 photomatz; 184, 188 Daniel Briem; 185 Ruben M Ramos; 186 Peter Leahy; 189 Kerrin Ingwersen.

ISBN 978-1-78755-776-5

Printed in China | Created, Developed & Produced in the United Kingdom

BEST-KEPT SECRETS OF
ALASKA

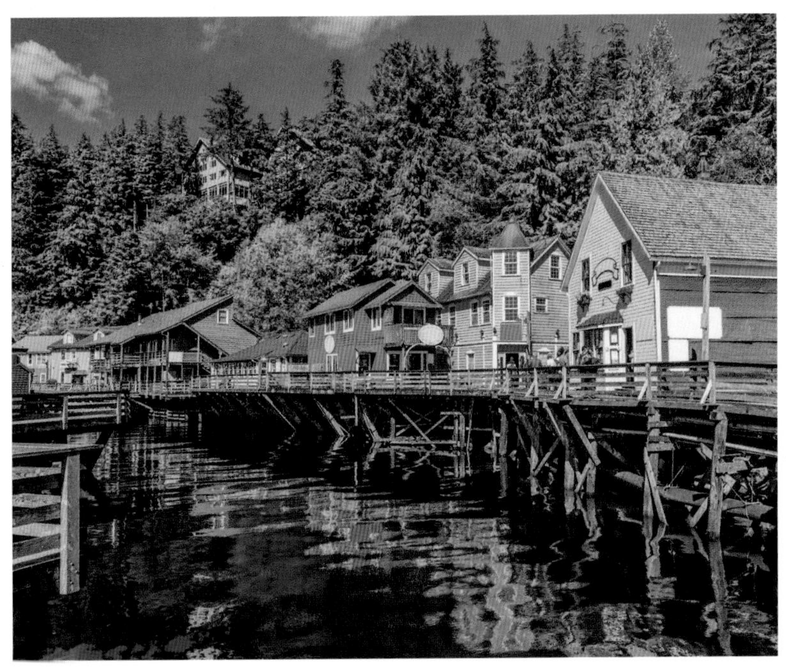

MICHAEL KERRIGAN

FLAME TREE
PUBLISHING

CONTENTS

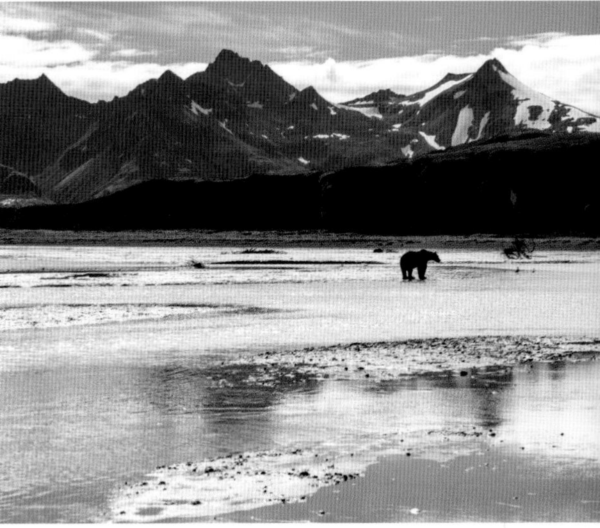

INTRODUCTION

'One learns that the world, though made, is yet being made. That this is still the morning of creation. That mountains, long conceived, are now being born, brought to light by the glaciers, channels traced for coming rivers, basins hollowed for lakes.' John Muir (1838–1914) is famous as the father of the United States' National Parks – and, arguably, of the modern environmental movement as a whole. Dunbar-born Muir brought a Scots-Presbyterian seriousness to his studies of nature and geology; and a religious reverence to his response to the great outdoors. What he was able to appreciate in the wilds of Alaska was that Nature was not just a static 'scene' but a dynamic process.

Up to a point this is obvious and always true: in any environment we see cycles of life and death and reproduction; of erosion and deposit; decay and natural growth. In Alaska, though, the most basic structures of nature are being built before our eyes. Volcanic activity is literally bringing new rocks, new landforms into being; glaciers, creeping at an immensely slow and yet still-measurable speed down open mountainsides, are shaping the landscapes of the future in real time. And all against a background of Edenic emptiness. Granted, the state has a population approaching three quarters of a million now. So vast is it, however, covering an area of 1.7 million square km (660,000 square miles), that all those people could be spread out very thinly. Overall population density for the state struggles to reach 0.5 (people) per square km (1.1 per square mile). Given that 290,000 of those people live in Anchorage alone, that leaves an awful lot of empty space.

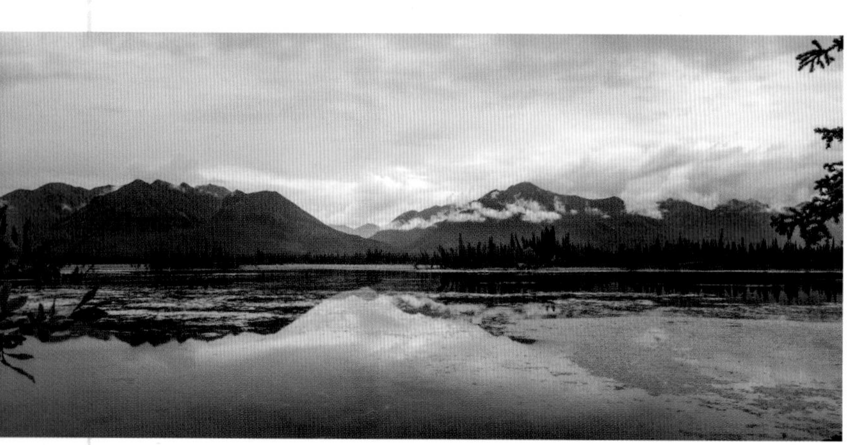

What of an Adam and Eve for this Eden? Hard as it may be to believe now, Alaska did play a pivotal role in the peopling of the Americas. At the height of the last glaciation, 20,000 years ago, much of the world's moisture was locked up in ice and the sea level was anything up to 120 m (400 ft) lower than it is today. One consequence of this is that the Bering Sea did not exist. Instead, a wide grassy plain extended between eastern Siberia and Alaska. The landmass we think of as North America was broader, too, spreading well beyond its present shoreline to take in a great deal of the continental shelf. The whole history of human life in the Americas is believed to have begun in Beringia, when early peoples migrated across this dry land bridge. To take up Muir's metaphor again, if humanity was not actually created in Alaska, it certainly had an important 'morning' here.

The word 'migration' is maybe misleading for what was surely an extremely gradual, trans-generational and almost certainly unconscious and uncoordinated movement. Its participants were a multitude of unconnected communities whose lifestyles as hunter-gatherers were inherently nomadic. They relocated all but constantly as they followed caribou or musk-ox herds or prospected for fresh-berry or shellfish stocks. It is unlikely, then, that they saw themselves as 'migrating' anywhere – in hindsight, though, from our modern perspective, that is what they did. Ultimately, as generations passed and they pressed onward, they populated the Americas, from British Columbia to the Amazon; from Martha's Vineyard to Tierra del Fuego.

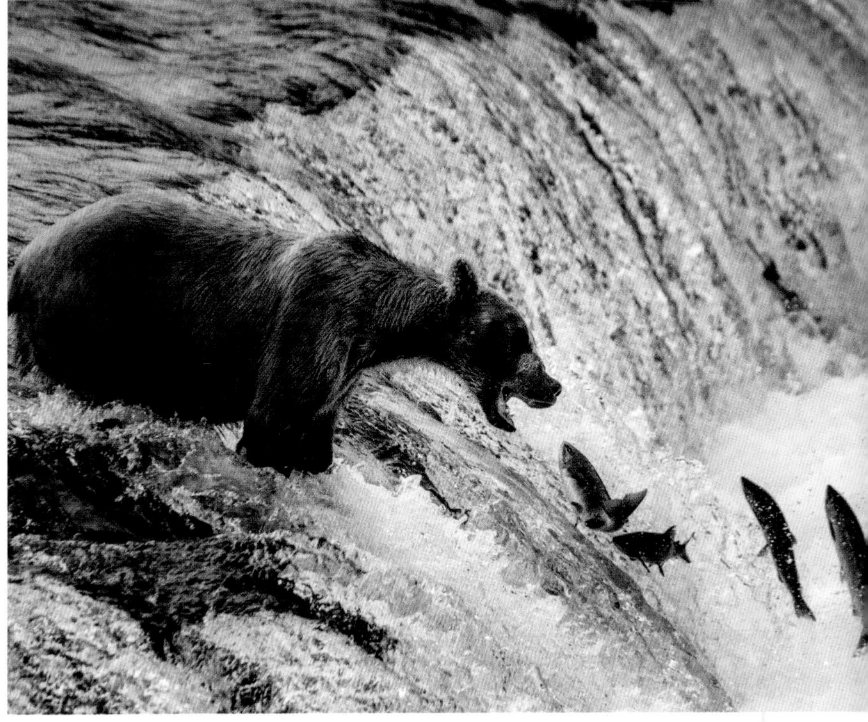

That this migration took place is indirectly attested by archaeological finds from throughout the Americas, starting a little further south, and dating from around 16,000 years ago. The lack of more immediate evidence in Alaska proper is accounted for by the fact that, at a time of heavy glaciation in the upland interior, people on the move would naturally have kept to the coastal plain – an area which has now, of course, been seabed for centuries. It is believed that Alaska's Native peoples came across from Siberia by the same route, but in a later wave. Maybe a much later wave: they might well have island-hopped their way here after the sea level had once more risen. The Aleuts of Alaska's far south-west have certainly been coast dwellers, comfortable at sea; so have many of the Iñupiat, an Inuit people of the Arctic North. The Yupiit of central Alaska, close kin with people to be found in eastern Siberia, also seem to have arrived by sea, and expanded into the interior up the river system.

Subsequent incomers were also to approach Alaska from the ocean. Russian merchants had been coming to the outlying islands to trade for furs for a few decades before more formal exploration began with the Englishman Captain James Cook (1728–79). He came here in 1778 in the course of his third expedition to the Pacific, just beating the Spanish commander Juan Francisco de la Bodega y Quadra (1744–94), who sailed this way in 1779. The appearance of potential competitors may

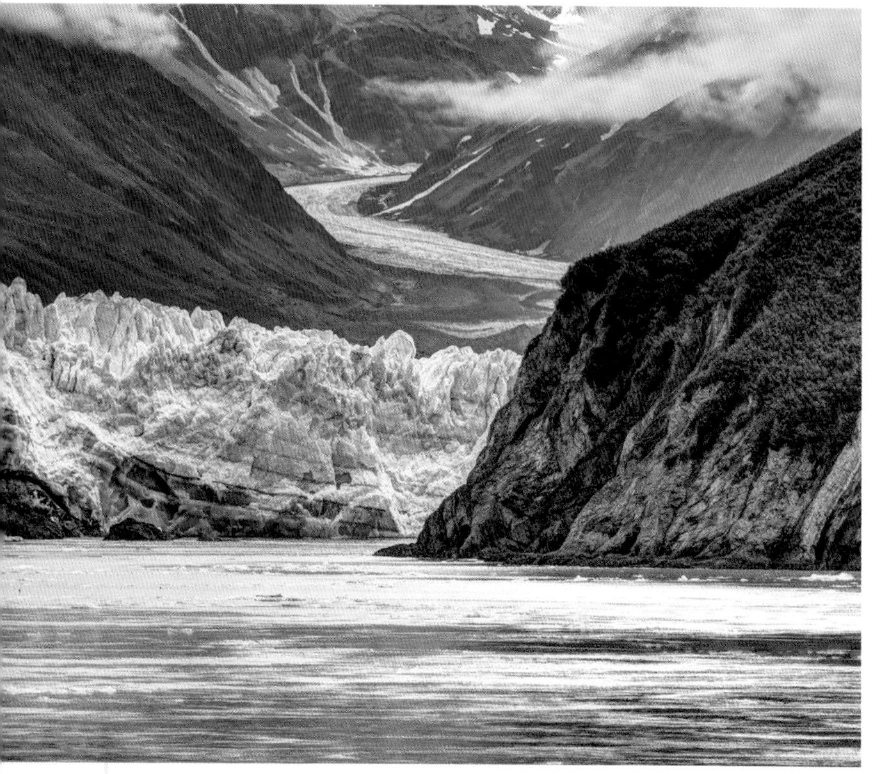

possibly have helped to galvanize the Russians, who began actively to colonize this coast.

Even then, they did not venture any distance inland. There were no rich farmlands to tempt long-term settlers. Here for furs, the Russians for the most part simply dropped anchor in estuaries or sheltered bays and let hunters from the interior come to them downriver. Over time, though, their operations did expand. By 1784 they had set up a permanent trading post on Kodiak Island. Others were to follow as the years went by. Missionaries came, converting many of Alaska's peoples to Orthodox Christianity and initiating them into their version of European culture. By 1804, there was a colonial capital at New Archangel (now Sitka; *see* page 156).

The idea of a Russian America did not seem quite so counter-intuitive as it does these days (when the geographical incongruity has been underscored by memories of the US–Soviet Cold War). Granted, Alaska was on a different continent from its imperial proprietor, but then Canada was much further from England, its far-northwestern regions scarcely explored, let alone settled or brought to British order. Even so, it was clear by the middle of the nineteenth century that Alaska was not adding greatly to Russian prosperity or power, so in 1867 they sold the territory to the United States.

Many Americans were not happy at the $7.2 million price of the Alaska Purchase when it went through, and for several decades their scepticism seemed well-founded. It was not the remoteness of what was now called the 'Department of Alaska', or even its ambiguous administrative status, that bothered them. Much of the modern Midwest had yet to be taken formally in hand. (We are reminded of this situation in the decision of Huckleberry Finn at the end of Mark Twain's (1835–1910) novel to 'light out for the Territory', beyond the Mississippi River, at that time technically an 'Unorganized Sovereign Territory of the United States'.) The question was one of how valuable an acquisition Alaska had been. Furs and fish apart, it was not a draw to new settlers in the way the rolling expanses of the Great Plains – wheatfields in waiting – clearly were.

The discovery of gold was to change all that – albeit only very slowly at first, with isolated finds by pioneering prospectors in the early 1890s. By the end of the century, though, the Gold Rush was in full swing. Many of the tens of thousands of men and women pouring into Alaska through this period were merely in transit: the Klondike, where the richest of the finds were concentrated, was across the border in Canada's Yukon. Even so, the US Territory's economic geography was radically reconceived in response to this influx of travellers, ports like Skagway expanding and a network of trails (and, subsequently, railways) taking shape. Besides, major finds were being made on Alaskan soil as well, as prospectors fanned out across the country. Boomtowns arose – even if, in most cases, they quickly fell.

The campaign for statehood gathered momentum in the years following the Second World War, in which, of course, the Aleutians had been a theatre (or at least a sideshow) of fighting. The immediate commencement of the Cold War in 1945 only heightened Alaska's strategic importance, close as it was to the Soviet Union across the Bering Strait. It was not a wave of patriotic fellowship, however – or even a geopolitical calculation – that finally precipitated the Americans to embrace their territory. Oil was discovered at Kenai's Swanson River on 19 July 1957, and on 4 July the following year President Eisenhower (1890–1969) signed the Alaska Statehood Act. The new state, the 49th (Hawaii would make up the half-century in August 1959), was born amid another boom, then. It has never really had to look back since. It has, however, had to work hard to reconcile its mineral wealth with its natural inheritance. That has not always been an easy balance to maintain.

Ultimately, though, while his environmentalist disciples have had their concerns, John Muir's description of Alaska has held up well. Or, rather, his acknowledged inability to describe it: 'Fain would I describe the glories of those months in the ice-world – the beautiful and terrible network of crevasses, the clustering pinnacles, the thousand streams ringing and gurgling in azure channels cut in the living body of the glacier, the glorious radiance of sunbeams falling on crystal dale and hill, the rosy glow of the dawn and sunset, the march of the clouds on the mountains, and the mysterious splendor of the auroras when the nights grow long … But this would require a volume, while here I have only space to add – Go to Alaska, go and see.'

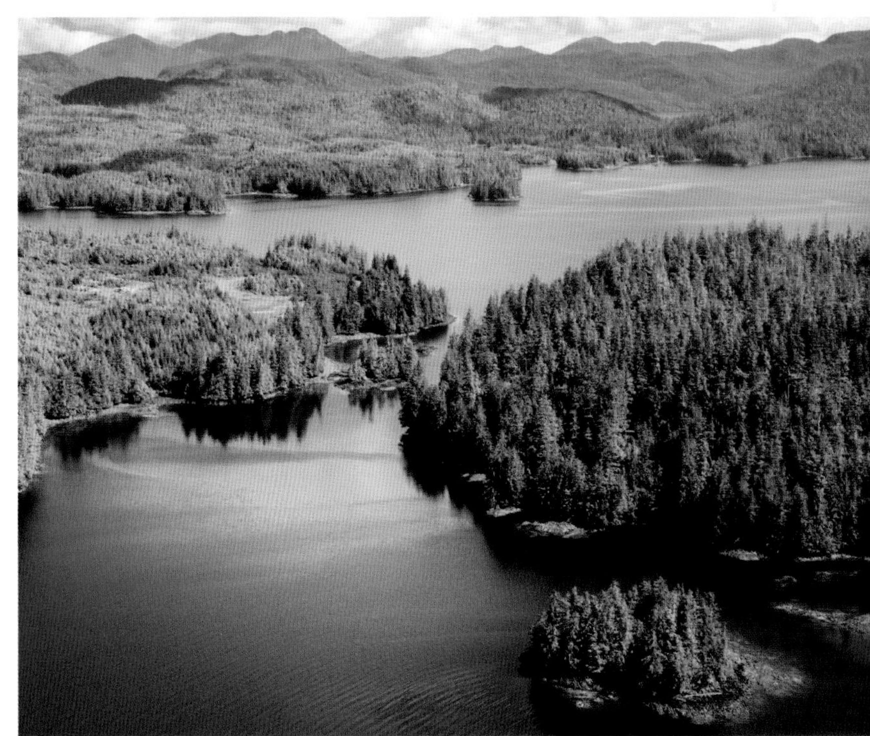

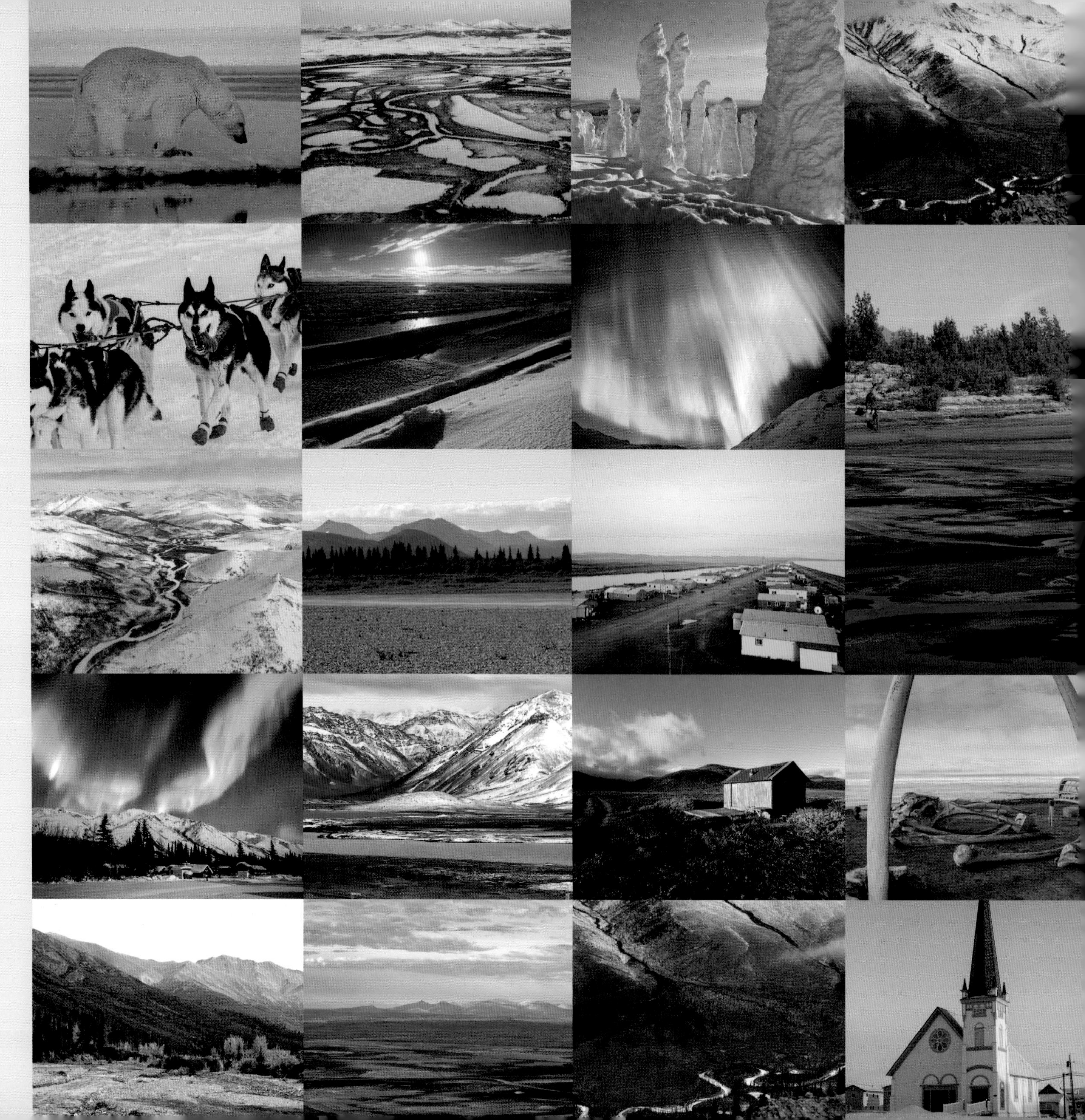

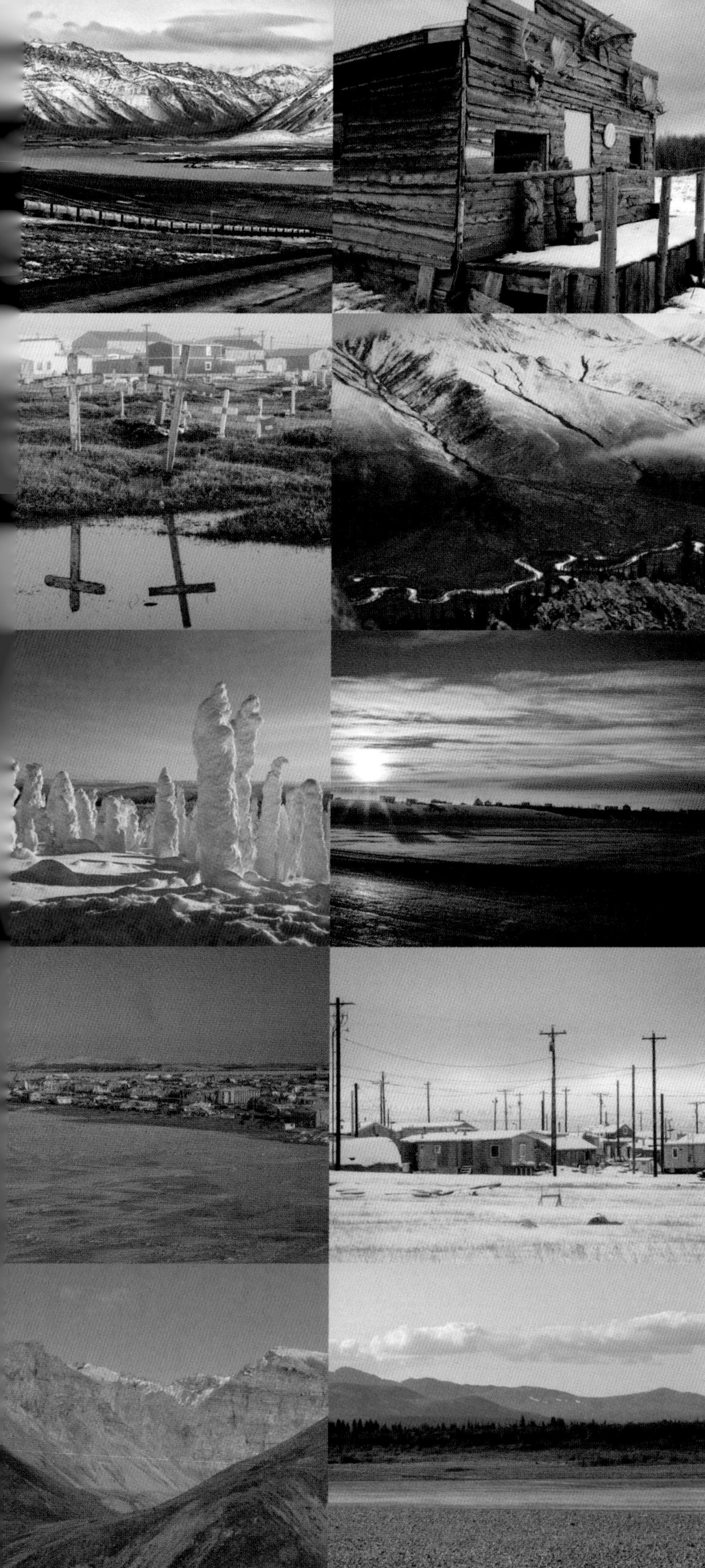

ARCTIC ALASKA

Rugged, austere, harsh and hostile … such are the terms in which Alaska's Arctic North is typically characterized. And, as far as it goes, that is fair enough. Temperatures up here barely break into positive figures at the very height of summer, plunging to –40°C/F or lower in the coldest months. It can snow at any time of year, and as for the much-vaunted 'midnight sun' of summer, that is, of course, counterposed by months of unrelenting winter gloom.

For the most part, the earth is icebound: when the warmer weather comes, the first few centimetres from the surface do thaw for a few short weeks and the tundra bursts into flower and fruit. But the summer is over all too soon, to be replaced by deepening dark and chill. Life here seems to be hanging by a thread. In human terms, then, this is indeed an environment to be feared. Its Iñupiat people have survived here for so many centuries only by developing very special skills. And yet, to represent this region so negatively is to miss not only its breathtaking beauty but its great fragility; its vulnerability before a range of immensely serious environmental threats.

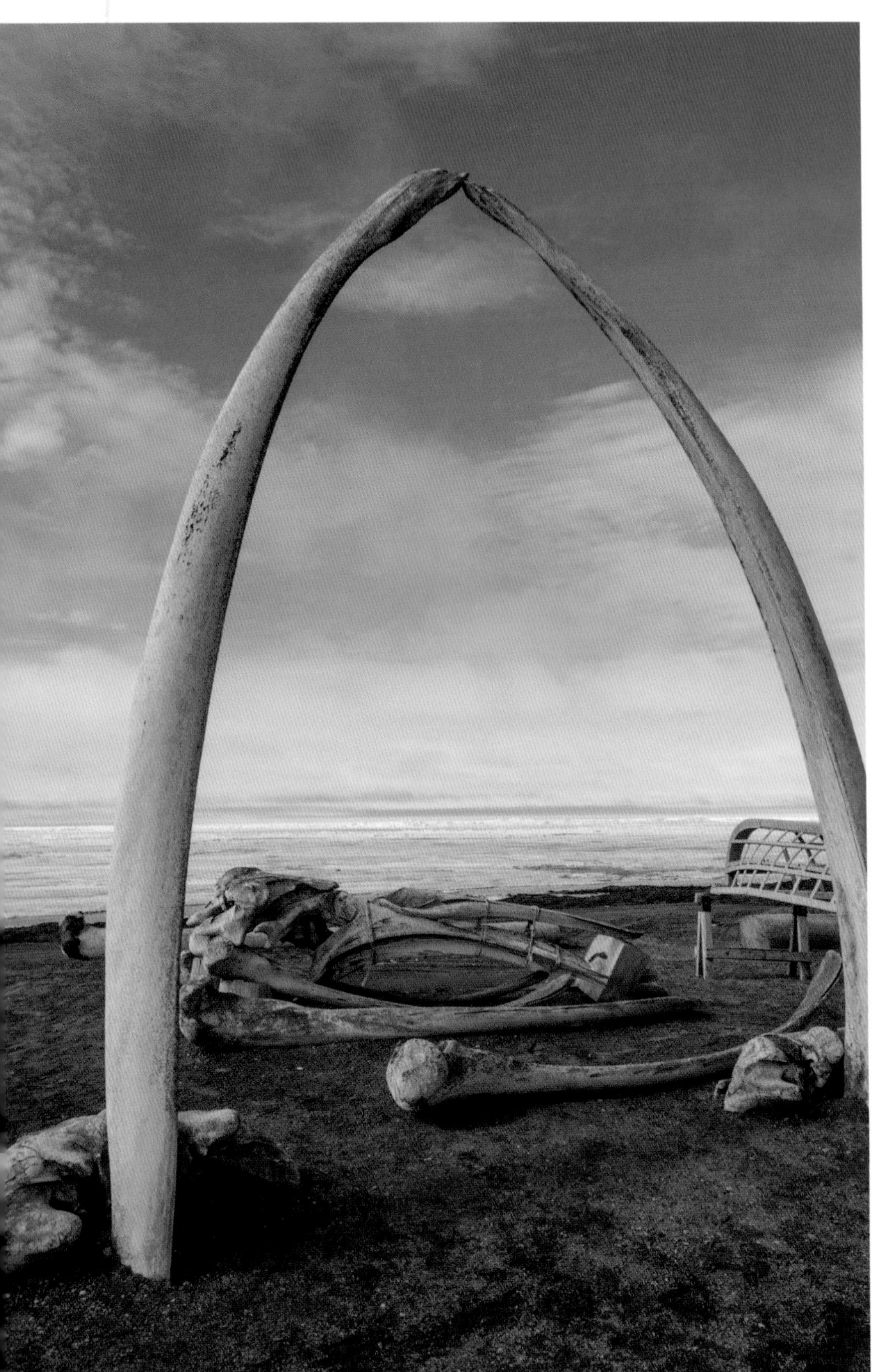

WHALE BONE ARCH, UTQIAGVIK

Arctic

Set in its own little park of whalebone, a pair of arching jawbones makes a fittingly dramatic portal for Alaska's Arctic North. With a population of just over 4,000, Utqiagvik does duty as the capital of Alaska's North Slope. For a century or so it was known as Barrow, in honour of a now-little-known nineteenth-century British aristocrat who had promoted exploration of the region. The decision by its citizens in 2016 to give it this Iñupiat name ('A Place for Picking Wild Roots') marked an important shift in their cultural and political priorities.

CEMETERY, UTQIAGVIK

Arctic

Crosses lean at crazy angles where the soggy surface layer of the tundra has thawed in the summer heat. Permafrost preserves the dead from decaying underneath. The normal rules of human existence, of life and death, do not necessarily prevail up here in the Arctic, a unique – and in many ways mysterious – environment. Even harder to assess is the impact that the gathering climate crisis is going to have. The idea of 'global warming' may seem remote to the point of ridiculousness here, but is the permafrost as permanent as we have always assumed?

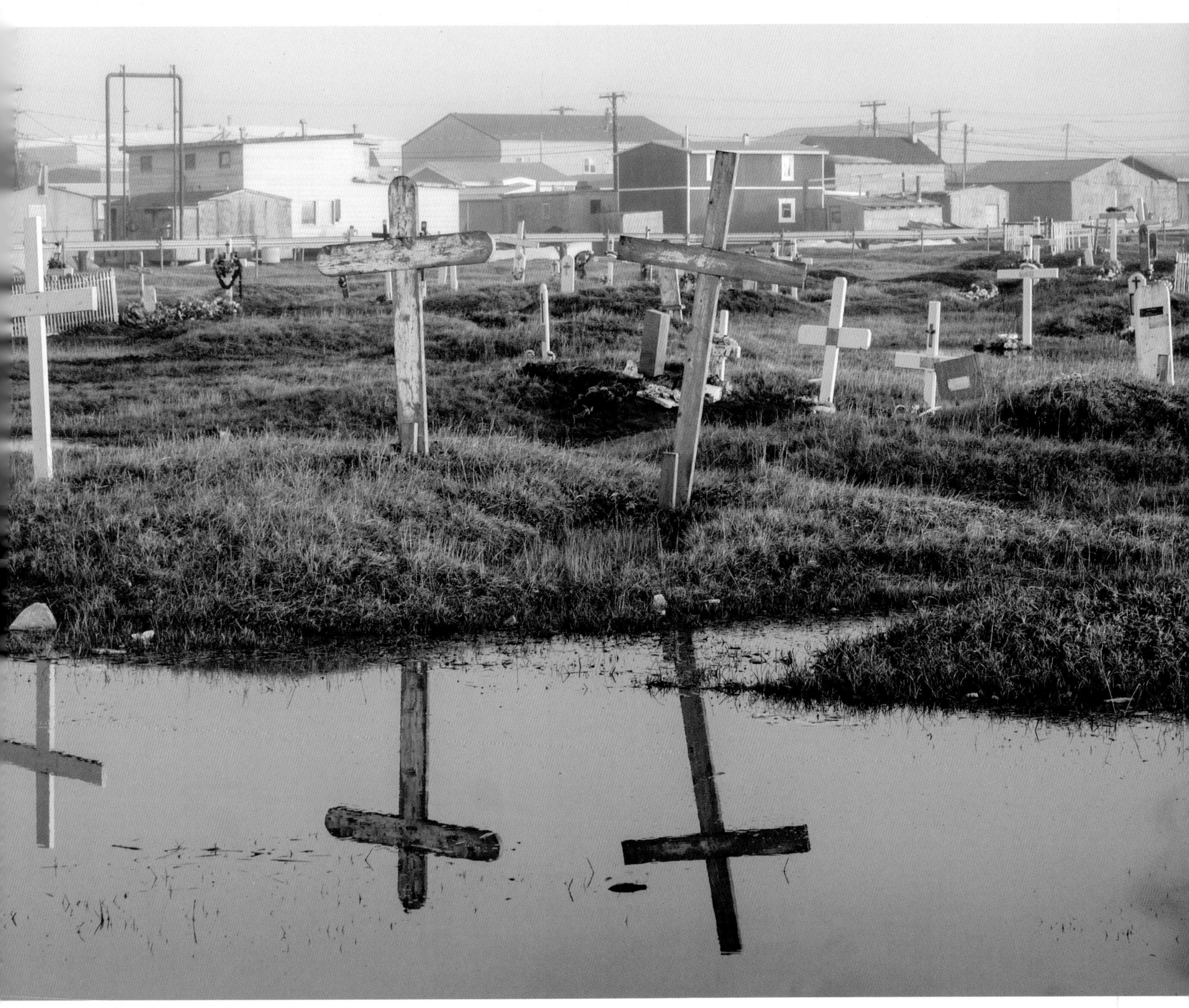

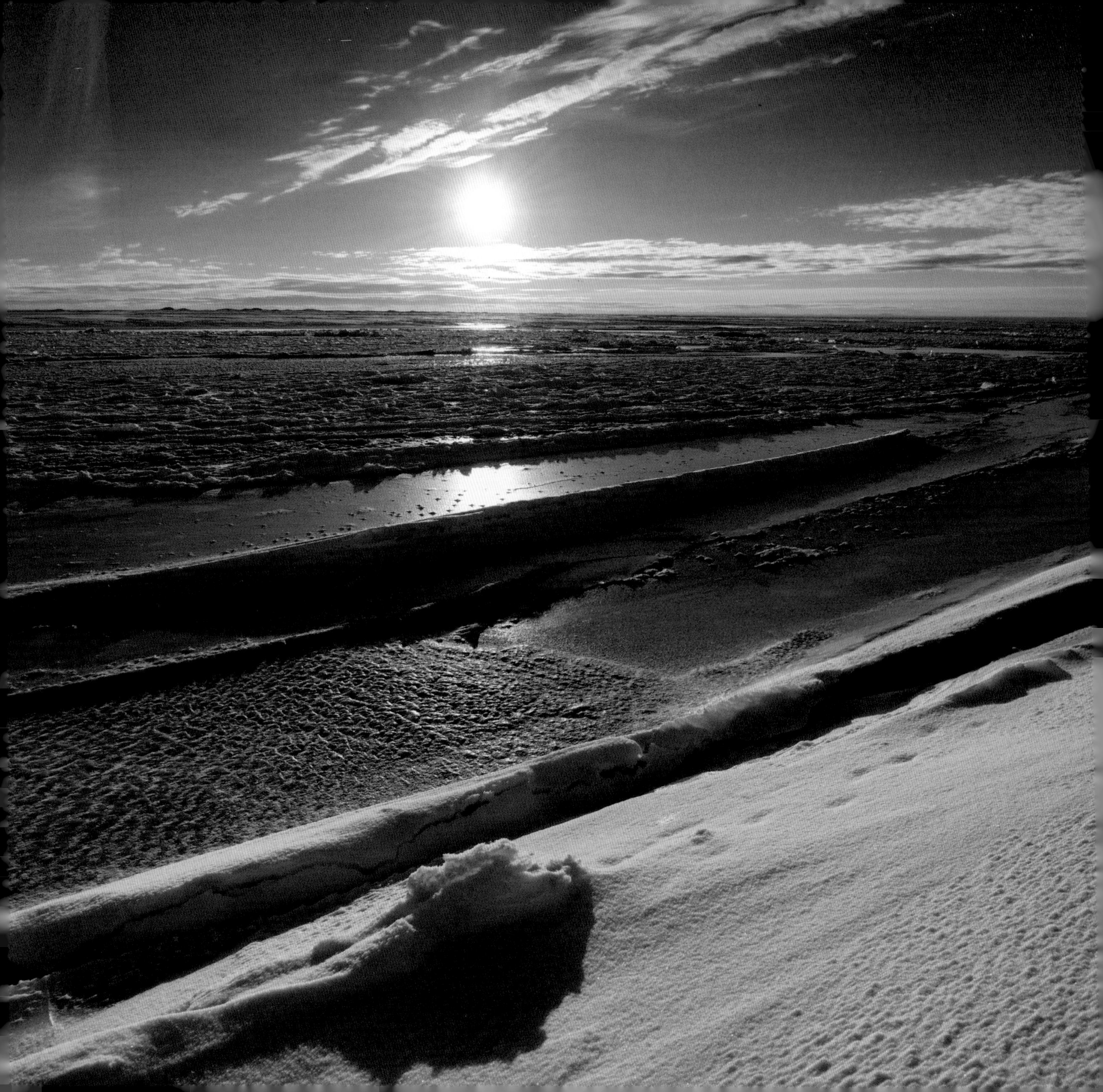

SEA ICE, PRUDHOE BAY

Arctic

Having risen in the Brooks Range (*see* pages 22–27), the Sagavanirktok ('Sag') River snakes its way across the North Slope all the way down to the Beaufort Sea. At 70°19'32"N, Prudhoe Bay, where it emerges, is northerly even by Alaska standards. And so, we see this scene, which could hardly be more stereotypically 'Arctic': the coastline blurred beneath a cloak of snow; the sea surface curdled with congregating ice floes; and all eerily illuminated by the creeping rays of a low sun.

HOUSES, KAKTOVIK

Arctic

Telegraph poles tower above functional-looking single-storey huts in Kaktovik, a tiny Iñupiat settlement clinging to the coast of Barter Island. The symbolism is strong: we all want to stay in touch, maybe, but out here – hundreds of miles from the next significant settlement, marooned amidst ice and snow and sea and more ice – it is that much more important to keep in contact with the world. Caribou hunting and whaling were always the economic mainstay here; the latter has been replaced by tourism in recent years.

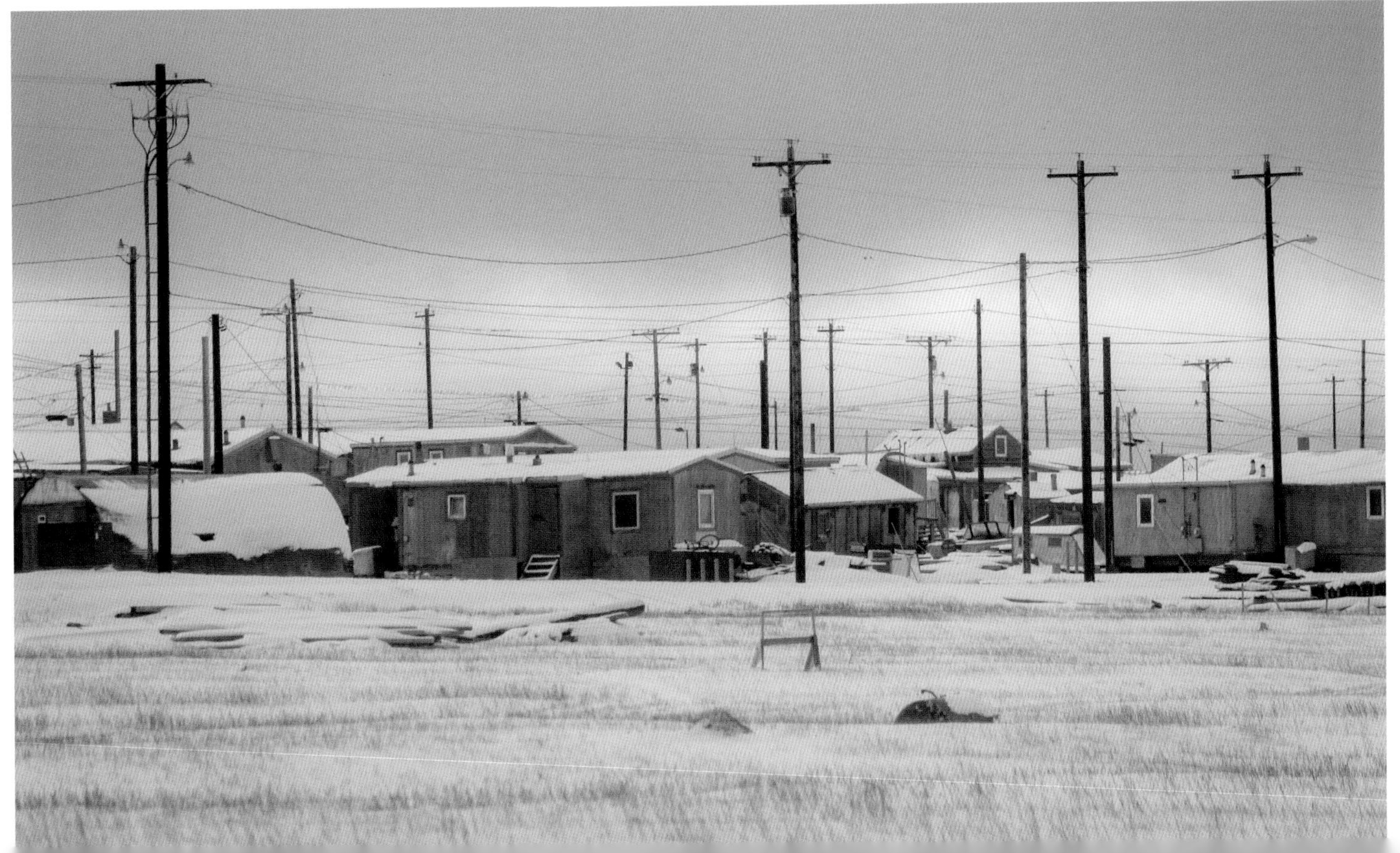

'ENCHANTED FOREST', ARCTIC CIRCLE

Arctic

Over and over again, in Arctic Alaska, it is brought home to us how precarious existence is, how fine the knife edge is on which we balance between life and death. Like fairytale princesses imprisoned by some witch's spell, these trees stand cloaked in frozen snow, 'locked in' for months on end by the winter freeze. What can they do but endure, patiently awaiting the moment when the spring thaw comes and – however briefly – they are released again? And yet how joyful that liberation will surely be when it is attained!

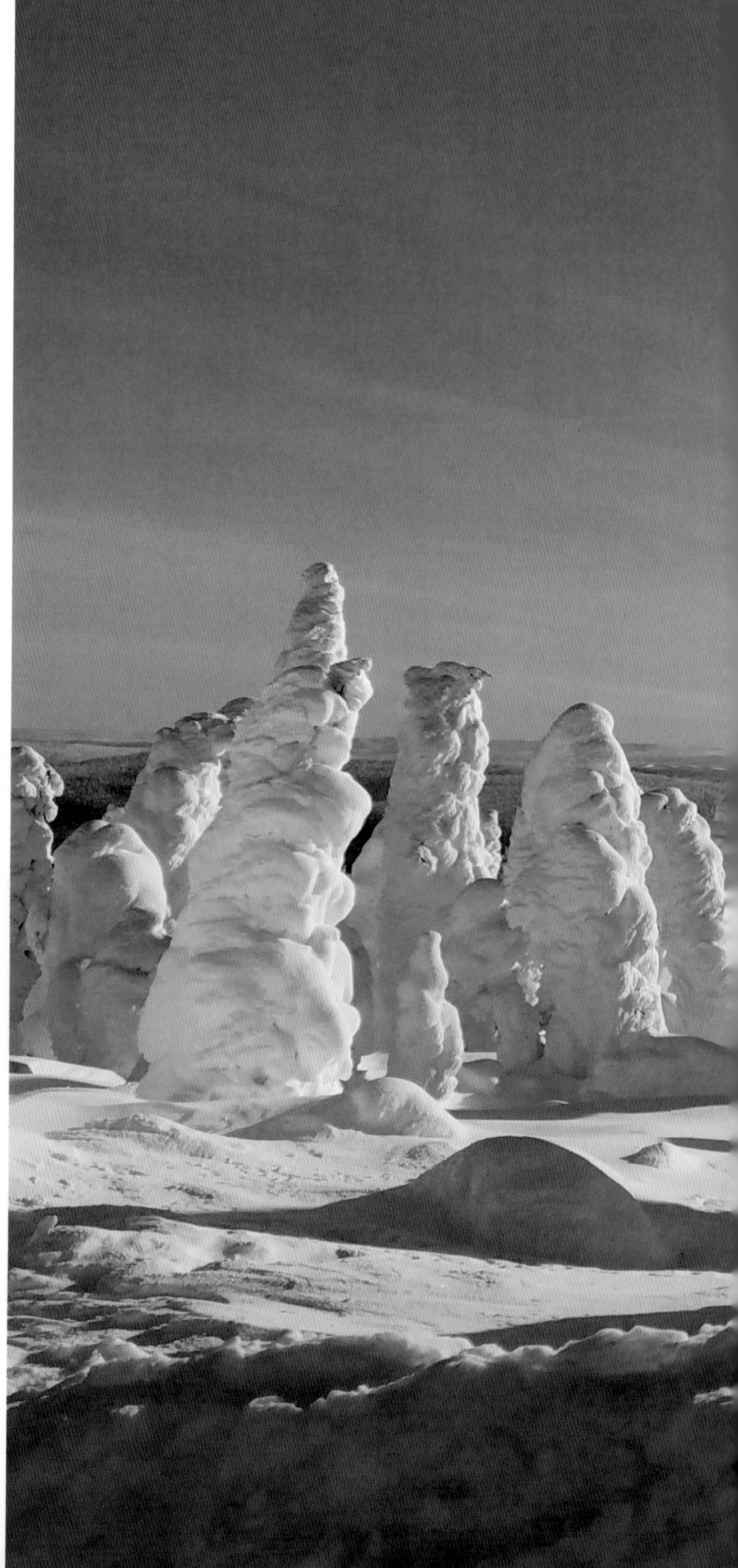

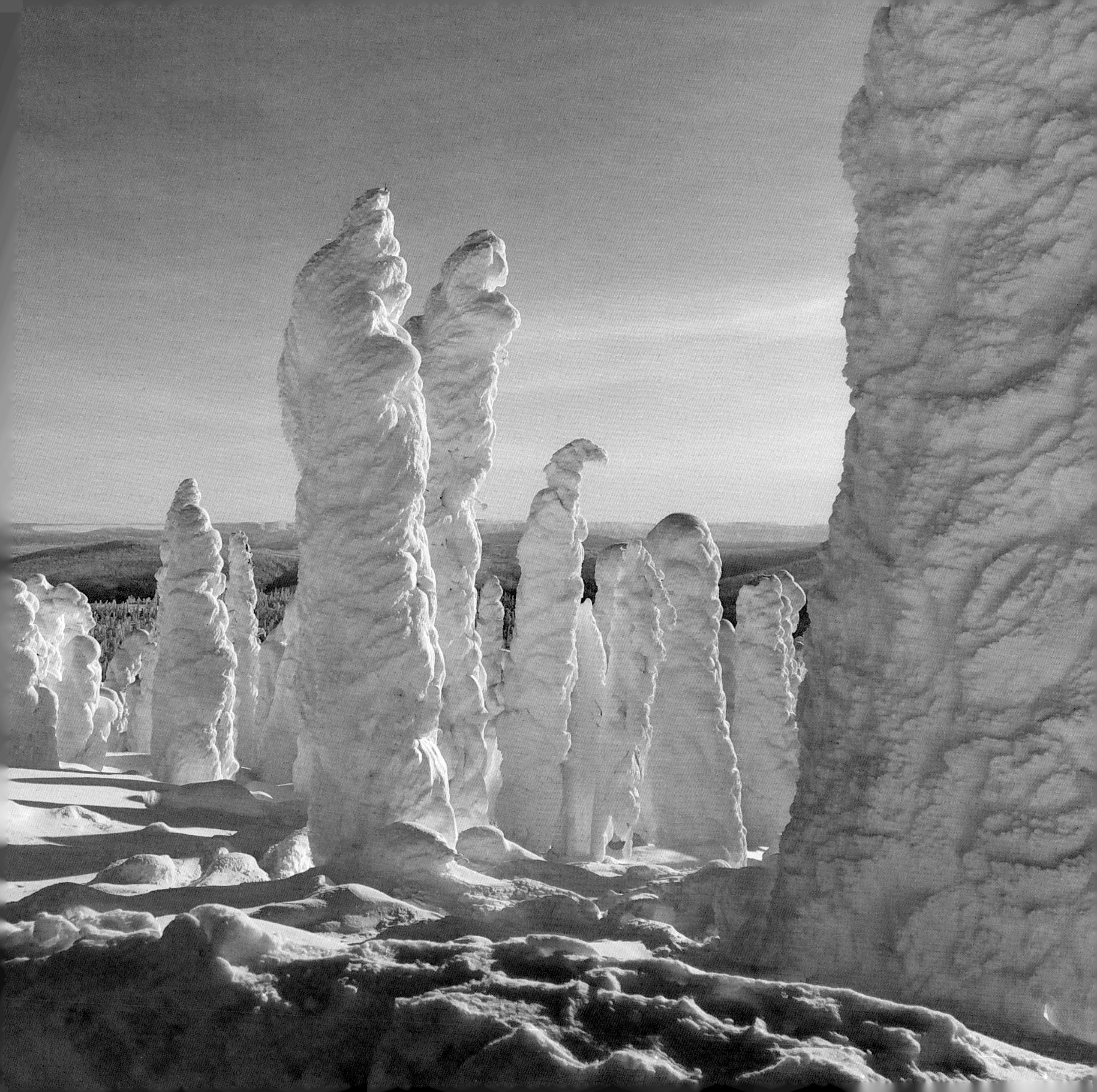

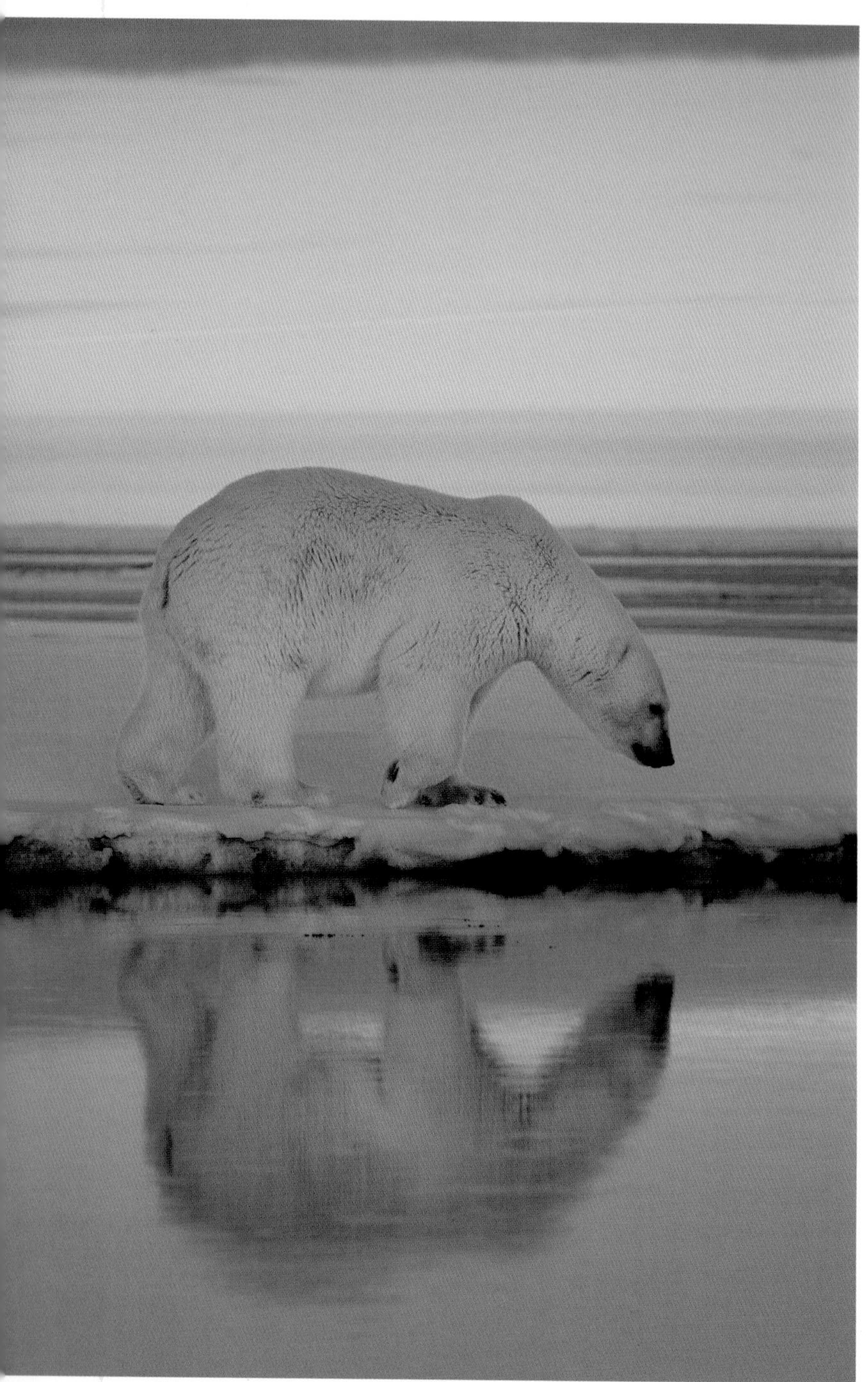

POLAR BEAR, BARTER ISLAND, KAKTOVIK

Arctic

It is not one of the state's official symbols, but the polar bear may still be seen as emblematizing Alaska, in both its exhilarating beauty and its endangered status. Like Alaska, it is big and frightening (polar bears are quite capable of aggression on occasion); like Alaska it is deeply vulnerable. Numbers in the southern Beaufort Sea declined by 40 per cent between 2001 and 2010 alone. One of Kaktovik's outstanding tourist 'draws' these days is the opportunity the place provides for seeing this thrilling creature in the wild.

AURORA BOREALIS, DALTON HIGHWAY

Arctic

A spectacular lightshow fills the sky. We may scarcely see the sun itself for much of the year in these Arctic latitudes, but that does not mean its benefits are not felt at all. For it is from the sun that charged particles are blown this way by a solar wind, colliding with atoms of oxygen, nitrogen and other gases in the earth's upper atmosphere. They flash in a range of colours – bright, evanescent and enchanting – in the phenomenon known as the aurora borealis or the 'northern lights'.

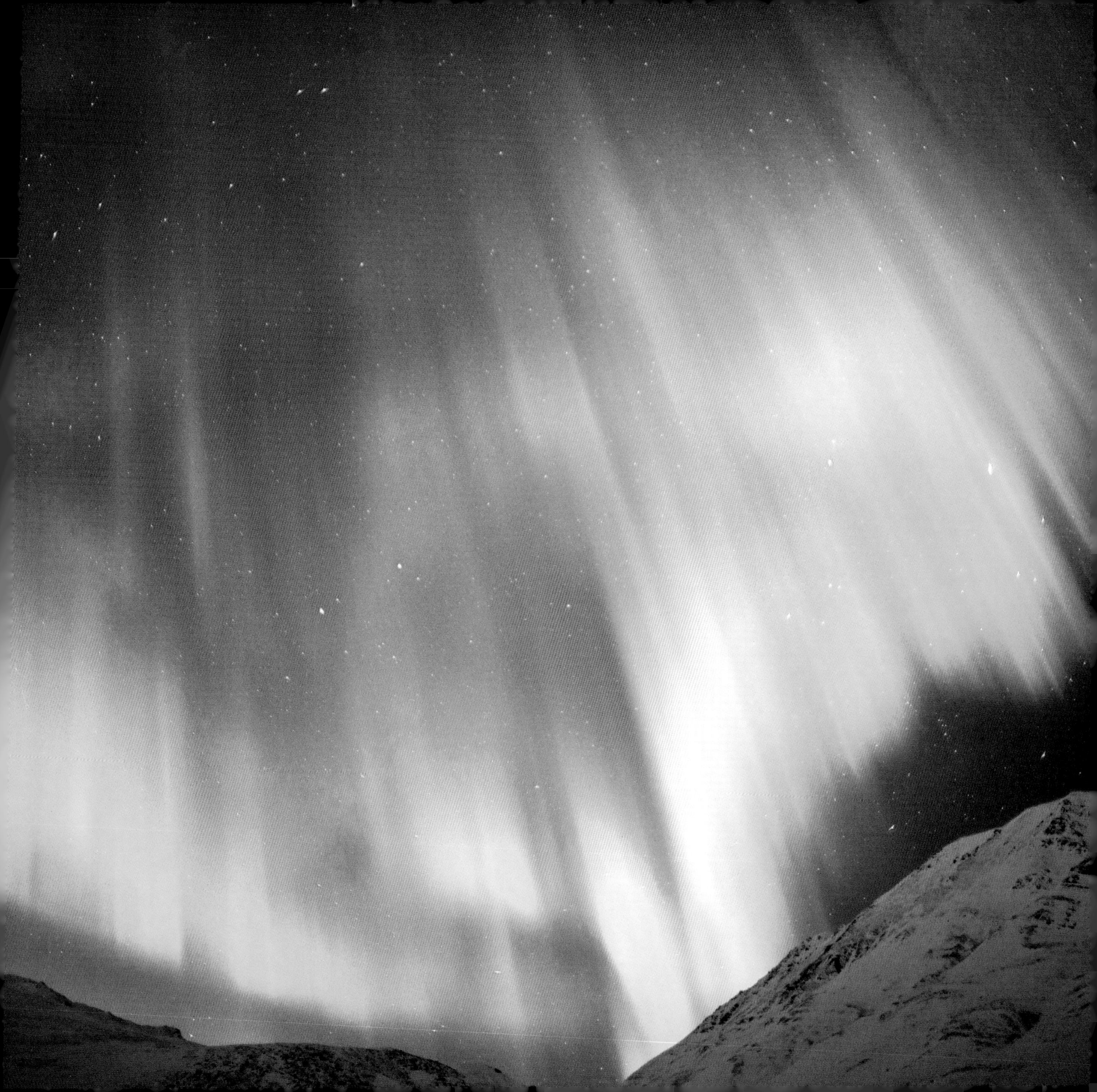

TRANS-ALASKAN PIPELINE, DALTON HIGHWAY

Arctic

Anywhere else, one might naturally assume that this important oil pipeline had been built along the line of the highway. But this is Alaska, where the mineral-extraction cart is invariably placed before the historical horse. The Dalton Highway is the main road across the North Slope, cutting straight inland, due south from Prudhoe Bay, until it links up with the Elliott Highway, north of Fairbanks. It was built to facilitate maintenance to the pipeline. Alaska's modern history has centred on a succession of mineral manias, from the nineteenth-century Gold Rush to the oil boom.

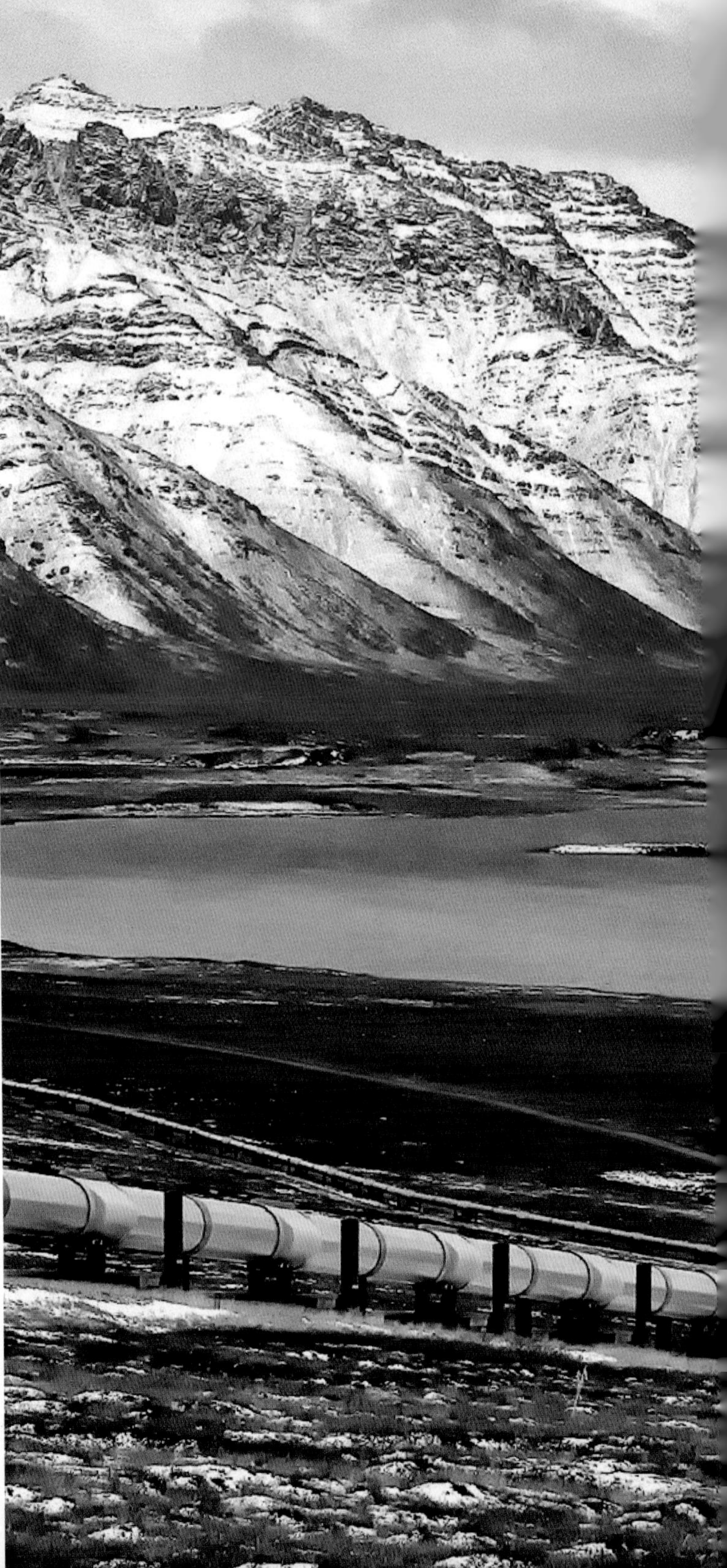

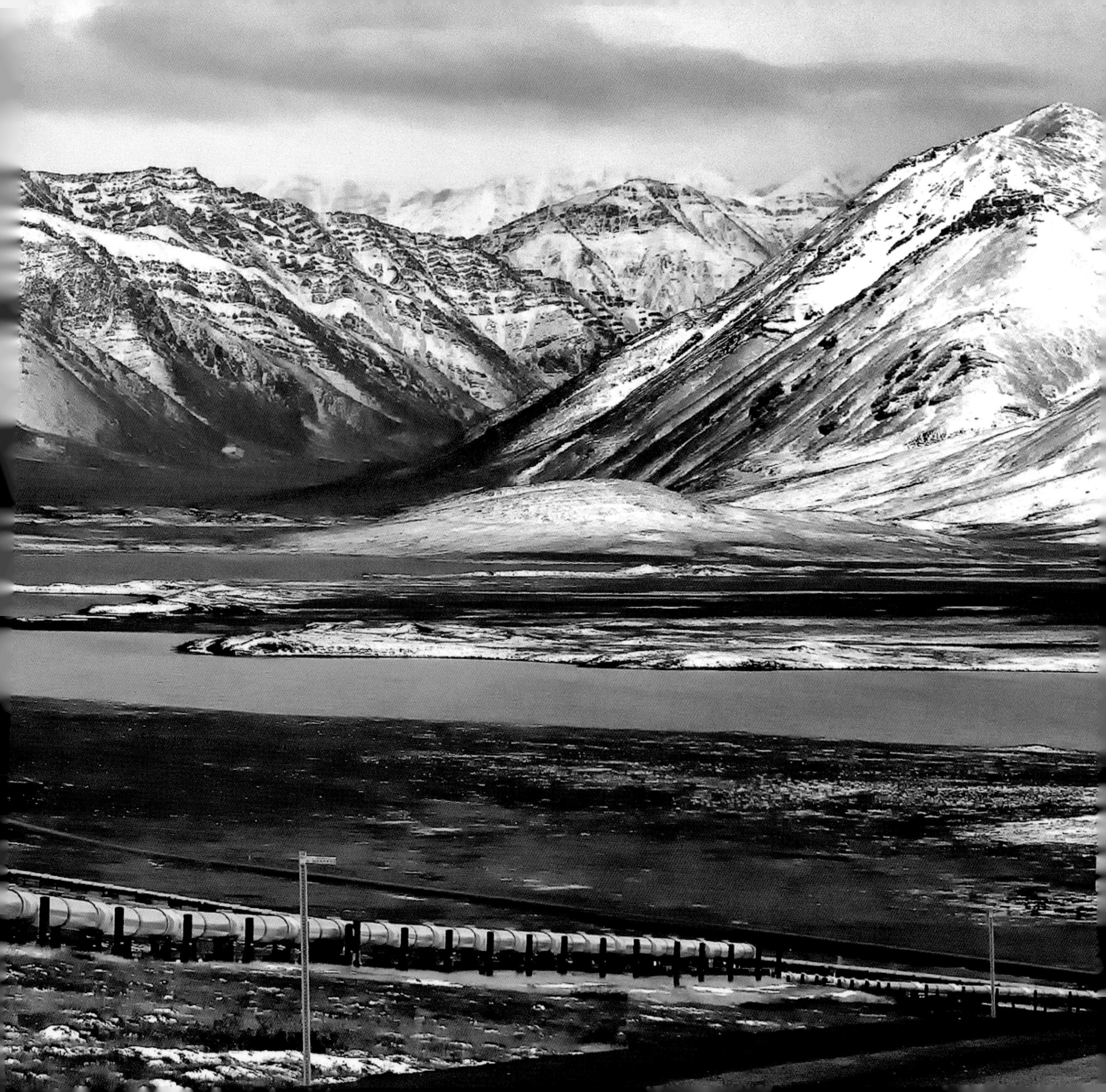

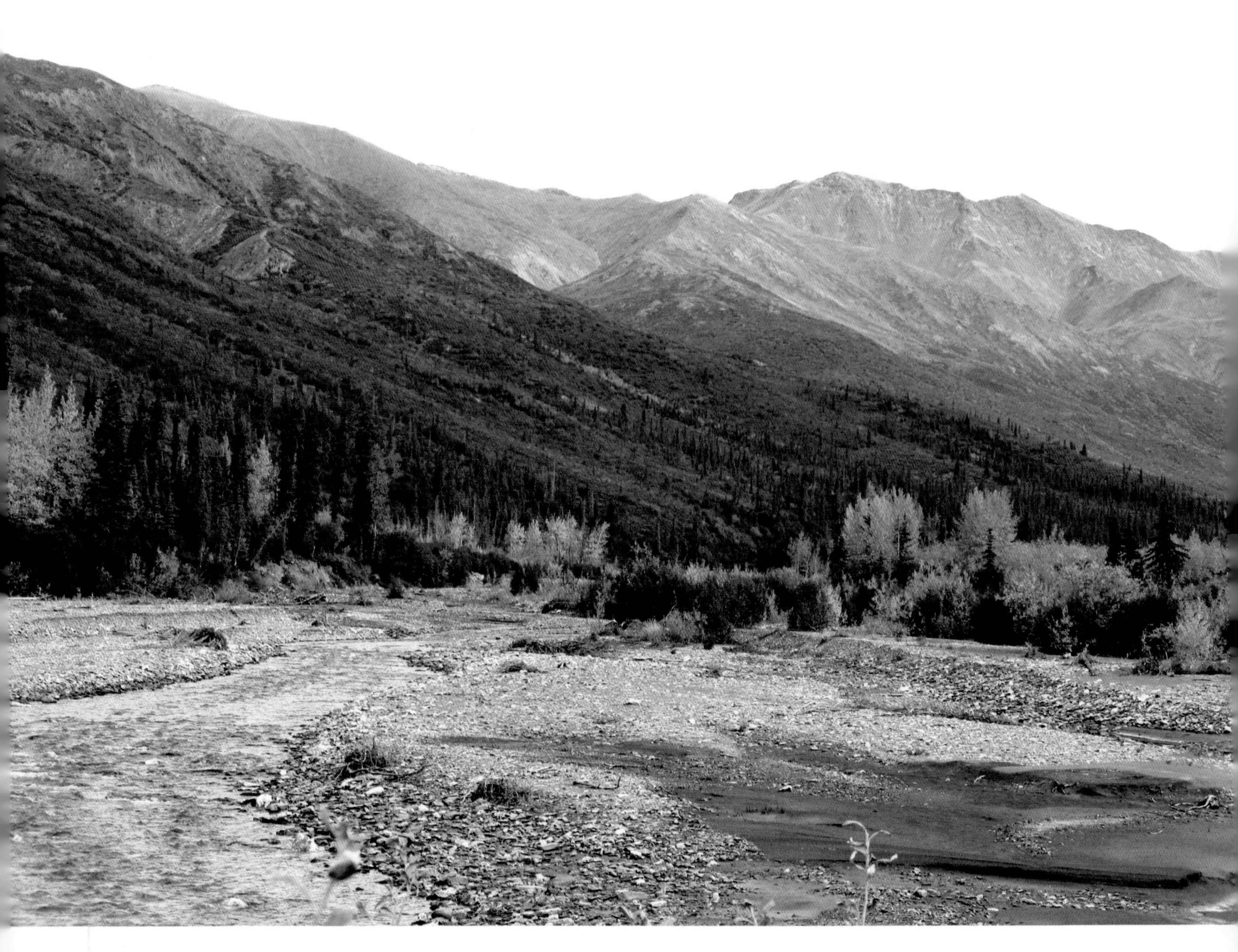

BROOKS RANGE FROM DALTON HIGHWAY

Brooks Range

Rising to heights of up to 2,736 m (8,976 ft), this 1,100-km (700-mile) mountain range can be seen as the northernmost extremity of what is known as the Western Cordillera. Thrown up by the collision of great tectonic plates, this long chain of mountain ranges runs all the way down the Americas' Pacific coast, through the Rockies to the Andes and Tierra del Fuego in the far south. Largely uninhabited, the mountains of the Brooks Range are a haven for wildlife, and as we see here, an area of simply staggering natural beauty.

ANAKTUVUK PASS, GATES OF THE ARCTIC NATIONAL PARK

Brooks Range

A bleak, intimidating landscape, it might seem, but it supported the Nunamiut for centuries. Semi-nomadic caribou hunters, they ranged widely in their pursuit of subsistence, but they returned to their base here between their forays. Unlike their fellow Iñupiat, they lived entirely inland and have been hit hard by the decline in caribou stocks in recent decades. Today, like other Iñupiat, they have had to adapt to changing times. Increasingly, Anaktuvuk has become a tourist centre. The United States' northernmost national park, the 'Gates of the Arctic' was designated as such in 1980.

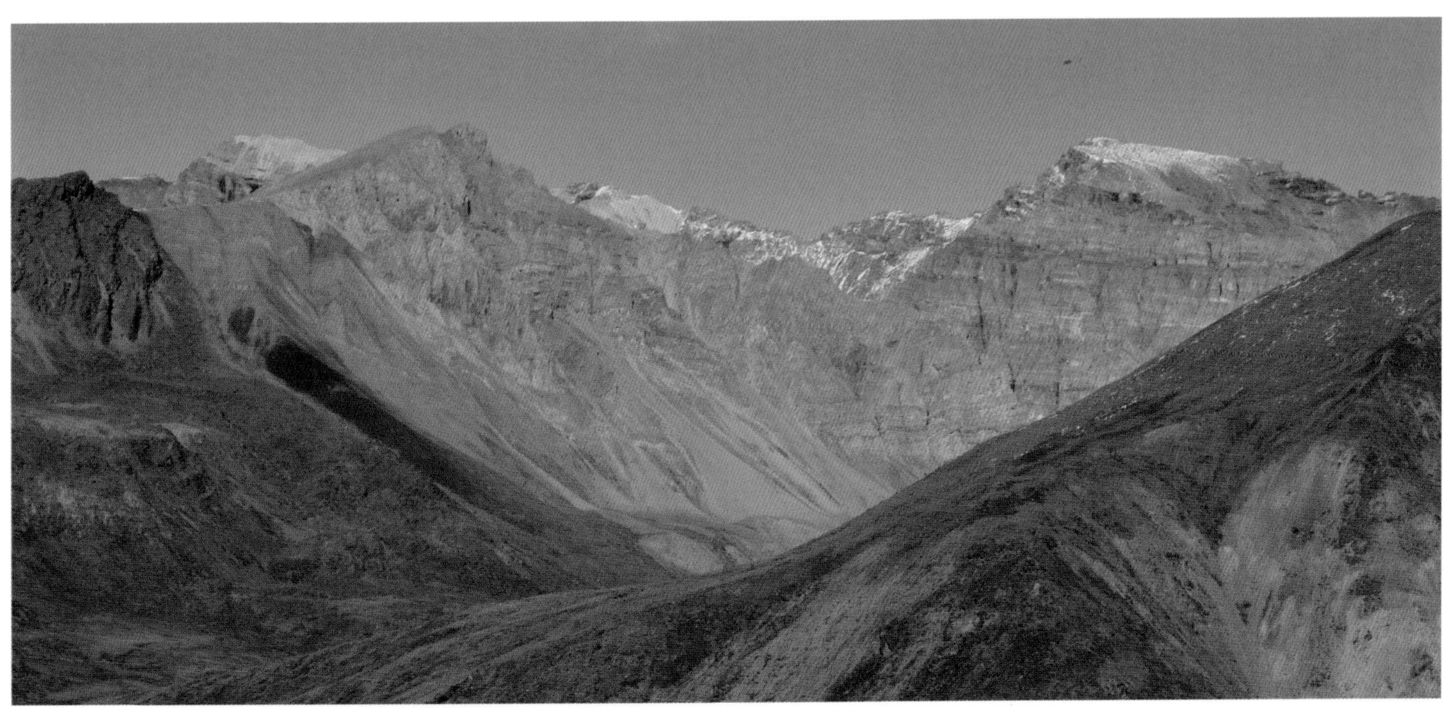

NORTHERN LIGHTS, WISEMAN VILLAGE

Brooks Range

Famous for his memoir, *Arctic Village* (1933) naturalist Robert Marshall (1901–39) first came to Wiseman in 1929, choosing it on the grounds that it 'seemed on the map to be the most unknown section of Alaska'. He enjoyed his stay so much that he subsequently spent the best part of a year and a half here, finding its human inhabitants still more intriguing than its wildlife. Unforgettable characters … yet surely formed as people by their proximity to nature – at its vastest, most awe-inspiring, most unforgiving.

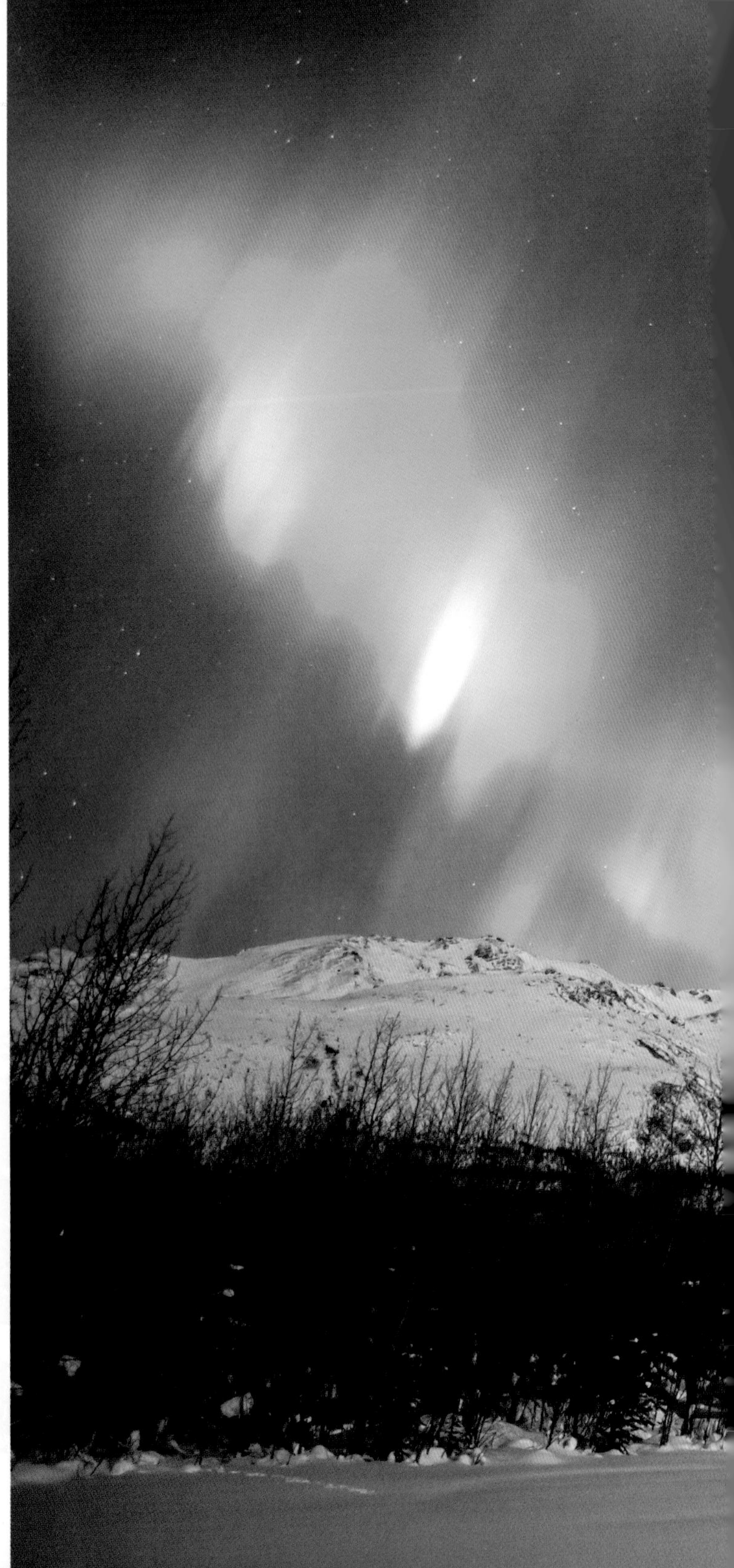

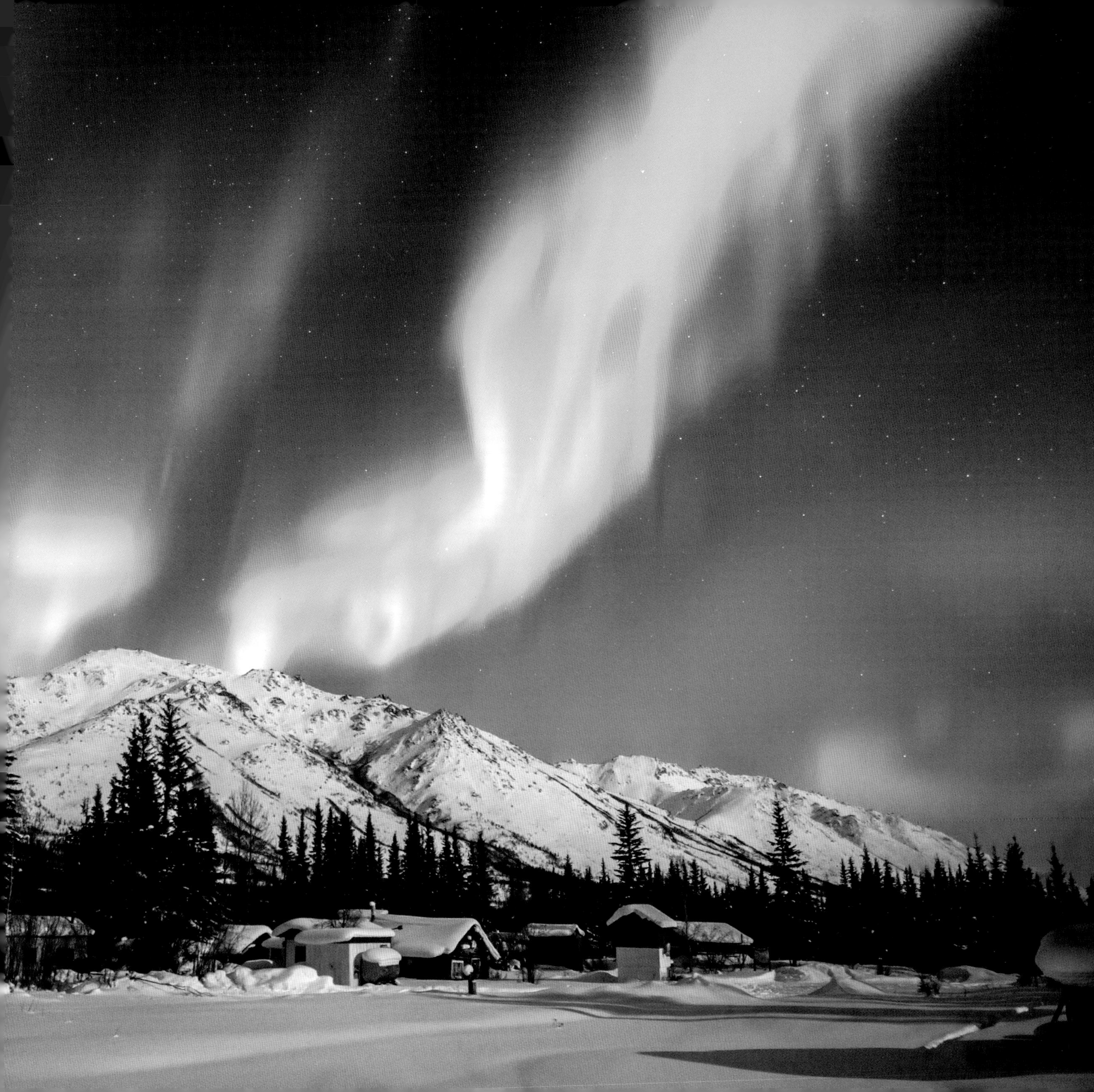

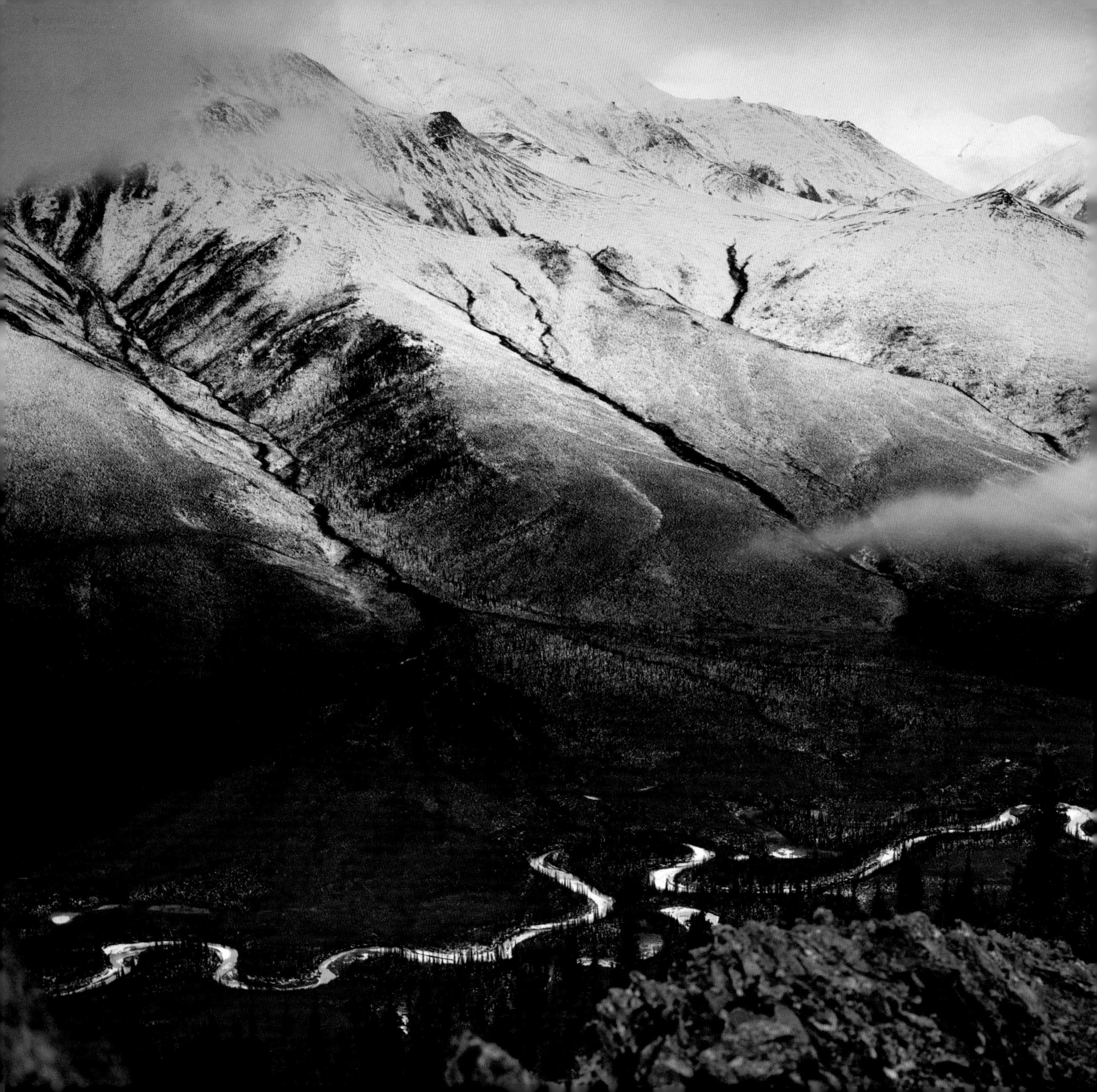

ENDICOTT MOUNTAINS, GATES OF THE ARCTIC NATIONAL PARK

Brooks Range

The lightest dusting of snow seems to soften the rough, rocky edges of the rising slopes of the Endicott Mountains, the central section of the Brooks Range. A tributary of the Koyukuk River (itself a tributary of the Yukon), Wiseman Creek follows its winding course below. As so often in northern Alaska, it is hard to say whether this scene is more uplifting or intimidating: there is something seriously unsettling about its austere beauty – its un-warming palette of ochres, tans, greens and greys.

COLDFOOT

Brooks Range

Slate Creek, as it was called then, was a product of the 1899 Gold Rush. It was renamed the following year, allegedly because a certain prospector, heading boldly northward, had thought better of his purpose here, got 'cold feet' and turned back. For those prepared to stick it out, there were certainly riches to be found. The boom lasted six years, which was very good. Since then the place has barely survived: that it does so still is down to its role as a waystation for truck drivers traversing the Dalton Highway between north and south.

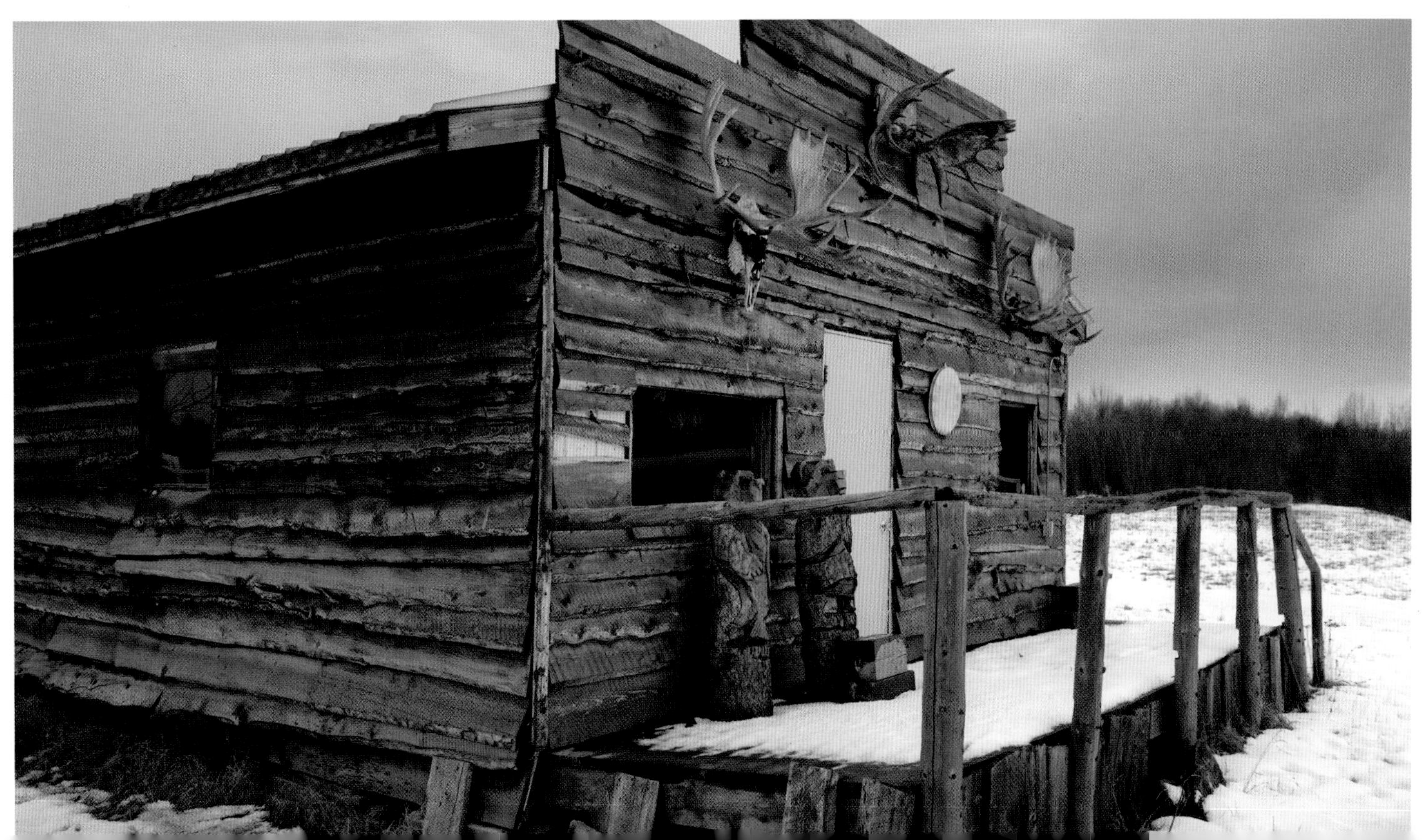

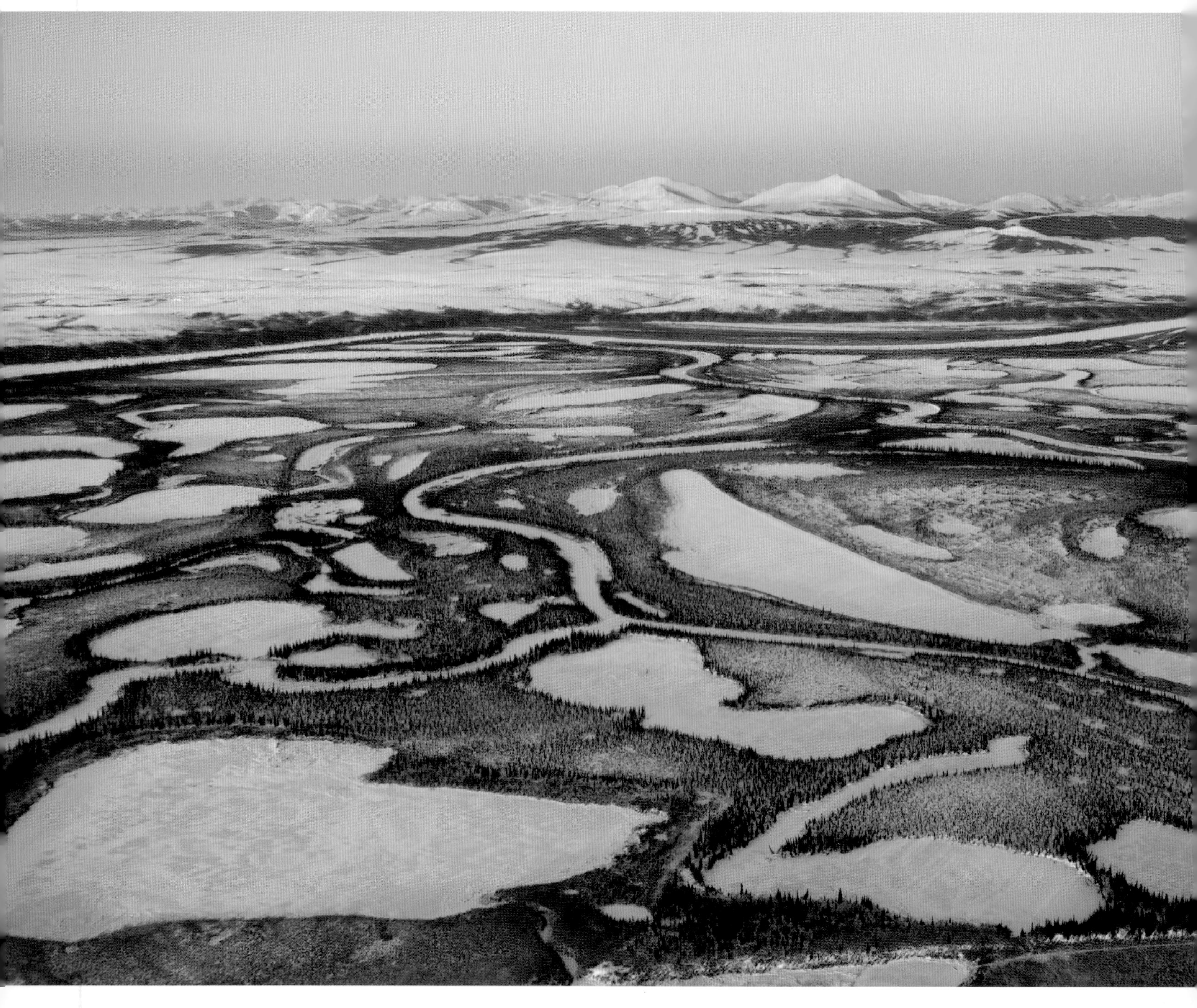

SUNSET OVER POINT HOPE

Western Arctic

Tikarakh, the Iñupiat called it: the word means 'pointing finger', and it was well-chosen, a glance at the map makes clear. The settlement stands near the westernmost end of a lengthy sand spit. This in its turn forms a natural barrier all but shutting off the mouth of the Kukpuk river delta, a labyrinth of lagoons and twisting channels. Factor in the lurid light of a lowering sun and a reflective layer of ice and snow and it all adds up to a weird and not-quite-earthly-seeming scene.

CAPE KRUSENSTERN NATIONAL MONUMENT LANDSCAPE

Western Arctic

Human beings are believed to have inhabited this lagoon-pitted coastal plain and the limestone bluffs above it for more than 5,000 years. Bleak as it may first appear, this is rich ground for hunter-gatherers, offering access to everything from musk oxen to wild green plants, from caribou to berries, and every sort of seafood, from seals to salmon, from whales to shellfish. All, of course, had their different seasons and their different pros and cons (harvesting berries was extremely laborious while whaling was dangerous): together, though, they gave the Iñupiat a decent living.

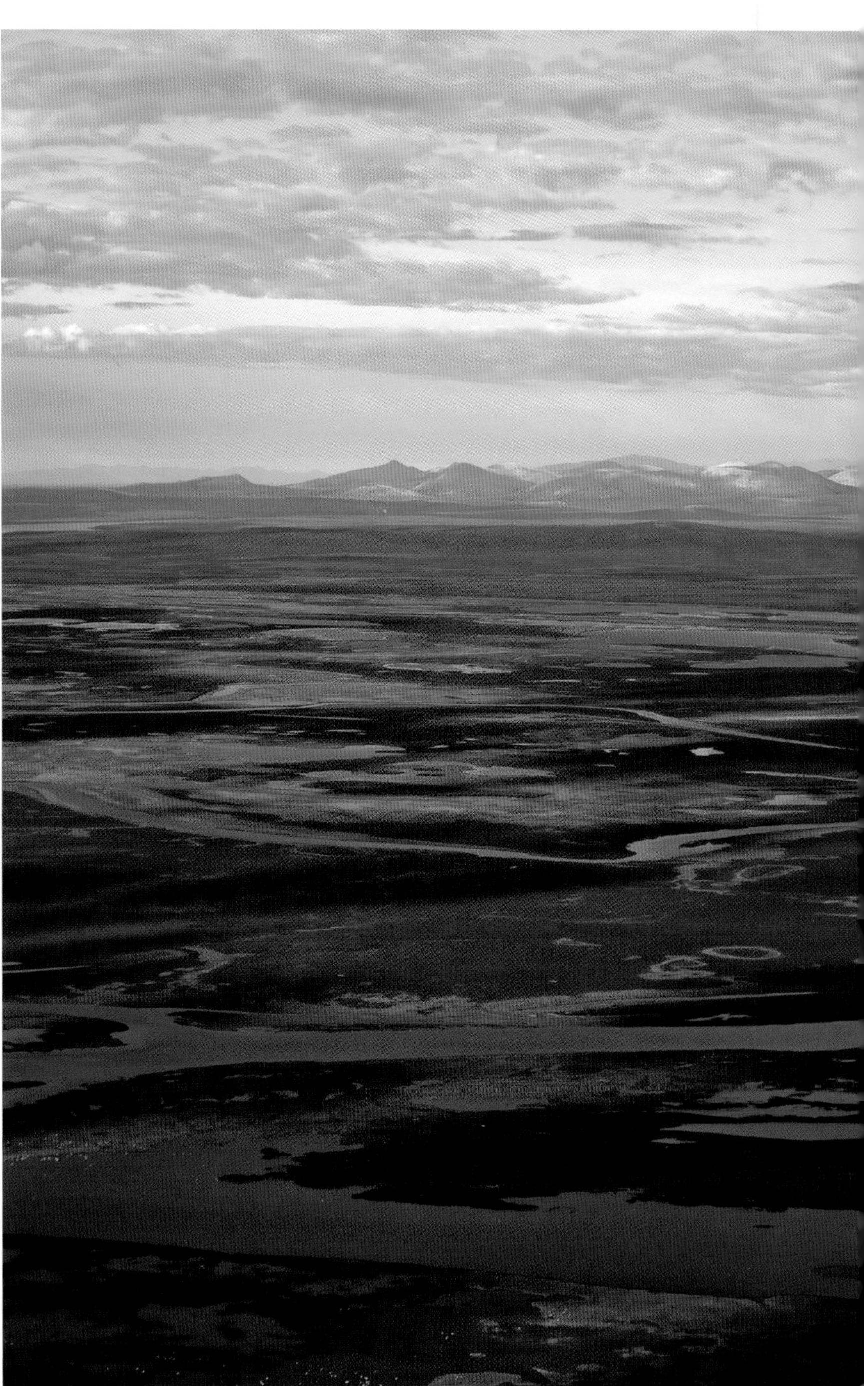

KOBUK RIVER, KOBUK VALLEY NATIONAL PARK

Western Arctic

Kobuk, 'big river', the Iñupiat called it, and they were not exaggerating. Not only does it run westward for 451 km (280 miles) from its source in the Endicott Mountains to the Bering Strait, it is deep, and consequently navigable, for much of its length. In rough wilderness areas like Alaska, rivers were always important as transport and

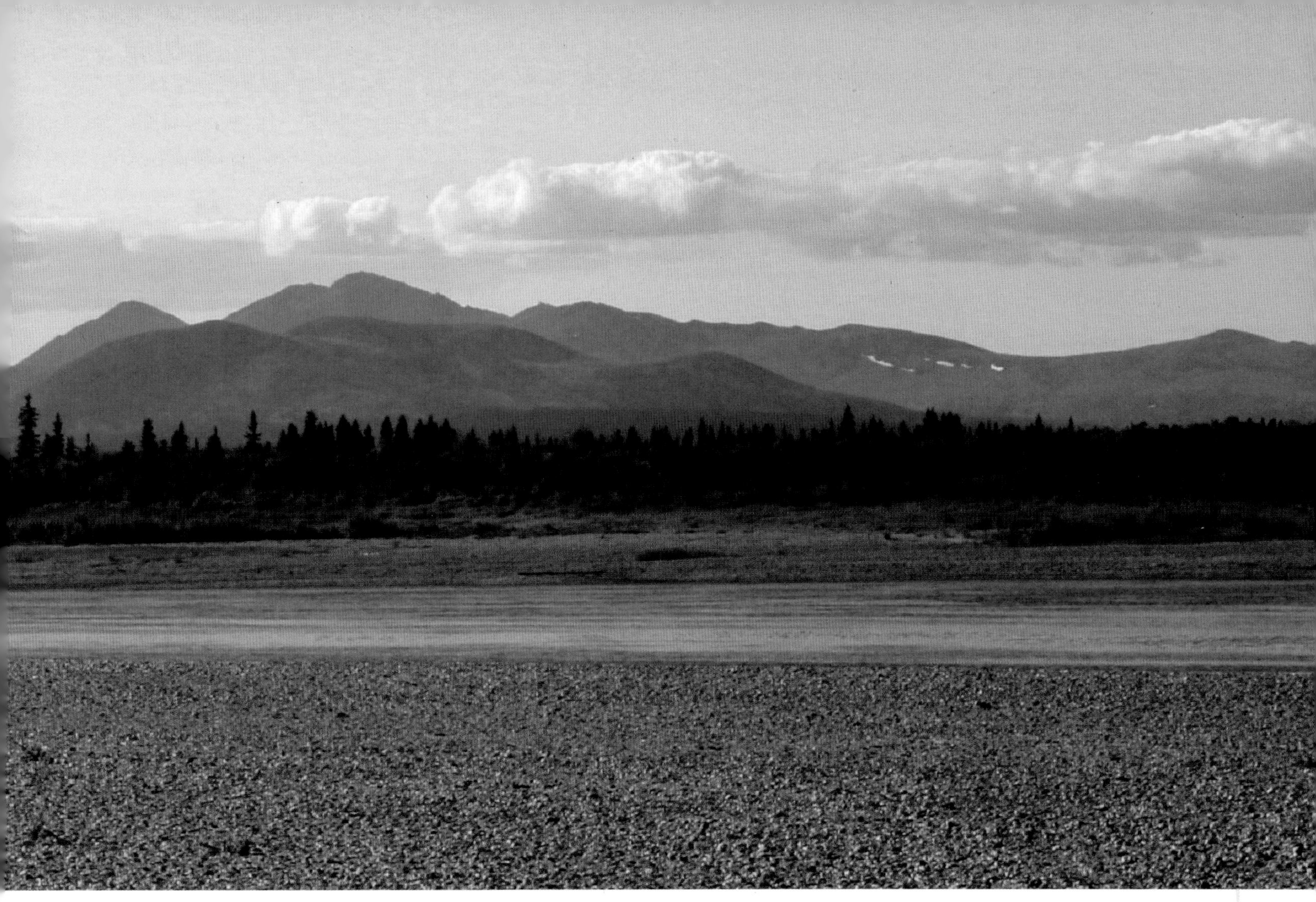

communications routes, as much for the early Iñupiat as for the European explorers and prospectors of more modern times. Well upriver at Onion Portage, archaeologists have found evidence of human occupation for more than 10,000 years.

MOOSE, KOBUK RIVER

Western Arctic

The moose is iconic, an emblem of Alaska, though it is generally the bull we see, with his impressive antlers. Here, though, more mundanely, we have a cow and calf, beating a hasty retreat up a muddy, scrub-covered bank. The reality is that, down the generations, big beasts like this (the caribou too) were the cornerstone of the hunter-gatherer economy, at least inland. Catching and killing them might be hard and hazardous, but one kill could feed a small community for many days, as well as yielding precious sinew, hide and bone.

COLD WINTER SUNRISE, KOTZEBUE

Western Arctic

With a population of just over 3,200, Kotzebue would scarcely qualify as a city anywhere else, but it is a major metropolis by Western Arctic Alaskan standards. Its location was key, on the shores of the Kotzebue Sound (named for the Baltic German Otto von Kotzebue, who in 1816 explored this coast on behalf of Russia). Several important rivers reach the sea here, and people from up their valleys would come down here to trade. These same advantages would later bring Russian and American traders here for furs.

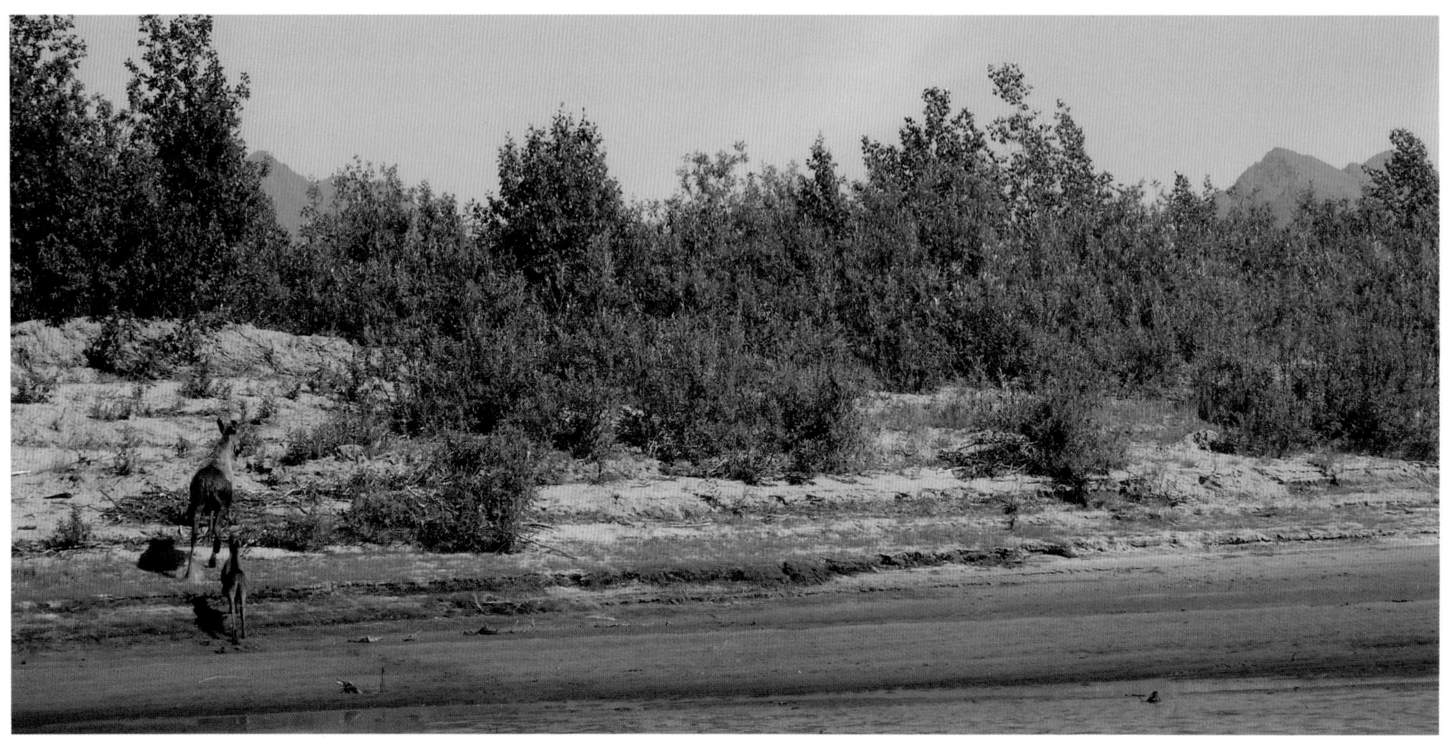

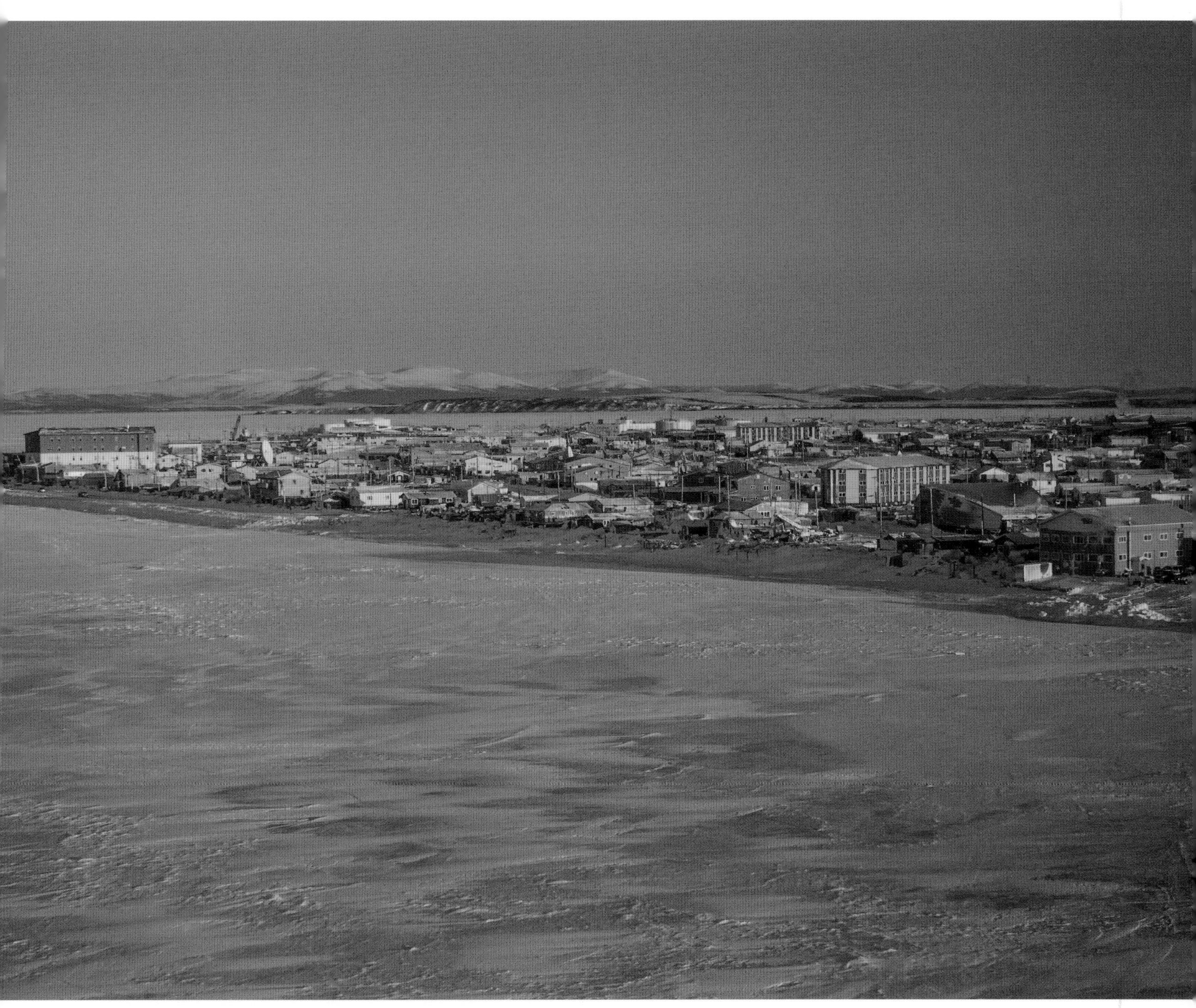

KOYUKUK RIVER, KOYUKUK NATIONAL WILDLIFE REFUGE

Western Arctic

This region was the last word in remoteness in 1855, when US Army officer, Lt. Henry T. Allen (1859–1930), led an expedition of the Koyukuk. His explorations here paved the way for prospectors, who came here in a dribble, which turned into a flood with the first gold finds in the 1890s. The Rush was over as soon as it had begun. Today this region is treasured chiefly for its wildlife, which includes caribou, moose, wolves, black and grizzly bears, beavers, lynx and a great many other species. And, of course, its extraordinary beauty.

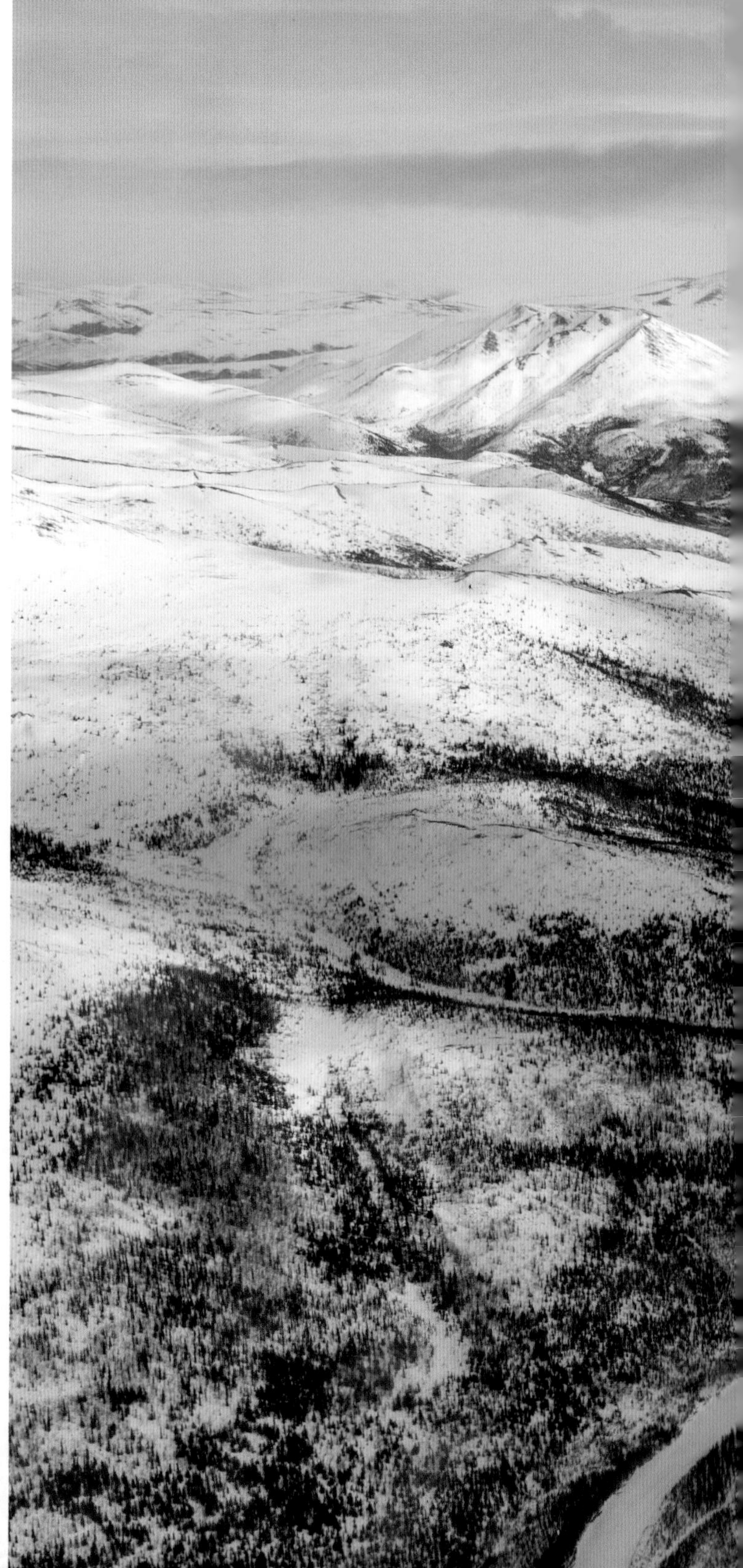

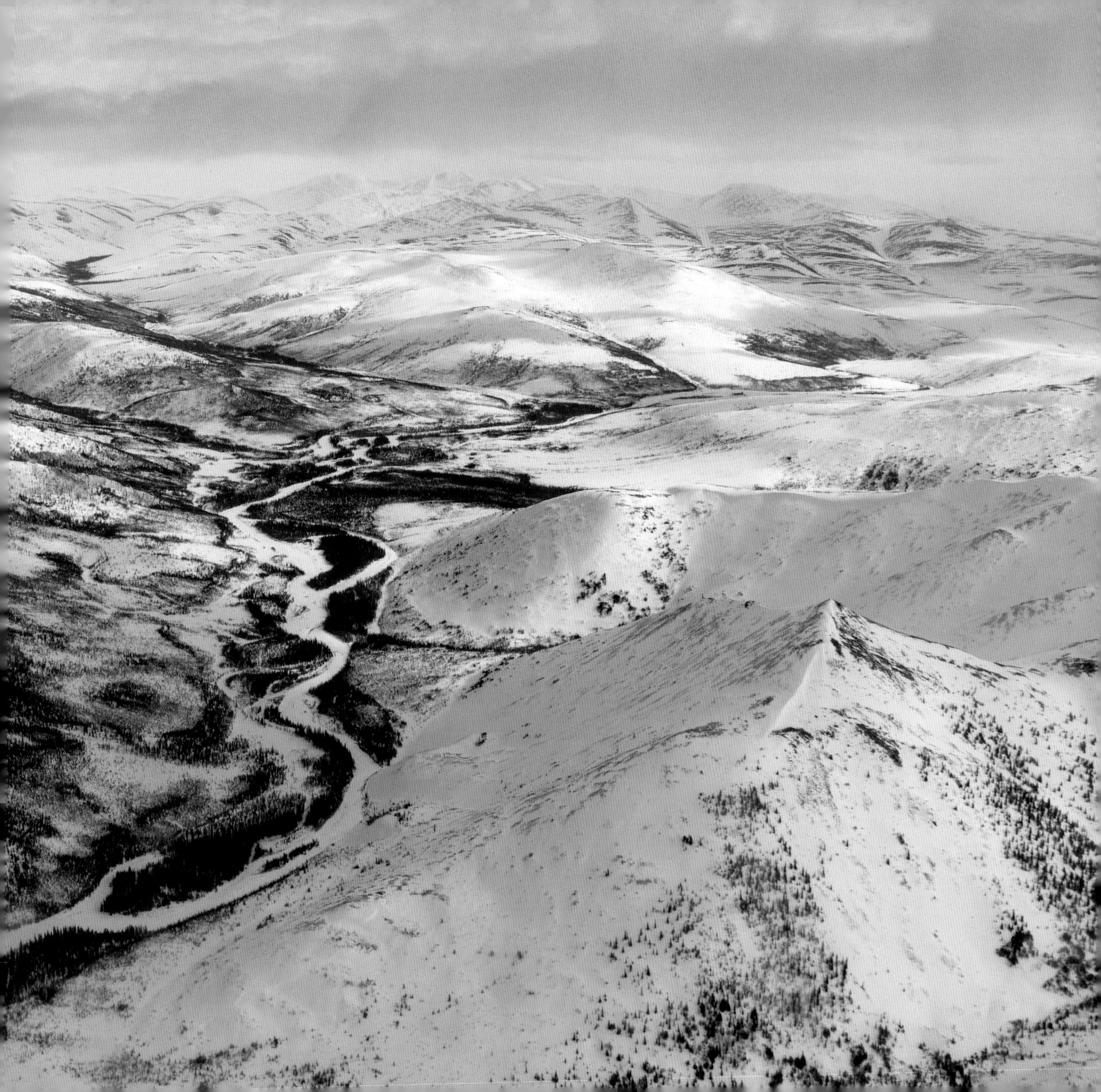

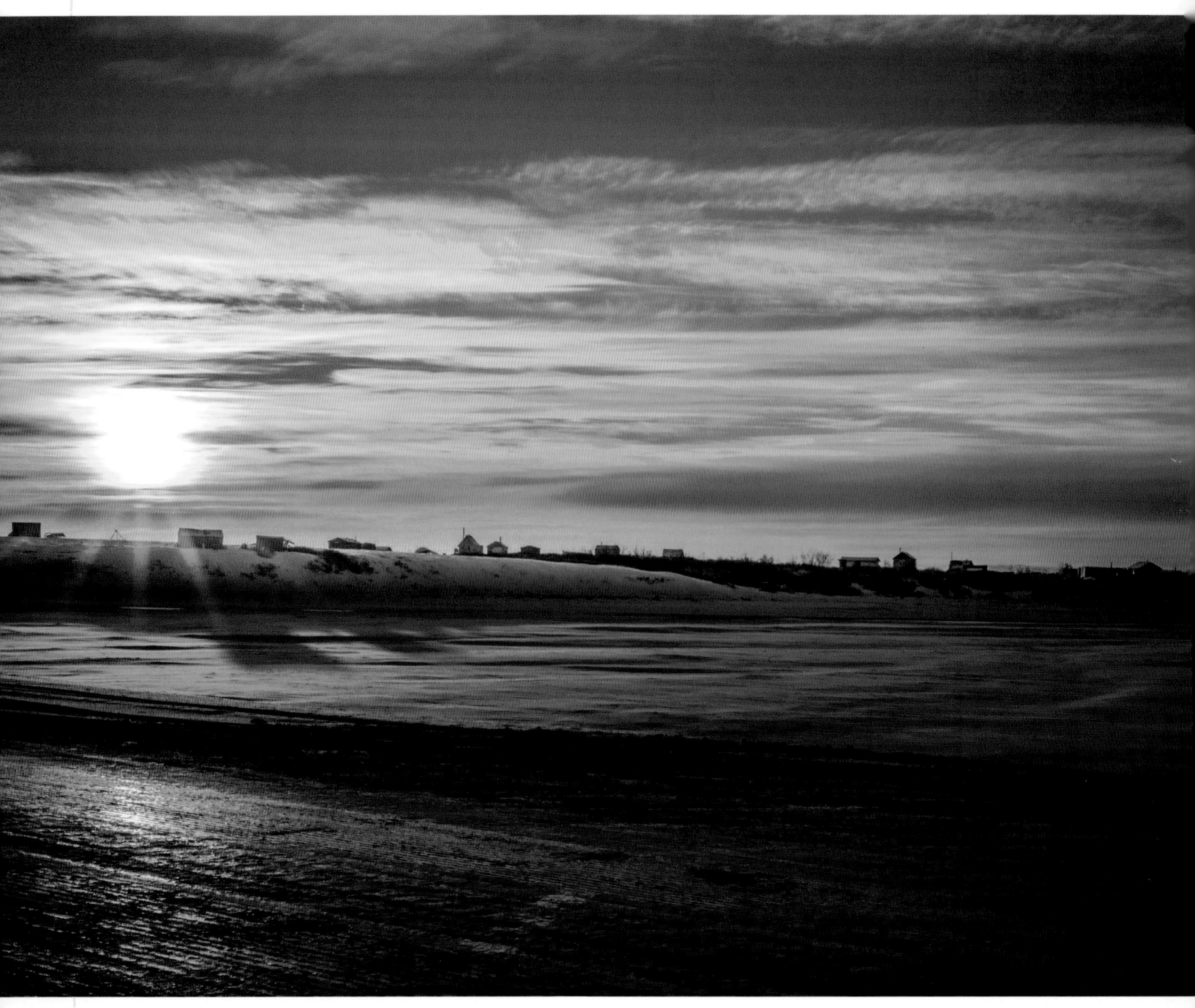

NOME SPIT, NORTON SOUND

Western Arctic

A long and level sand spit stretches out from Nome, whirled there from beaches up the coast by the near-constant winds. It is empty now, as it was for centuries before, but in 1899 it was home to some 10,000 gold prospectors. They lived in a tent city here, frantically panning for gold among the gravel; overwhelmingly, they ended up going home, broken and embittered. There is still a significant town here, but it is content to be a quiet coastal community, with some of Alaska's most beautiful sea views.

OLD ST JOE'S HALL, NOME

Western Arctic

Nome did not die when the Gold Rush ended, partly because the gold itself was not exhausted: in tiny but cumulatively significant quantities, it is extracted industrially to this day. Things settled down to a more sedate pace and, while not exactly prospering, Nome at least survived. The Second World War brought a brief boom as a staging point for flights to the Soviet Union – at this time a US ally – but the Cold War, and renewed stagnation, soon ensued. Today it is hanging in there, a regional transport hub and occasional stopping-off place for cruise liners.

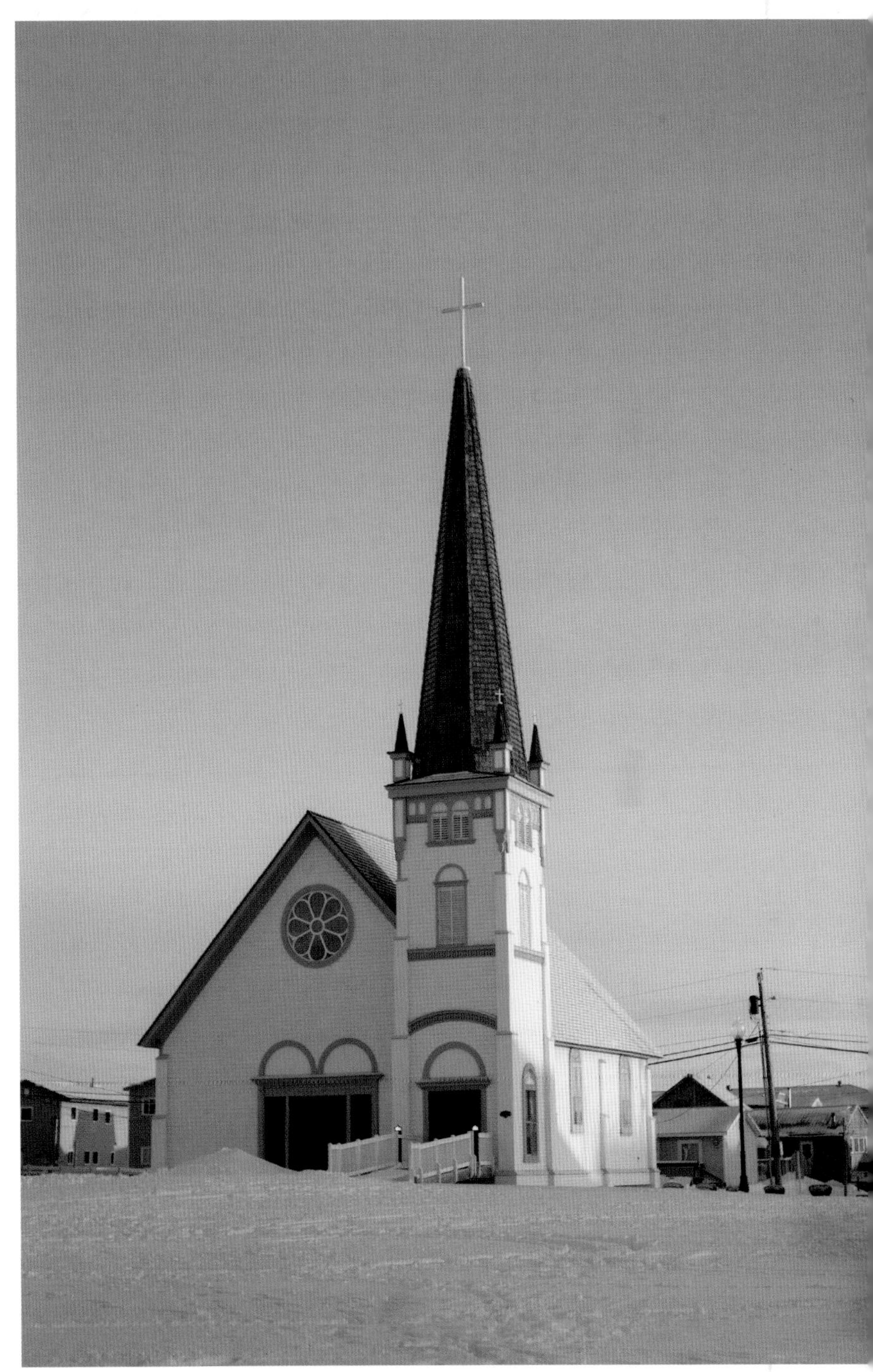

IDITAROD TRAIL, NOME

Western Arctic

'Mushing – winter travel in the Arctic', Robert Marshall (*see* page 24) explained, was 'one of the genuine joys in the life of most Koyukukers'. And, it seems, they were not by any means alone. The Iditarod Trail Sled Dog Race is not just one of the sporting world's most wildly improbable events but one of its most gruelling. And one of Alaska's most popular. Teams of huskies 14-strong have to haul a sled 1,509 km (938 miles) from Anchorage to the finish line in Nome (the record time stands at a little over eight days).

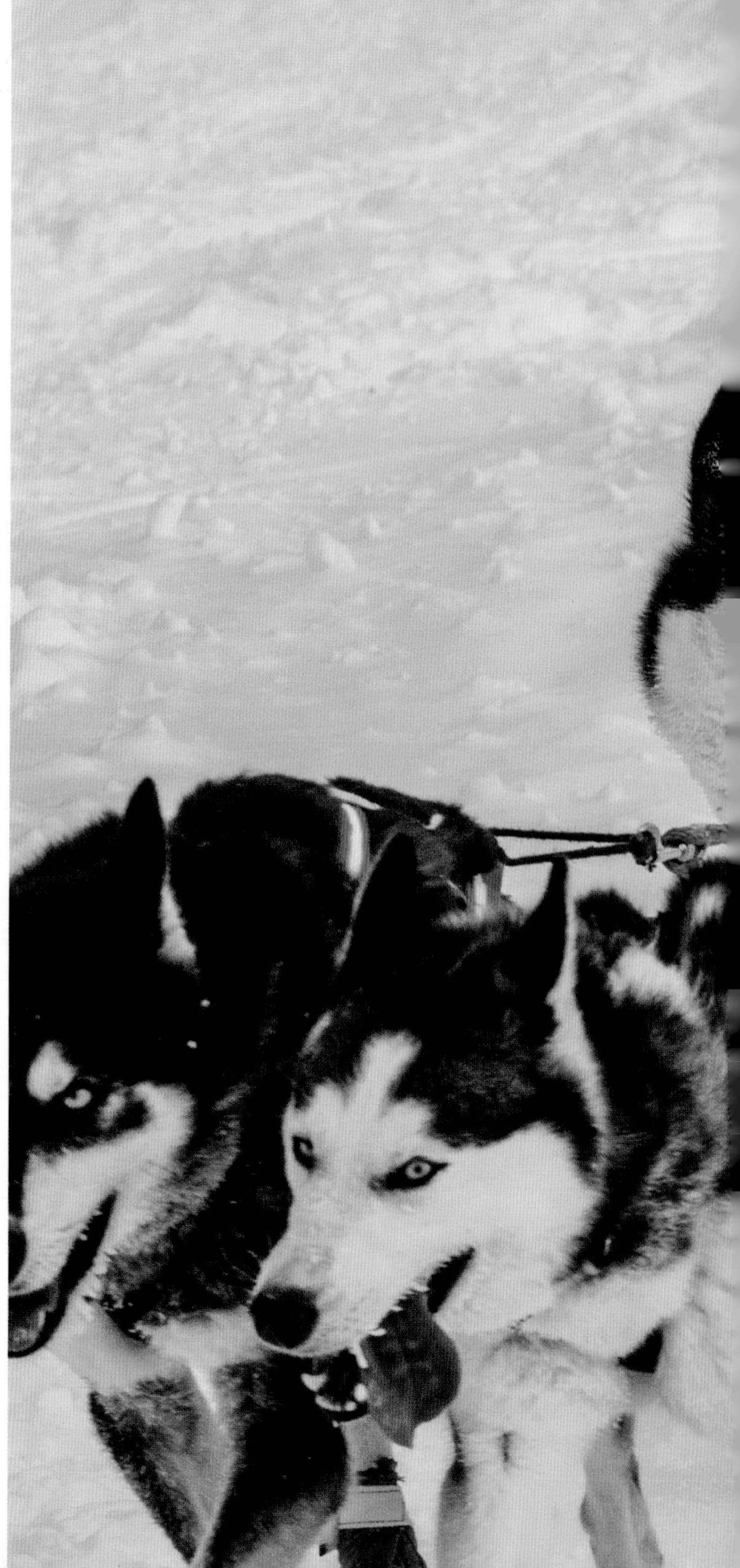

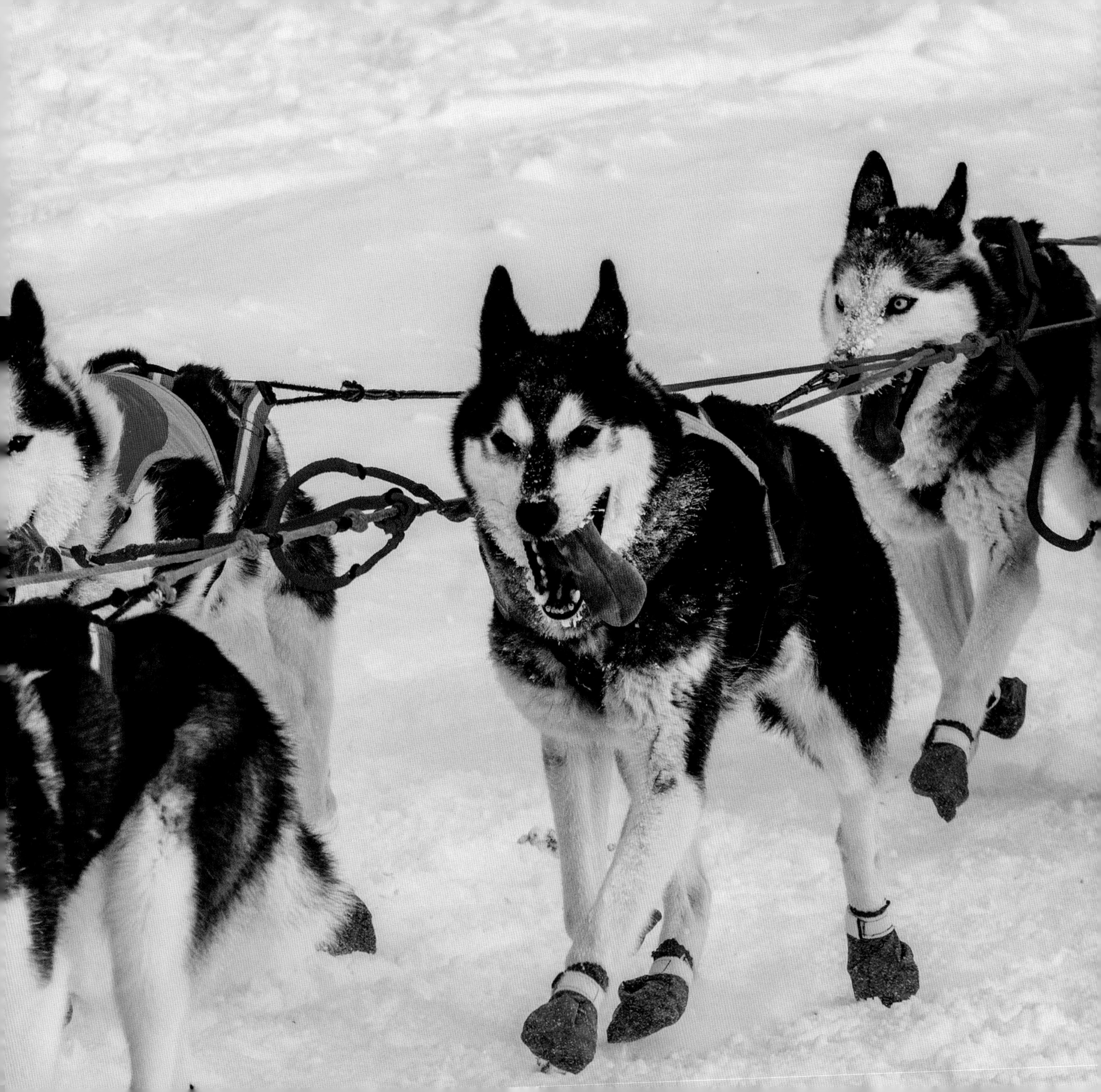

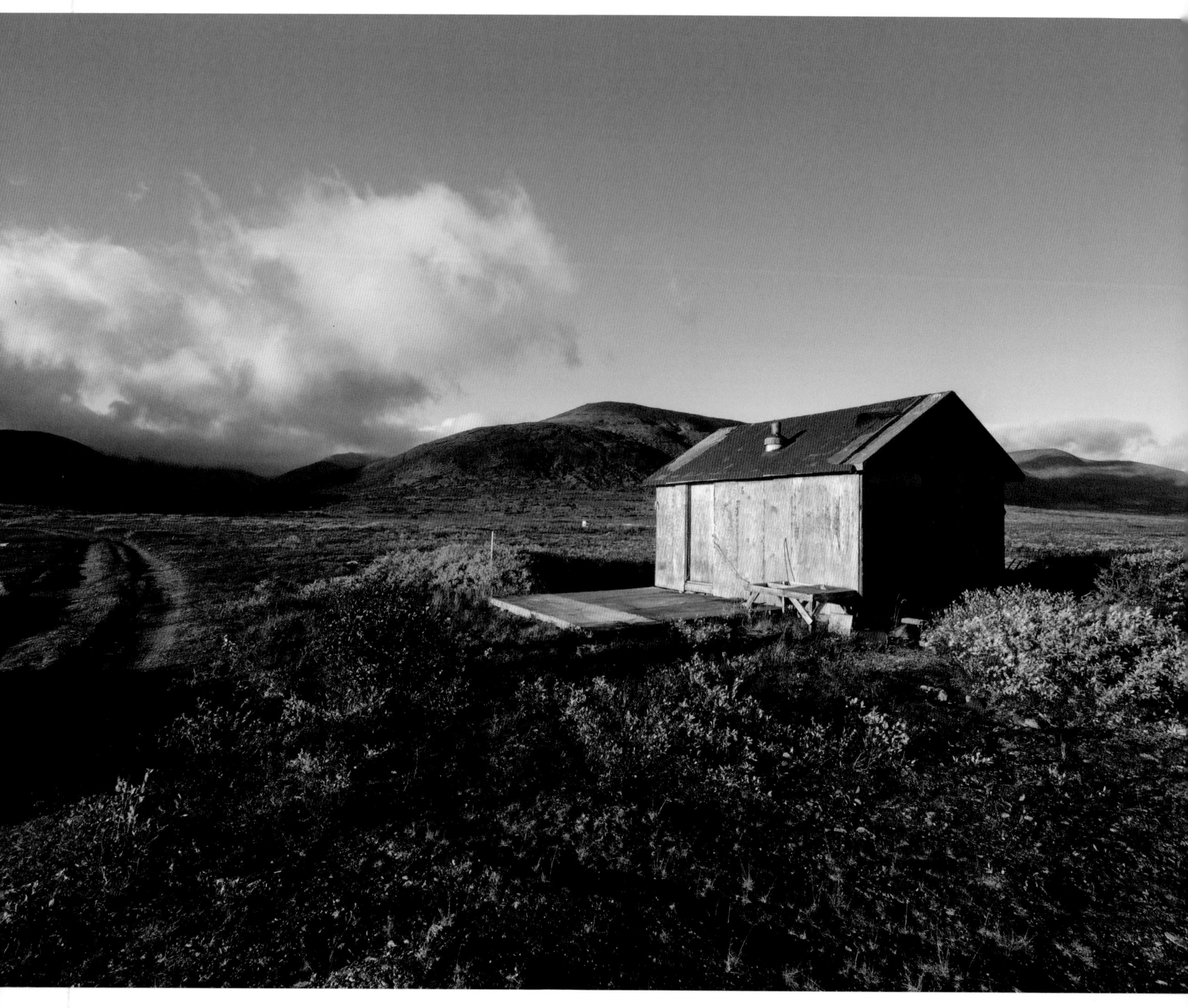

ABANDONED MINING HUT, NOME

Western Arctic

If only a derelict hut could talk … though it hardly bears thinking about the kind of tragedies it would have to relate – of families left; hopes dashed; fortunes lost (or found and squandered); violence and fraud. And ultimately unedifying: innocence is one thing, naive greed another, however difficult the lives being left behind. Today it is more uplifting, perhaps, to focus on the poetic pathos of this russet-roofed structure set in a sumptuous evening landscape, glowing gold (ironically) under a declining sun.

SHAKTOOLIK

Western Arctic

As we have seen (*see* page 12), 'global warming' is manifesting itself in some of the earth's coldest places. Shaktoolik is another case in point. This settlement stands on a narrow peninsula, with Norton Sound on one side and the waters of the Tagoomenik River on the other. On the seaward side, there is constant erosion, and the fear of a catastrophic storm swell; on the landward, there is danger when the river is in flood. It is a lively community, and its people are happy here, but how long can they stay?

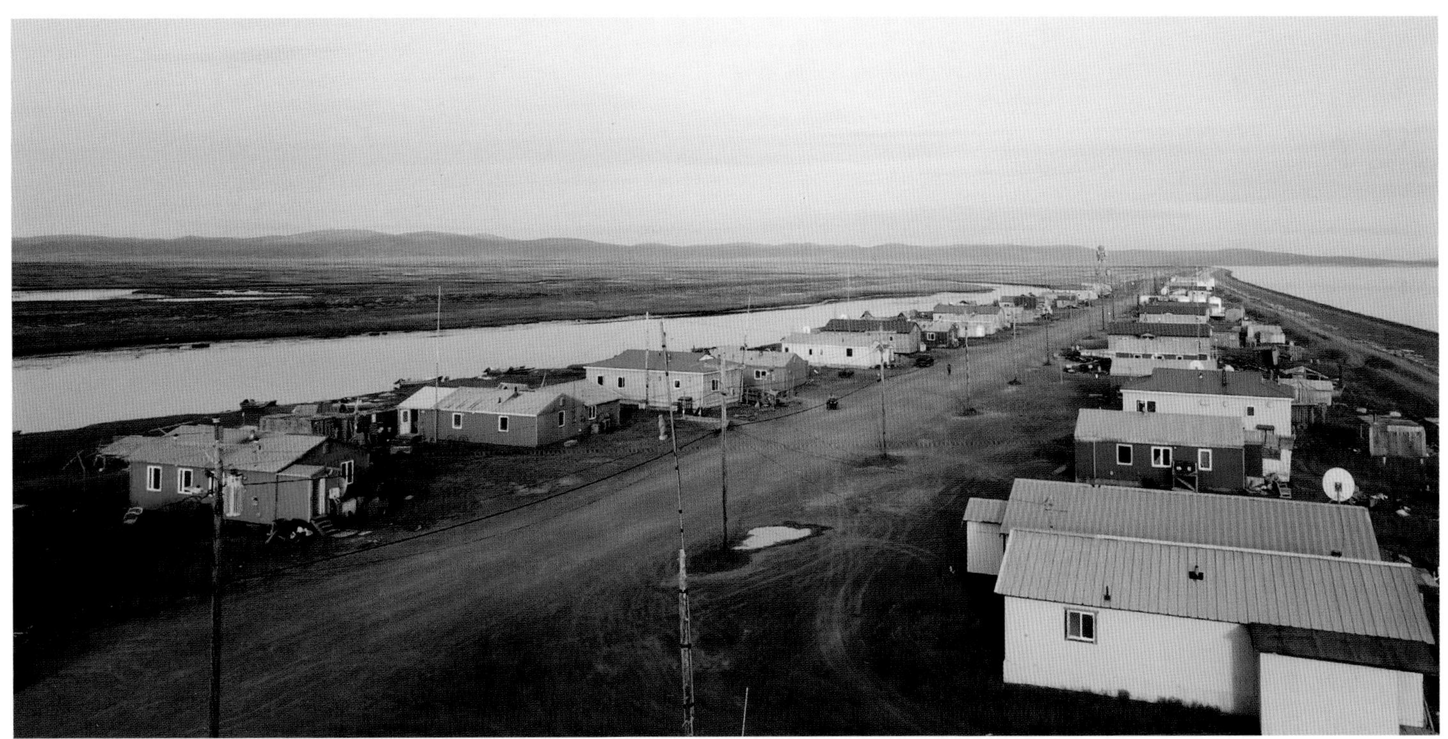

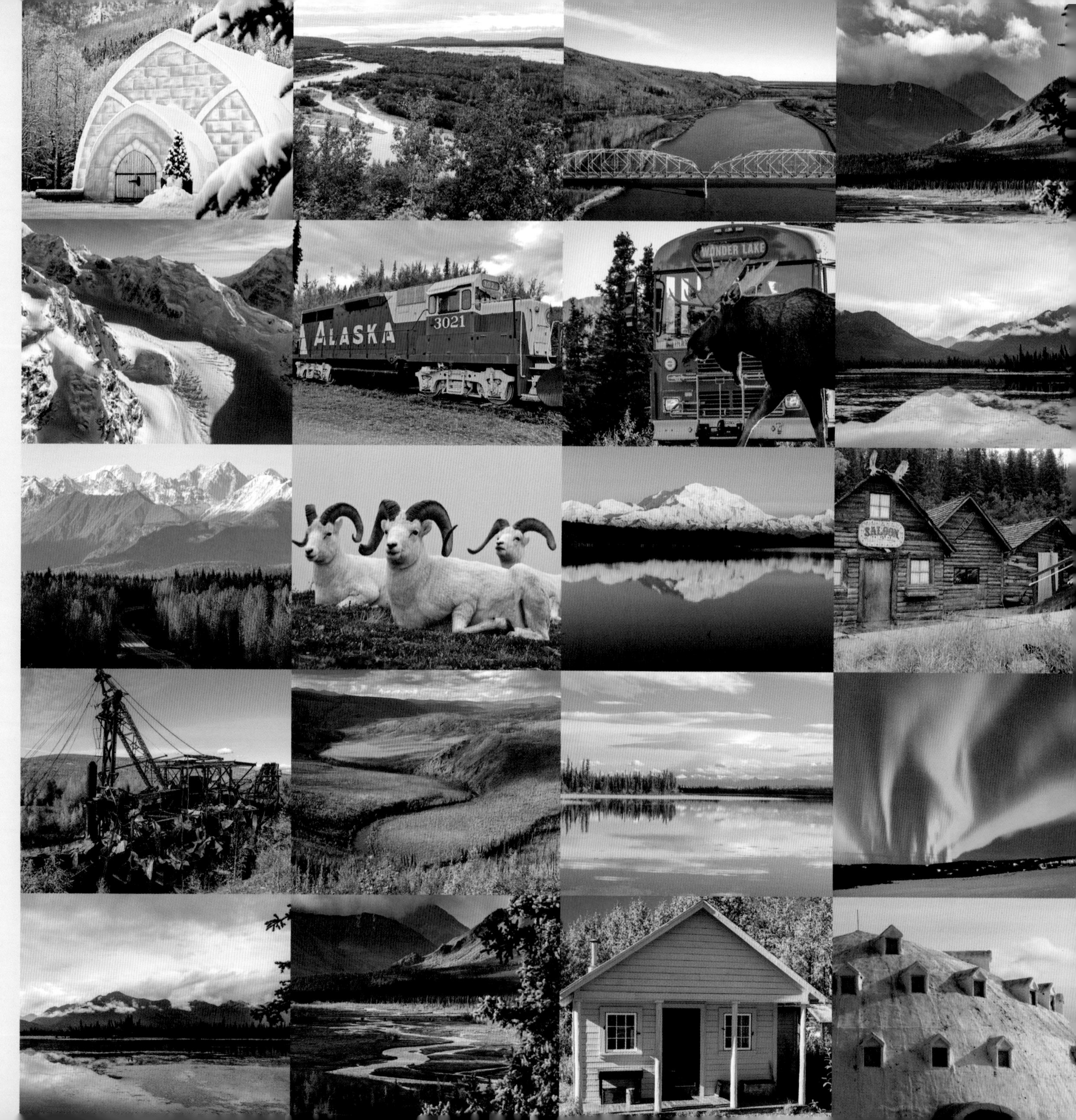
ALASKA
3021
WONDER LAKE
SALOON

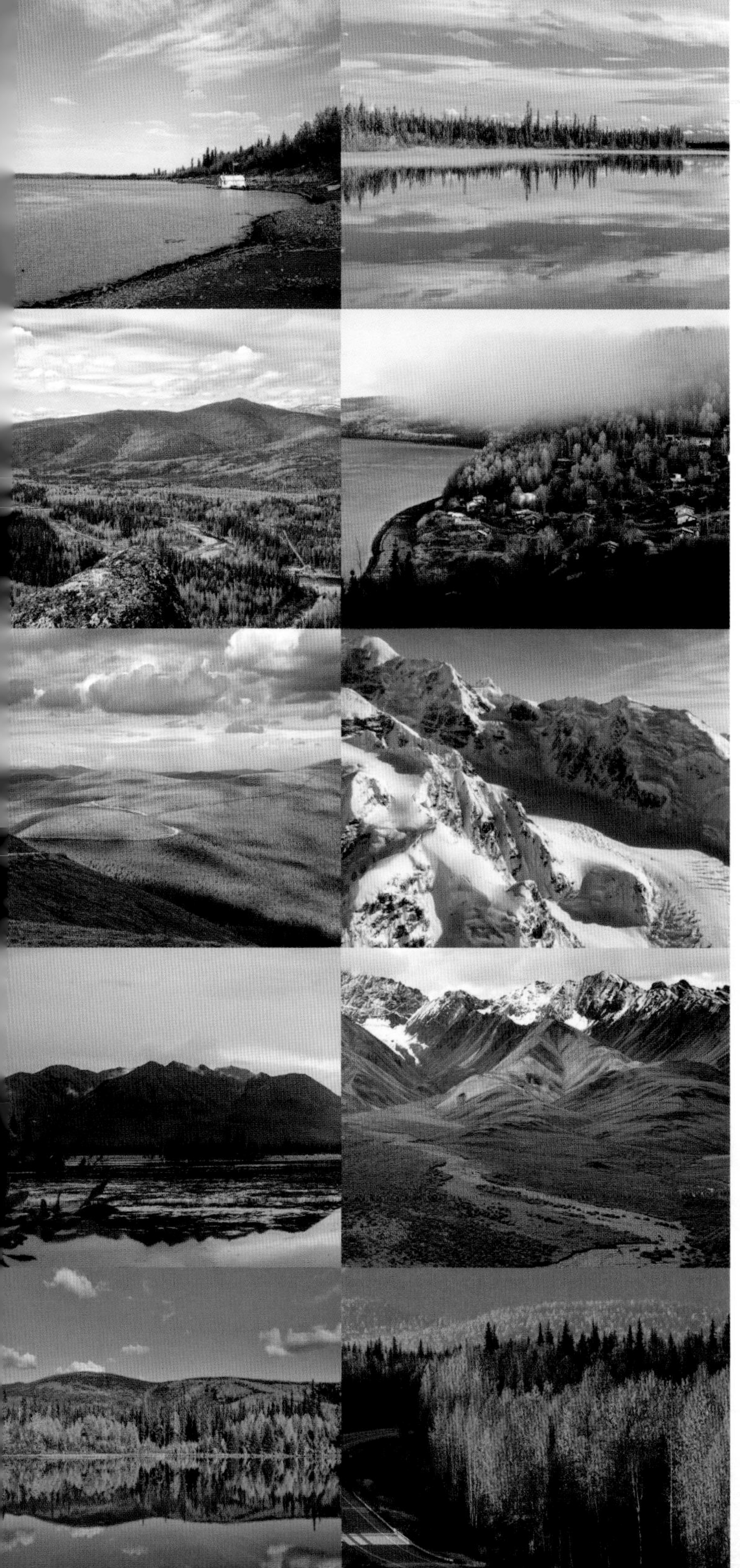

INTERIOR ALASKA

Venture any distance south below the Arctic Circle in Alaska and you will find yourself in a very different-looking country. Not least because you encounter a new 'biome' here. The treeless tundra with its permafrost is replaced by what is known as 'taiga', from the Siberian name given to northern Russia's endless expanses of coniferous forest. Except at the highest altitudes here, the landscape is cloaked with conifers (predominantly spruce), with the odd stand of deciduous trees like birch and aspen. A richer, apparently more welcoming landscape, then – but it would be naive to conclude that it was necessarily much kinder.

Thanks to the effects of what geographers call 'continentality', the Interior can actually be much colder than the Arctic North. Water responds relatively slowly to temperature changes, so the ocean insulates coastal regions, restricting both rises and falls in temperature. So inland areas see more extremes: in Alaska's case, temperatures can fall below the –50°C (58°F) mark in winter, then soar in summer to 38°C (100°F). Beautiful, but every bit as dangerous as the Arctic North, the Alaskan Interior must be treated with immense respect.

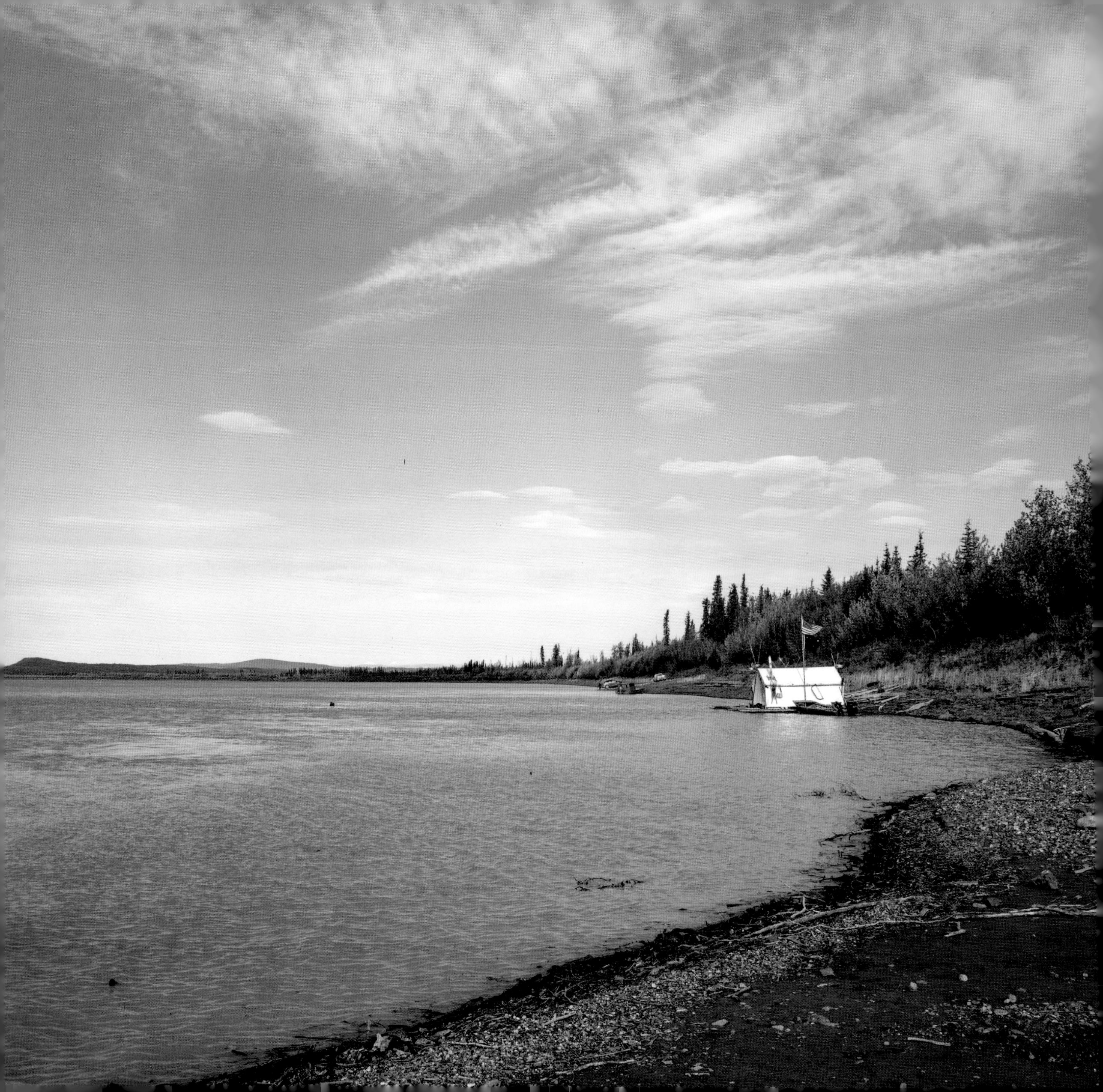

YUKON RIVER CAMP

Northeastern Interior

Yukon Territory may be in Canada (and the river for which it is named may rise in British Columbia) but for most of its 3,190-km (1,980-mile) length, the Yukon flows from east to west through Alaska's heart. Miners heading for the Klondike Gold Rush (1896–1903) voyaged up this way from the Pacific, but for a century or so now it has all been a bit quieter. The Yukon has throughout this time supported one of the world's most important salmon fisheries, though this, in its turn, is now under threat from climate change.

GOLD DREDGER, STEESE HIGHWAY

Fairbanks

The section of Alaska Route 2 that runs north–east from Fairbanks to the city of Circle is officially known as the Steese Highway, in honour of General James G. Steese, a military engineer and sometime President of the Alaska Road Commission. It was built to service the mines and river dredges of a region with a history of extraction going back to Gold-Rush days. Abandoned installations like this one are frequently to be seen along the road, but a fair few still remain in active use.

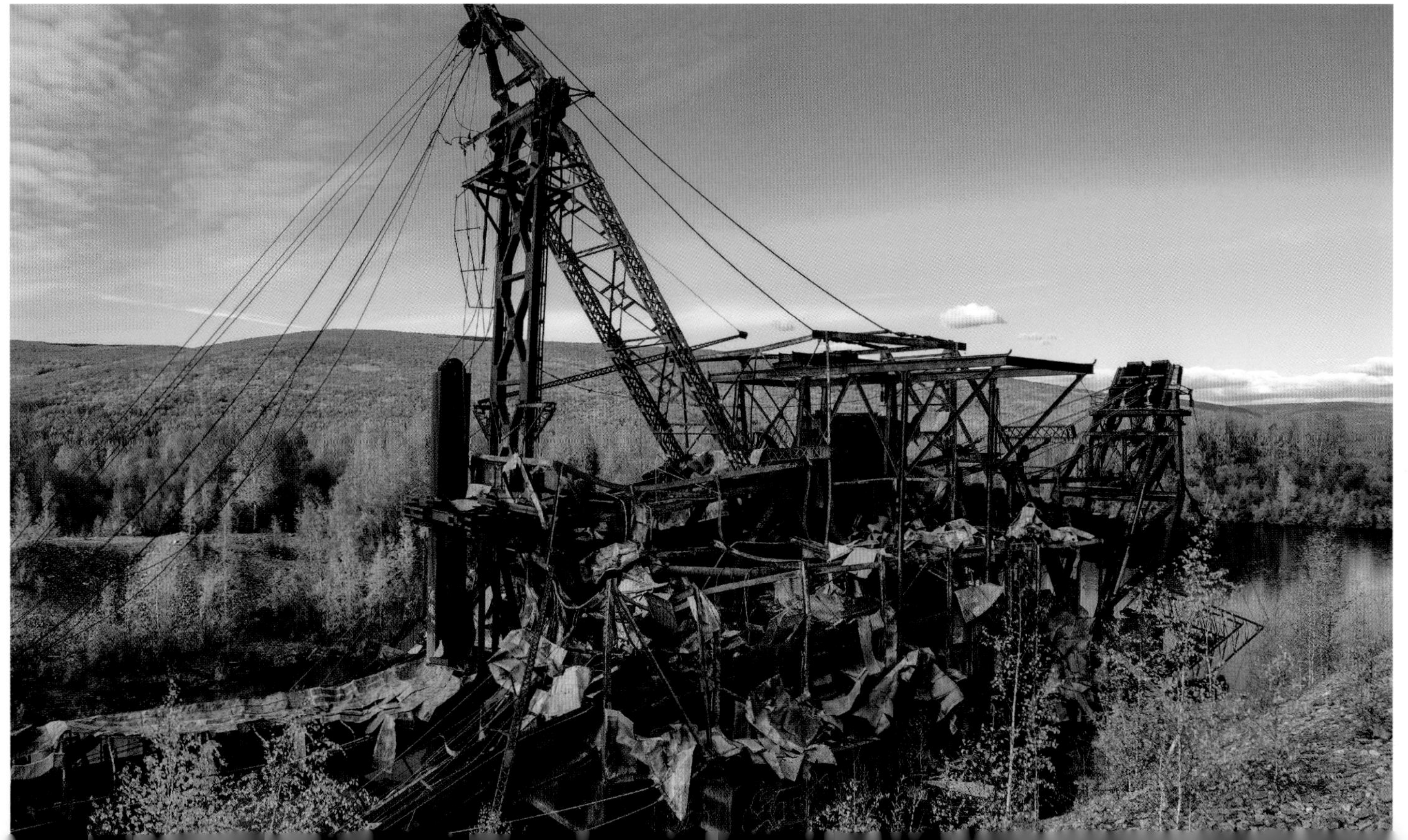

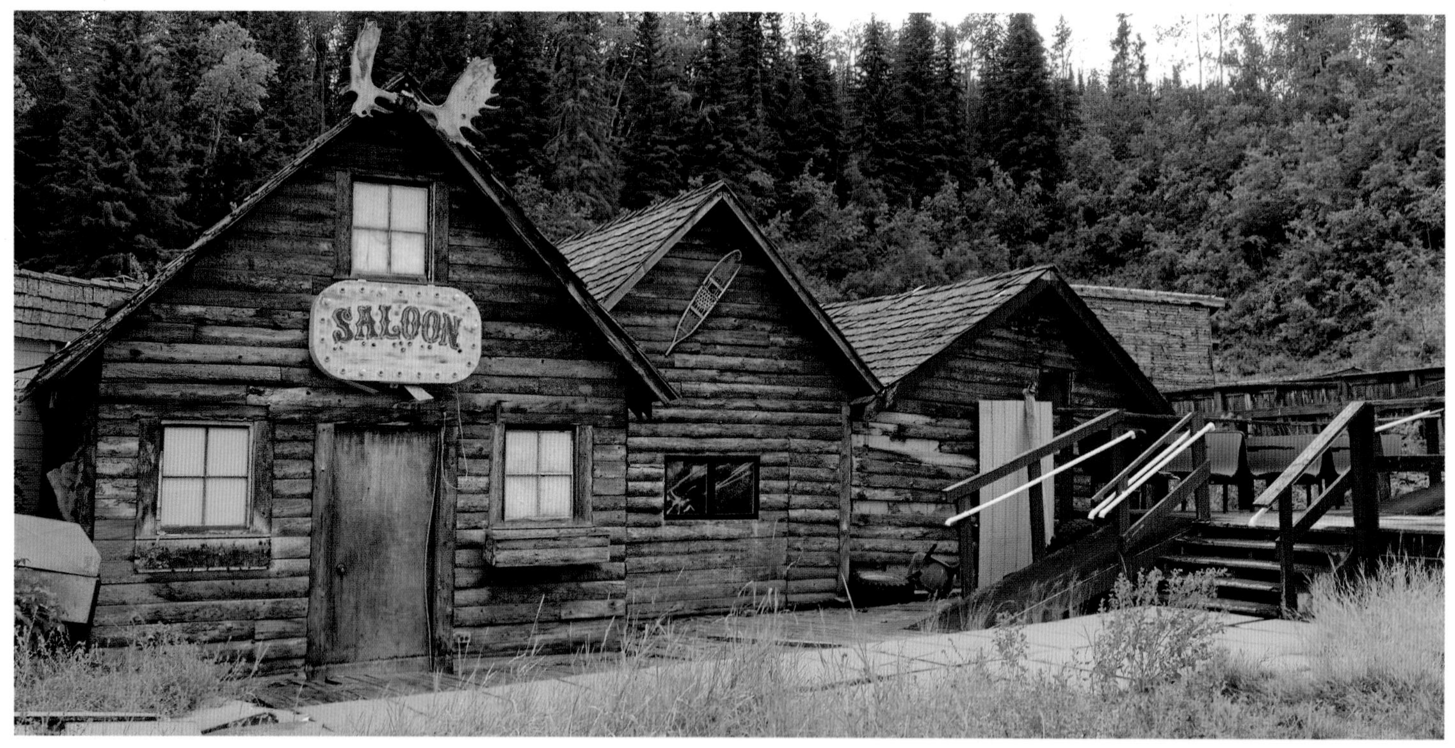

CIRCLE HOT SPRINGS, STEESE HIGHWAY

Fairbanks

The men who opened up this country were prospectors first and geographers a very poor second: they were in important ways confused about where they were. A town named Circle stands some 48 km (30 miles) north of this little spa, and even *that* is some 80 km (50 miles) below the actual Arctic Circle. So popular were these springs in their early-twentieth-century heyday that a landing strip was built nearby. The resort here has been closed for some years now, but it is still possible to bathe in the geothermal springs.

AURORA ICE MUSEUM, CHENA HOT SPRINGS

Fairbanks

The enterprising owners of the Chena Hot Springs have done their best to diversify their spa's appeal by opening an ice museum on the site. It features the fantastic (and frequently fantastical) work of ice-sculpting couple Steve and Heather Brice: exhibits include everything from a giant-sized chess set to some full-size figures of jousting knights on horseback and it is all illuminated in the colours of the aurora borealis by special (also ice-carved) chandeliers. You can even have a cocktail served to you in a 'glass' of ice....

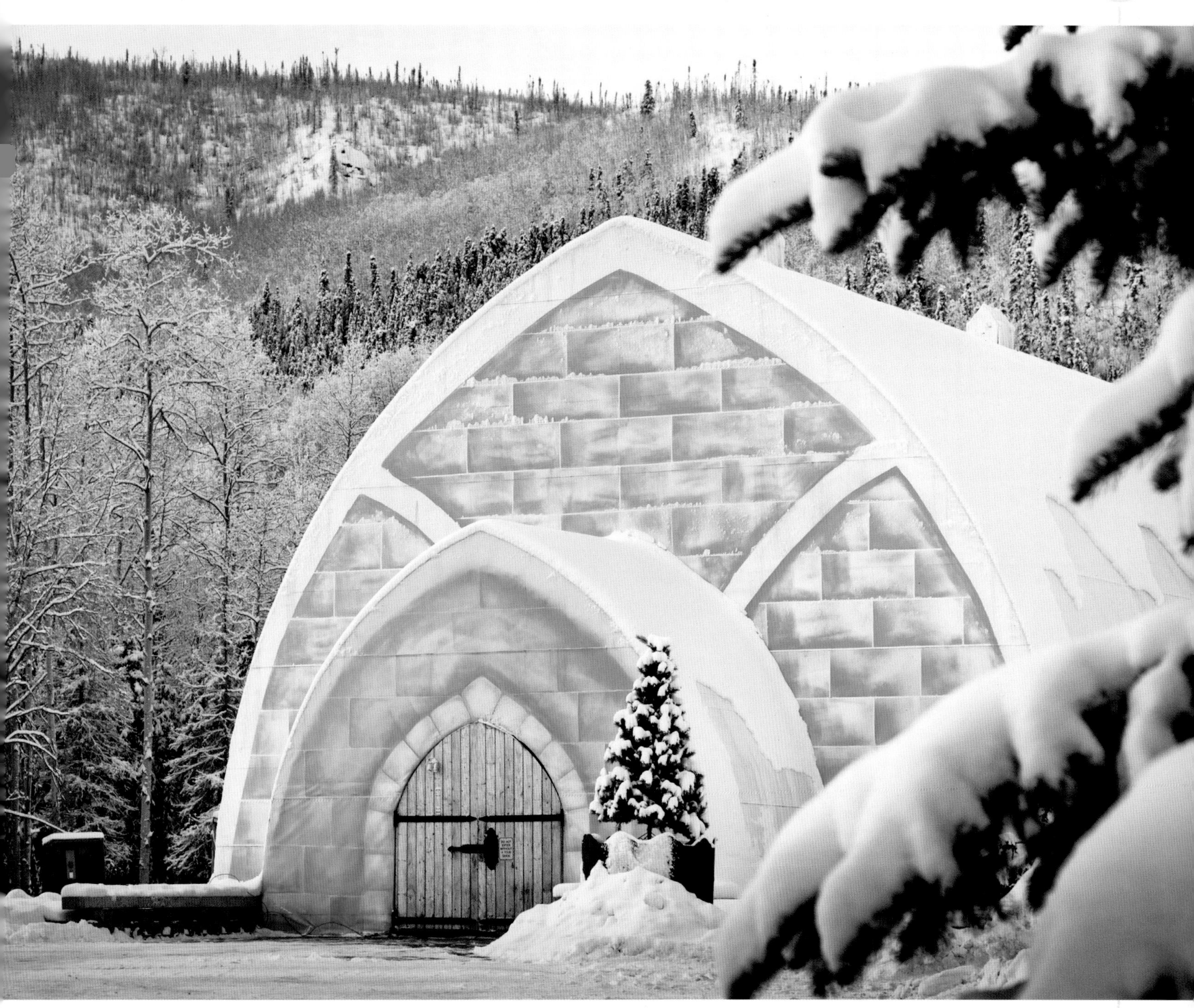

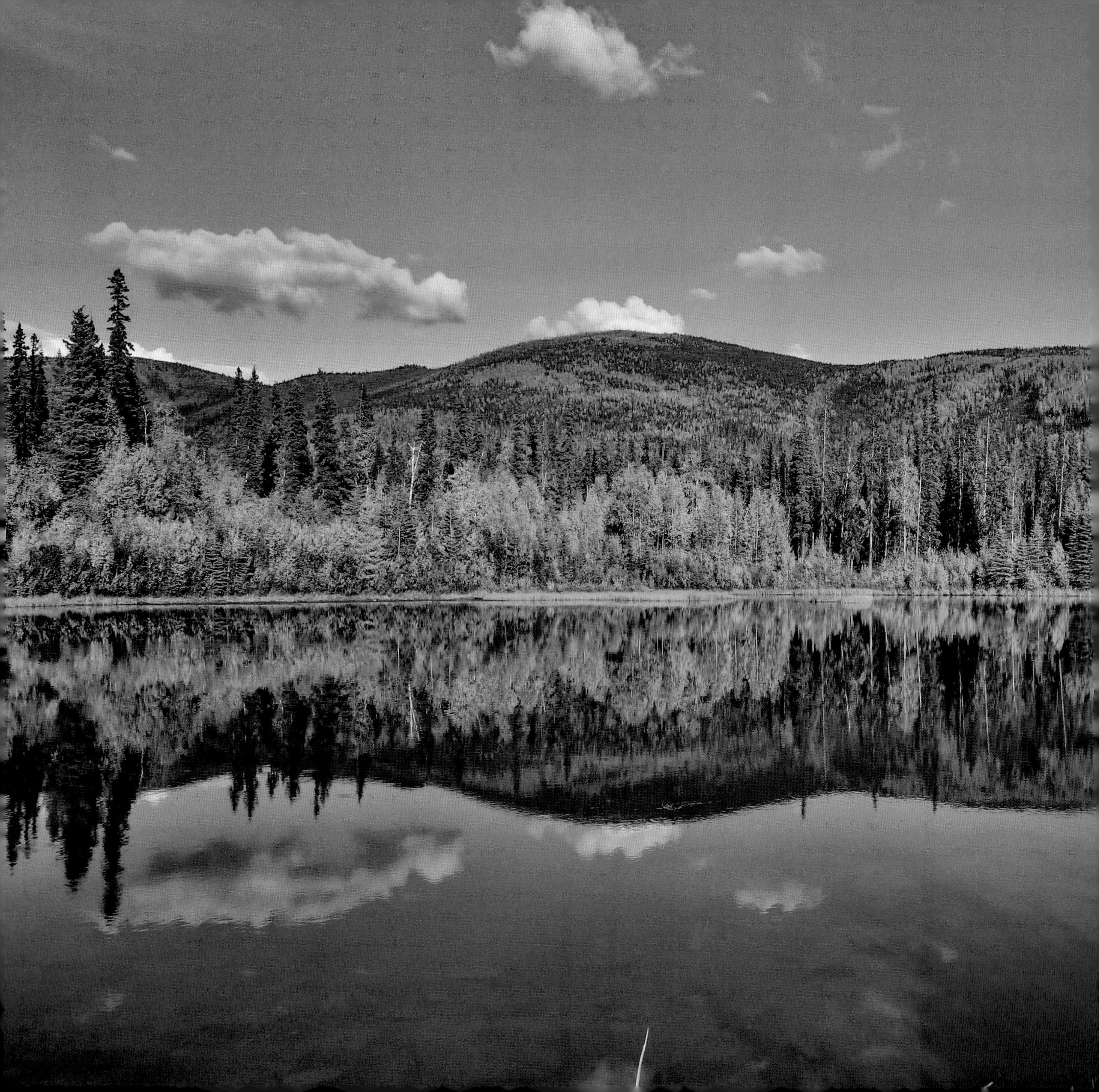

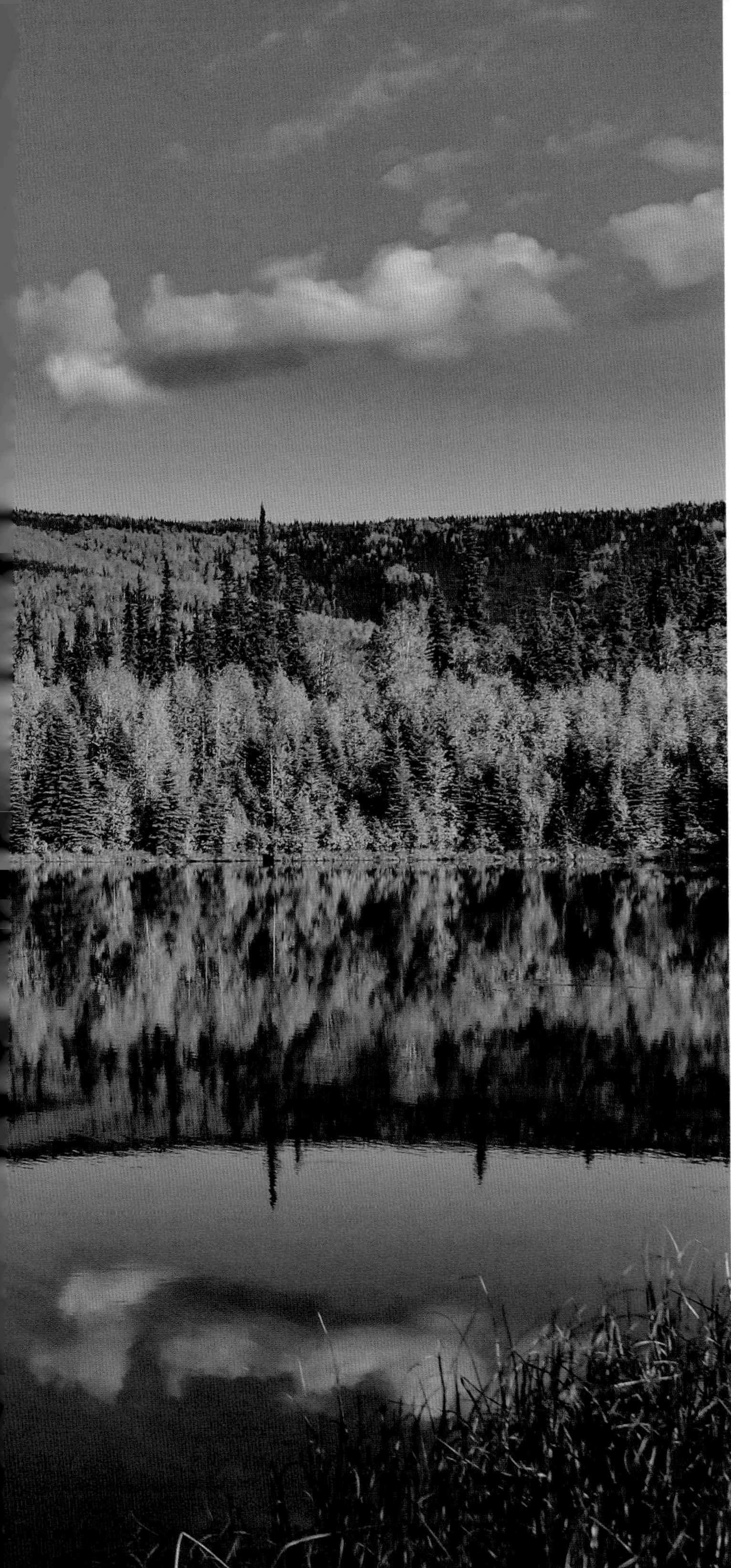

48 MILE POND, CHENA RIVER STATE PARK

Fairbanks

It is not especially long or large, in fact: this is the 48 Mile Pond by virtue of its lying alongside the 48-mile marker on the Chena Hot Springs Road north-east of Fairbanks. What it lacks in length, however, it more than makes up for in beauty, reflecting the woods that crowd along its banks. It shows to best advantage the subtler (and, paradoxically, 'warmer') colours of the Alaskan autumn. While conifers are considered evergreen, that is something of an oversimplification, even if they do not actually lose their needles in the season of supposed 'fall'.

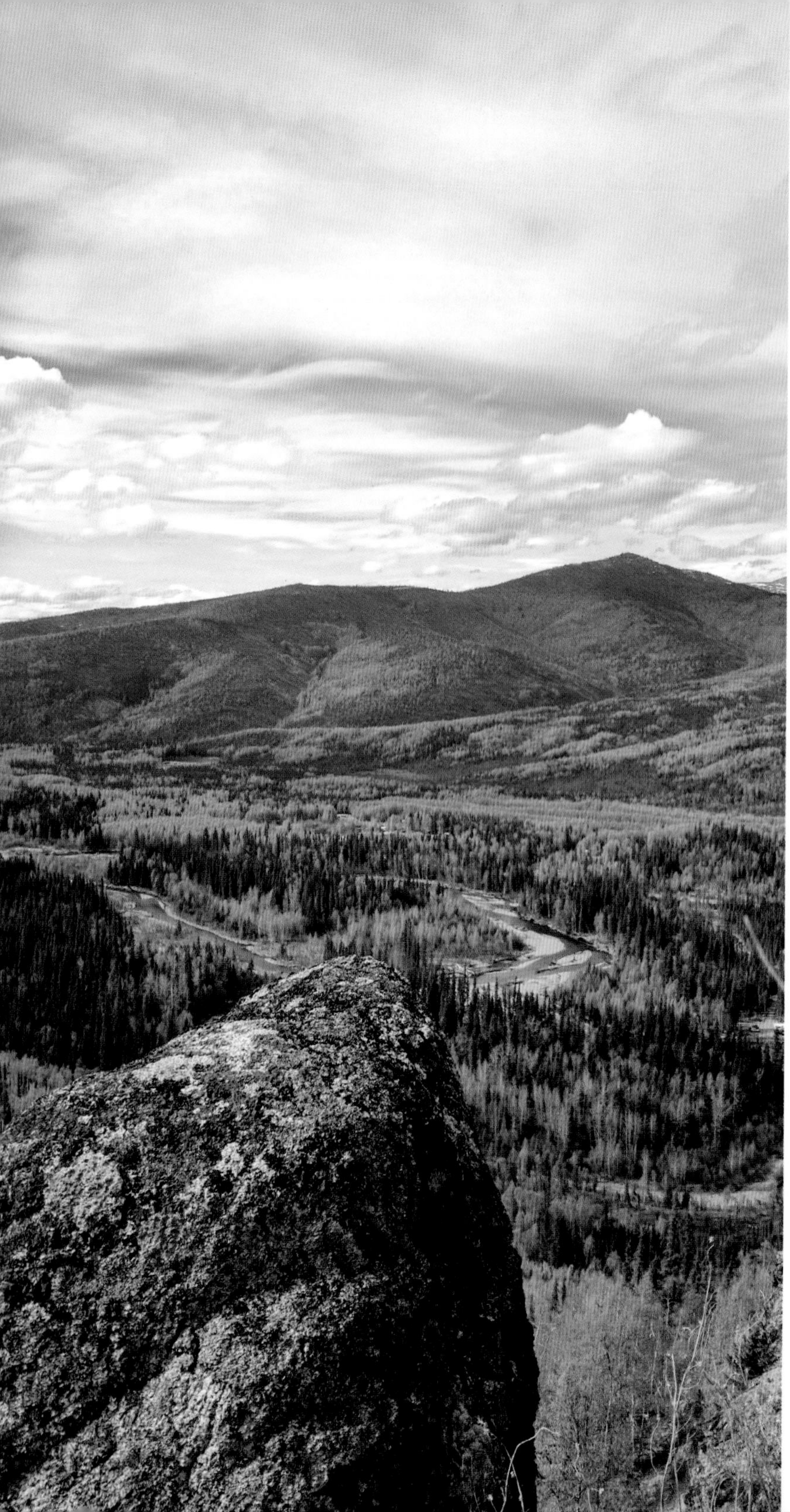

ANGEL ROCKS, CHENA RIVER STATE PARK

Fairbanks

Such is the roughness of the terrain round here that the hike through the forest to the Angel Rocks is hard, though it is only 6 km (3½ miles) each way. From its starting point, the trail climbs quickly through 270 m (900ft); at its highest point, it is 530 m (1,750 ft) above sea level. It is definitely worth the effort, though: the lookout on this granite outcrop commands the most stunning vistas across a deeply wooded valley. The ultimate Alaskan view, it might be said.

NORTHERN LIGHTS

Fairbanks

Shimmering, strangely coloured curtains displace the darkness of the night, casting a mysterious tinge over the bright white ice below. In between, the lights of the city wink. The Interior's major urban centre, with a population topping 31,000, Fairbanks advertises itself as the 'aurora capital of the world'. People have been coming here to enjoy the Northern Lights for many years, of course: now aurora tourism is an industry in its own right. The University of Alaska here even runs an online aurora forecast.

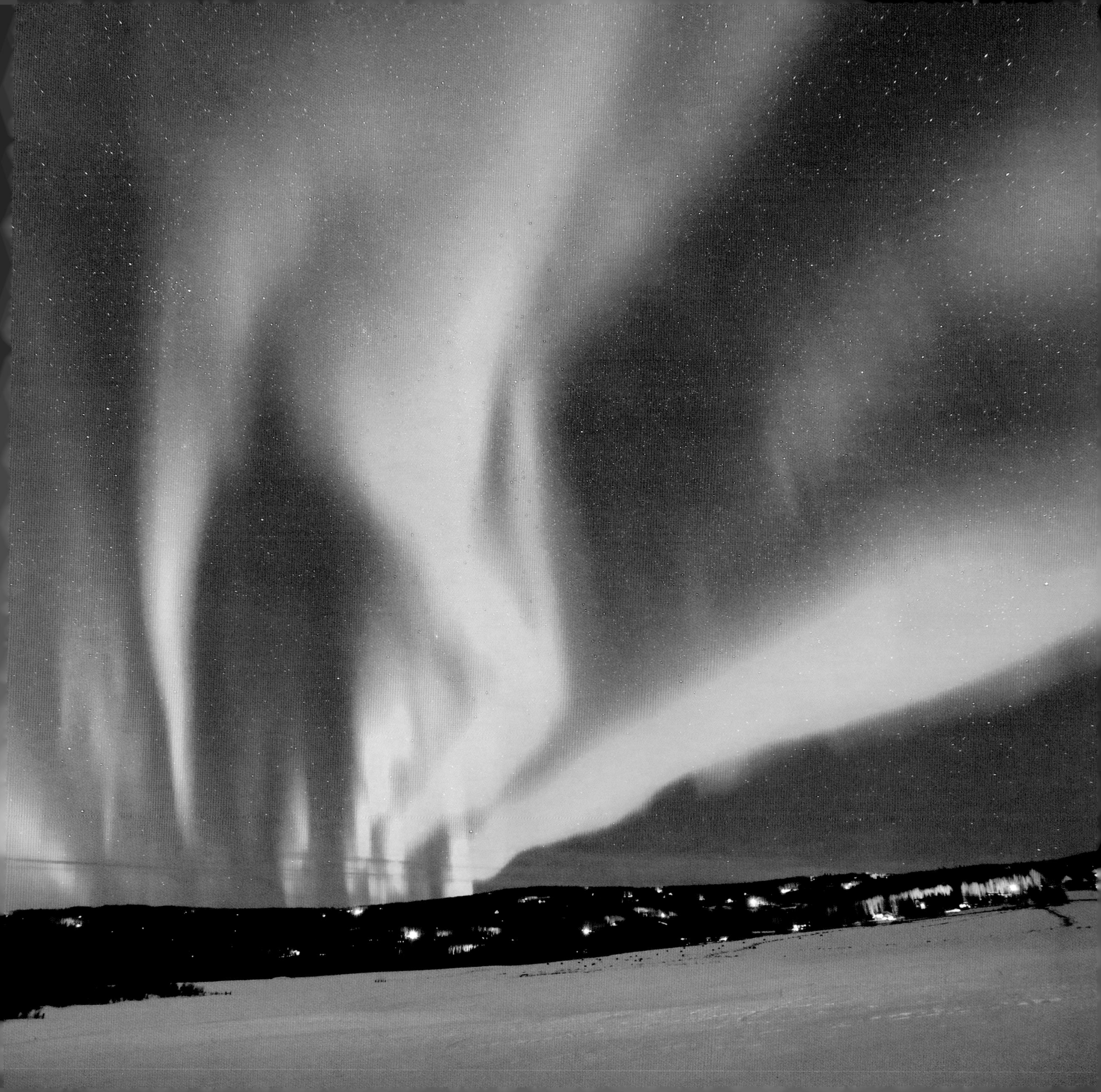

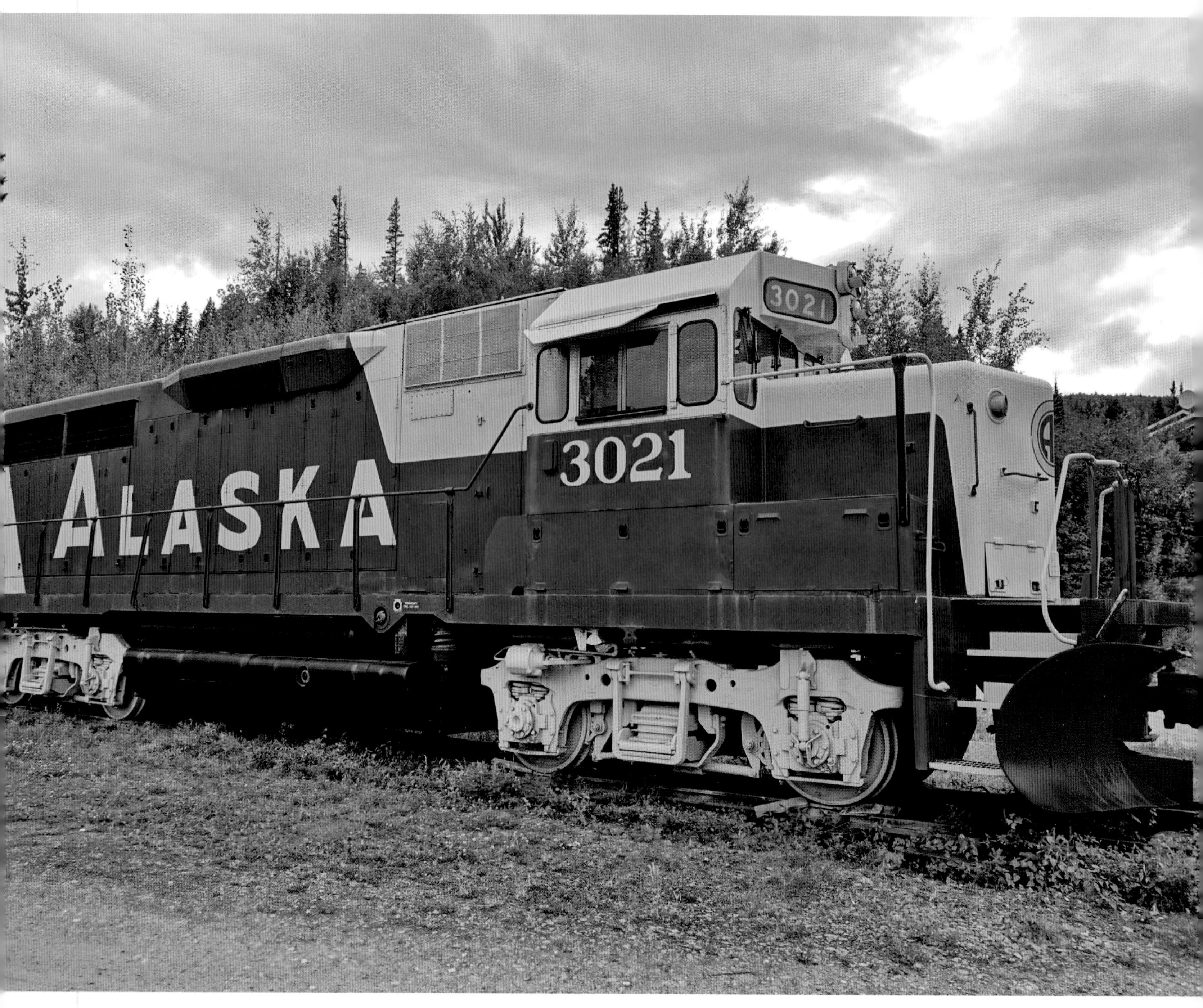
3021
ALASKA
3021

AURORA EXPRESS

Fairbanks

All aboard...! This locomotive is static now, like the assorted antique carriages lined up behind it on a set of sidings on this thickly wooded hillside. But why would you need to go anywhere, when you can stand still in such style, staying and sleeping in such lovingly reproduced and lavishly furnished period-splendour, with views out over Fairbanks and the Tanana River Valley? And, of course, when you know that after darkness falls the world's greatest lightshow, the aurora borealis, will come to you?

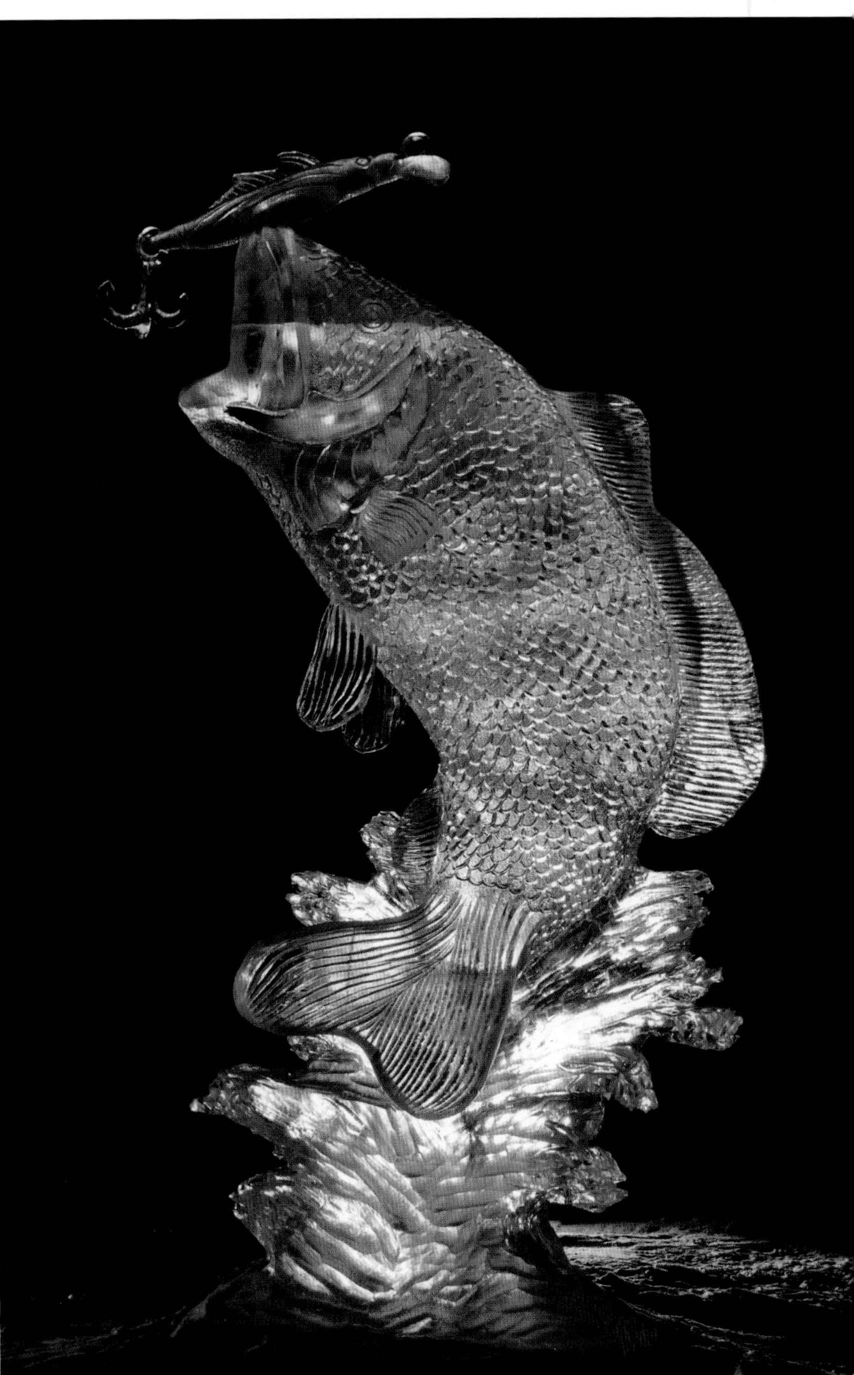

WORLD ICE ART CHAMPIONSHIPS

Fairbanks

If life gives you lemons, the saying goes, make lemonade.... Life gave Alaska prodigious amounts of ice. Hence the inauguration in 1989 of the Ice Art Championships, now attracting teams of sculptors from far and wide. It is tempting to say 'from around the world', but colder countries have naturally predominated: recent winners have come from Finland, Russia, China and Japan. And, of course, from Canada and the United States, especially Alaska, where ice art has become a real area of cultural interest.

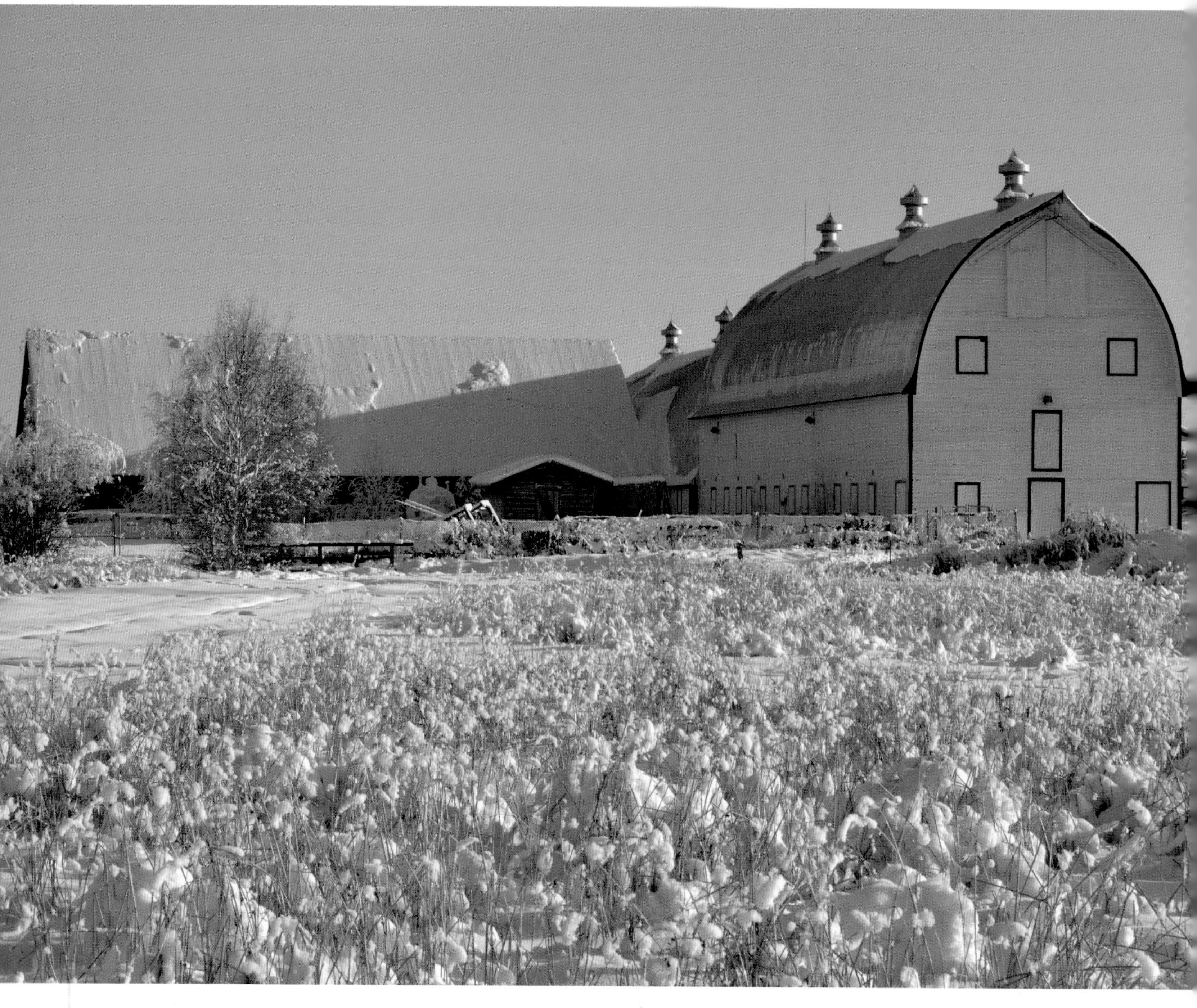

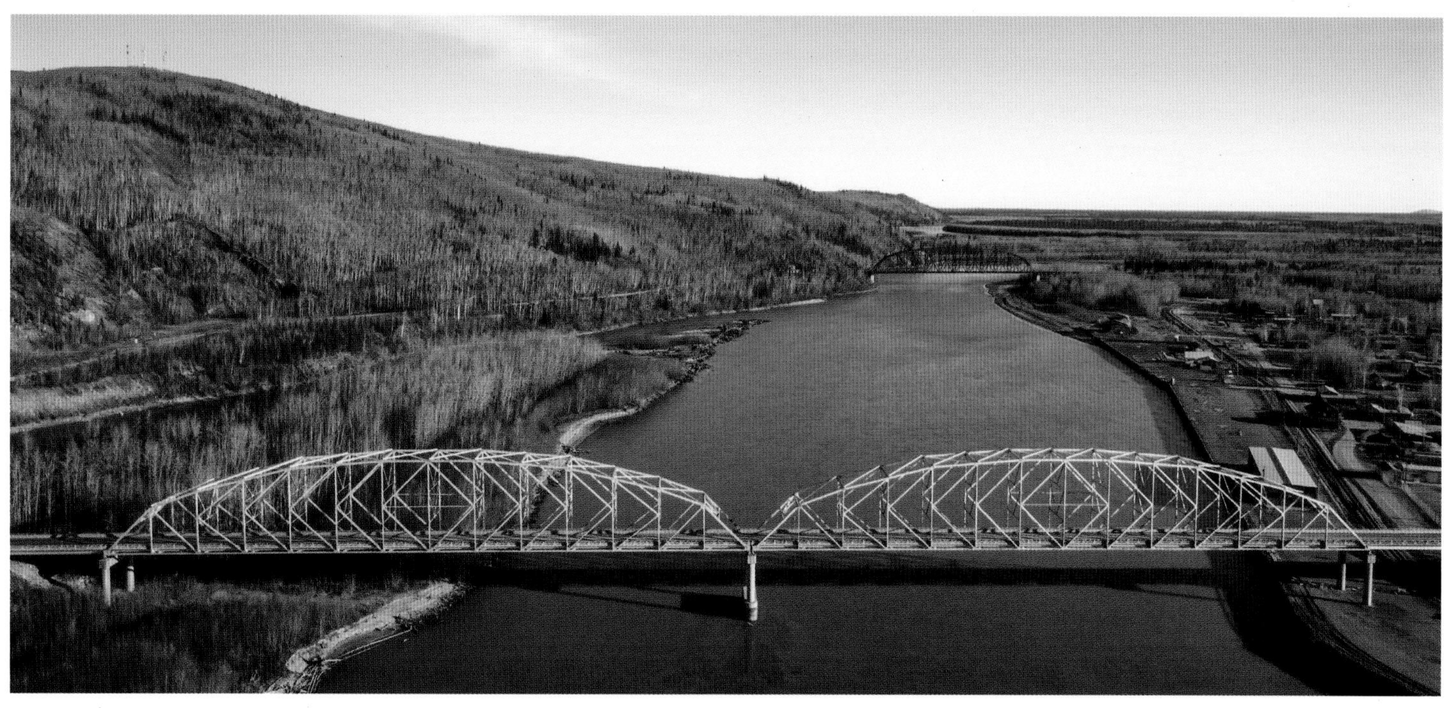

CREAMER'S FIELD MIGRATORY WATERFOWL REFUGE

Fairbanks

Charles Hinckley started a dairy farm here as long ago as 1904; the aptly named Charles Albert Creamer (1889–1974) took over in 1938 and built this barn. He also, however, put out his surplus grain to feed the flocks of geese, ducks, cranes and other birds who used his 890 hectares (2,200 acres) of open pasture, wetlands and wooded stands as a staging post on their long journeys of migration. Since his death, it has been adopted by the state as an official waterfowl refuge.

MEARS MEMORIAL BRIDGE, NENANA

Fairbanks

Some 80 km (50 miles) downstream of Fairbanks on the Tanana, this handsome bridge carries the Anchorage–Fairbanks section of the Alaska Railroad 201 m (700 ft) across the Tanana River. Its opening in 1923 by Warren G. Harding (1865–1923) marked the first visit to Alaska by any US President, and the start of Nenana's heyday (all too brief) as a railway town. It was named in honour of Colonel Frederick Mears (1878–1939), trained as a military engineer with the US Army, then chief engineer of the Alaska Railroad.

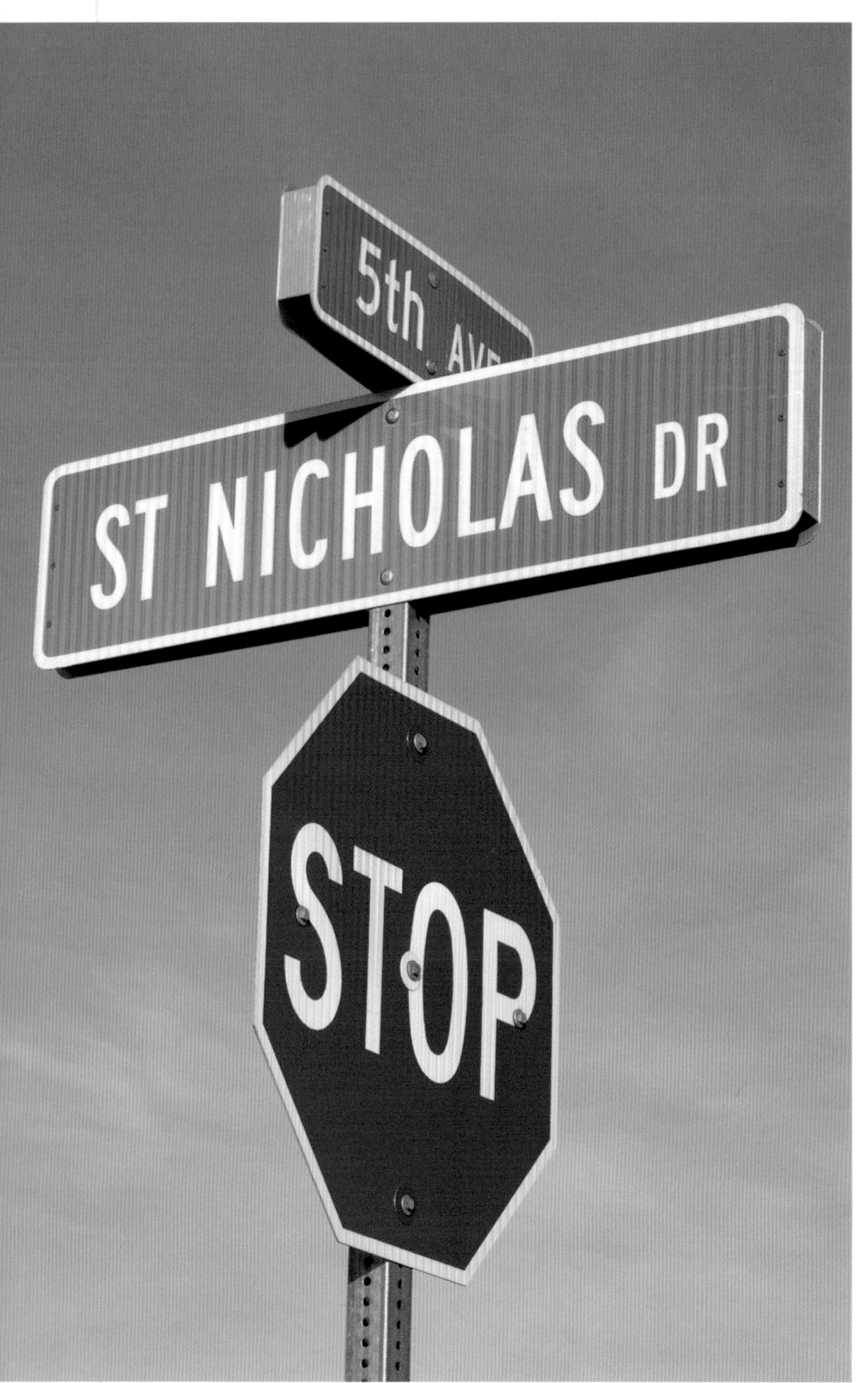

STREET SIGN, NORTH POLE

Fairbanks

No Grinches allowed … It is not even in the North of Alaska, let alone above the Arctic Circle, and is pushing 3,000 km (1,700 miles) from the real thing. Even so, North Pole – as it was named by entrepreneurially minded locals in the 1950s – milks its spurious connection with Father Christmas for all it is worth. There are candy-cane-style streetlights; giant reindeer and Santa statues; and umpteen shops catering to all your (real and imagined) Yuletide needs. The post office does a roaring trade postmarking and forwarding Americans' Christmas cards.

RUBY, YUKON RIVER

Western Interior

This once-prosperous settlement has seen a century of slow decline. Like so many such places along the Yukon Valley it was established in the Gold Rush (1906–10), but found a function as a lumbering centre when that fever passed. Even so, those of its sons who shipped out so eagerly to go and fight in two world wars were not so keen to come back at the conflict's end. Ruby would have been a ghost town had Native families from its periphery not trickled in to take over the best of the abandoned homes.

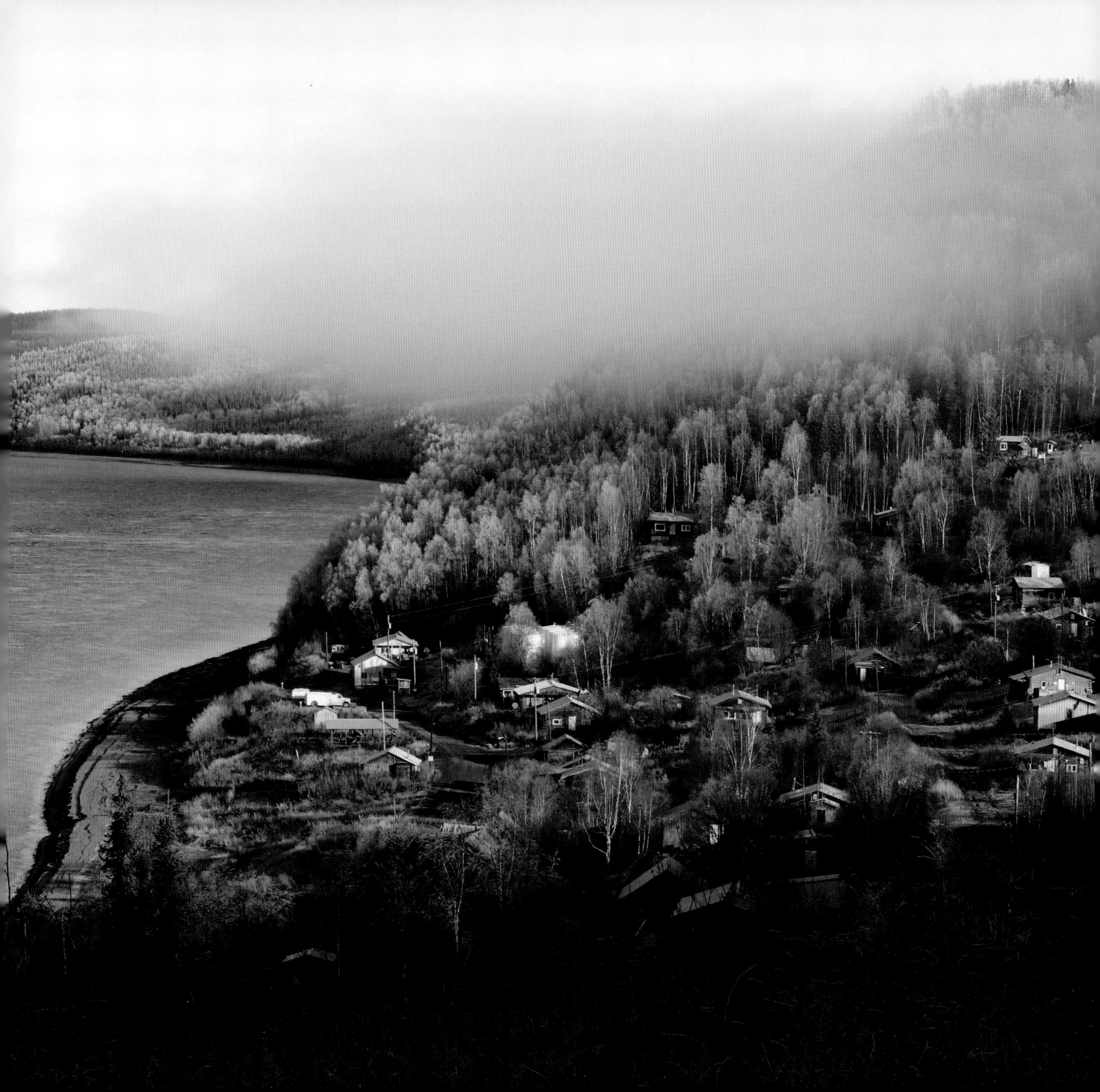

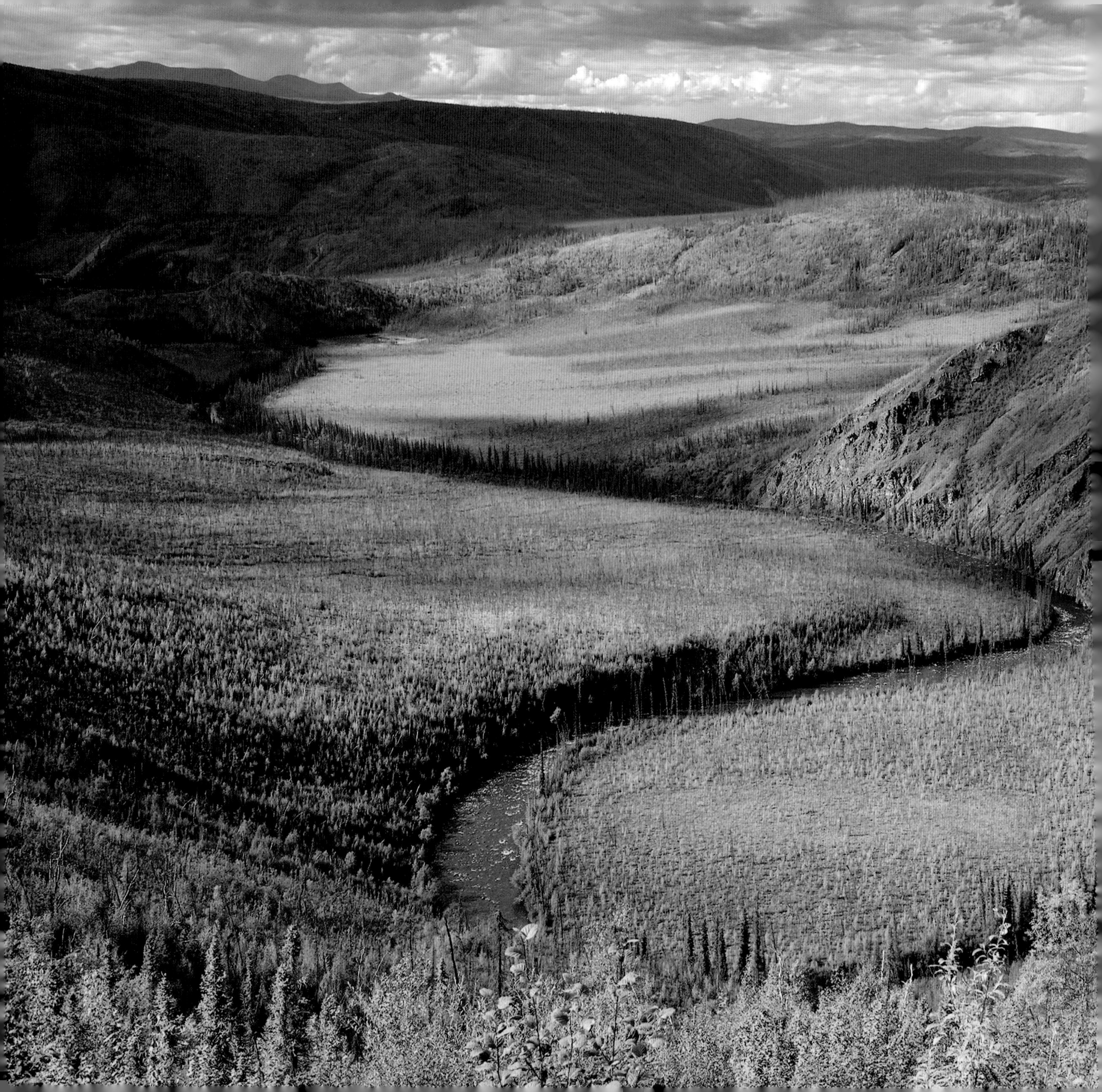

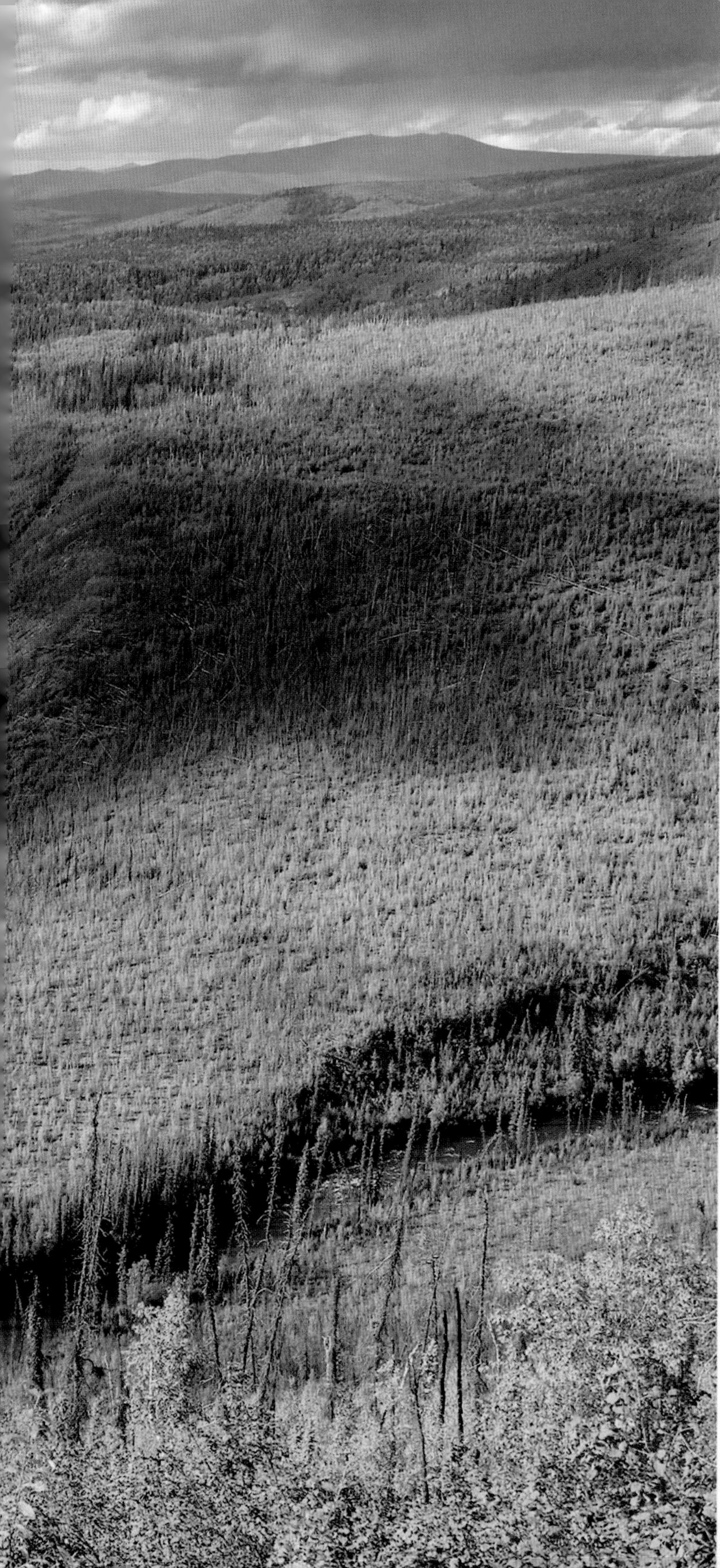

WALKER FORK RIVER, TAYLOR HIGHWAY

Alaska Highway

The Taylor Highway is a 260-km (160-mile) section of the Alaska Highway (Route 5) south-east of Fairbanks. It starts at Tetlin Junction and ends at Eagle, to the north-east. So cold and snowy does it get down here that the Highway is closed to wheeled vehicles not just for the deep-winter months, but for more than half the year, between October and April. On the other hand, when it *is* traversable, the views it affords are unrivalled. Here we look along the wooded floodplain of the winding Walker Fork River.

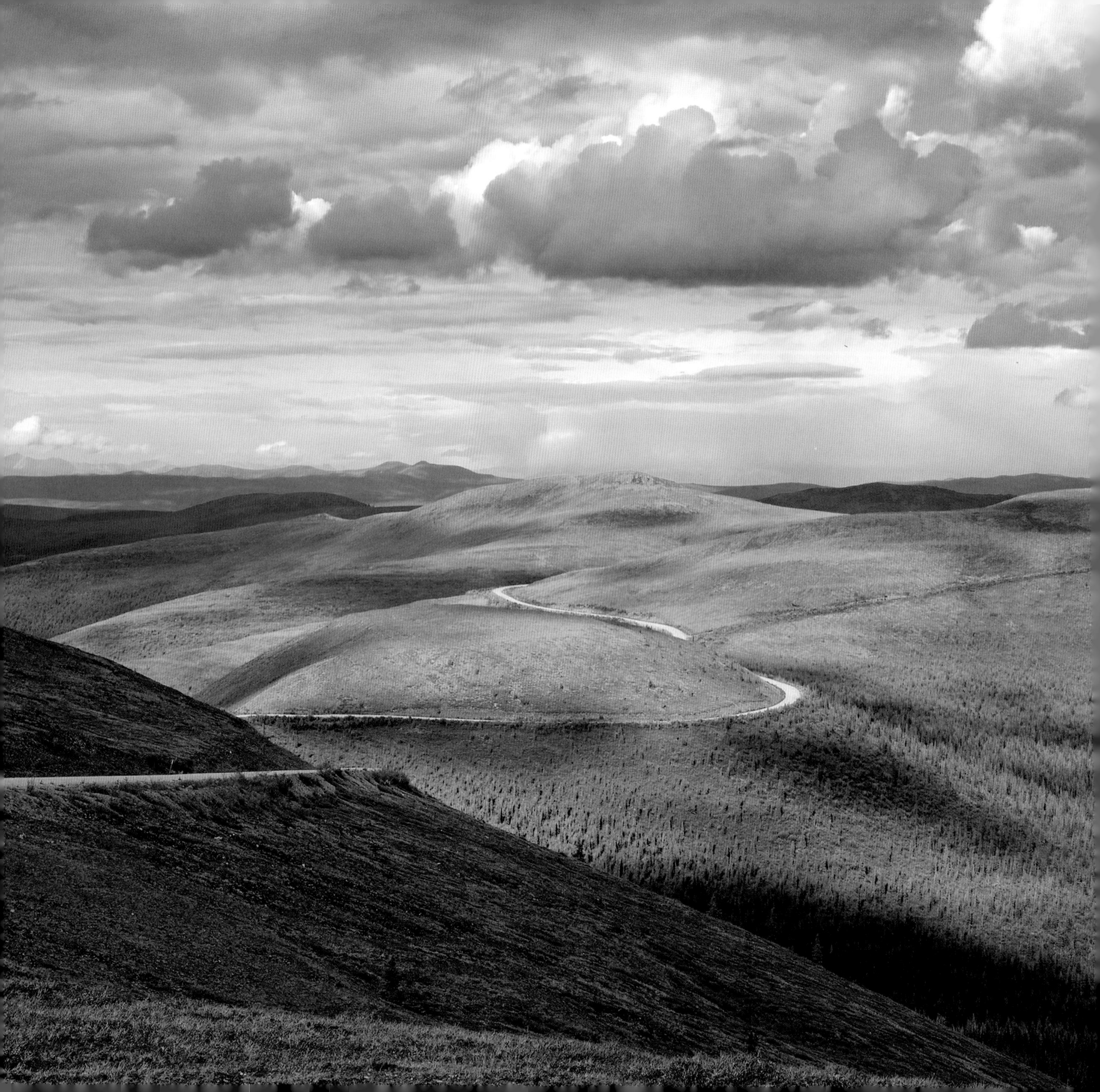

TOP OF THE WORLD HIGHWAY

Alaska Highway

For much of its 127 km (79 miles), this road runs through Canada's Yukon Territory, its eastern terminus the town of Dawson. Its western, Alaskan, section – some 21 km (13 miles) in length – joins the Taylor Highway (*see* page 59) near Jack Wade. It takes its title from the fact that, not only is it among the northernmost major roads to be found on earth, but also its winding course avoids the valley bottoms for the (more exposed, but less likely to be snowbound) upland heights.

SCULPTURE, CHICKEN

Alaska Highway

With well over 30 designated 'ghost towns' in Alaska, Chicken is perhaps doing well to have a population in single figures. Like so many settlements here, it was established in the 1890s at the time of the Gold Rush; as elsewhere, the boom times came quickly to an end. At a low-key level, though, the search for gold has been able to continue: the year-round population (seven in the census of 2010) swells significantly during the summer months.

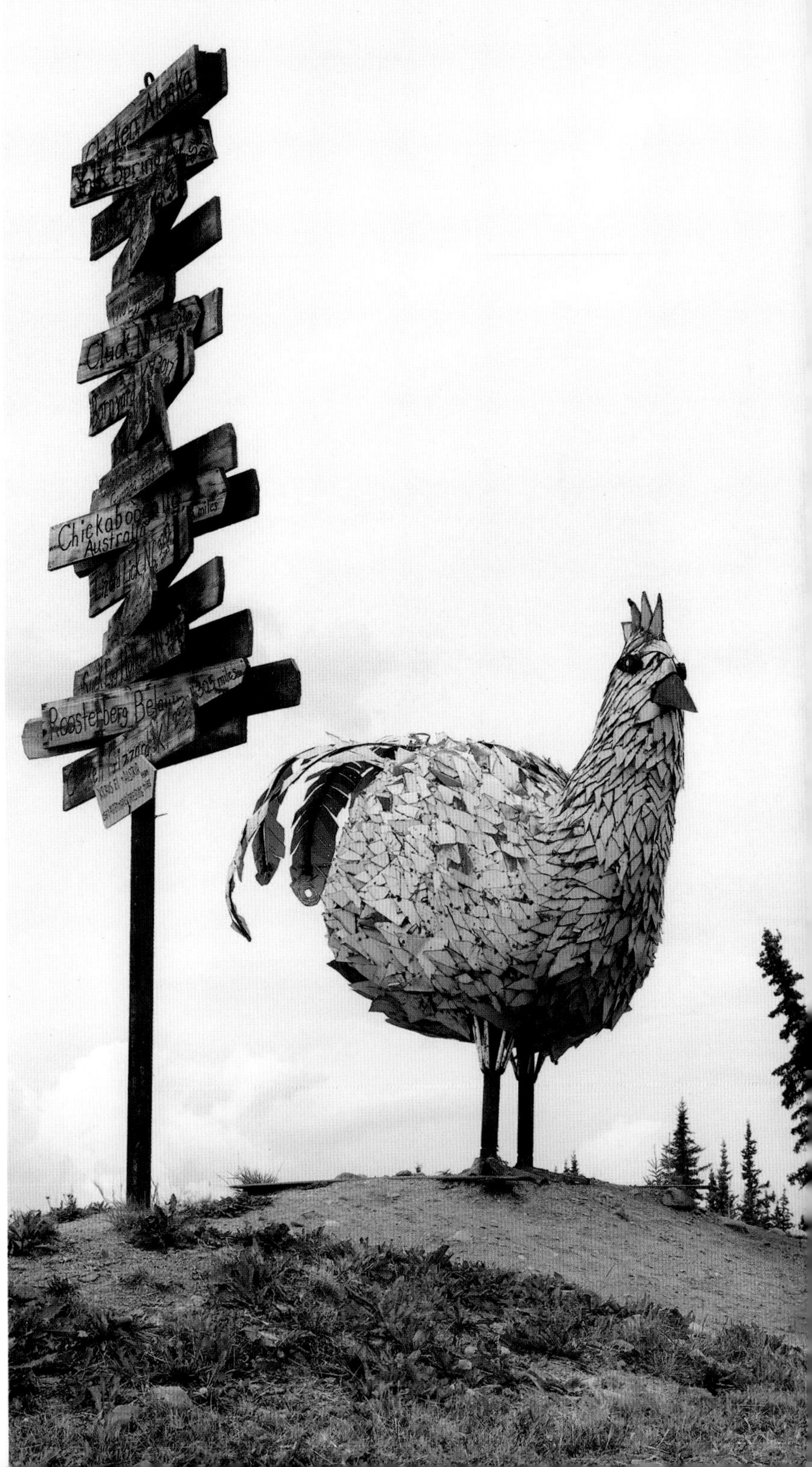

POKER CREEK BORDER CROSSING, EAGLE

Alaska Highway

The Top of the World Highway crosses the Canadian–Alaskan border here, the most northerly crossing point between Alaska and the Yukon Territory. And consequently, as the sign explains, the United States' most northerly border control. Though only opened in 1971, this US-built, log-cabin-style structure is now boarded up, having been replaced in 2001 by a larger joint US–Canadian construction. Given its comparative quietness, it is easy to lose sight of the sheer length of the Alaska–Canada border: 2,475 km (1,538 miles).

TANANA RIVER, RICHARDSON HIGHWAY

Alaska Highway

The Delta River joins the Tanana here, a little way north of the town of Delta Junction. You can see the confluence clearly from the road. Running north–south between Fairbanks and Valdez on the southern coast, the Richardson Highway followed the course of earlier trails and wagon tracks. Upgraded in the 1920s (though it was paved completely only in the 1950s), it is Alaska's oldest modern major road. It constitutes what is now Route 4 from Valdez to Delta Junction; Route 2 from there to its terminus at Fairbanks.

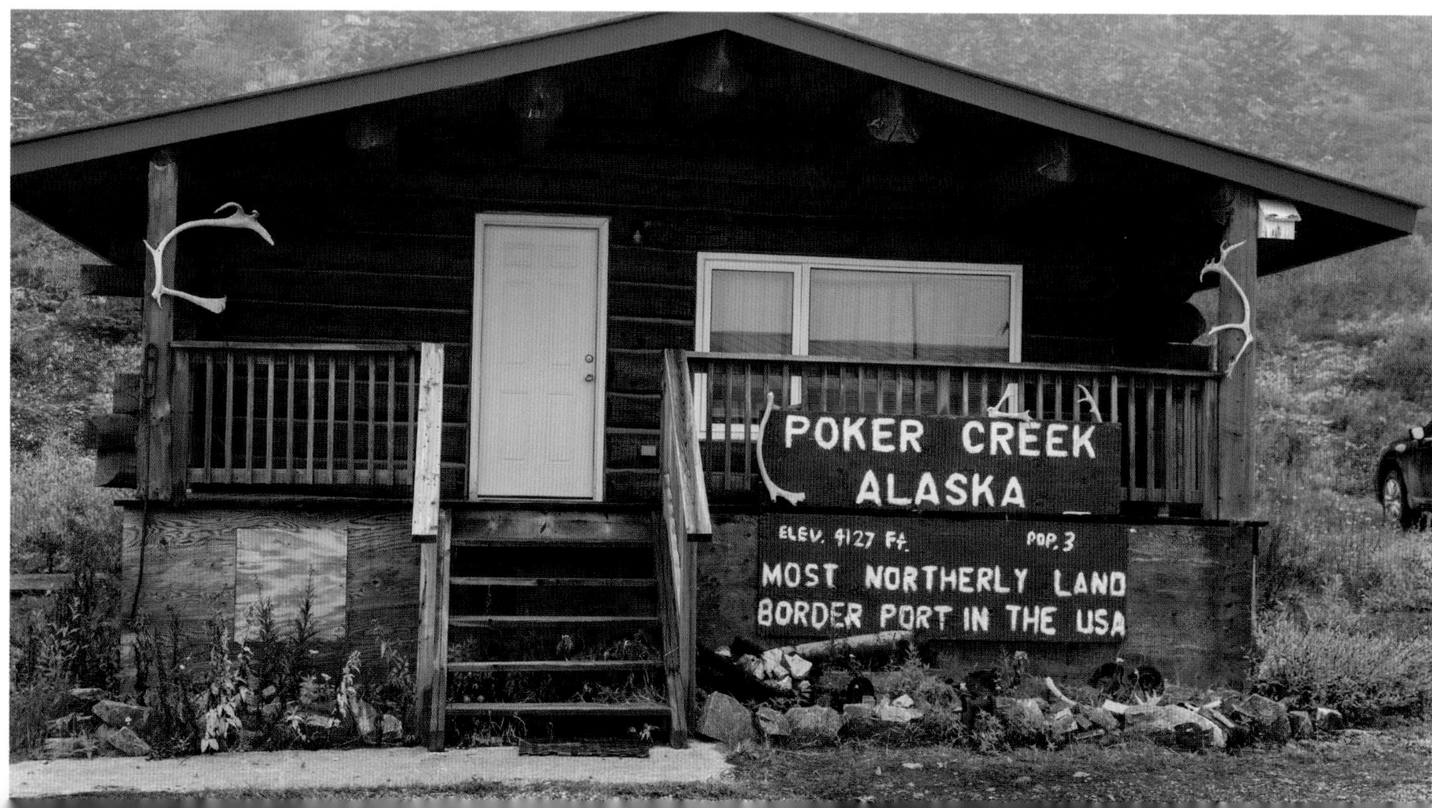

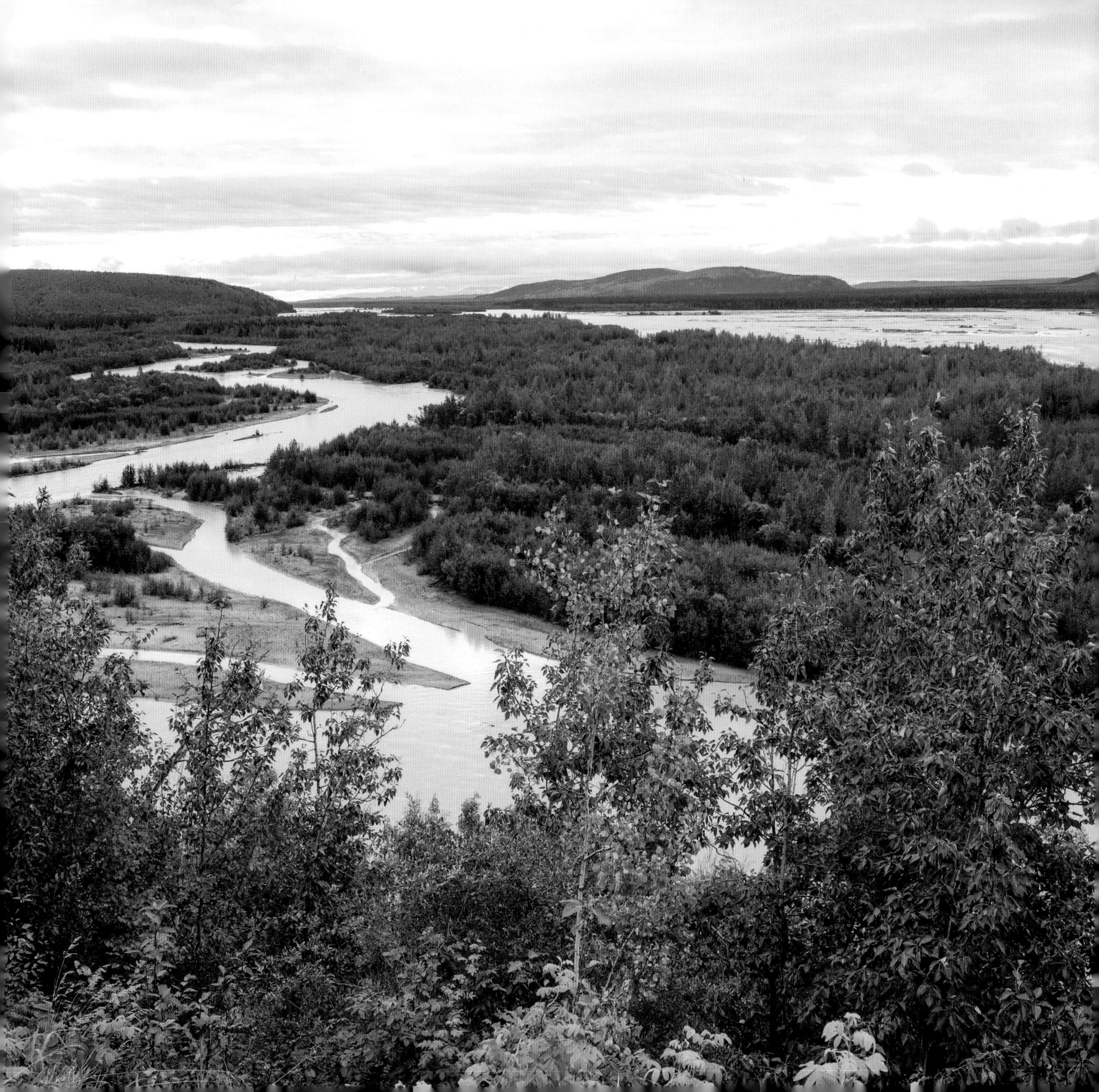

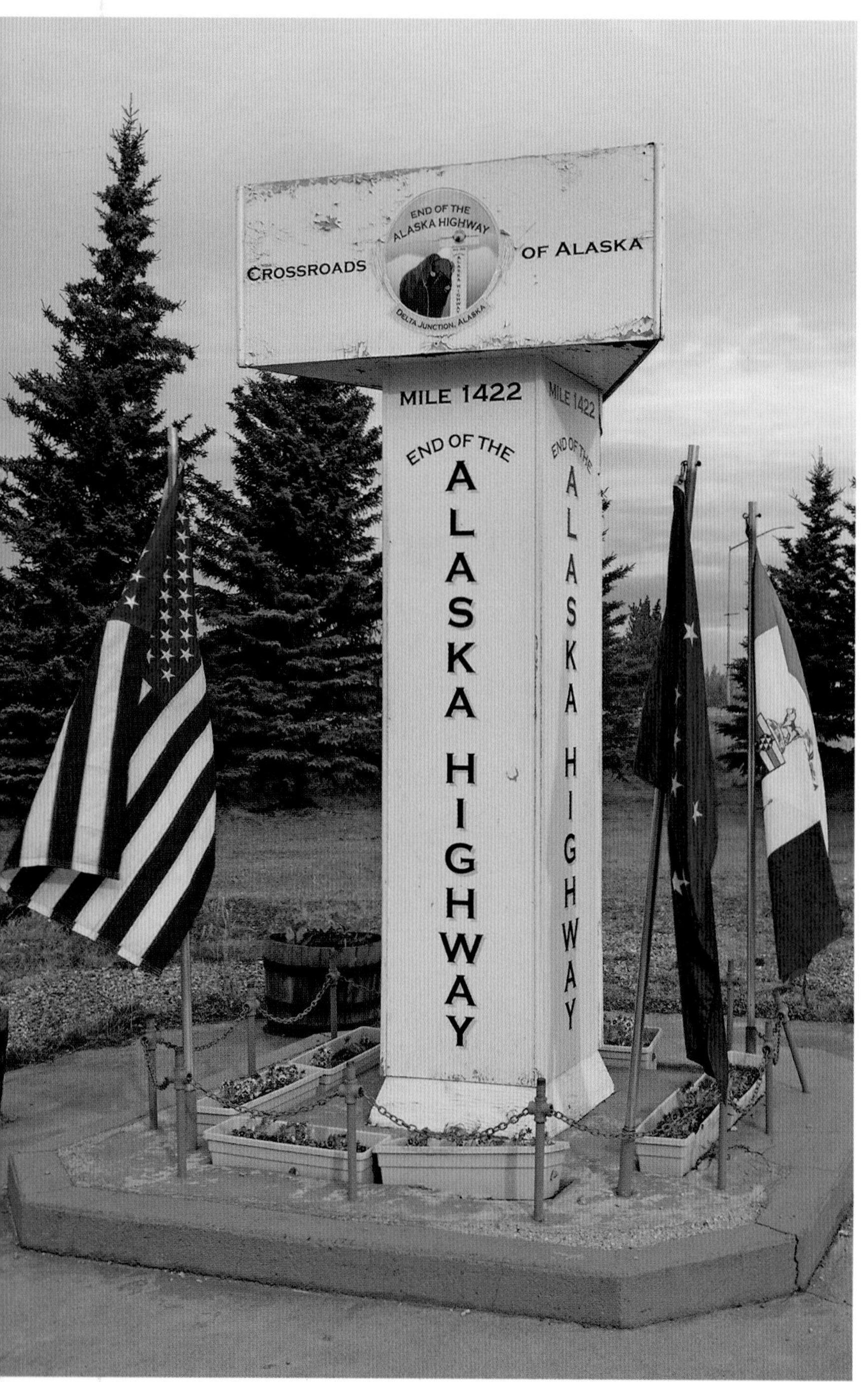

MILEPOST, DELTA JUNCTION

Alaska Highway

Alaska's relation to the 'Lower 48' has always been anomalous. Symbolic and strategic considerations alike helped drive the patriotic decision to build a connecting highway during the Second World War. Canada was agreeable, but had no stake in the road's success, so did not participate in construction or help with funding. This is, then, an 'all-American' road, at least from its start in Dawson Creek, BC. Pushing its way northwestward up through otherwise quiet areas of inland British Columbia, it links up with the Alaskan system here at Delta Junction.

DEADMAN LAKE, TETLIN NATIONAL WILDLIFE REFUGE

Alaska Highway

The clouds that cross the heavens here, and the trees that line the lakeshore, are perfectly reflected in the mirror-still surface of the waters. Along with woods and lakes like this, the Tetlin National Wildlife Refuge has a broad variety of biomes – including streams, rivers, extensive wetlands and, at higher elevations, Arctic-style tundra. Consequently, it sustains extensive populations of large mammals like wolves, black and grizzly bears and lynx; some rare fish and a wide array of migratory birds.

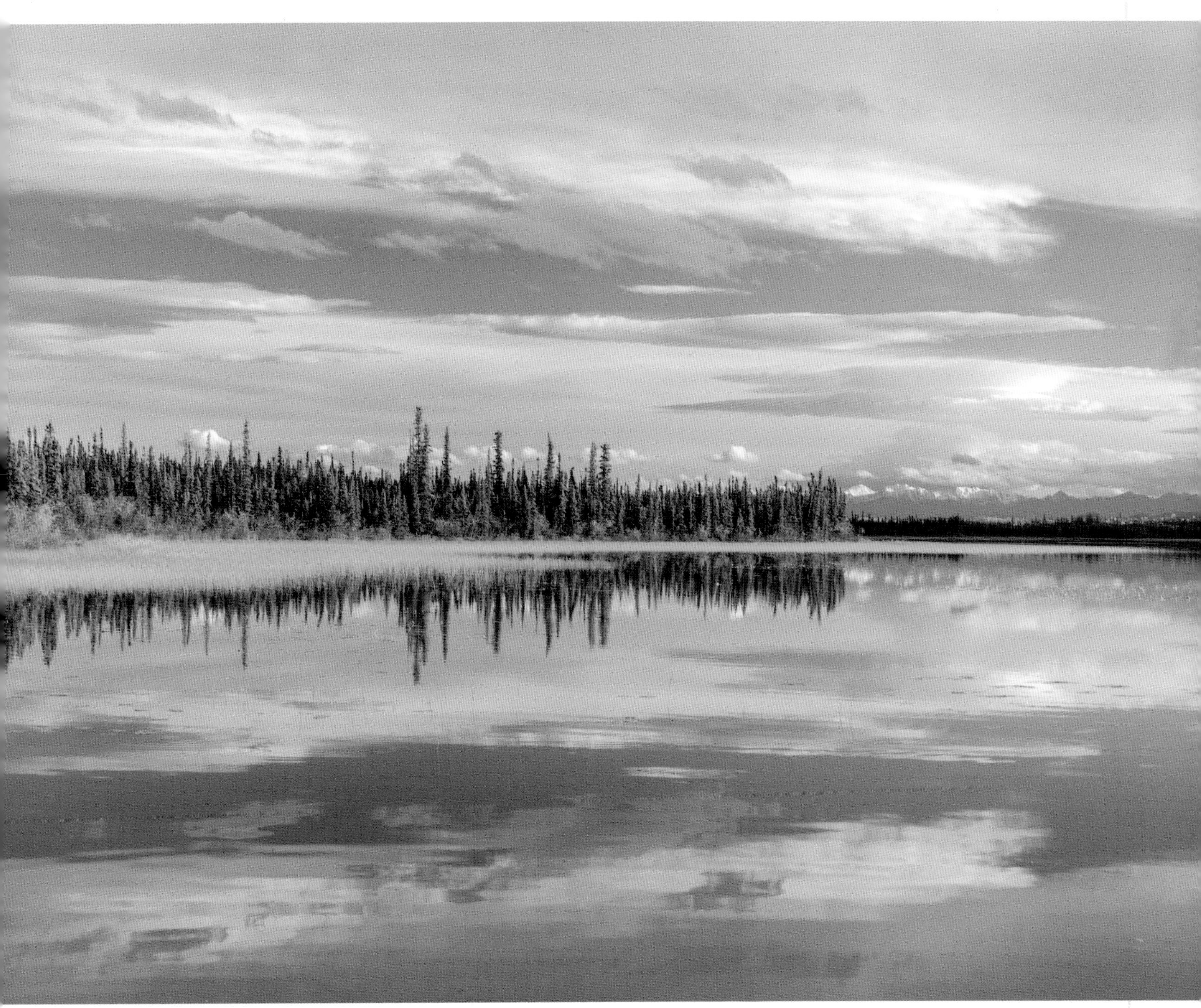

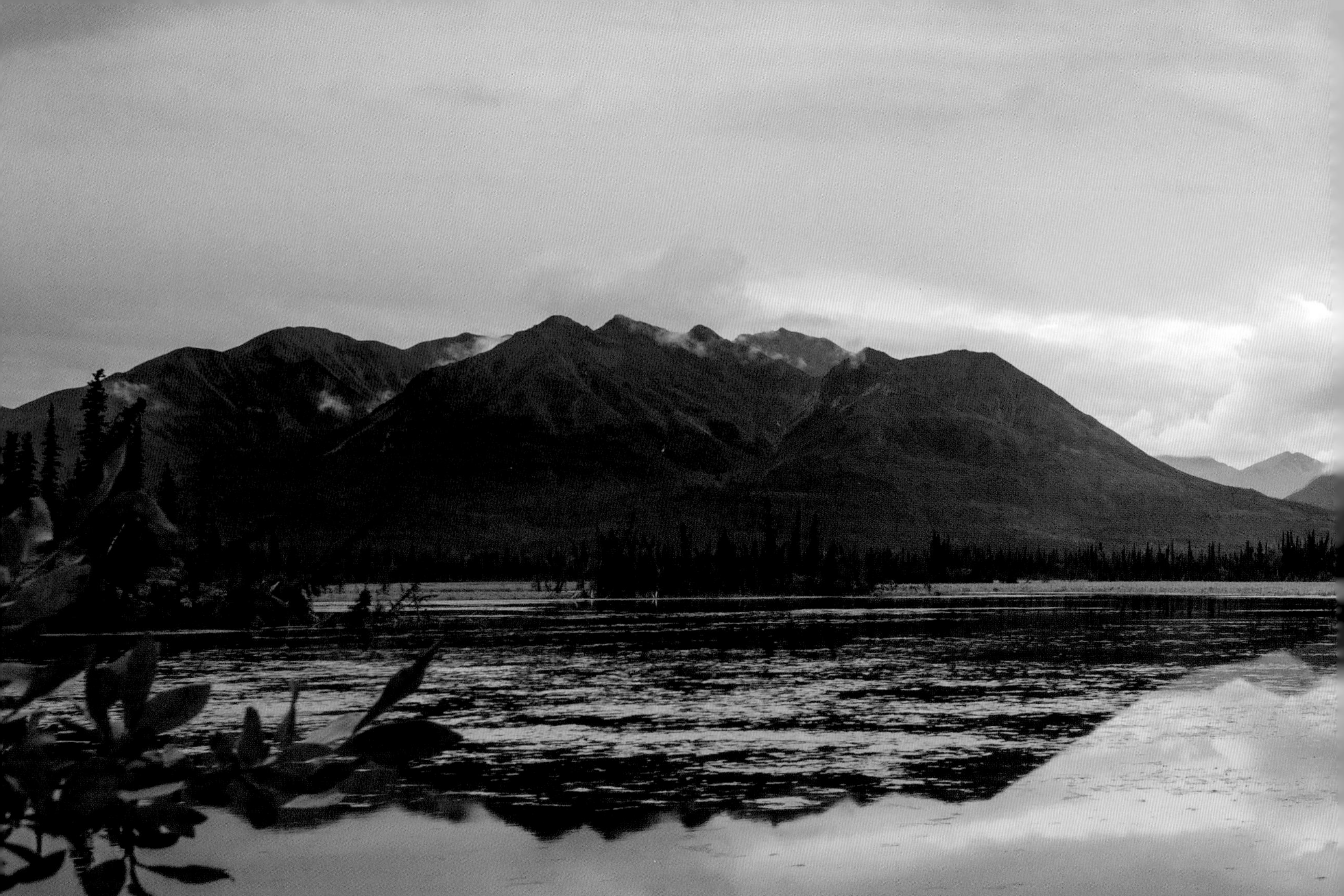

MENTASTA LAKE

Alaska Highway

There are two Mentasta Lakes: one is an actual lake; the other a nearby village; one this enchantingly beautiful natural scene; the other an economically and culturally hard-pressed human community. The predominantly Native-American population of Mentasta Lake, the village, have struggled for decades now with poverty and associated issues (family breakdown, drugs

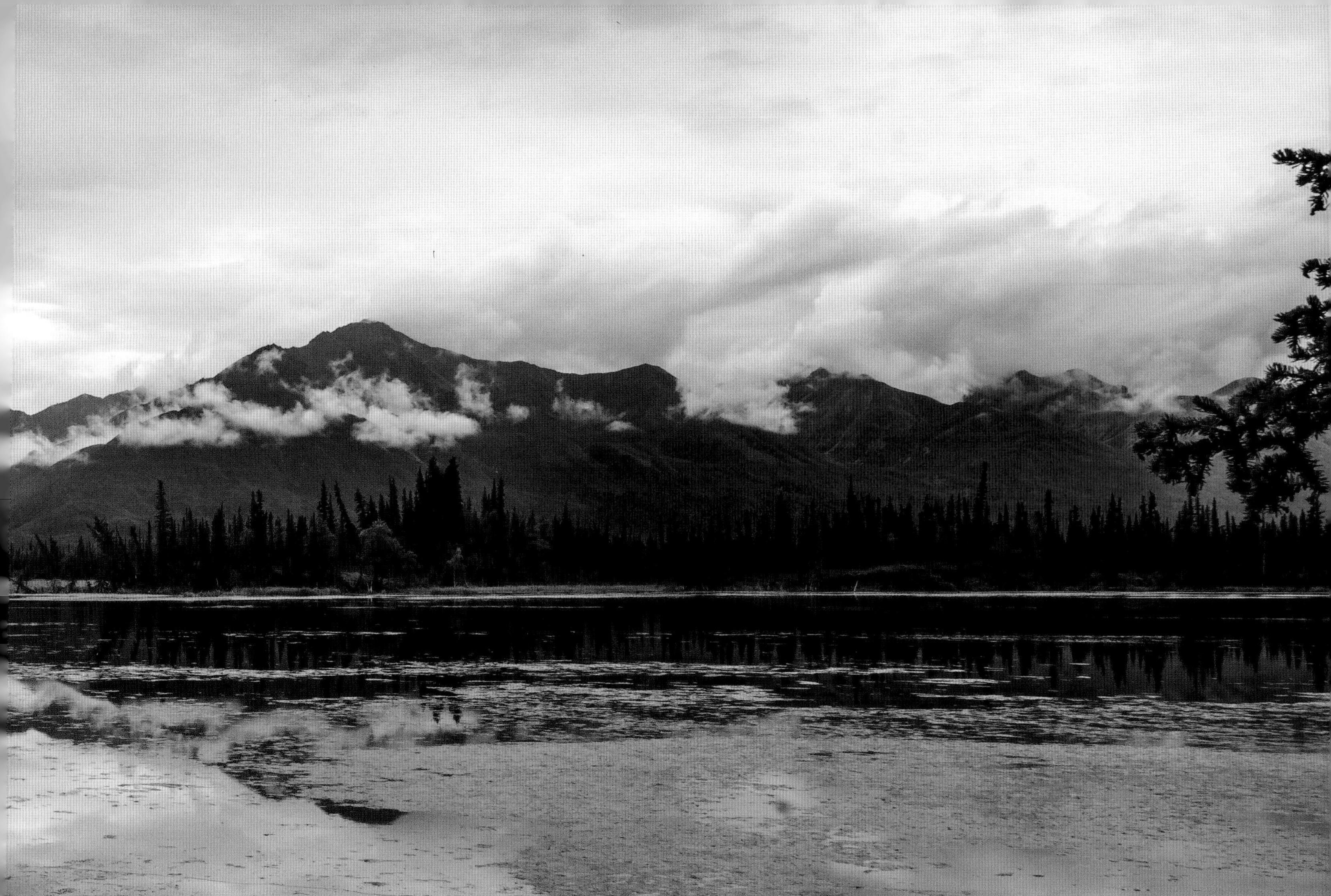

and alcohol....). Living in 'paradise' has certainly not brought them salvation. There is no greater challenge for Alaska, looking forward, than that of finding a way for its founding peoples to live well and happily in this most bountifully blessed of states.

DALL SHEEP, SAVAGE RIVER

Denali National Park

There are more exciting species, maybe, but these wild sheep have been part of the northwestern ecology for millions of years; their protection was the main justification for the creation of the Denali National Park in 1971. Not that there were no other good reasons for this beautiful bit of wilderness to be preserved. Wildlife apart, more than 80 archaeological sites here have offered evidence of human habitation dating back 11,000 years. And then, of course, there is the iconic status of Denali, this special peak.

MIDNIGHT SUN, MOUNT DENALI

Denali National Park

North America's highest mountain rises to a height of 6,190 m (20,310 ft). For decades it was officially known as Mount McKinley. It bore this name in honour of the US President William McKinley (1843–1901), who took office in 1897 but was then assassinated at the start of his second term in 1901. Its Koyukon name simply means 'high'. Even so, it mattered sufficiently to local people that they campaigned long and hard for its official recognition, a goal they finally won in 2015.

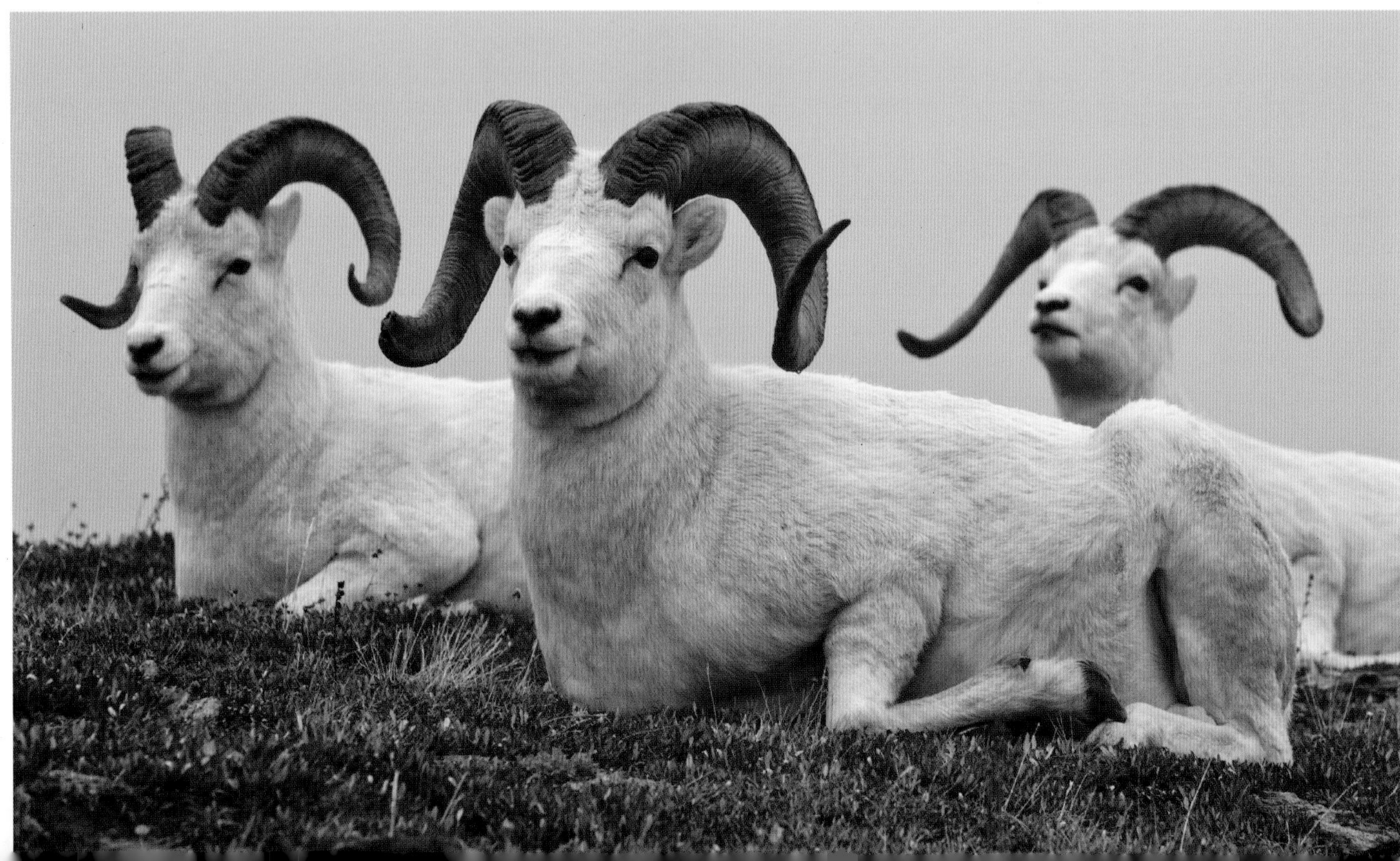

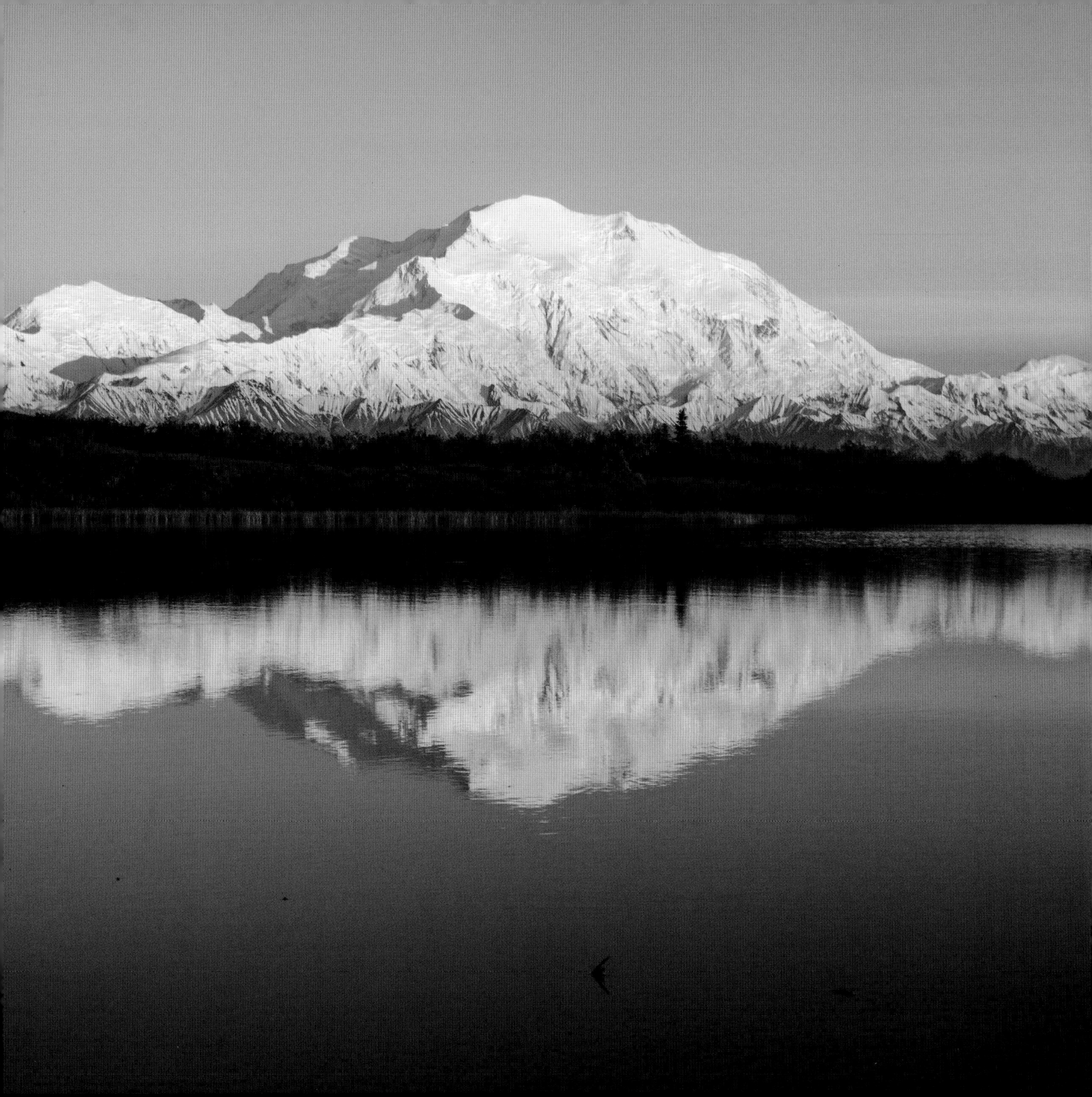

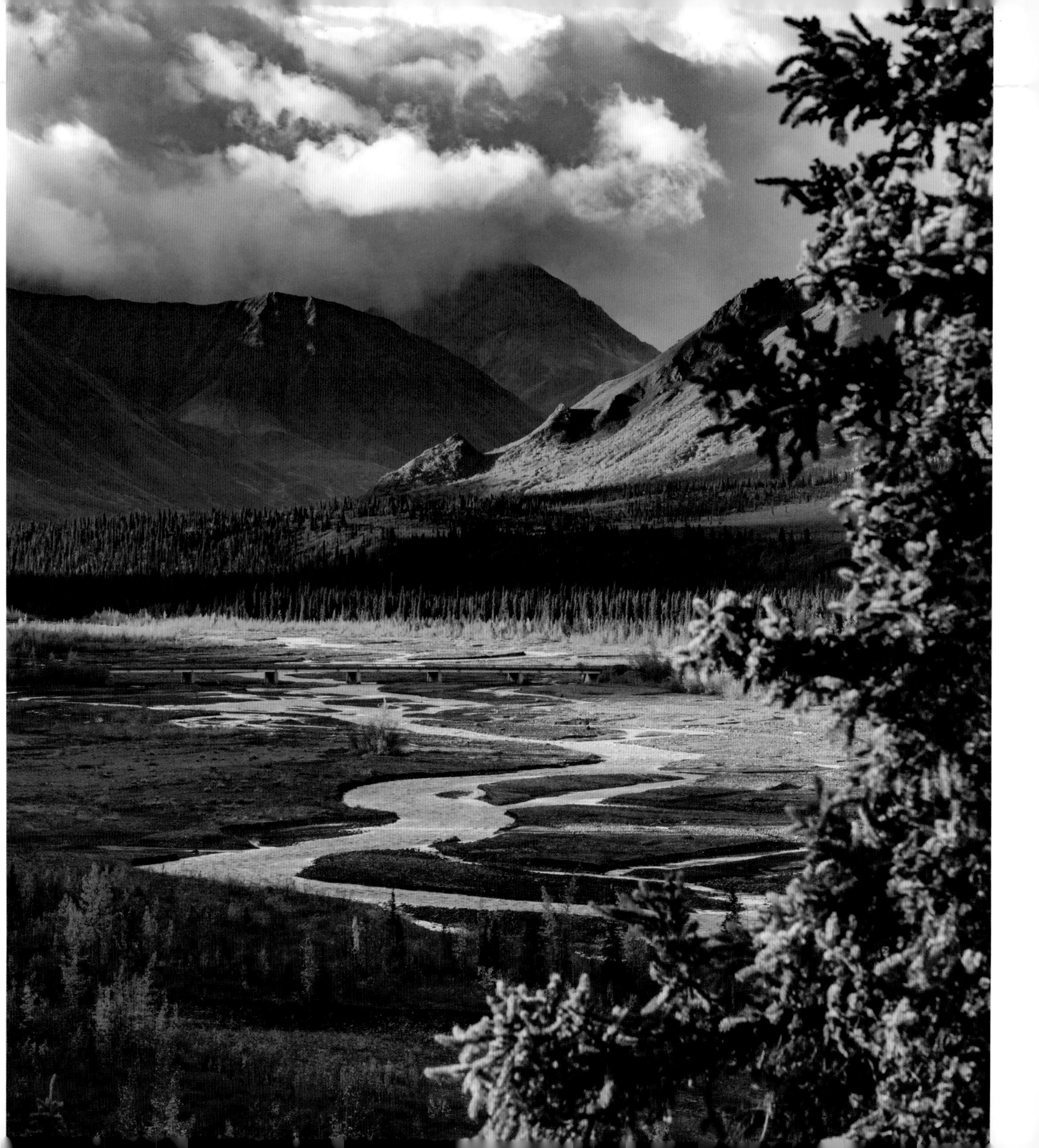

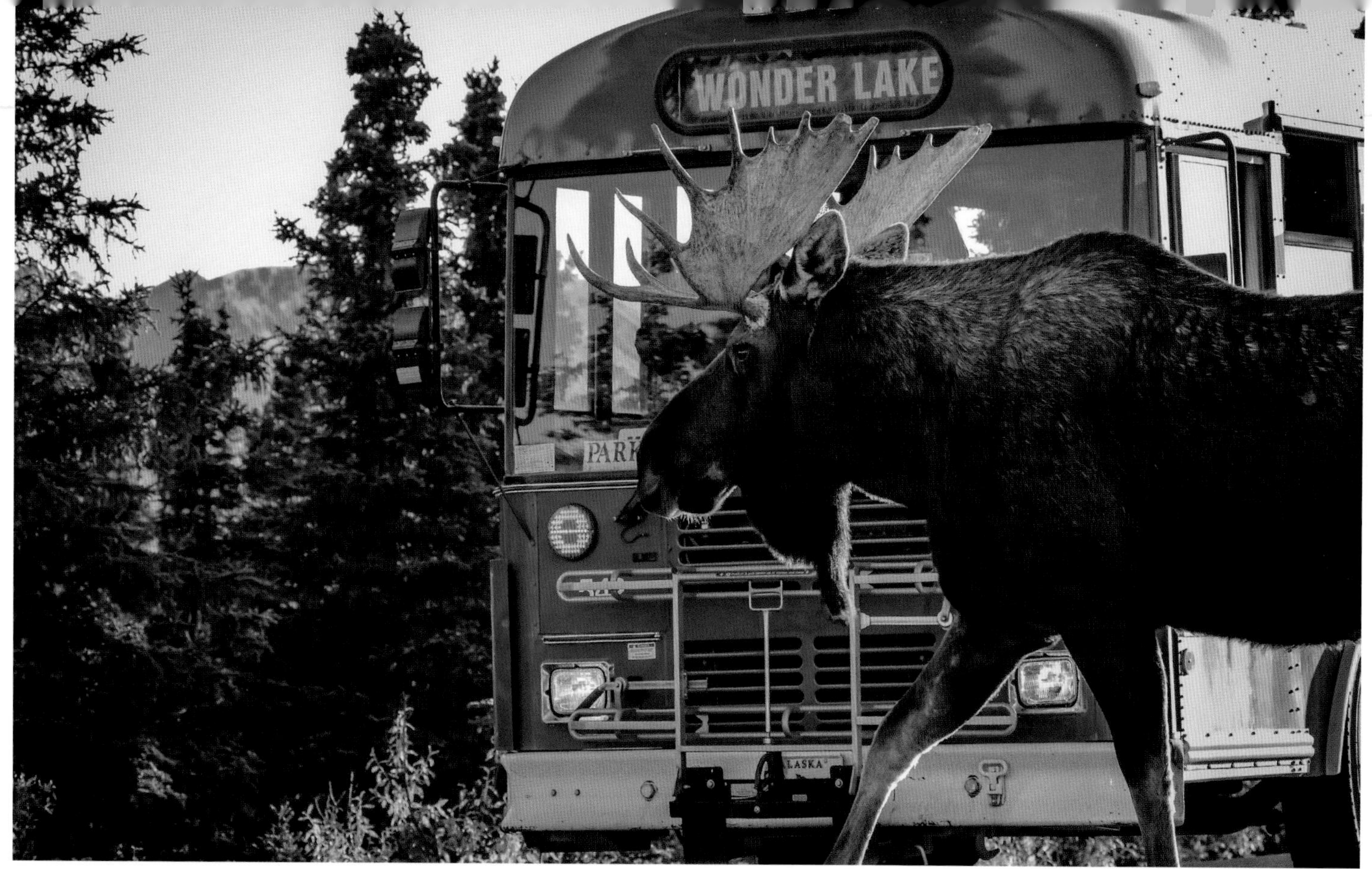

TEKLANIKA RIVER

Denali National Park

An atmospheric, even slightly eerie evening scene. Through much of its upper reaches, the Teklanika is a 'braided river', a web of winding channels separated out by banks and tiny islands. This effect is caused by variations in its flow as it twists and turns its way along its floodplain. While on the outside of its curves, the current is forced to flow much faster, creating erosion there; the slower-moving waters on the insides deposit silt and build up mudbanks.

BULL MOOSE

Denali National Park

It is a beautiful beast, there is no doubt; but a moose may weigh up to 725 kg (1,600 lbs) – three or four times the weight of a grizzly bear. And, while it may be a herbivore, it can be aggressively territorial. It must be treated with some caution, in other words. 'Stay at least 25 yards (25 m) or two bus-lengths away …' warns the Denali National Park Service website in its special 'Moose Safety' section. Unless, of course, as here, you *are* a bus. Though even then, it seems, you must give way.

MOUNT FORAKER AND MOUNT DENALI FROM PARKS HIGHWAY

Denali National Park

At 5,304 m (17,400 ft), Mount Foraker is Alaska's second-highest peak; seen slightly to the left of Denali here, and apparently in close proximity, it is actually 23 km (14 miles) away, though it belongs to the same Alaska Range. Running through the forest foreground here, the Parks Highway links Anchorage with Fairbanks. It was named for George Alexander Parks, from 1925 to 1933 the Governor of what was then of course still the 'Territory' of Alaska. It offers some of Alaska's finest views.

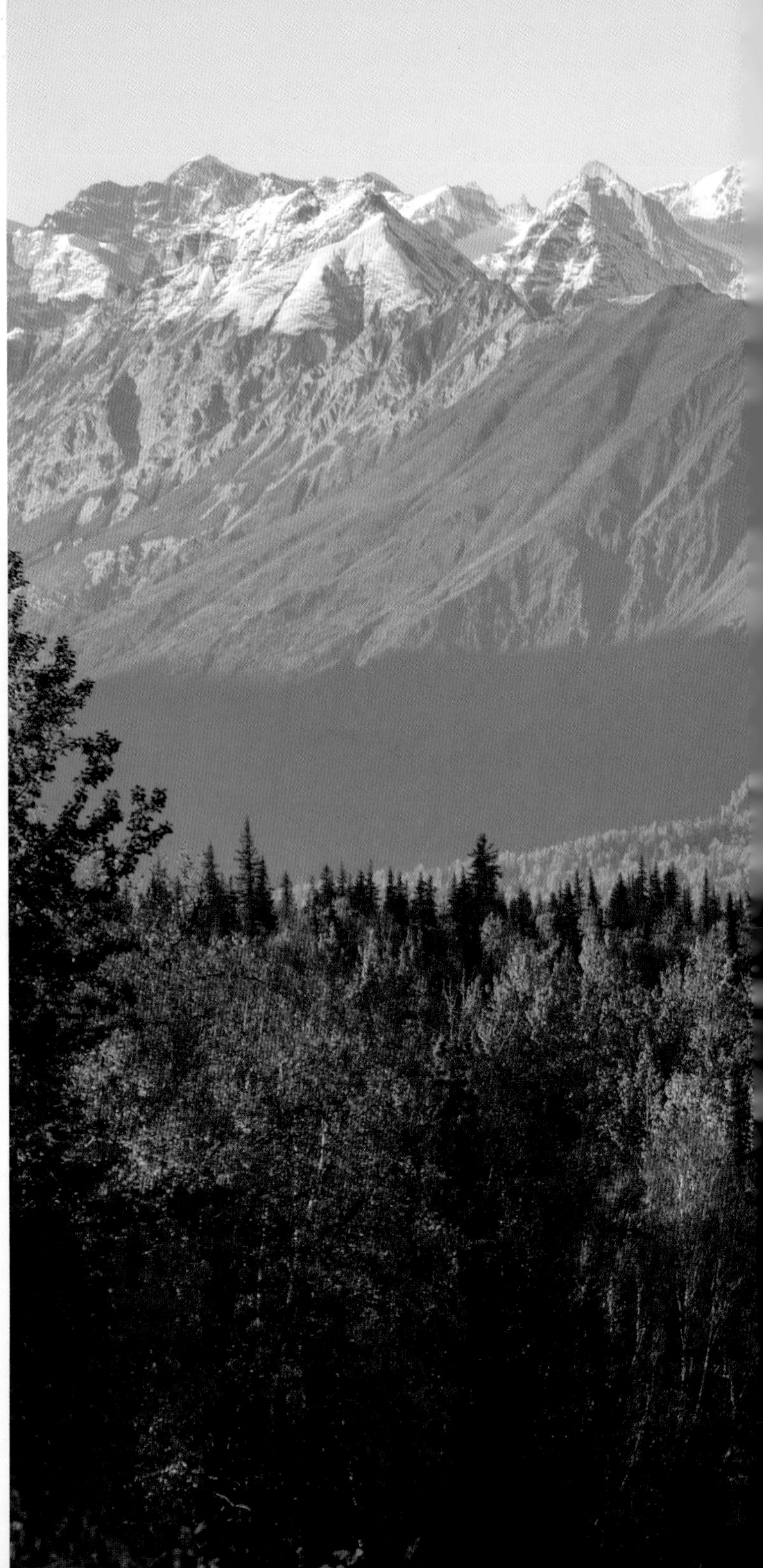

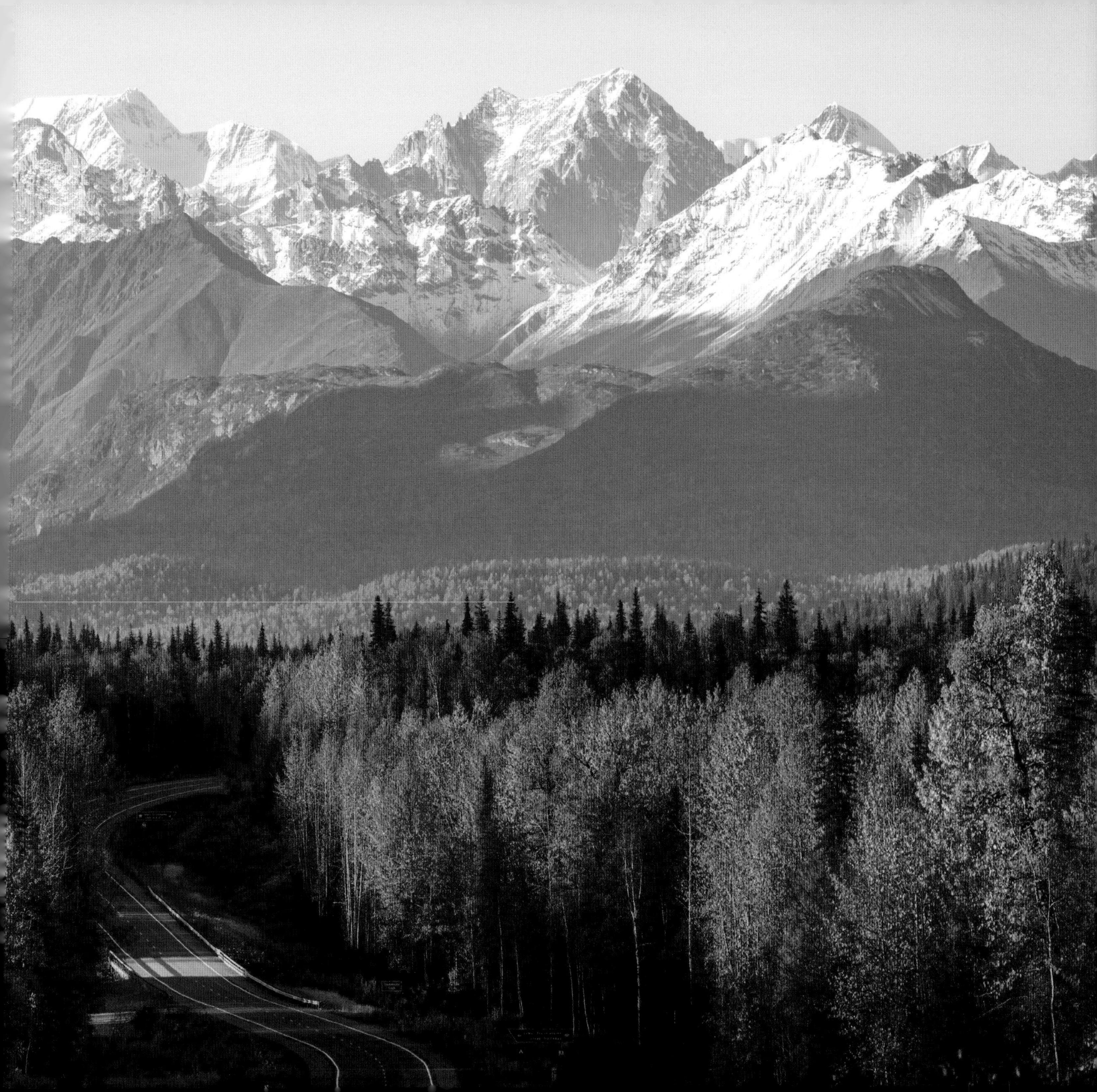

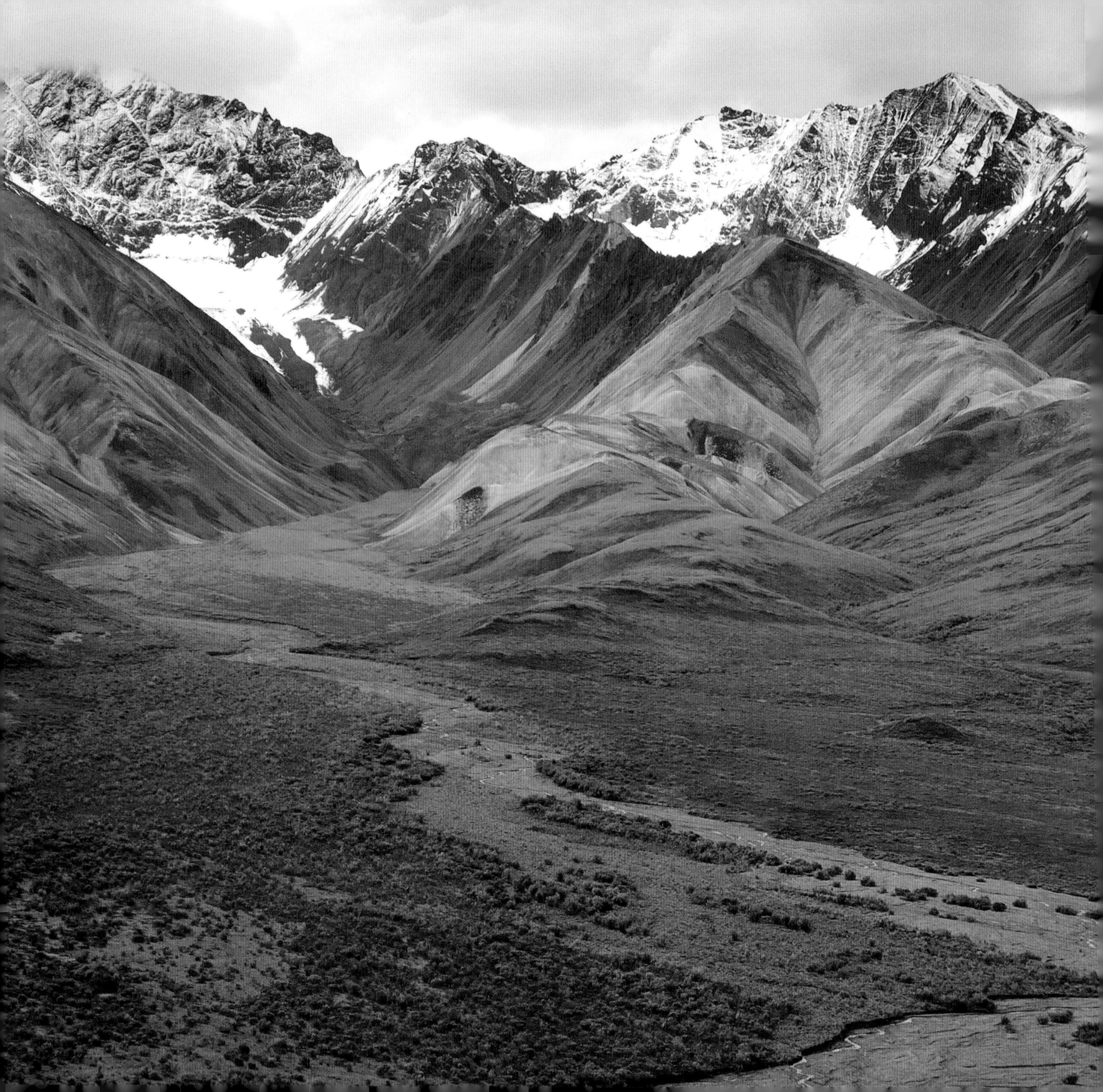

POLYCHROME PASS

Denali National Park

The hillside at the centre of this scene gives an example of the sort of multicoloured rock formations which have given this route through the Alaska Range its name. The road here rises to an altitude of 1,080 m (3,500 ft), sufficiently high for the ground beneath it to be tundra-like – boggy at the surface in the summer but frozen solid just a short way down. If this permafrost were to prove impermanent in the face of continuing climate change, much of this ground could collapse and slide away.

FANNIE QUIGLEY'S CABIN, KANTISHNA

Denali National Park

Frances Sedlacek (1870–1944) was born in a Bohemian settlement in Nebraska. She left at sixteen to seek her fortune further west. Drawn up here by the Gold Rush, she staked 28 of her own claims before she married in 1918 and carried on mining long after that. But it is her prowess as a hunter that has been the basis for her enduring fame, driving her dog sled on expeditions after caribou, moose and bears. And as a drinker, a wearer of men's clothes and a user of profanities. An all-round bad example – and inspiration.

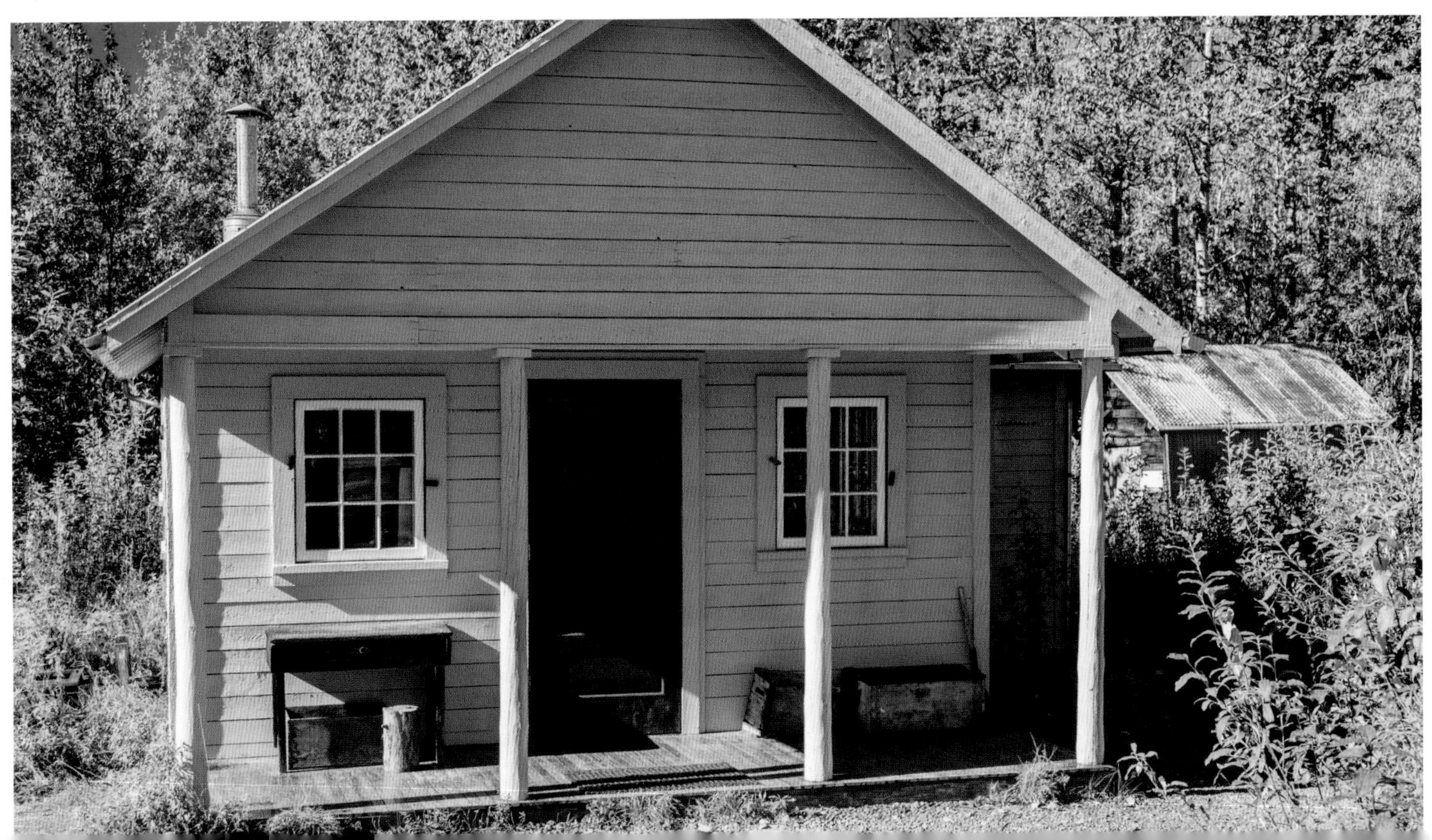

KAHILTNA GLACIER

Denali National Park

Though only one of five glaciers to start on the upper slopes of Denali, Kahiltna is the longest by some way. Beginning 3,150 m (10,320 ft) above sea level, it creeps down over a distance of 71 km (44 miles) between the South Buttress of Denali and Begguya (or Mount Hunter). Finally, at a height of around 300 m (1,000 ft) it melts and makes its way onward down the slopes as the Kahiltna river. Glaciation made the Alaskan landscape – and up here it has continued to do so.

IGLOO HOTEL, CANTWELL

Denali National Park

The entrepreneur who built this giant concrete hummock beside the Parks Highway, 35 km (22 miles) south of Cantwell had visions of an entire 'igloo city'. Fortunately, perhaps, the planning officers intervened. Even the hotel he settled for was never actually to open: it couldn't meet the required building codes. And so, since the 1970s, it has sat here rotting slowly, a mute memorial to disappointed dreams. A memorial too, however, to the inspirational force of human whimsy and the irrepressible power of the imagination.

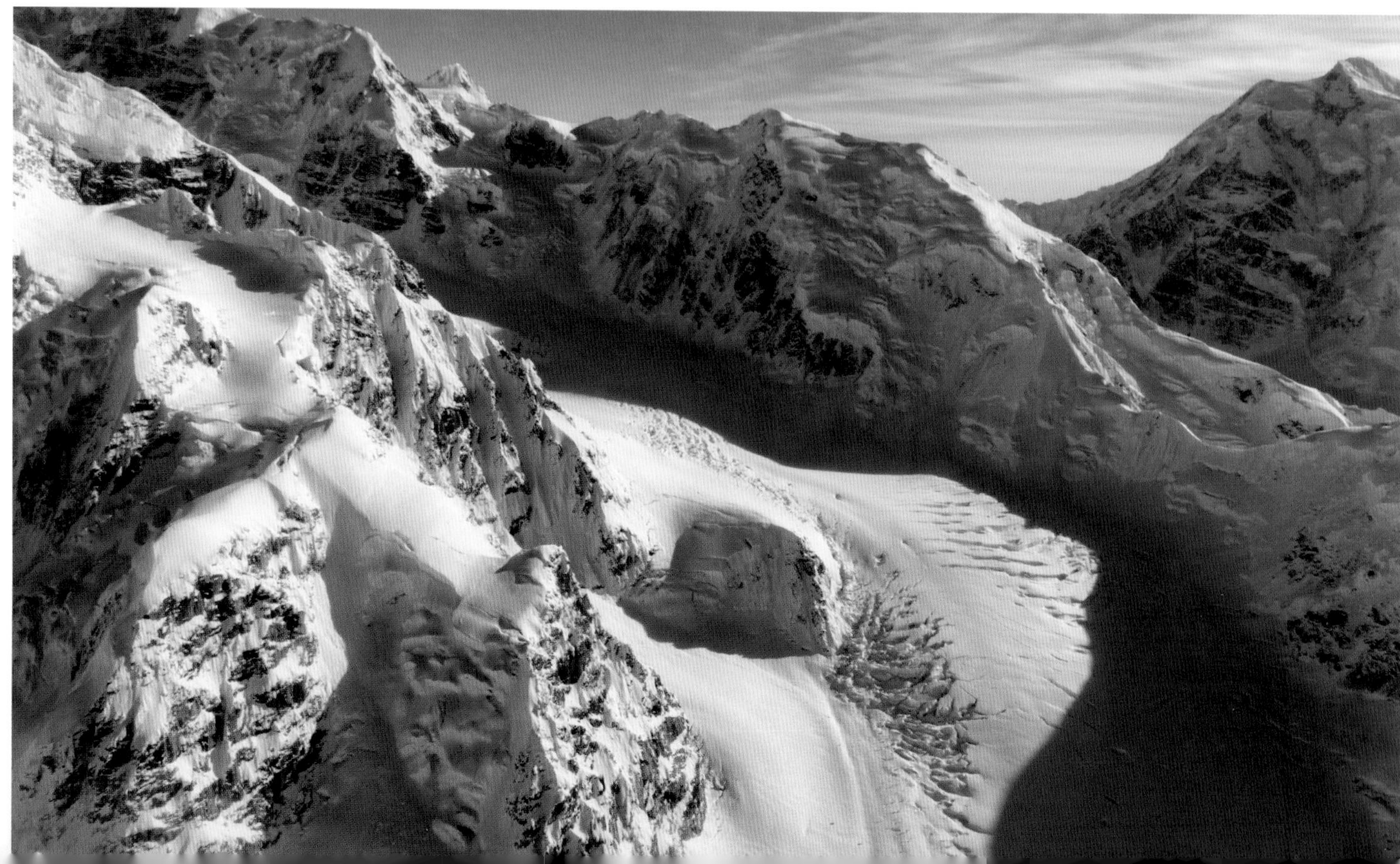

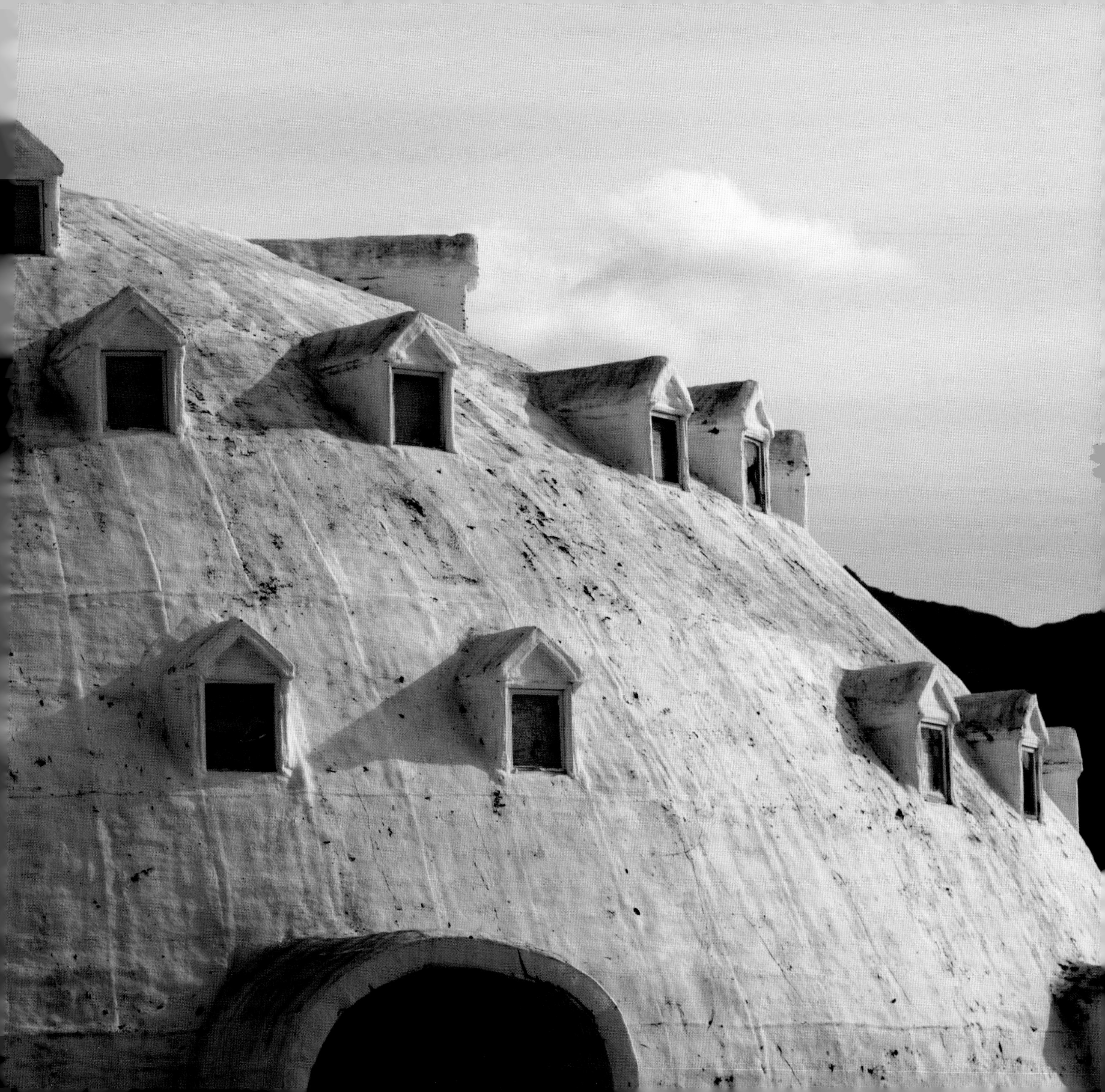

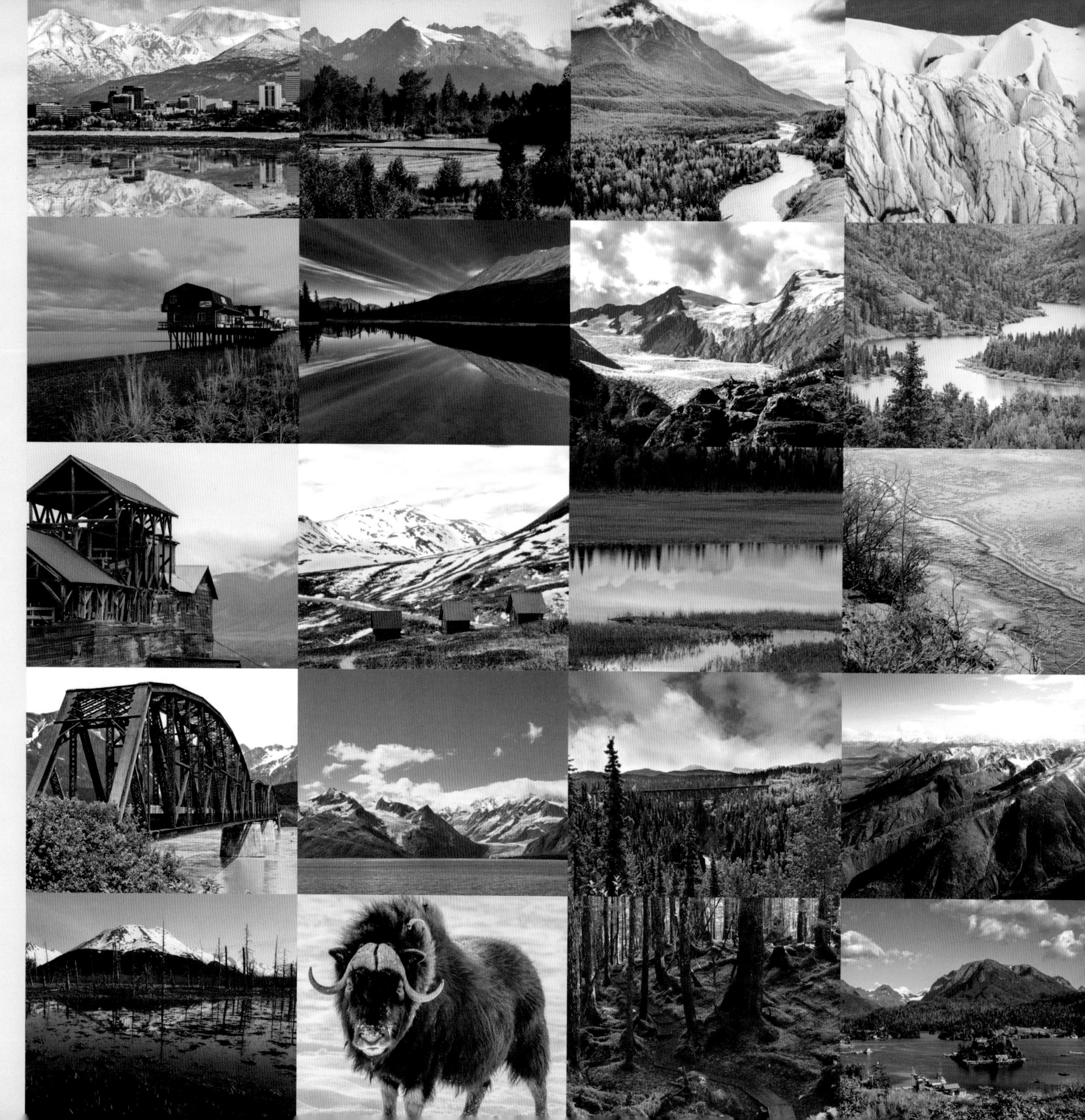

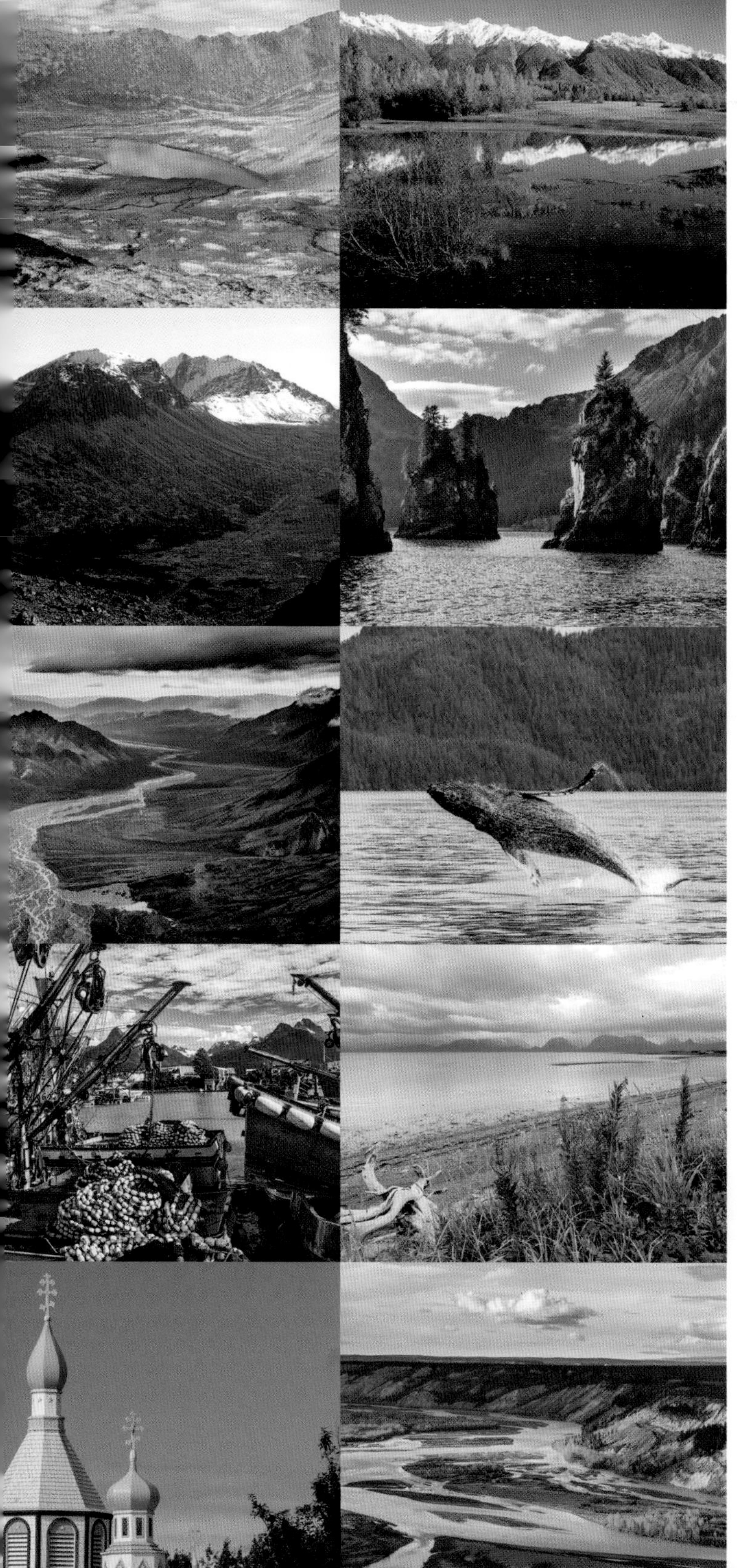

SOUTHCENTRAL ALASKA

Extending inland from the Gulf of Alaska, this region encompasses much of the state's most populous areas, including its most important urban centre. More than half of Alaska's people live in and around the great city of Anchorage, which accordingly exerts an enormous pull, politically and culturally, within the state. One obvious implication of this is that other areas are overshadowed, and consequently overlooked – including areas of this same Southcentral region. Many of Alaska's most stunning scenery is to be encountered here.

The Copper River, in its upper reaches, runs through what amounts to wilderness; the Chugach Mountains are substantially unspoiled. Just a stone's throw away from Anchorage across the water, the Kenai Peninsula juts down into the Gulf for 240 km (150 miles). Along with significant towns, it has great tracts of mountain and forest, lakes and streams. To the east, beside Prince William Sound, stands the great oil port of Valdez; but there are tiny fishing villages and Native settlements here, too. Altogether, the Southcentral region offers the Alaskan experience in all its inexhaustible variety and vitality. History and hope for the future; sublime outdoor scenery and quaint little villages; bustling city streets and silent shores.

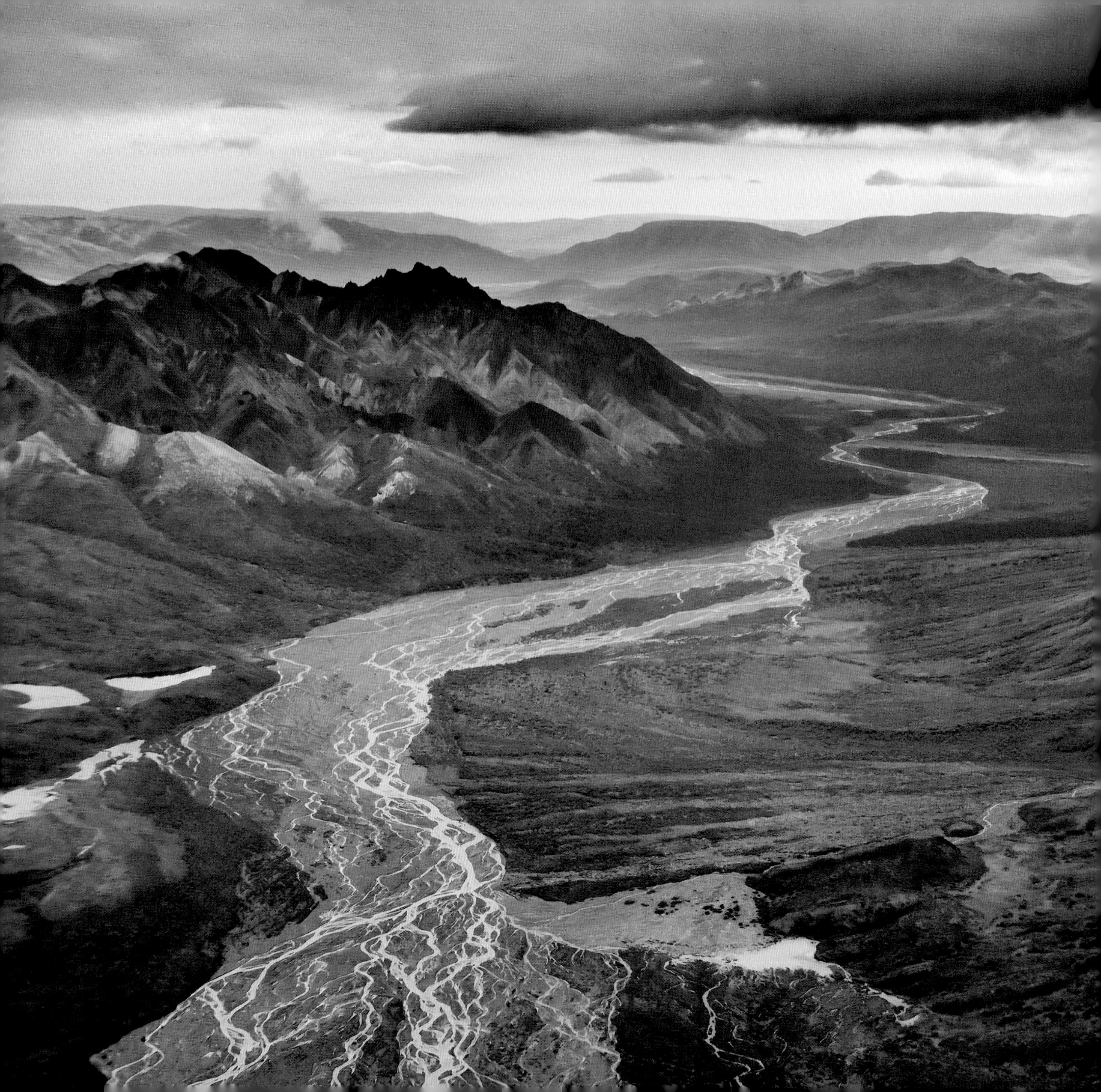

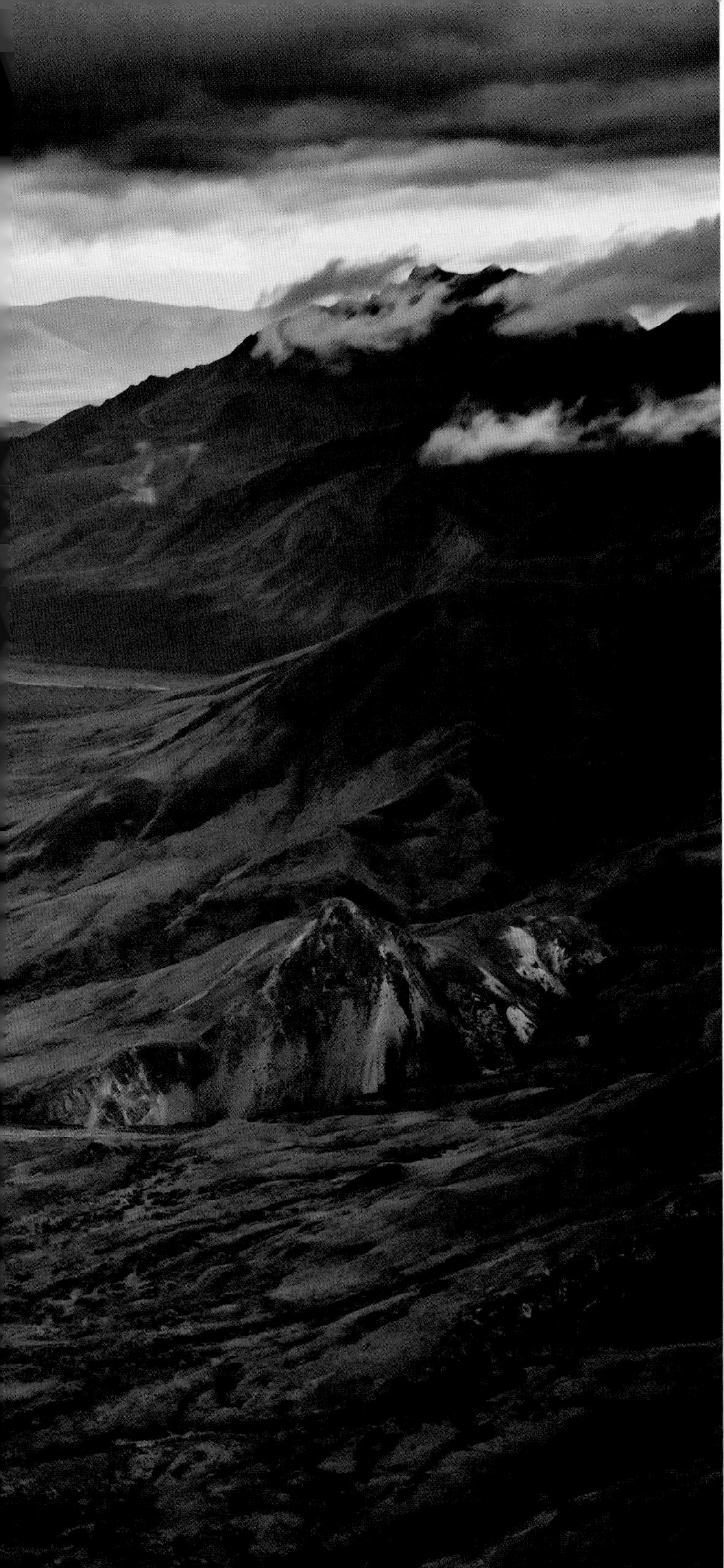

TALKEETNA MOUNTAINS, SUSITNA RIVER AND VALLEY

Mat-Su Valley

The Matanuska and Susitna Valleys, known jointly and colloquially as the 'Mat-Su', come together to form an open coastal plain. Nowadays this area is covered in market gardens and commuter communities serving Anchorage. But this is Alaska and even in the most suburban setting you are never really far from stupendous scenery. Dark clouds lower dramatically, rugged mountains menace, but the Susitna rushes on undaunted through its deep, wide valley. Colossal forces shaped this country, its geological construction 'finished off' by glacial action. The Alaskan scene will never be truly tamed.

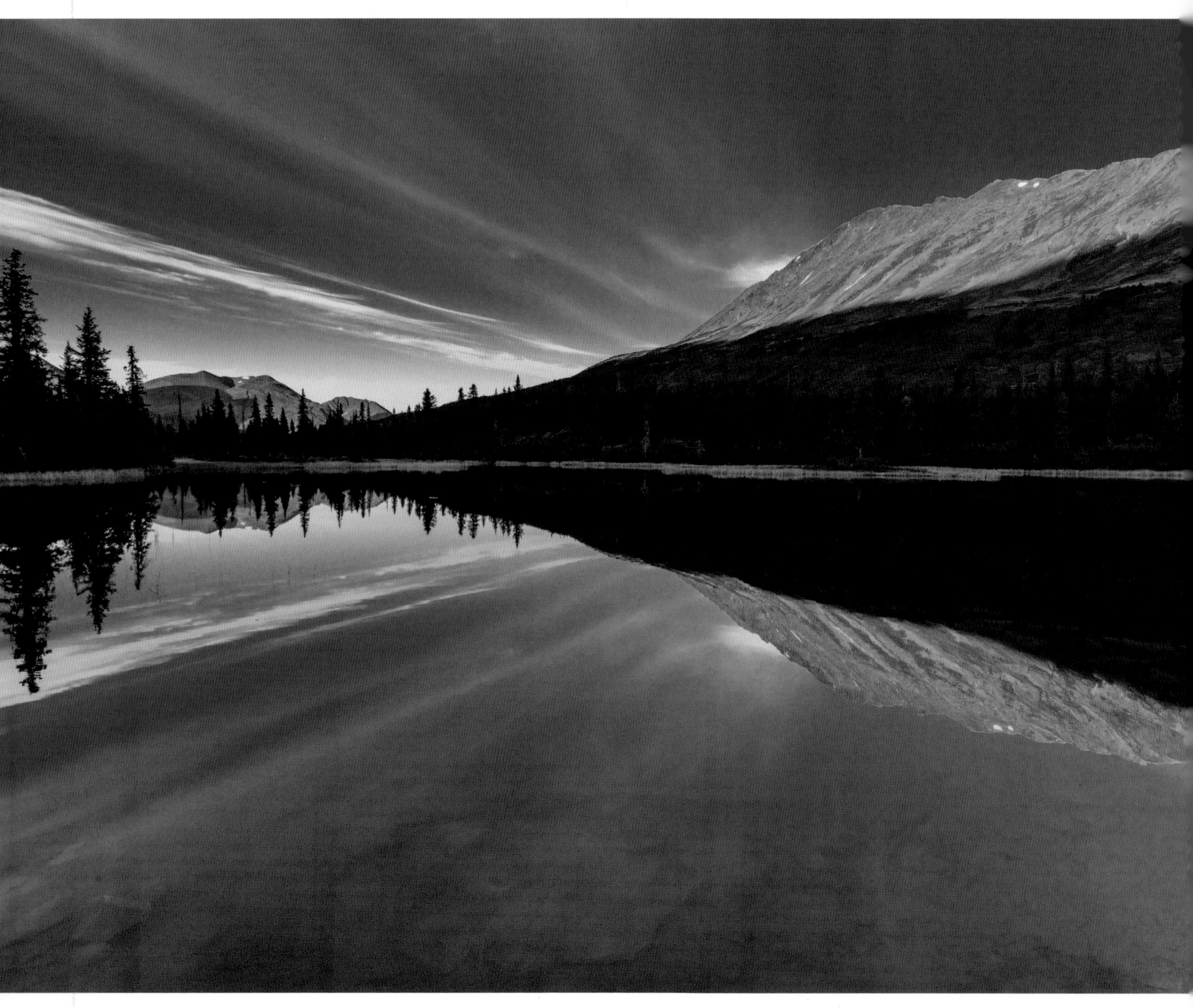

RAINBOW LAKE, WILLOW

Mat-Su Valley

A lakeside in the forest is the perfect place for reflection, far away from the bustle and the cares of daily life. Willow, as its name perhaps suggests, is not short of wooded sanctuaries. People from Anchorage like to come out here in summer to find a bit of peace and quiet and calm and beauty; those fortunate enough may well have weekend cabins here. (In the winter, it is a very different story: the Iditarod Trail Sled Dog Race – *see* page 38 – starts near here, just a short way outside the city.)

PETERSVILLE ROAD, TRAPPER CREEK

Mat-Su Valley

This 55-km (34-mile) road was once a miners' wagon trail. (Though nominally upgraded, it still has a great many of the bumps that prove it.) Now it offers an alternative 'backdoor' way to approach Denali. And, in the process, to enjoy some real wilderness-standard peace and quiet, just a couple of hours' drive from Anchorage. The views to be had are breathtaking, like this one out over wetland and forest to the mountains of the Alaska Range in all their jagged majesty.

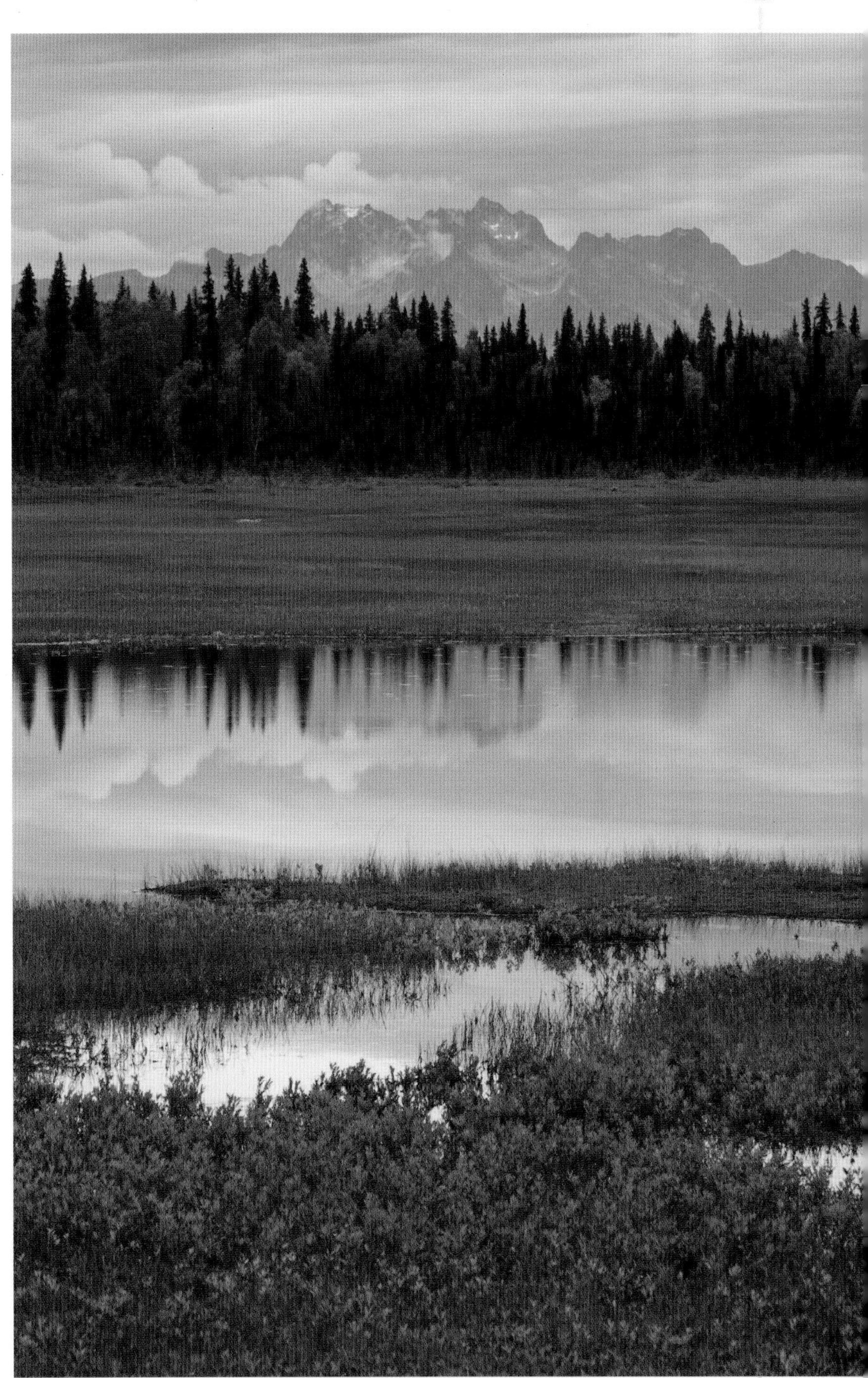

KING MOUNTAIN, NEAR SUTTON

Mat-Su Valley

Imposing as it appears in this view from the Glenn Highway, this 1,702 m (5,584 ft) mountain has no royal connection of any sort. Prospectors named it in around 1905 after one of their number, the otherwise-obscure Al King, who had a cabin on its slopes where the Kings River (no relation) met the Matanuska not far from here. Now a State Recreational Area, King Mountain abounds in campsites and picnic areas and has become a popular resort for weekend trippers.

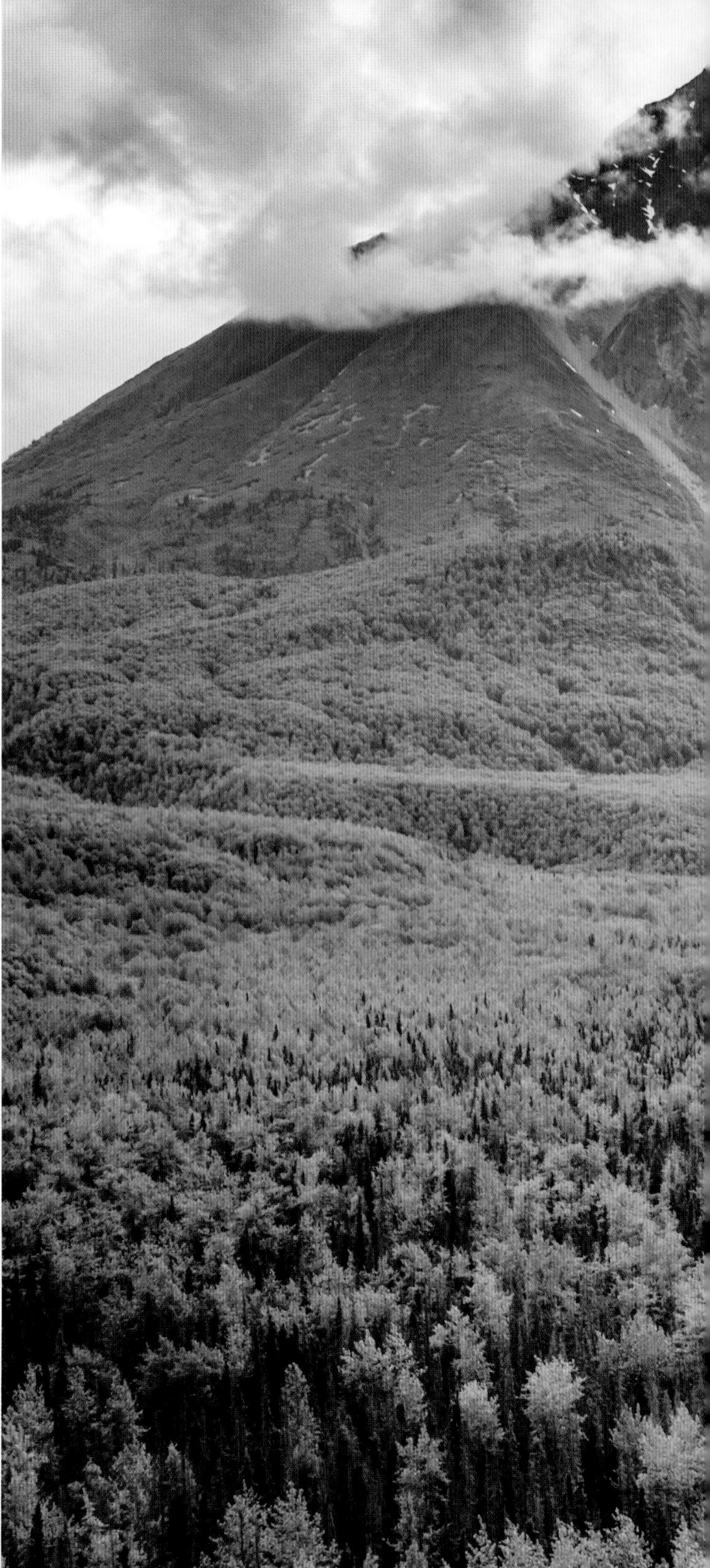

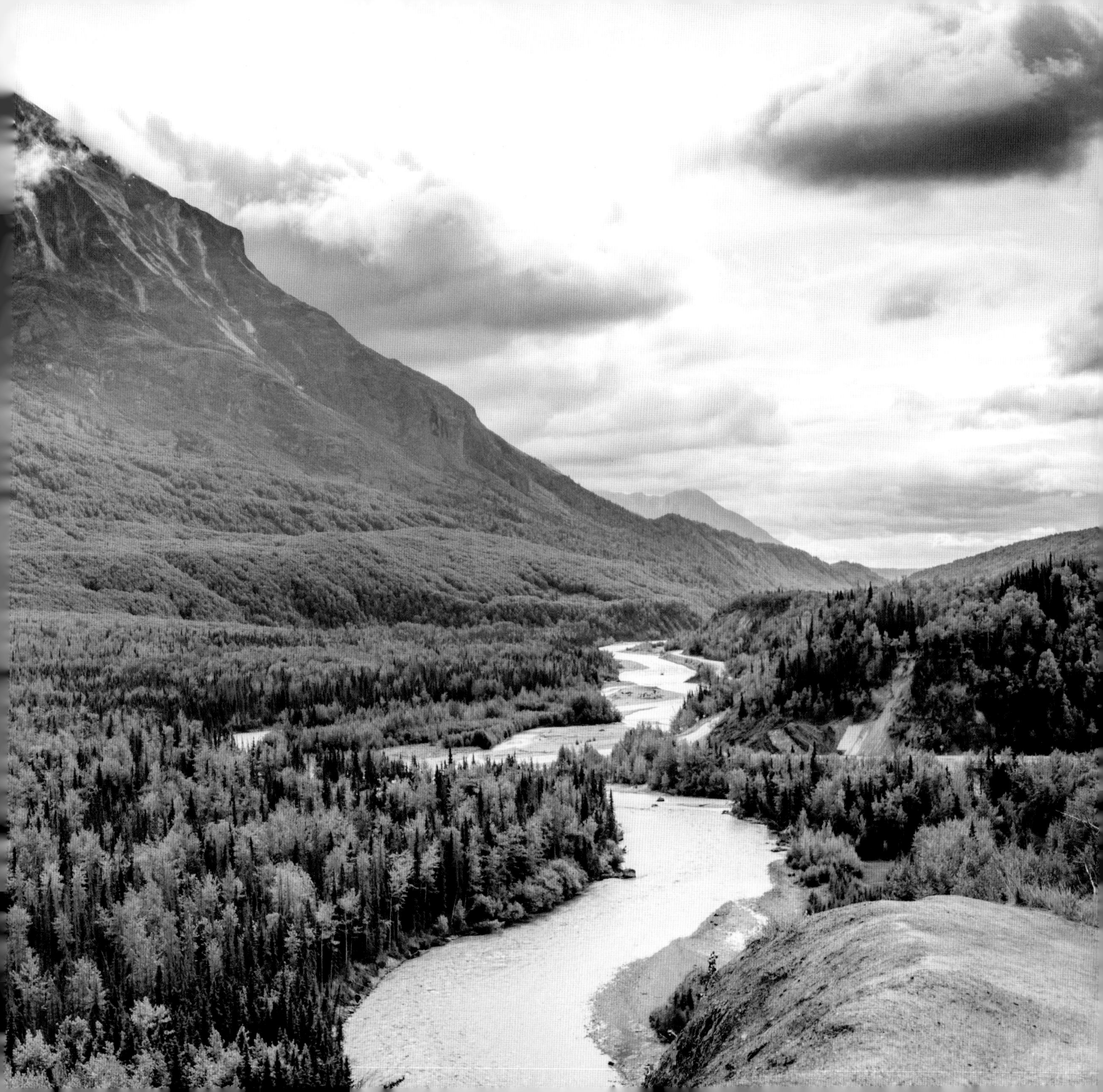

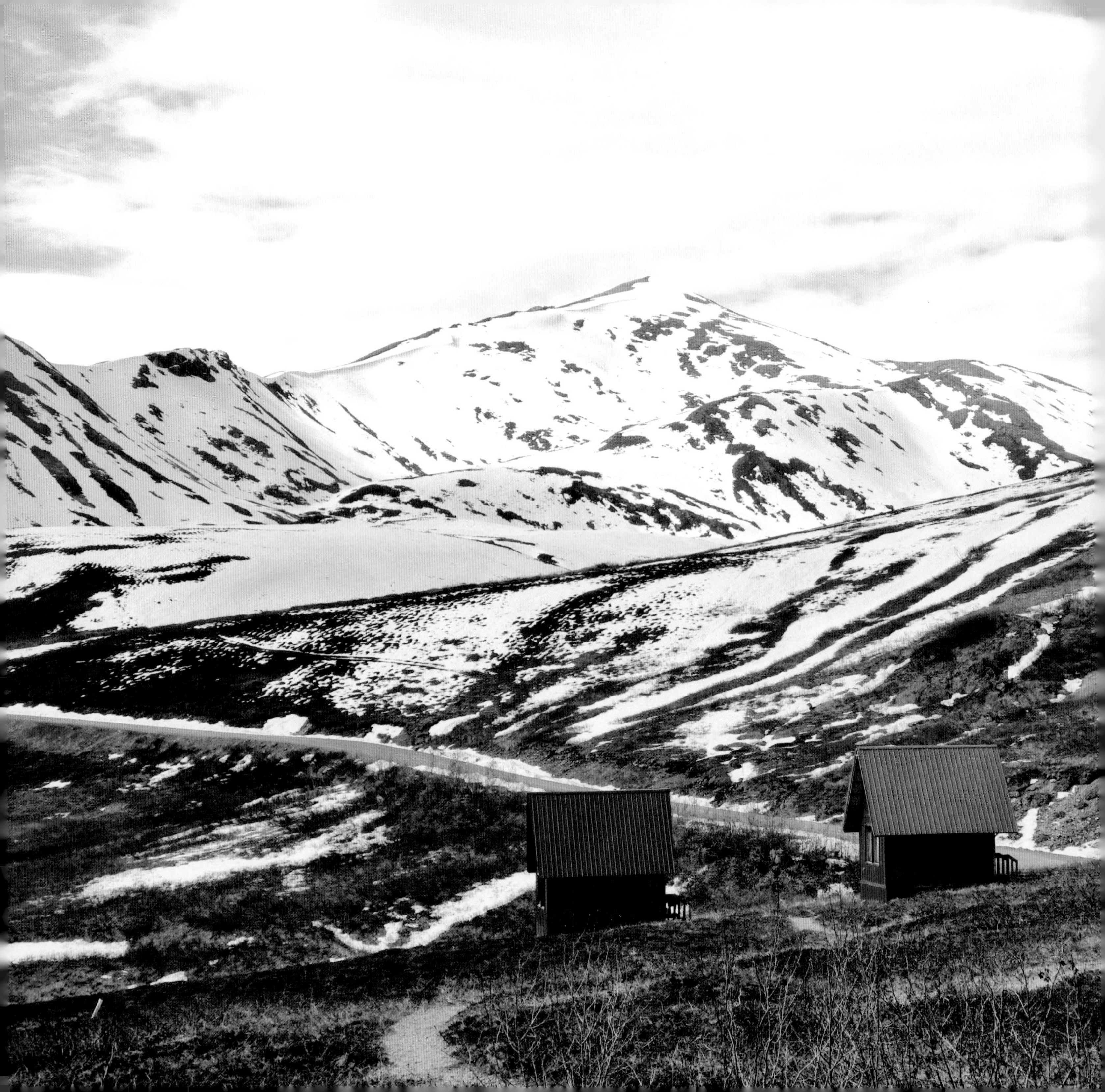

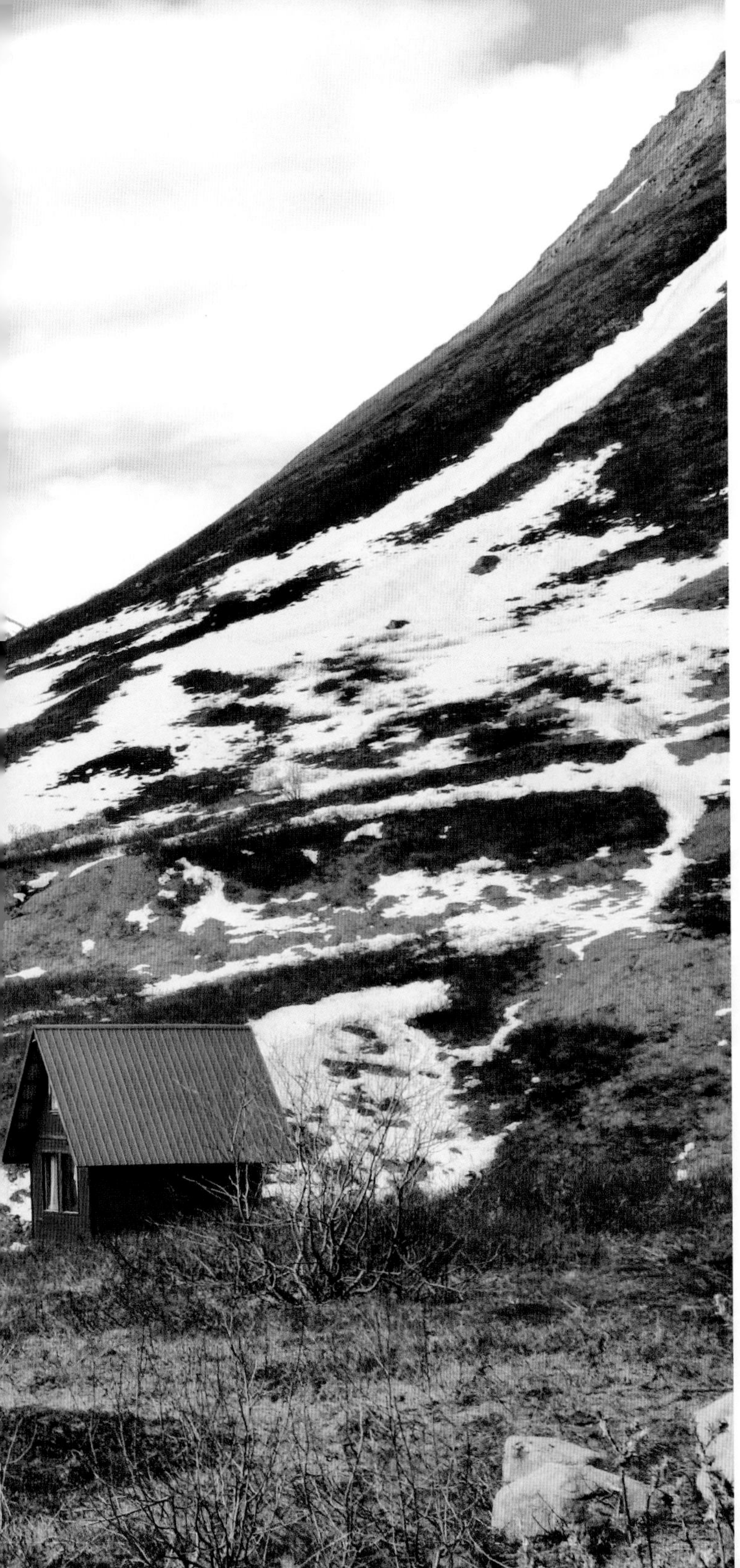

CABINS, HATCHER PASS

Mat-Su Valley

From Willow, a winding mountain road leads up into the Talkeetna Mountains (*see* page 81) and over the wonderfully scenic Hatcher Pass. The Independence Mines outlived the 1890s Gold Rush: not surprisingly, perhaps – gold was literally mined here, from clearly demarcated rifts in the rock below the ground, not simply panned for in the gravel of running streams. Even so, as time went on, reserves dwindled and rising costs made extraction unviable. The mines shut down in 1950, leaving these old cabins and some odds and ends of machinery behind.

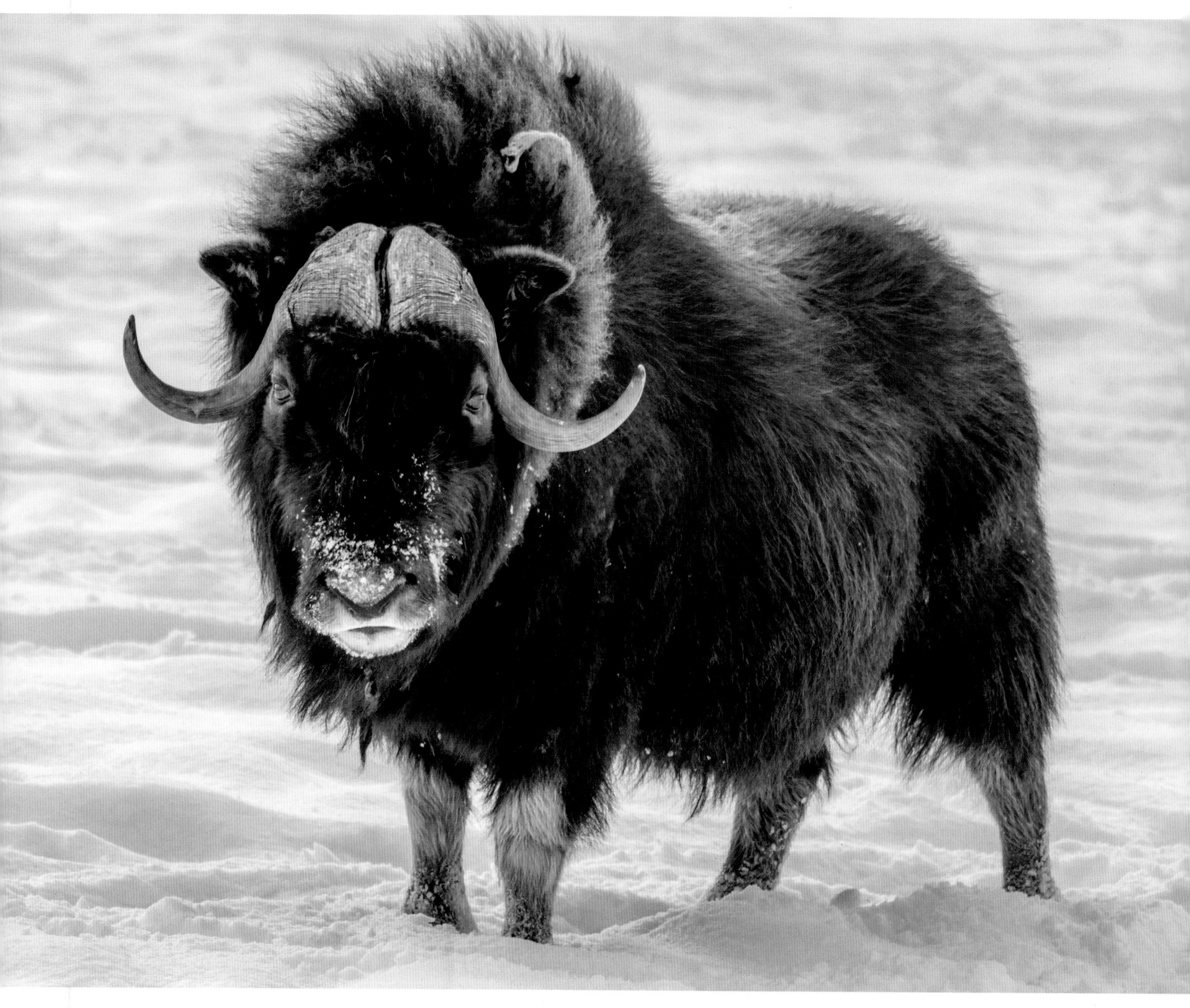

MUSK OX

Mat-Su Valley

There is a challenge in that look, no doubt, but this magnificent beast just wants to be left alone: all the more reason to give it a wide berth. Musk oxen *can* attack when they themselves feel vulnerable, though their first response is invariably to close ranks and bundle up together to face down the threat. For the most part, though, they just want a quiet life. They have not had one, historically, alas, being hunted to extinction in Alaska in modern times: they have only recently been reintroduced.

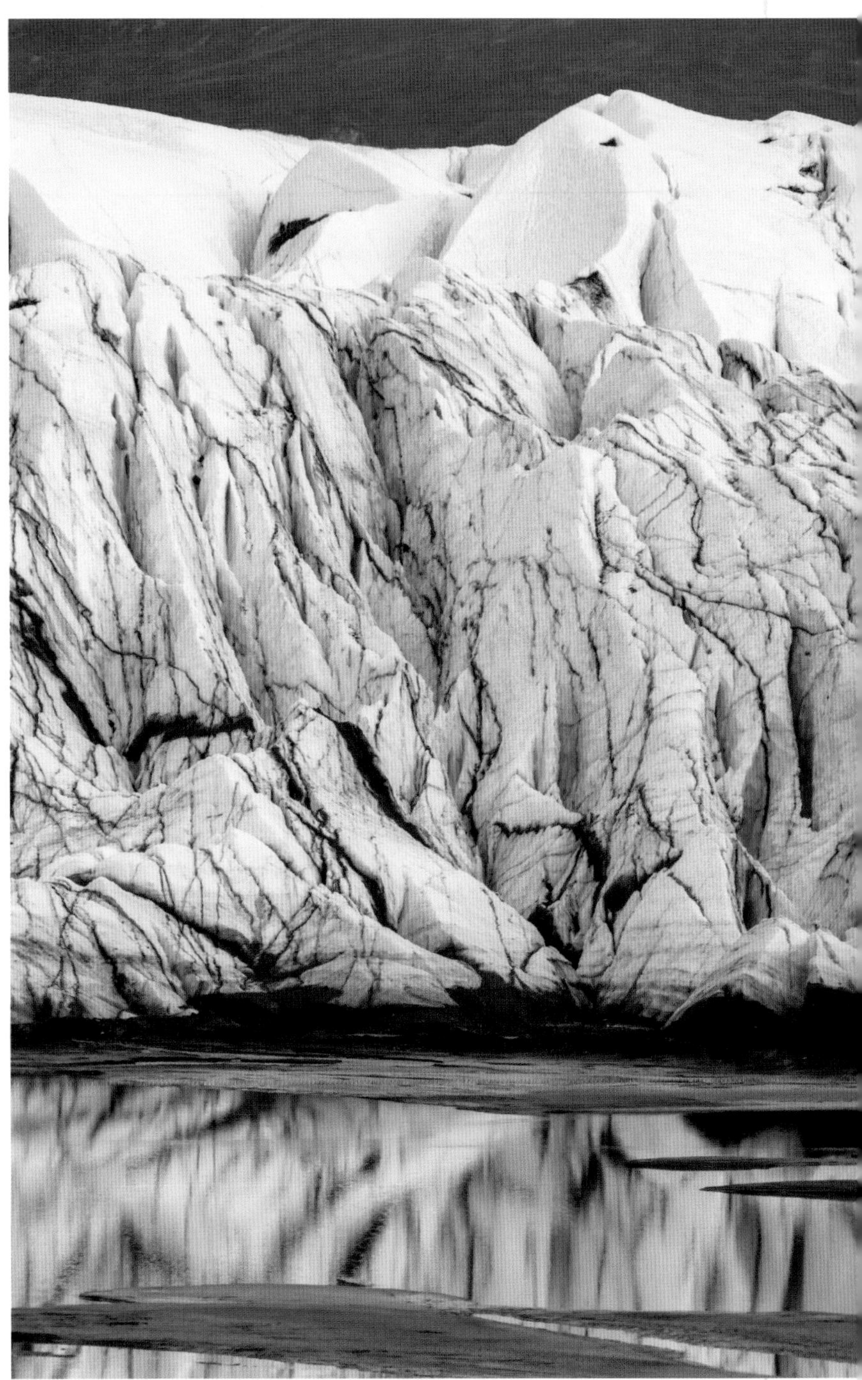

MATANUSKA GLACIER

Mat-Su Valley

You can hardly say it 'flows' – still less that it 'runs': even so, the Matanuska Glacier finds its way down from the heights of the Chugach Range at a speed of some 30 cm (1 ft) a day. Towards its terminus, after 42 km (26 miles), it spreads slowly out across the valley it has formed, to a breadth of over 6 km (4 miles). It is this end point that we see here, those grubby veins a reminder of the glacier's role in gradually rubbing away at and eroding the rock and earth across which it moves.

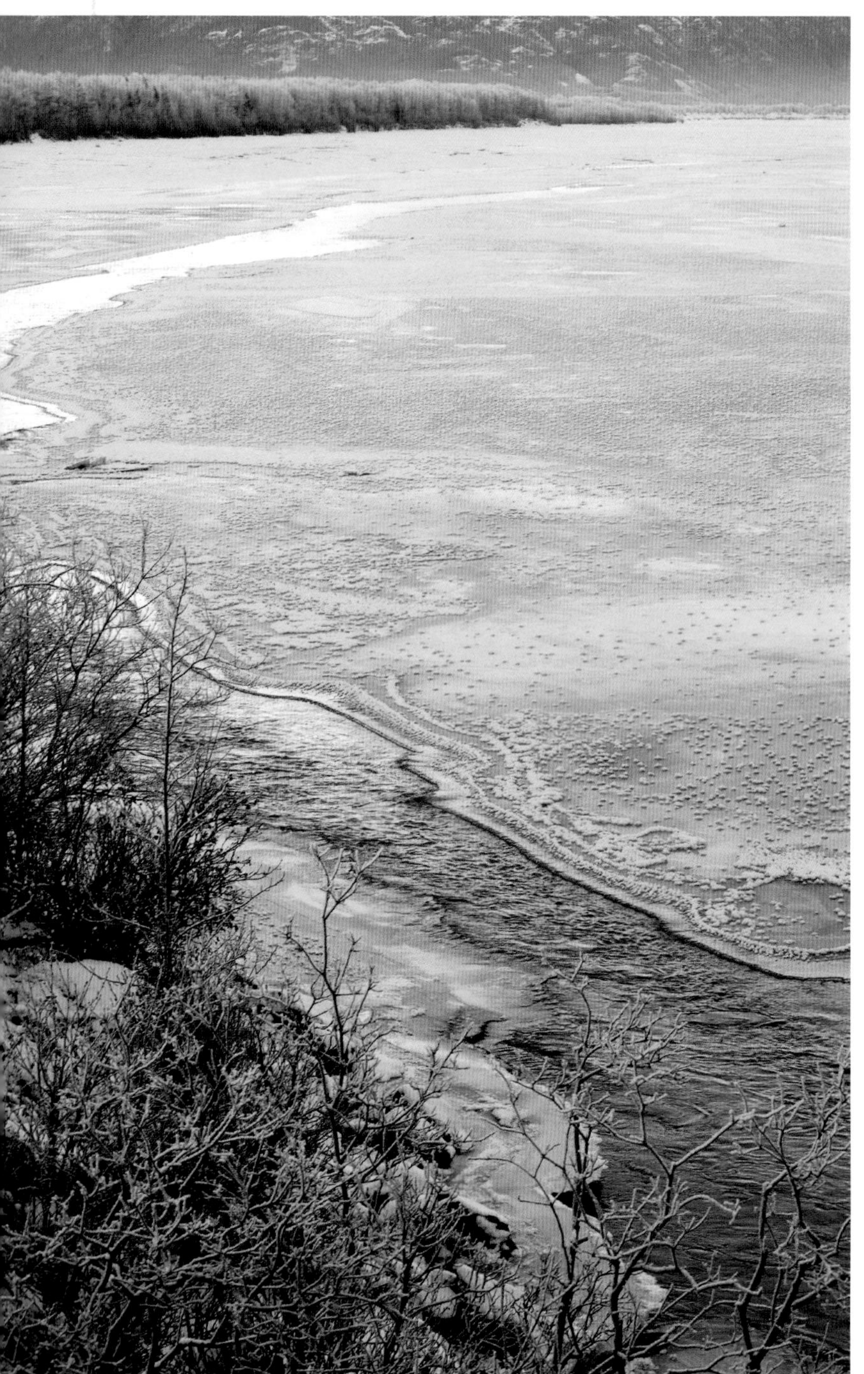

ICE, KNIK RIVER

Mat-Su Valley

It begins life as the Knik Glacier, and for much of the year this river is itself iced up – though of course the current continues to flow beneath the frozen layer. We see it here shortly before it reaches the sea at the Knik Arm, a branch of Cook Inlet, north-east of Anchorage. Winter casts a special spell over the Alaskan landscape, and this scene is no exception. Not that the Knik River's broad, tree-lined estuary is not in its own way beautiful in summer, but it does not have the sparkling, jewelled quality we see here.

MOUNTAINS, GLENN HIGHWAY

Copper River Valley

A section of Route 1, the Glenn Highway runs for 288 km (179 miles) between Anchorage in the west and Glennallen, where it meets the Richardson Highway, in the east. It was built during the Second World War, as part of the same patriotic and strategic effort that saw the start of work on the Alaska Highway (*see* page 64). Its utility apart, this road is celebrated for its scenic beauty, offering incomparable views of the Talkeetna and Chugach mountain ranges.

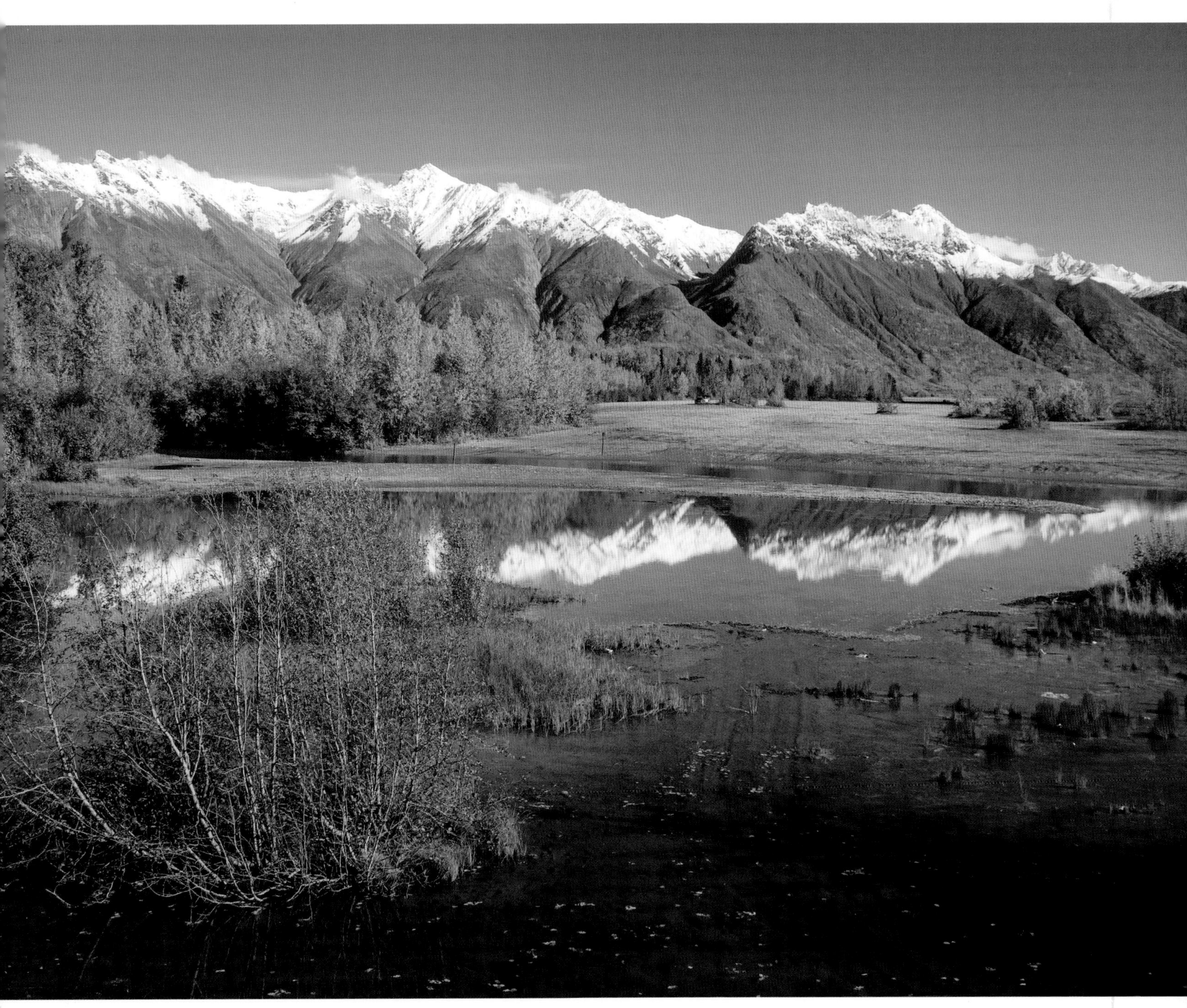

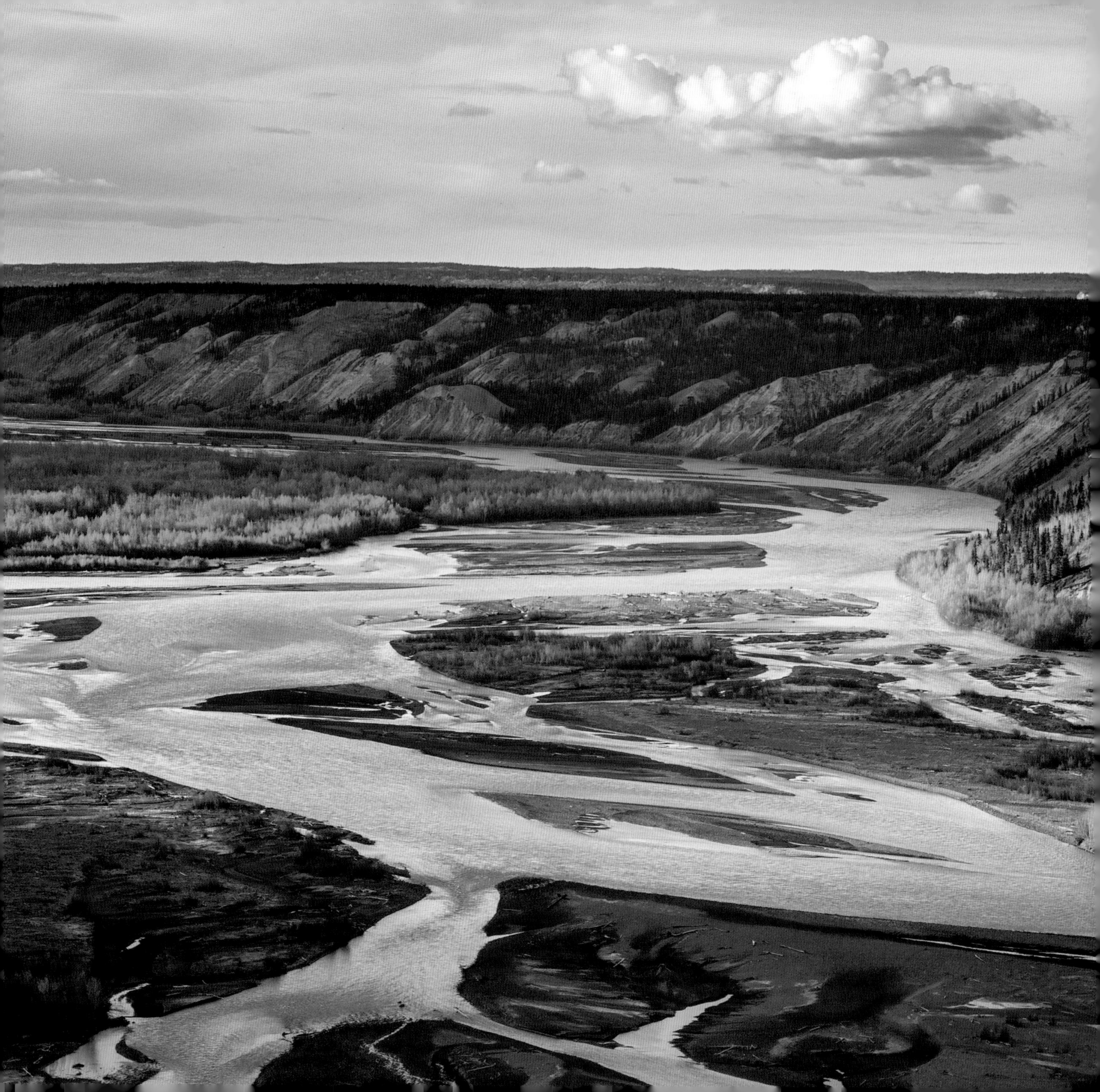

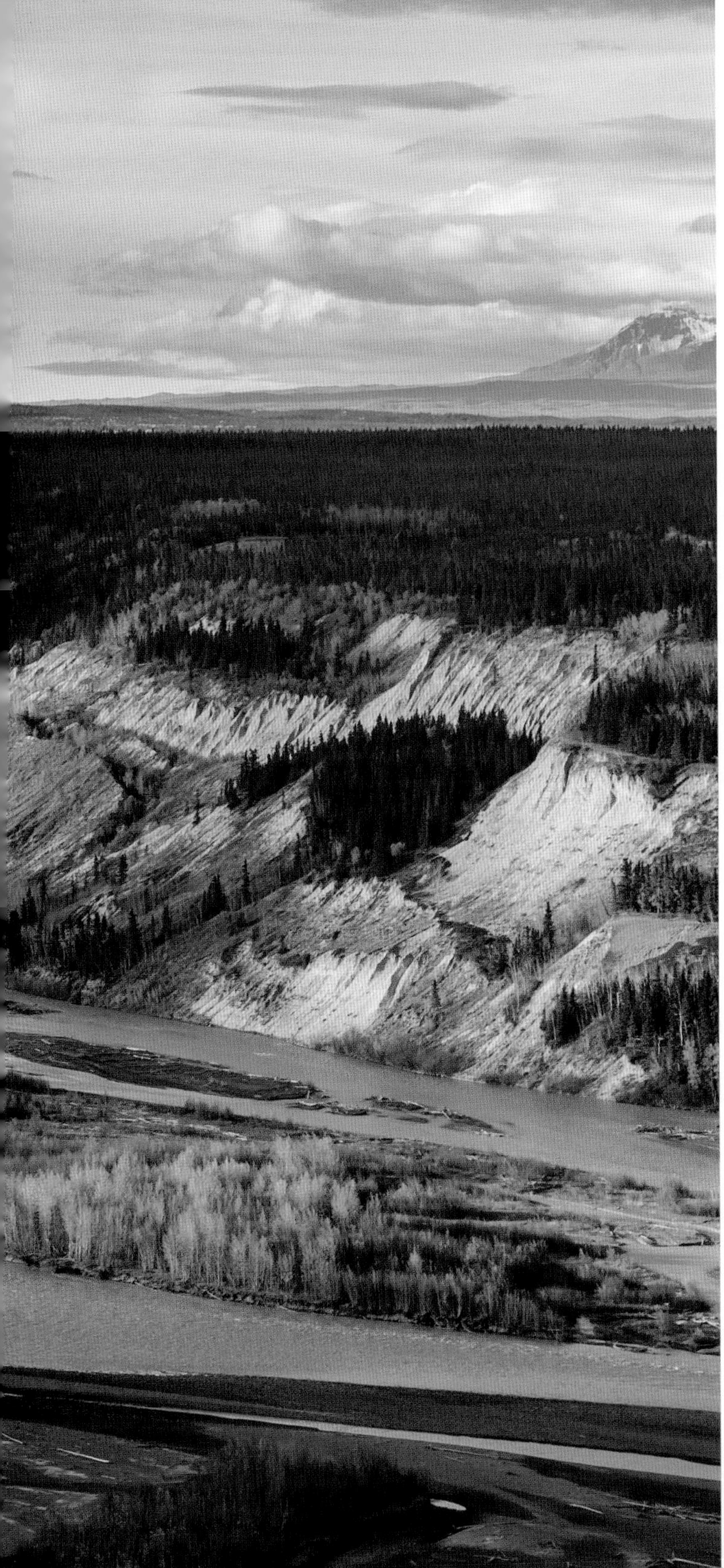

COPPER RIVER, WRANGELL-ST. ELIAS NATIONAL PARK

Copper River Valley

Living up to its name in the warming tones of an evening sun, the Copper River winds sluggishly down into its delta. This was the Copper River even to the area's first inhabitants, the Ahtna, who made full use of deposits of the metal to be found upstream. They were followed in this by Russian settlers in the region, as well as by Americans in more modern times. These days, however, the river is famous primarily for its salmon fishery. Handheld dip nets are used to catch the migrating fish as they pass by.

MOUNTAINS, WRANGELL-ST. ELIAS NATIONAL PARK

Copper River Valley

These mountains are high by any standards: they seem the more impressive, though, for the abruptness with which they seem to rise out of a comparatively level coastal plain. Mount St. Elias rises to 5,489 m (18,000 ft); Mount Wrangell reaches 4,317 m (14,000 ft). Its subsidiary summits are not that much smaller, a dozen peaks in the Wrangell range overtopping the 4,000 m (13,000 ft) mark. It is another world up here: an extensive ice field from which several glaciers start – even when the lower slopes are warm and fresh and green.

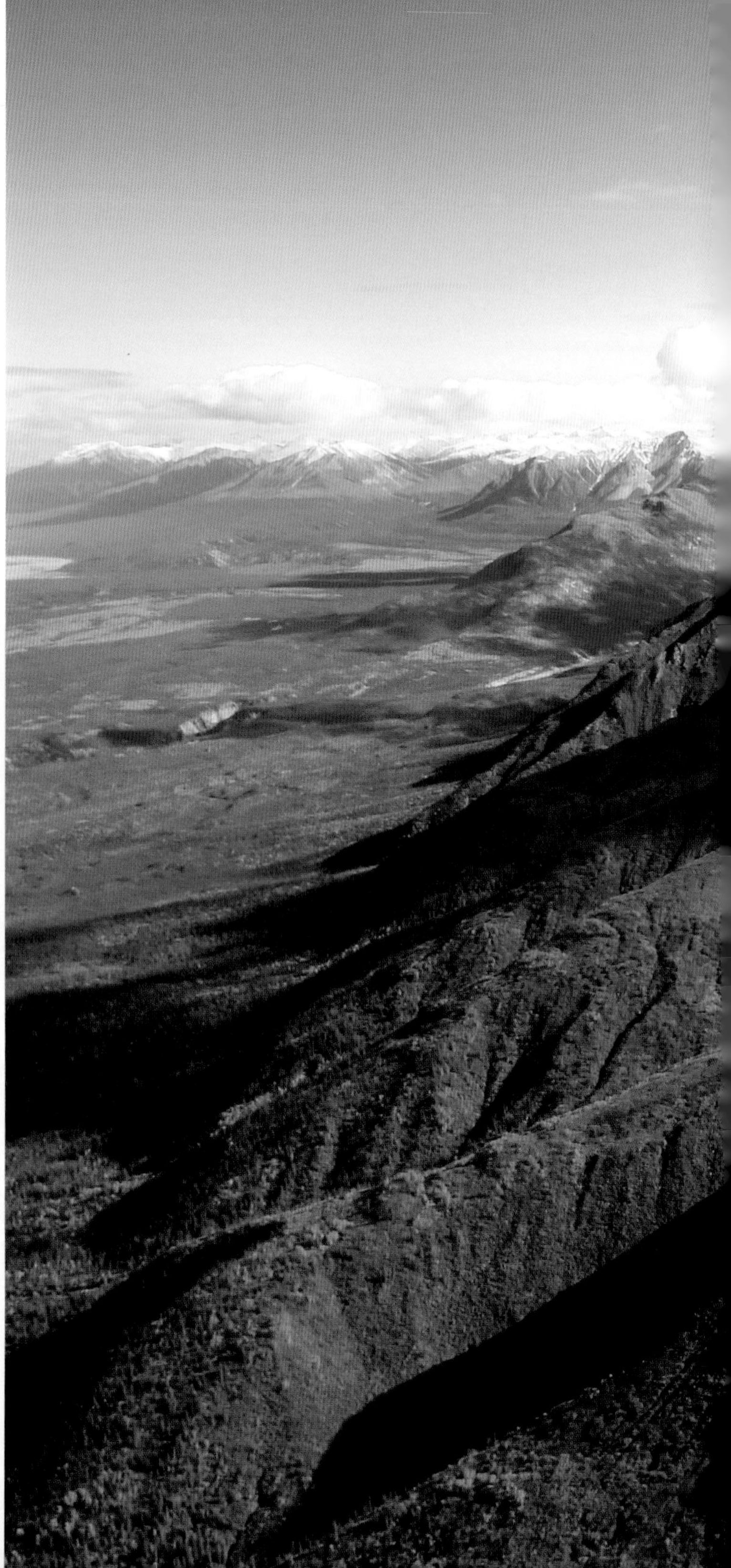

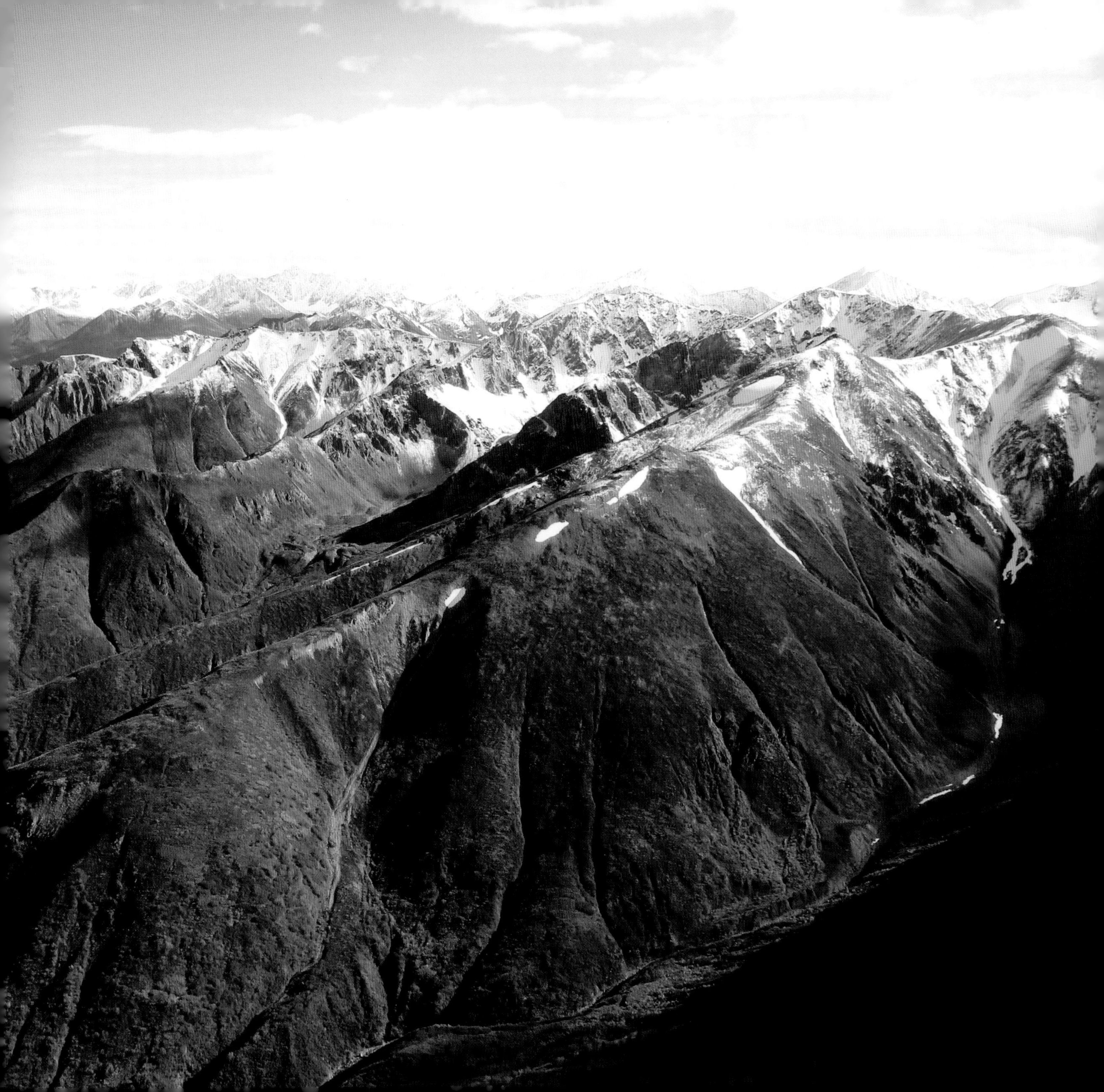

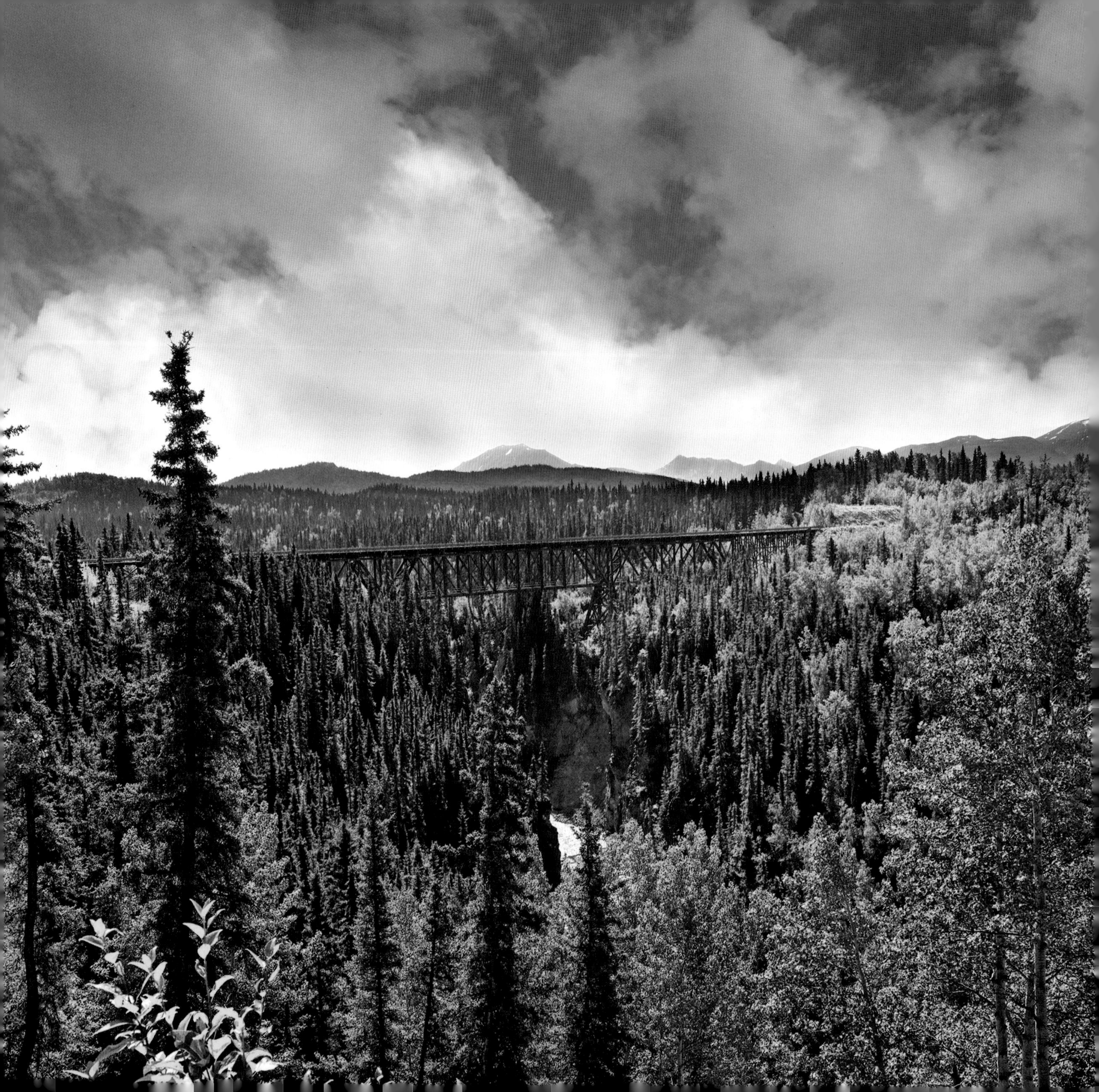

KUSKULANA BRIDGE, MCCARTHY ROAD, WRANGELL-ST. ELIAS NATIONAL PARK

Copper River Valley

Not much more than a gravel track, the McCarthy Road is still celebrated for its spectacular course, skirting the southwestern edge of the Wrangell Range. Running between Chitina and McCarthy, it follows the route of an abandoned railway line, linking up with Alaska's highway system at its northern (Chitina) end. This vertiginous trestle bridge, 160 m (525 ft) long, was built to carry the railway over the Kuskulana River, 75 m (230 ft) below. Now it is a highlight of one of Alaska's most rewarding scenic drives.

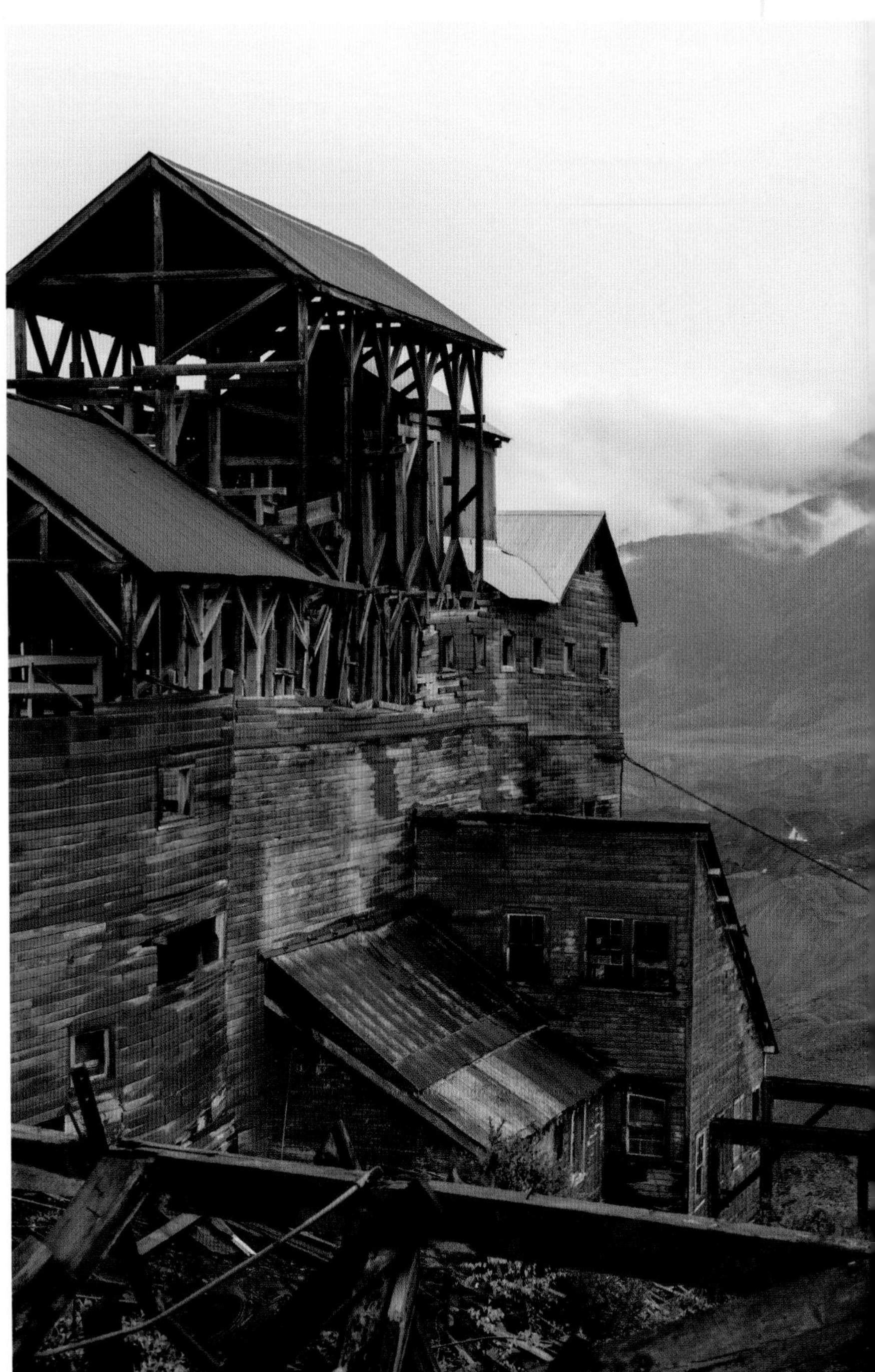

ABANDONED KENNECOTT MINE, WRANGELL-ST. ELIAS NATIONAL PARK

Copper River Valley

Dramatically situated high up on a mountainside above a glacier, this complex made history more than a century ago. Gifford Pinchot (1865–1946), Forest Service Chief, tried to prevent its opening, on the then-novel grounds that it would damage one of Alaska's most beautiful and sensitive environments. He won the support of President Theodore Roosevelt (1858–1919). Ranged against him, however, with Interior Secretary Richard A. Ballinger (1858–1922), were the Guggenheim and J.P. Morgan banking houses. Money won, but notice had been served of a new issue: 'conservation'.

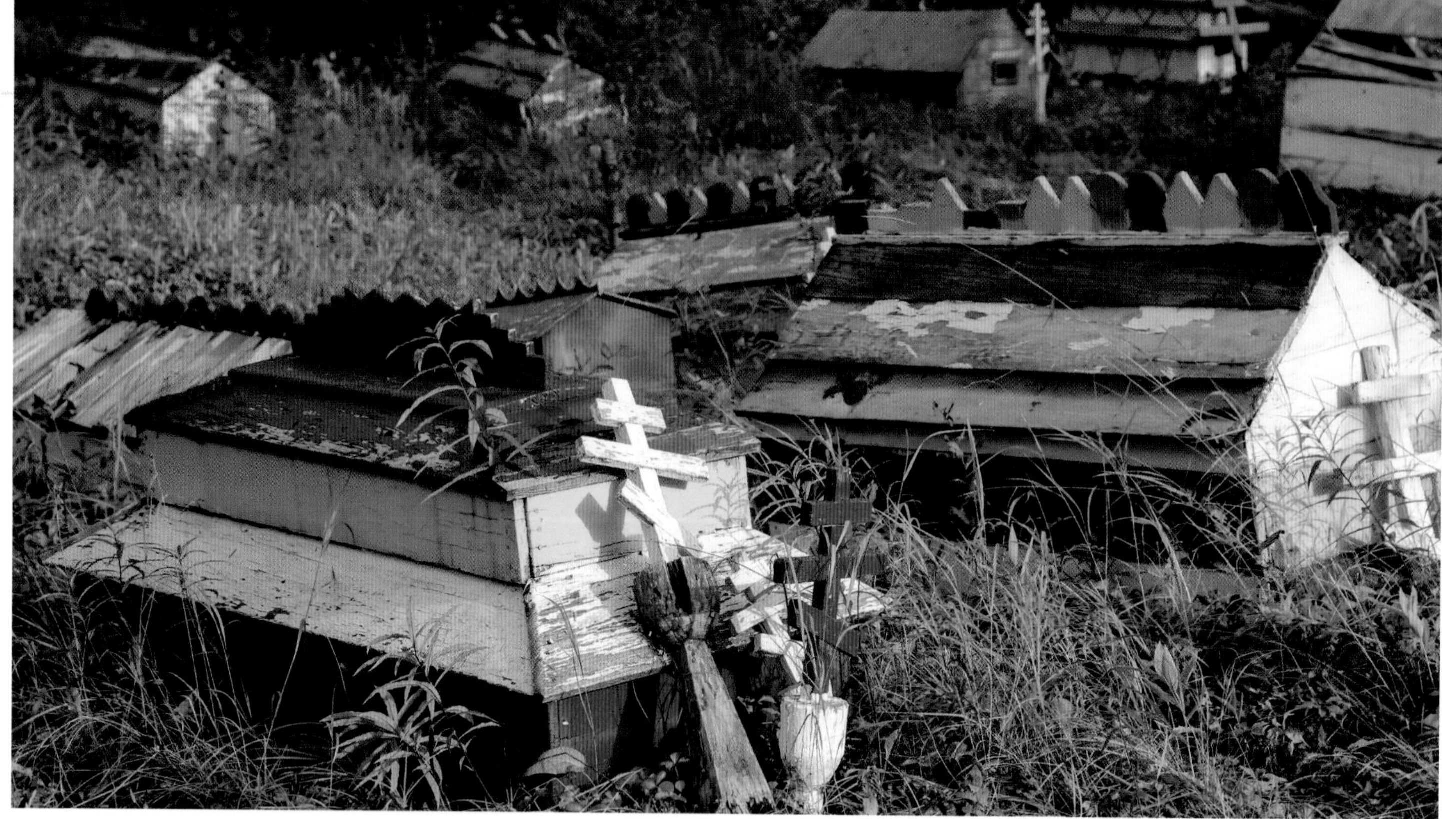

CEMETERY, EKLUTNA

Anchorage Area

A Native-American people, the Dena'ina, are believed to have lived here for 800 years. In the eighteenth century, though, the Russians came. They were followed, in the 1840s, by Orthodox missionaries, sufficiently persuasive to get the entire community to convert. Not, however, sufficiently to make them forsake their old faith entirely. Hence the brightly coloured 'spirit houses' on the graves in their cemetery. Such syncretism is not uncommon in these circumstances: think of the West African slaves who identified their traditional gods with their 'new' Catholic saints in Haitian *Vodou* or in Cuban *Santería*.

FLATTOP MOUNTAIN, CHUGACH STATE PARK

Anchorage Area

This 1,070 m (3,510 ft) peak is the most-climbed mountain in Alaska. But then it is also Anchorage's local summit, standing just beyond the city's eastern suburbs. Look back the way you came (typically from the Glen Alp trailhead, close to town), and your view from that famous flat top is of all that urban sprawl. To the east, though, you look out to the wild and lovely Chugach Mountains. Further to the north is the Alaska Range, with such towering peaks as Denali and Mount Foraker (*see* page 72).

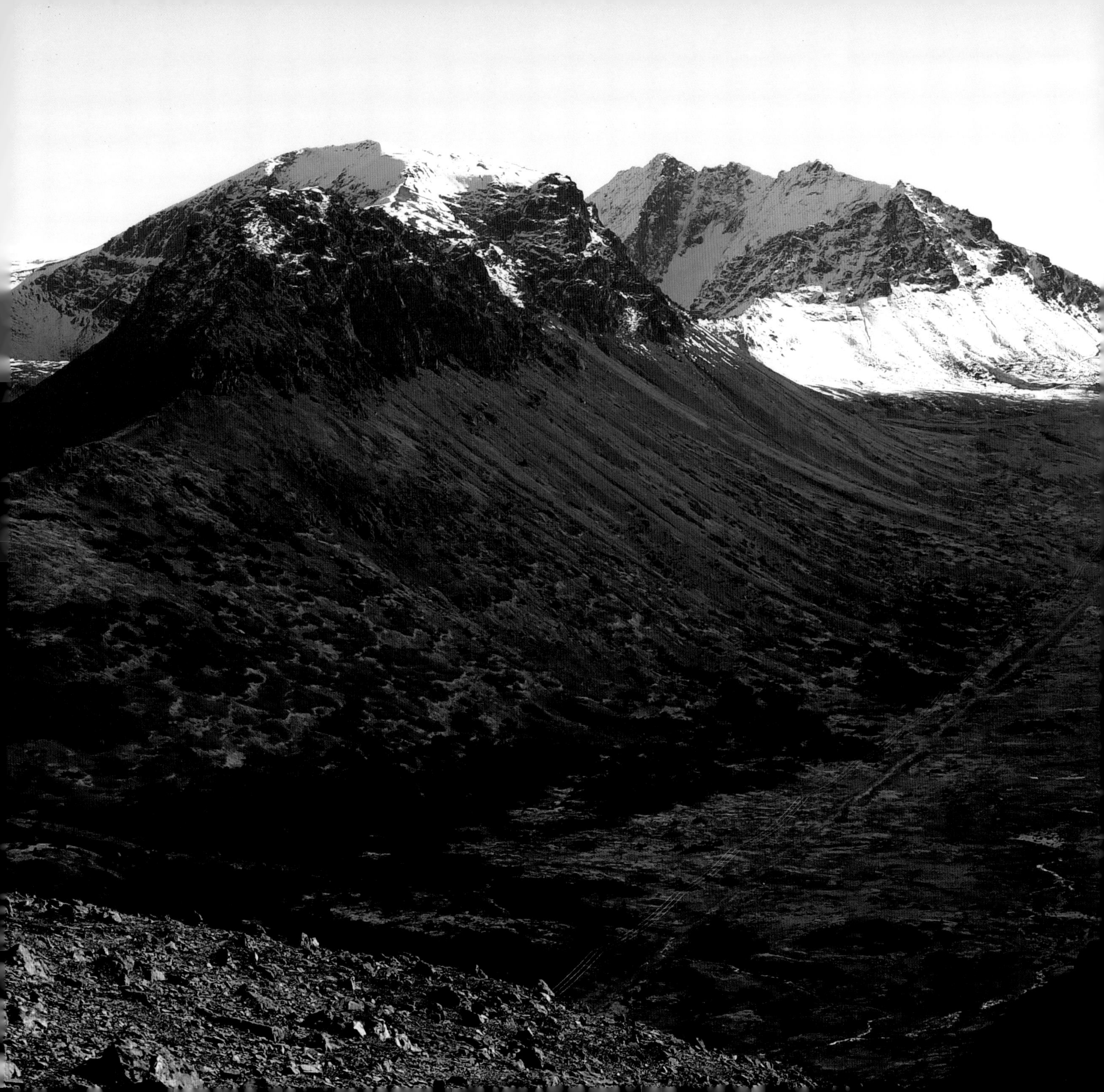

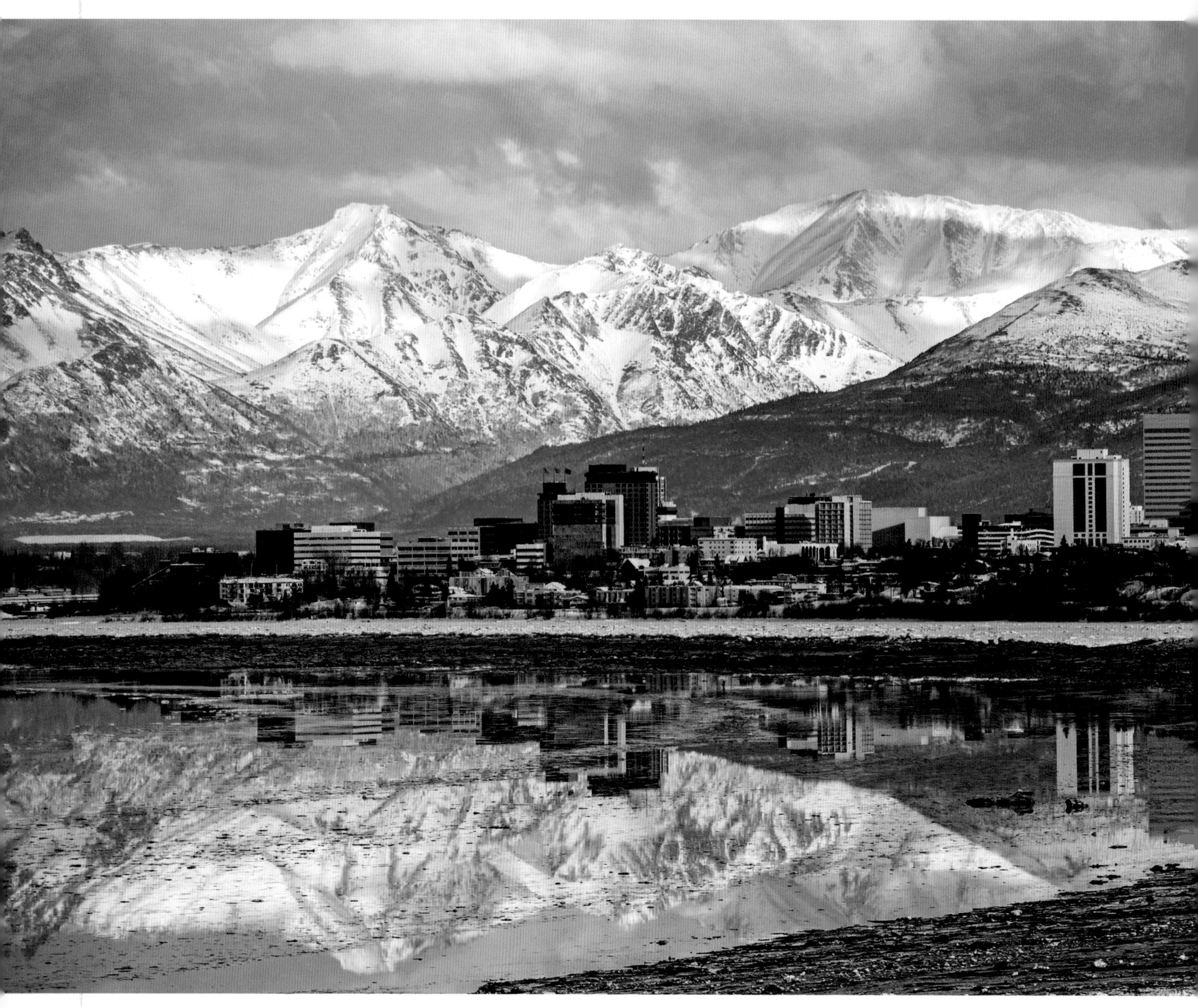

ANCHORAGE SKYLINE

Anchorage Area

Anchorage, a beautiful city? Building by building (with honourable exceptions), you might not say that. And yet, you have to admit, its setting makes it so. Here the mass of so many million tonnes of concrete, steel, glass and tarmac that make up any modern city are transmuted into something magical by mirroring waters, framing mountains and a lightening, lifting sky. And, of course, by winter's spell, somehow crystallizing everything it touches here into something special, something sparkling, crisp and clean.

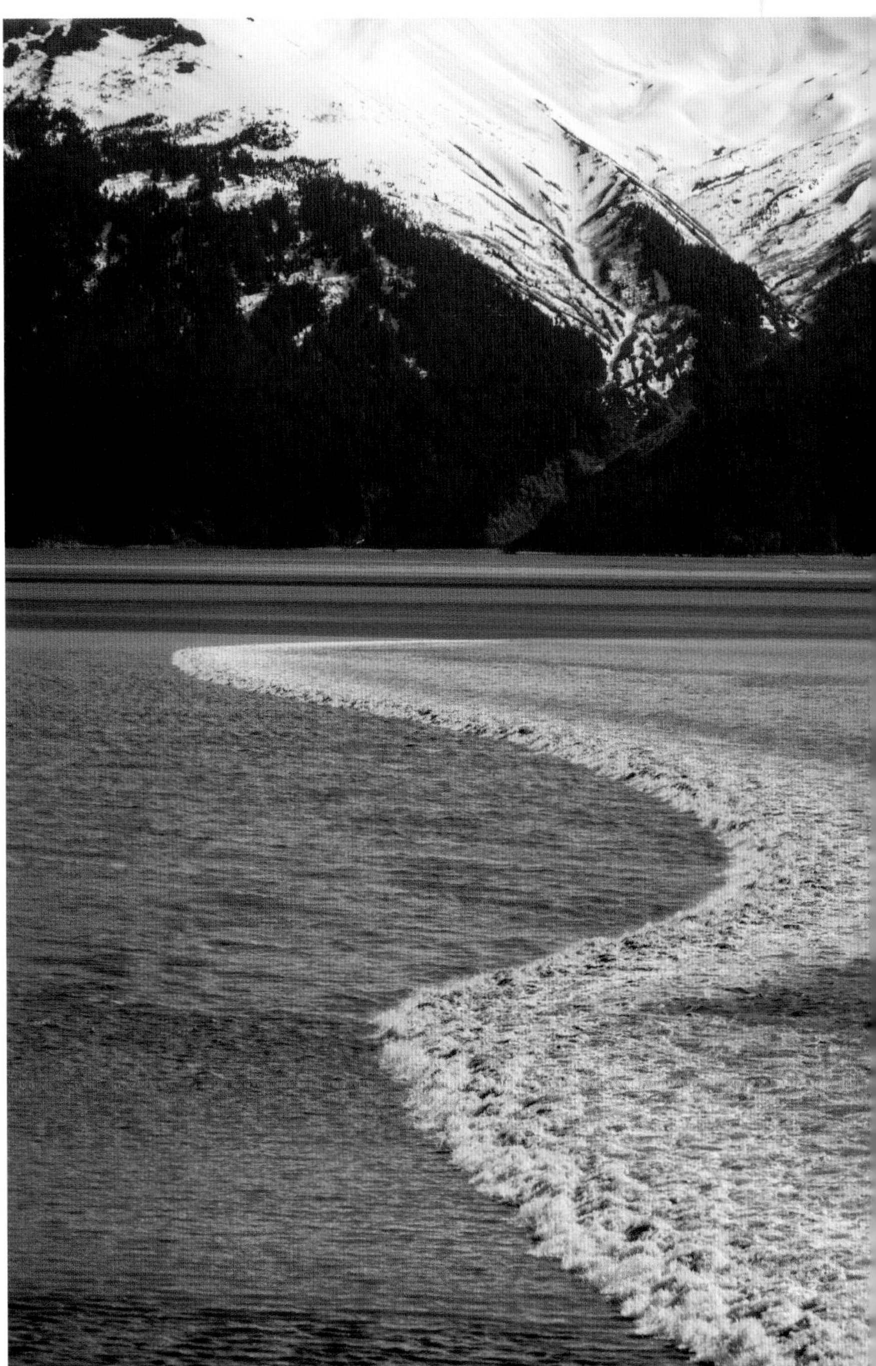

TIDAL BORE, TURNAGAIN ARM

Anchorage Area

Anchorage stands between two branches of water which stretch out from the top of Cook Inlet, like a pair of arms. The more northerly is Knik Arm (*see* page 90). The more southerly was named Turnagain Arm by the English naval officer William Bligh (1754–1817; later of *Bounty* fame). He came here in 1778 with Captain James Cook, after whom, of course, Cook Inlet as a whole was named. Turnagain Arm has a striking tidal bore which can reach heights of 3 m (10 ft) and speeds of 24 km/h (15 mph).

PORTAGE GLACIER FROM PORTAGE PASS, WHITTIER

Anchorage Area

An awe-inspiring sight: a solid river, looking powerful, unstoppable, impregnable. And yet, slowly but surely, it is in retreat. The visitor centre for the Portage Glacier was built in the 1980s on a site that offered stunning views of the ice wall across the lake. But a sign of changing times on a warming planet: the ice has withdrawn around a mountain spur and cannot be seen from the centre any more. Now you have to take a trip by boat.

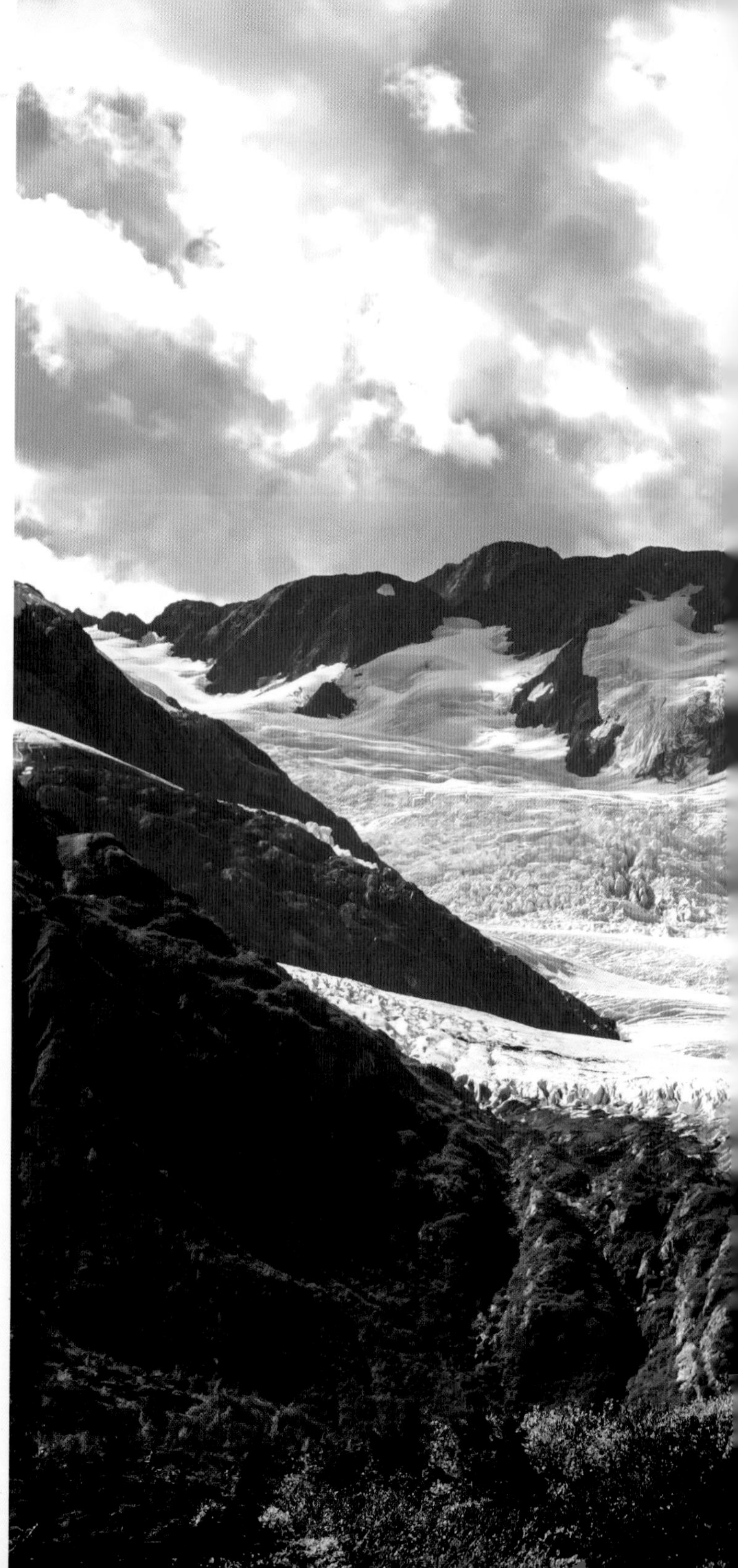

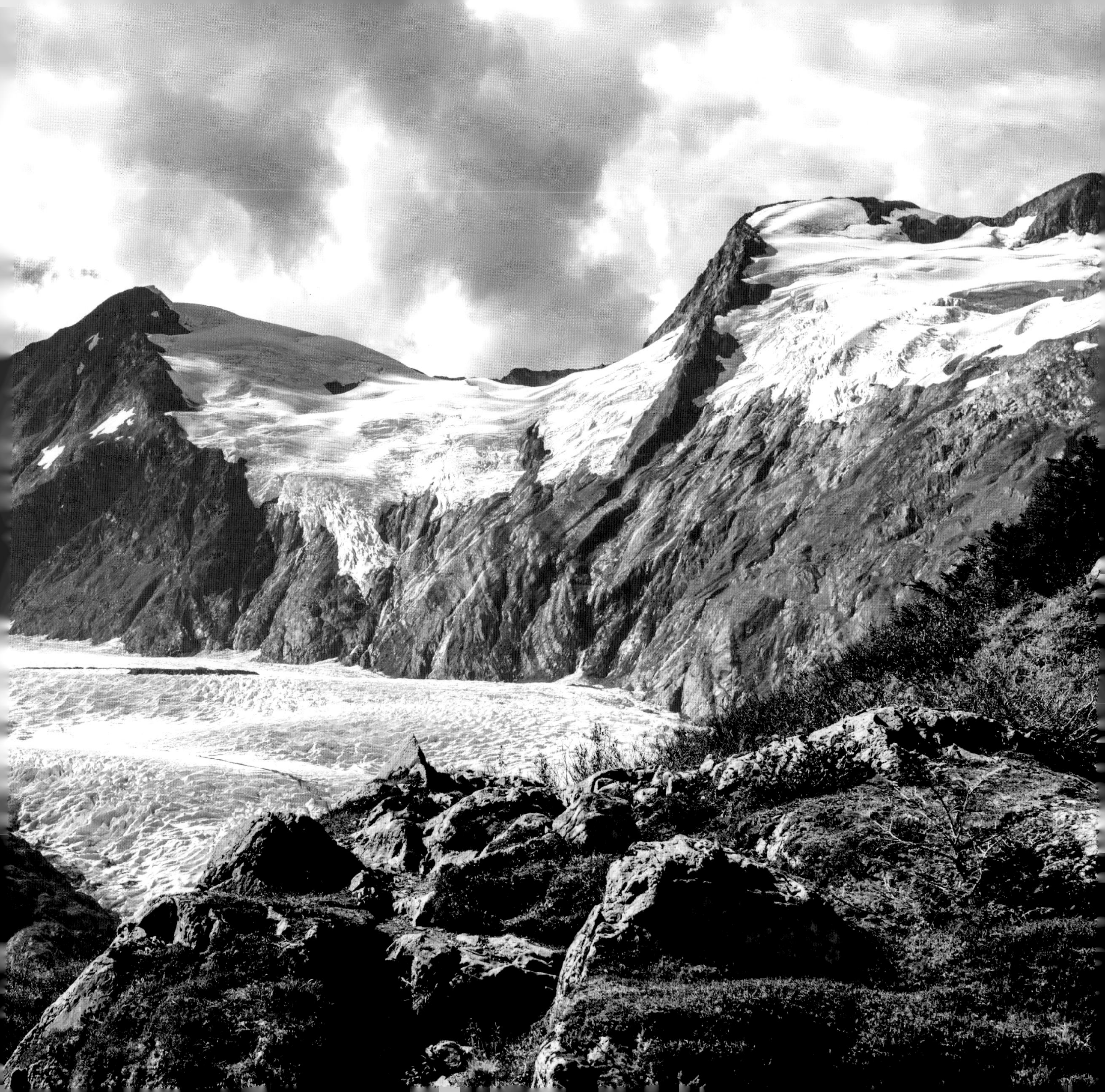

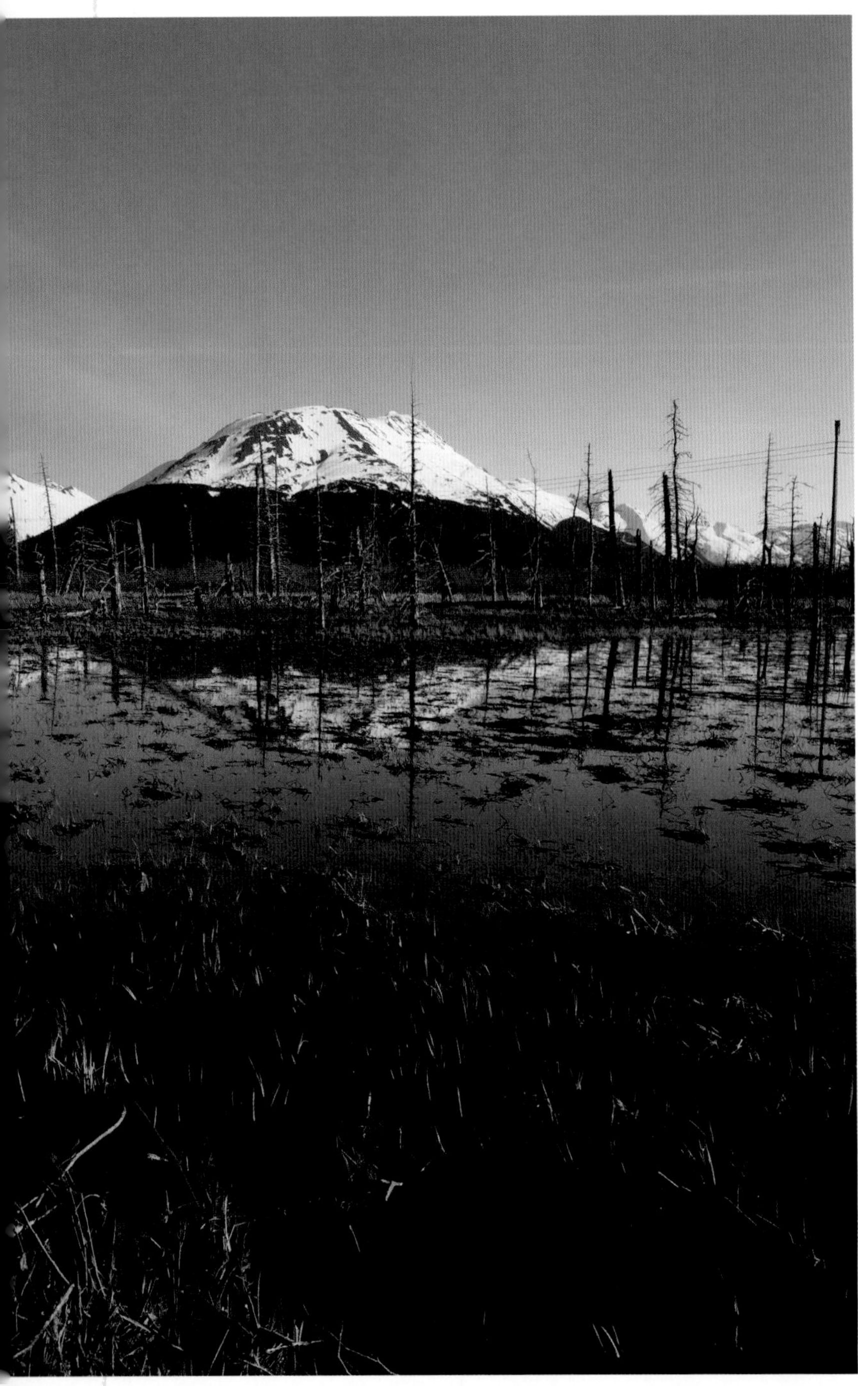

'GHOST FOREST', PORTAGE, TURNAGAIN ARM

Anchorage Area

Not content with picking up Portage and shaking it violently for several minutes, the Good Friday Earthquake of 1964 left the ground level 3 m (10 ft) lower than it had been. The settlement suddenly found itself below the high-water mark, being completely inundated at each full tide. Such buildings as were not simply swept away collapsed or slumped at crazy angles; they have all but disappeared in the decades since. All that is really left now is this forest of drowned trees, killed by the action of saltwater on their roots.

BUCKNER BUILDING, WHITTIER

Anchorage Area

In the Second World War, Whittier was an important port for munitions being brought in for the defence of Alaska. Troops had to be brought in to defend the port itself. General Simon Buckner (1885–1945) commissioned this reinforced barracks with room for a thousand men – but it had not been completed by the conflict's end. Construction went on into the Cold War and the Buckner Building was finally finished in 1953. Soon, however, it was coming to be seen as obsolete and was abandoned in 1966. It has been empty – and increasingly controversial – ever since.

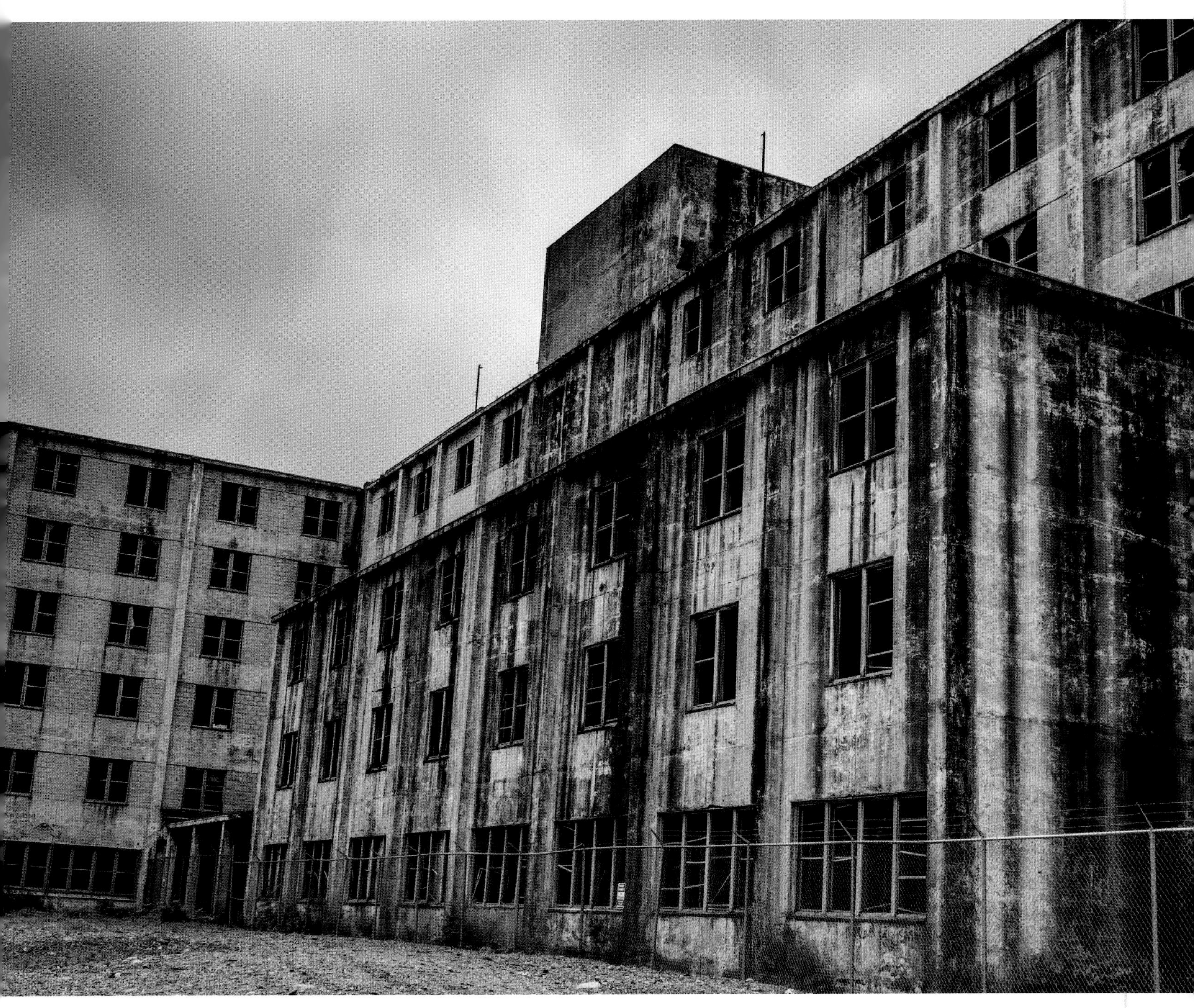

VALDEZ SMALL BOAT HARBOR

Prince William Sound

Tucked away, deep in a fjord, itself secreted at the north-east corner of Prince William Sound, with mountains all around, Valdez has the ultimate in sheltered harbours. While it is best known these days as marking the southern limit of the Trans-Alaska Pipeline, so a key terminal for tankers, it retains its role as an important fishing port. There have, of course, been conflicts. Fishermen are even now still struggling with the long-term consequences of the oil spill that resulted when, in 1989, the *Exxon Valdez* struck Bligh Reef, in Prince William Sound.

GLACIERS, CHUGACH MOUNTAINS

Prince William Sound

A wall of blue-grey rock, rising to a blue-white symphony in snow, ice, sky and cloud. Prince William Sound is hemmed in on three sides by the Chugach Mountains. Amidst their jagged, jumbled heights we see the white splashes that show where glaciers have, over countless centuries, slowly gouged and ground their way down the mountainsides to the melting sea. Of the 150 glaciers still to be seen among the summits around the Sound, seventeen 'tidewater glaciers' are still frozen when they reach the sea.

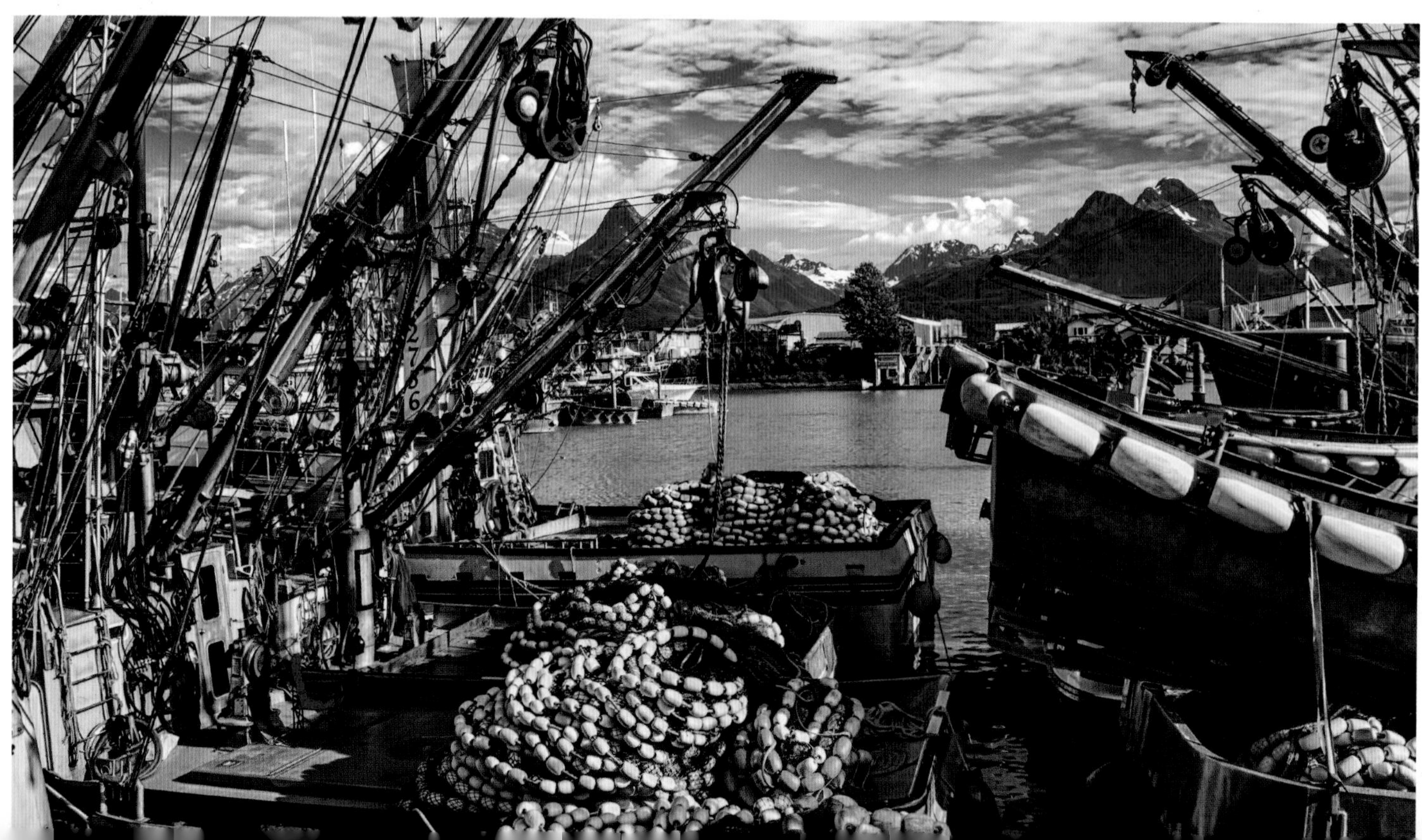

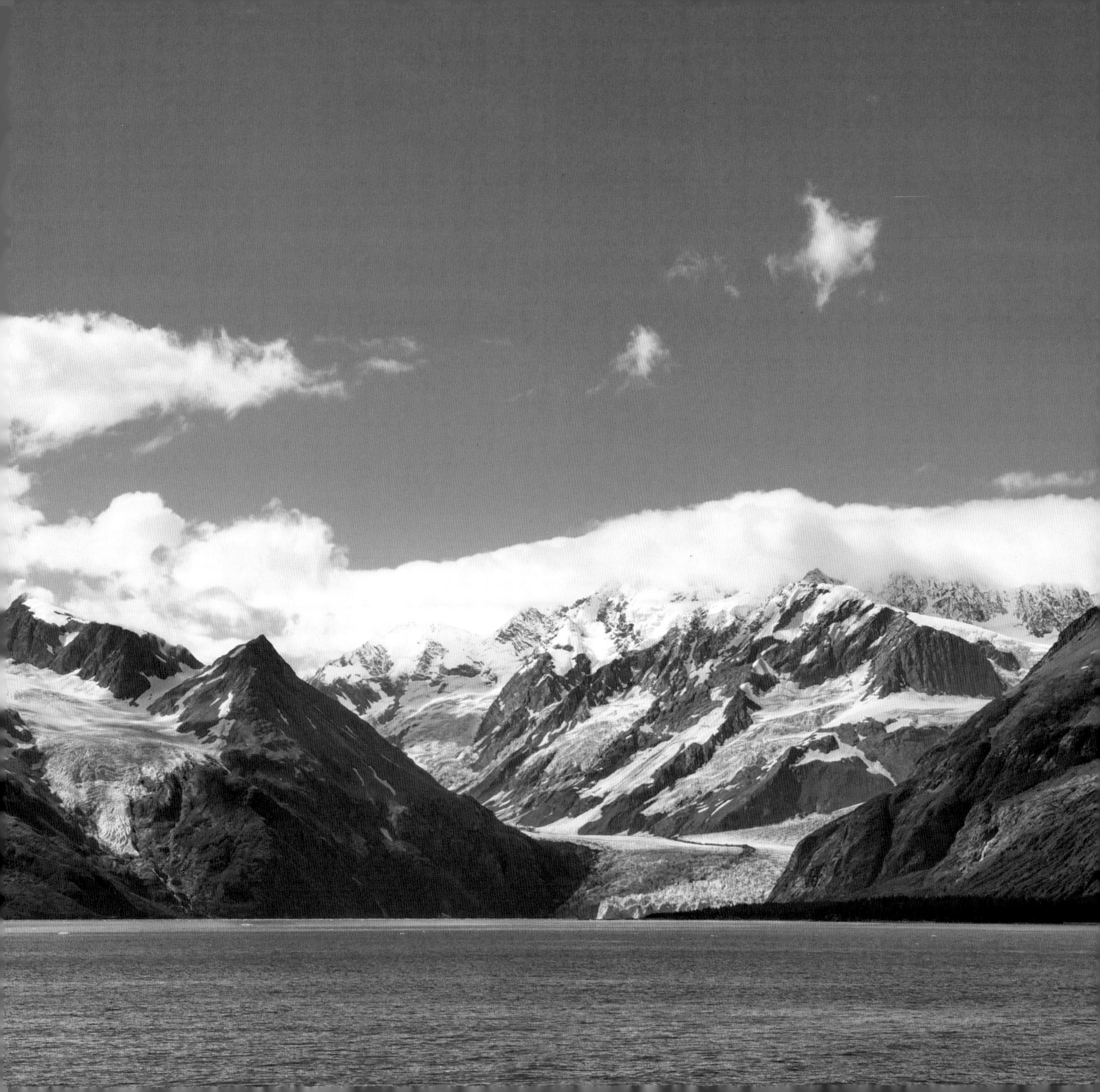

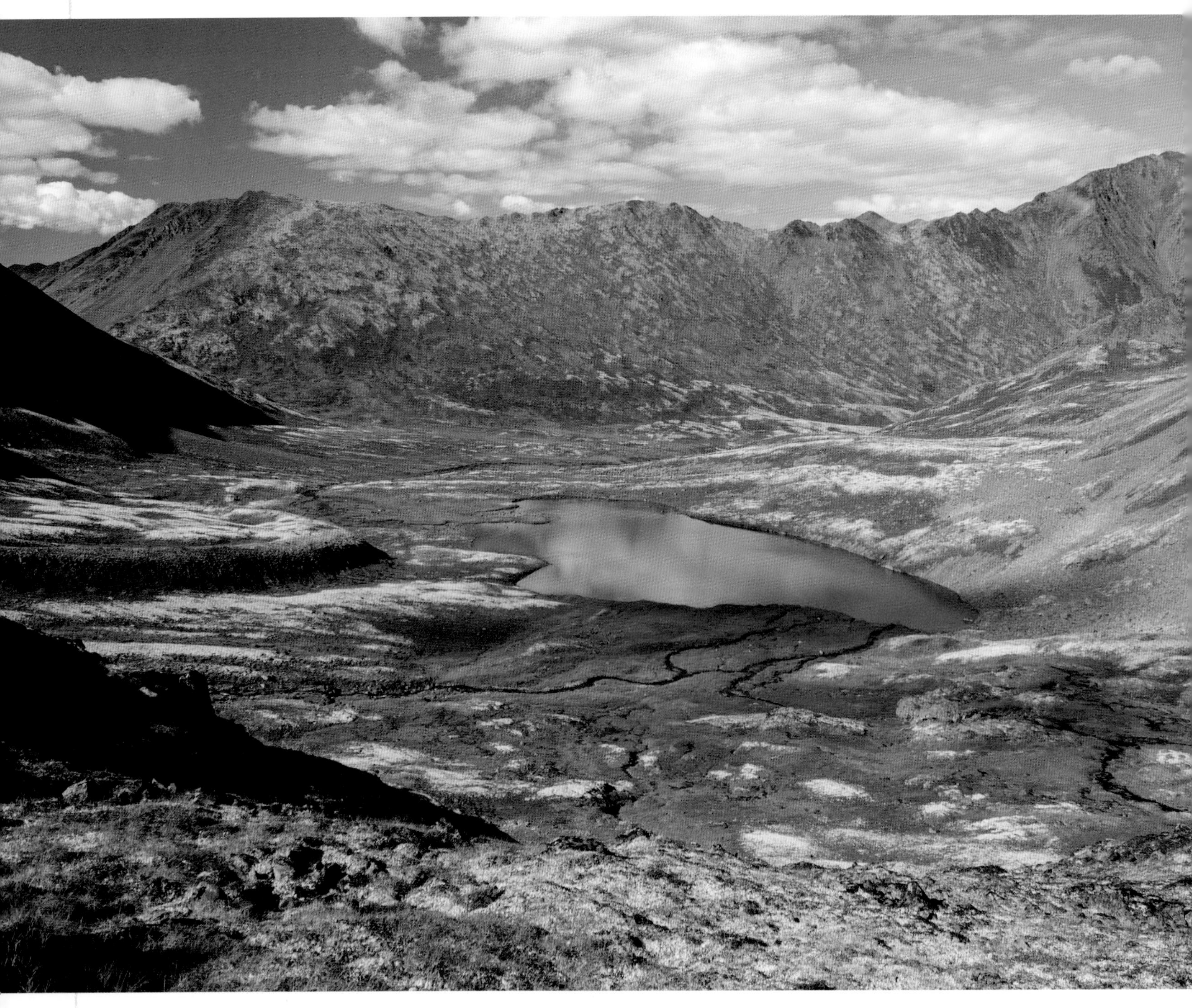

LAKE, CHUGACH NATIONAL FOREST

Prince William Sound

With its rugged, glaciated landscape, Chugach National Forest is full of challenging trails and lovely views. Glaciers carve out distinctive valleys, steep-sided but flat-bottomed. (A river cuts a narrow V, its sides eroded in their turn by streams.) The French call this a *cirque*, from the Latin word for 'amphitheatre'. In Scotland they're 'corries', from the Gaelic *coire*, 'cauldron'. Typically, the 'moraine' – the earth and debris pushed along by the ice – is left behind as the glacier finally melts. A raised lip results, behind which a corrie-lake or tarn like this may form.

HAYSTACK TRAIL, CHUGACH NATIONAL FOREST

Prince William Sound

Those inclined to doubt the old saying that it is the journey, not the destination that matters, should make the short hike up the Haystack Trail to the Copper River Outlook. Not to detract in any way from exhilarating views of the valley, all the way down to the delta and beyond to the Gulf of Alaska, but the real highlight here is the walk through the woods. Between blessed peace, the soft comfort of the mossy forest floor and the protective presence of these towering hemlock and spruce, the sense of something like spirituality is strong.

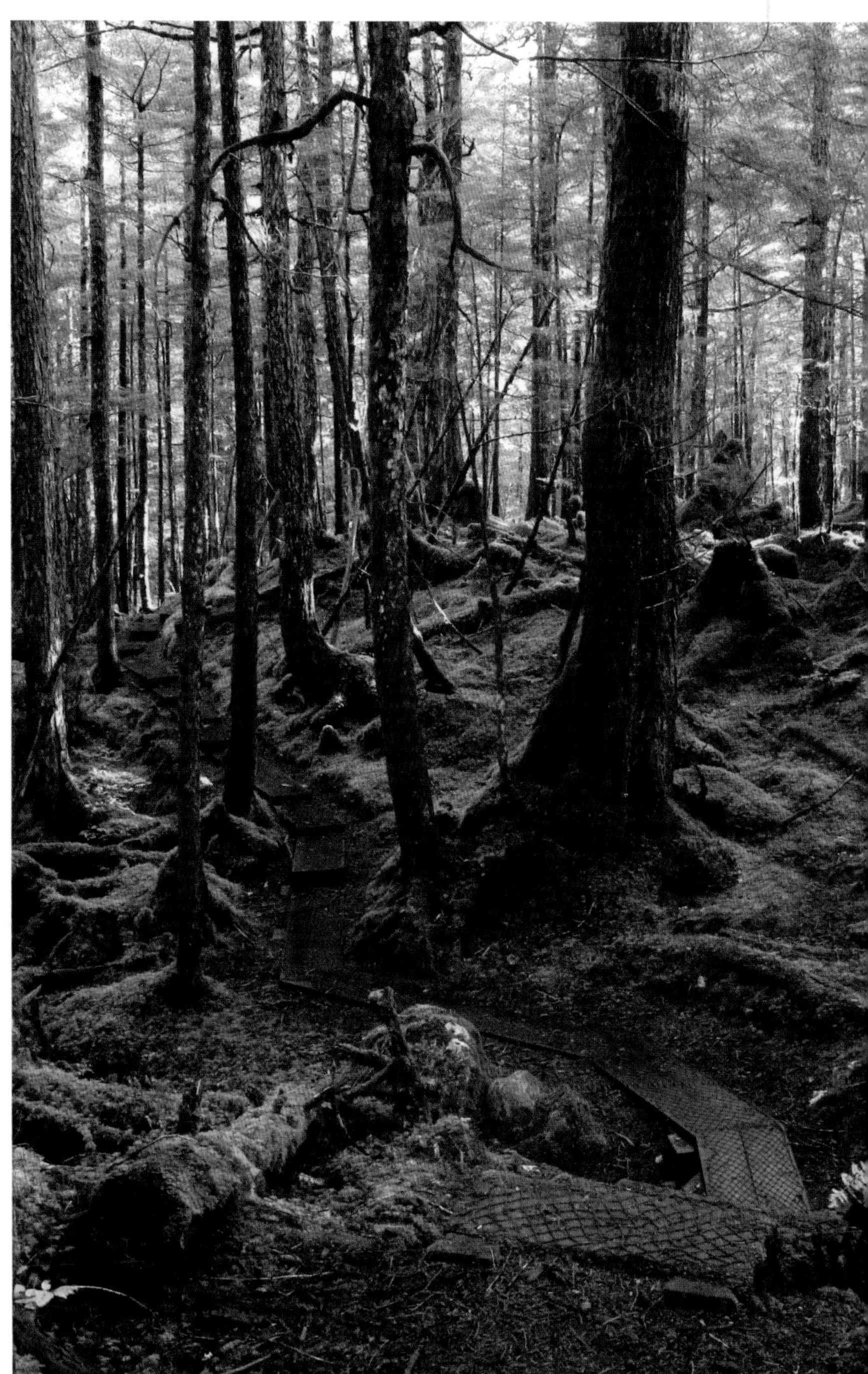

MILLION DOLLAR BRIDGE, CORDOVA

Prince William Sound

In our own times, maybe, a million dollars does not buy you that much bridge. In 1909, however, it seemed a lot. The cost (actually more like $1.4 million) was so high because this 470 m (1,550 ft) concrete-and-steel structure had to be robust enough to withstand the impact of the icebergs from the Miles Glacier upstream. For years it carried the trains of the Copper River and Northwestern Railway – bringing copper from the Kennecott Mine (*see* page 97). Since that closed in 1938 it has been adapted as a road bridge.

GOLD-RUSH-ERA CAFE, HOPE

Kenai Peninsula

Hope was aptly named: what is now a quiet, even sleepy settlement, a weekend winding-down place for over-pressured Anchorage-dwellers, was a frantic boomtown back in Gold-Rush days. It goes without saying that most of that original hope was dashed. The Seaview Cafe has certainly fulfilled the promise of its name, however. From here you can look out over the Turnagain Arm and see the westernmost mountains of the Chugach range sloping down, through snow and rock and forest, to the water's edge.

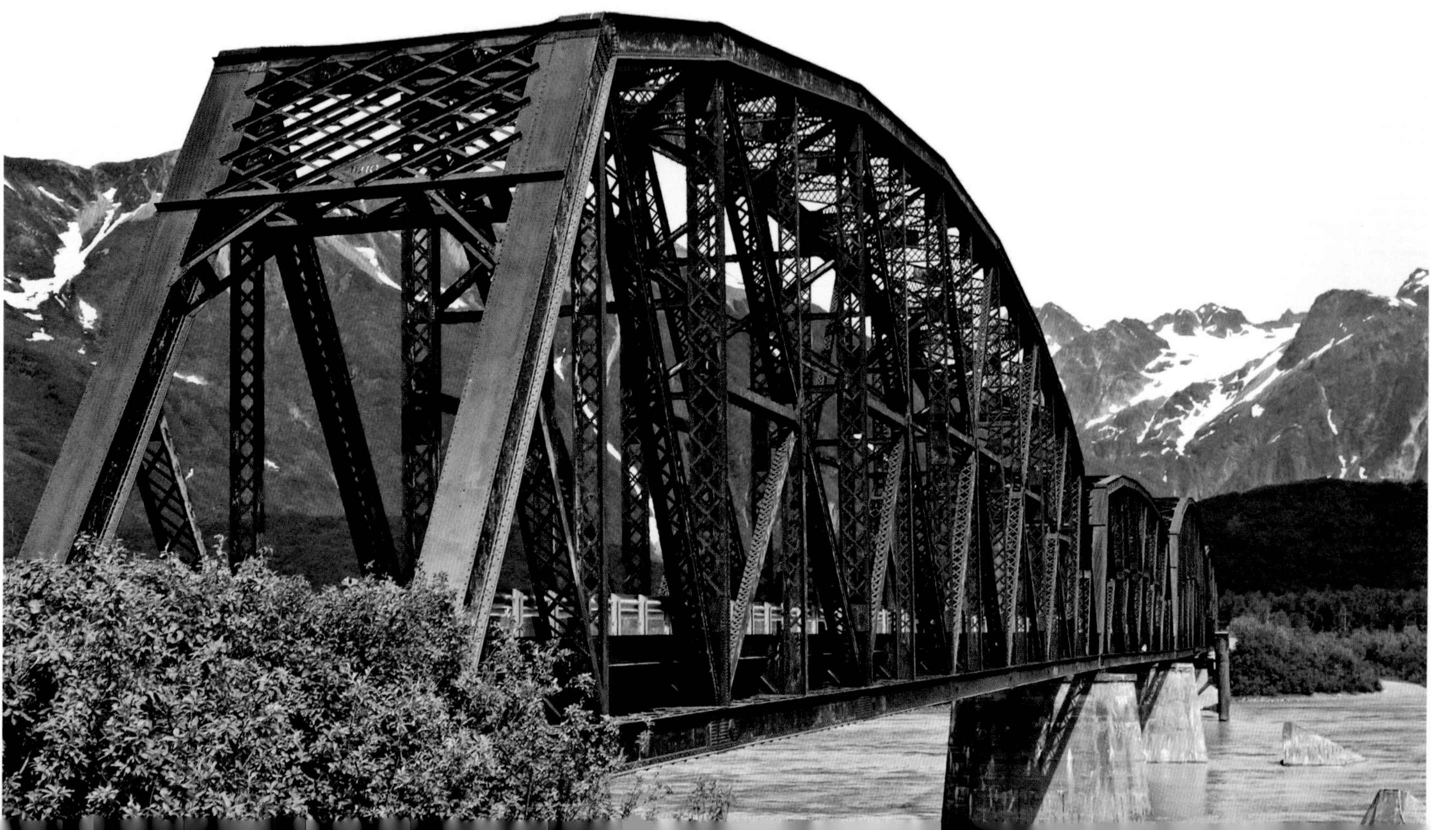

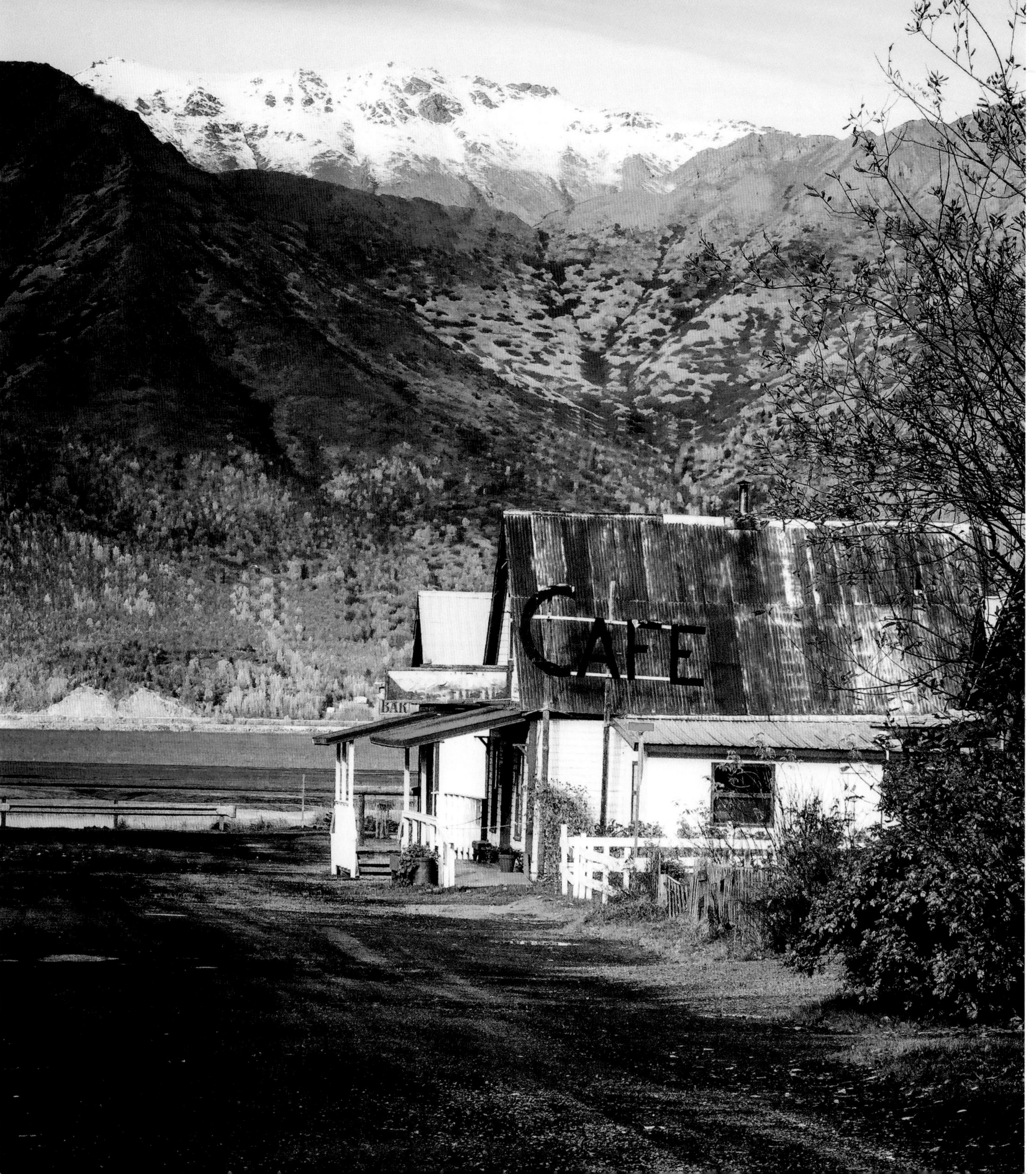
CAFE

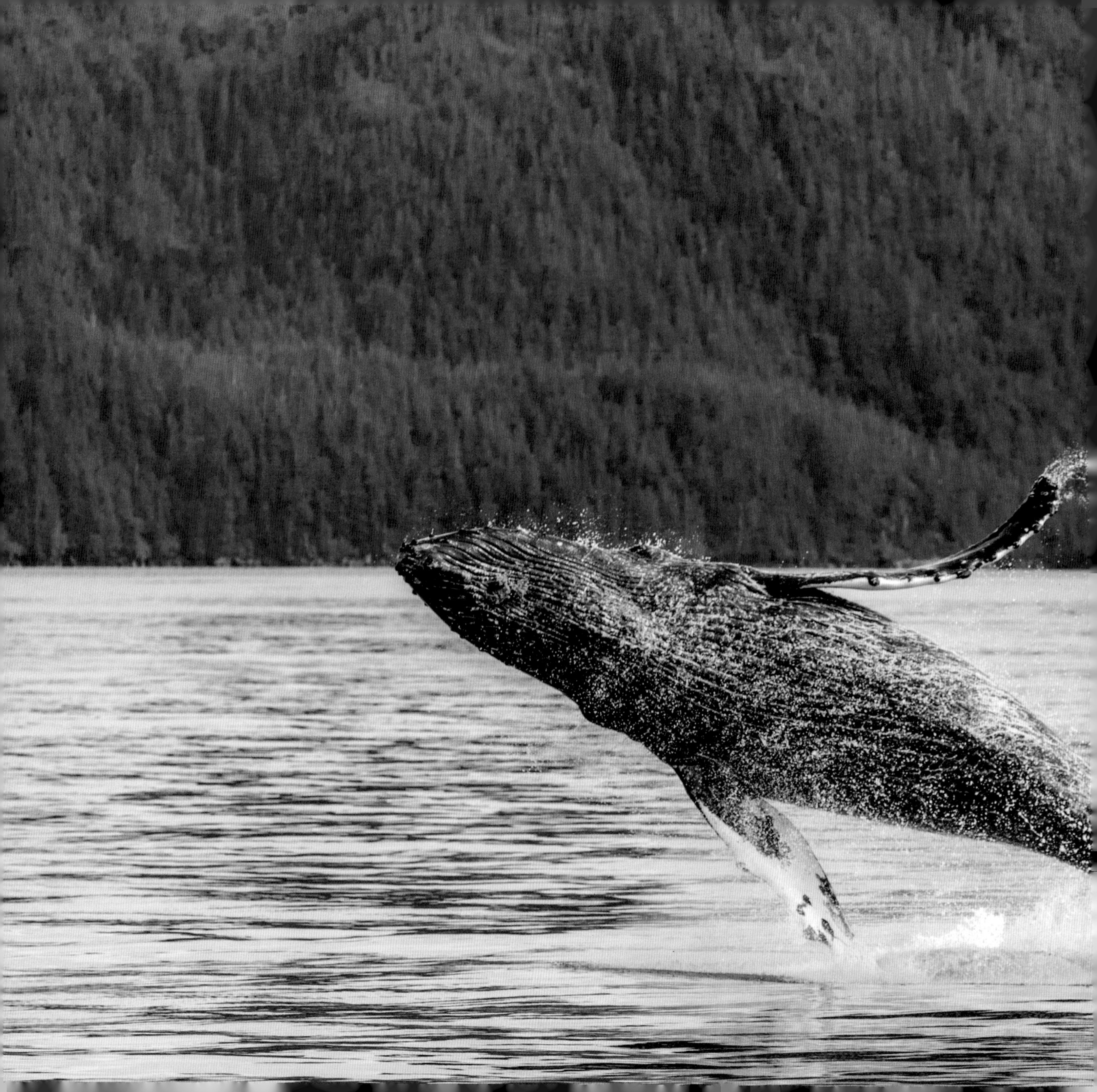

HUMPBACK WHALE, KENAI FJORDS NATIONAL PARK

Kenai Peninsula

The humpback whale breeds in the tropical waters around Mexico and Hawaii in the winter months, but between April and November it is often seen by whale watchers here. The fact that, for unknown reasons, it 'breaches' (leaps from the water) more often than other species, has made it the centrepiece-attraction for the wildlife tours that these days flourish in the Kenai Fjords. The strong likelihood of seeing a humpback or so offsets the risk of missing more retiring marine life, like sea otters, Steller's sea lions (*see* page 145), seals and other kinds of whale.

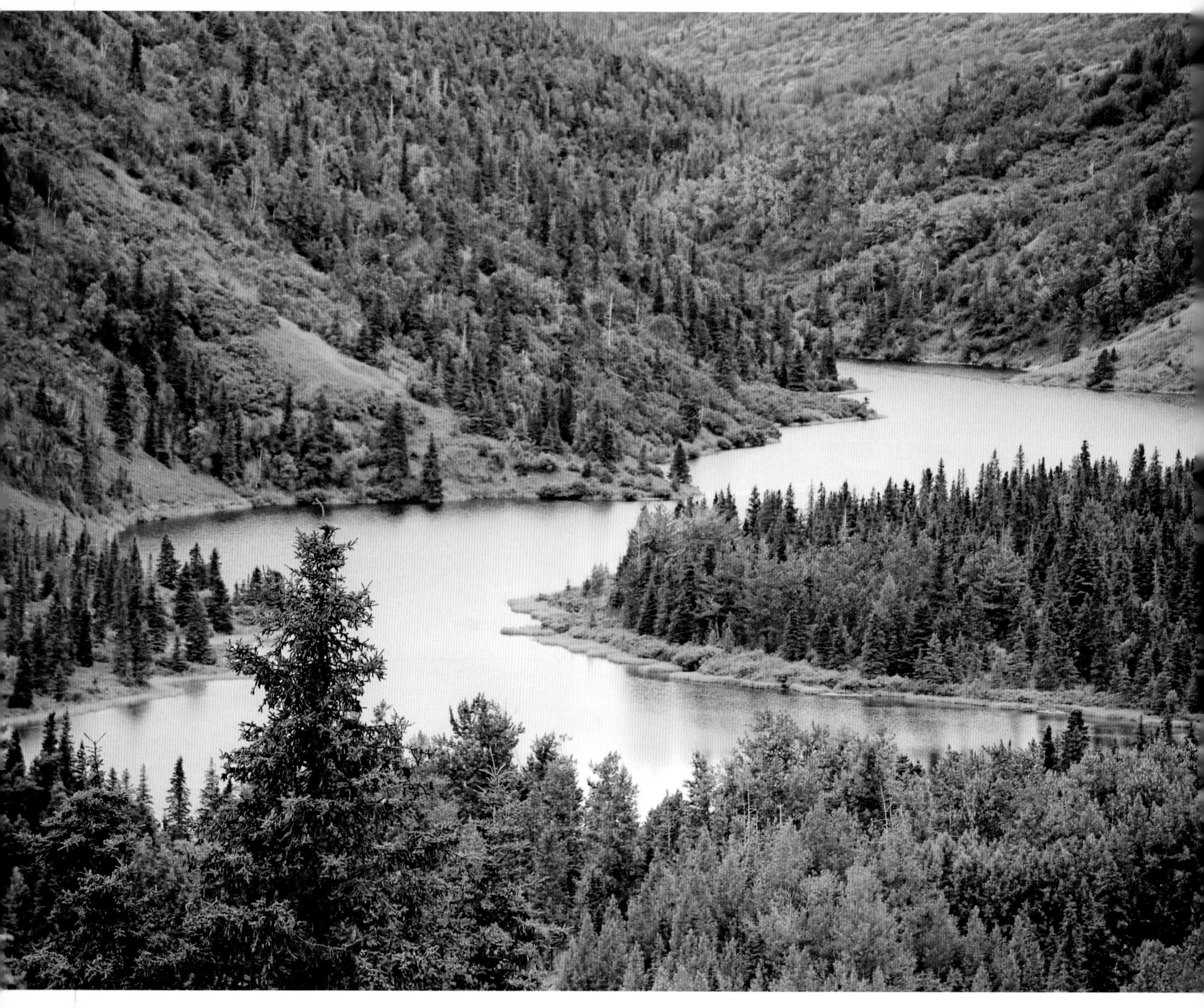

SWAN LAKE, RESURRECTION PASS, HOPE

Kenai Peninsula

A former prospector's path that's since become a route for seekers after less worldly treasures, like fresh air and inspiration, the trail over the Resurrection Pass rises to a height of 790 m (2,600 ft). At this altitude, you are walking through what amounts to a tundra valley, with mountains rising high and rugged on either side. Lower down, though, the way lies through a wonderfully wild and atmospheric forest, punctuated by lovely lakes and running streams. Swan Lake is rich in waterfowl, as its name suggests.

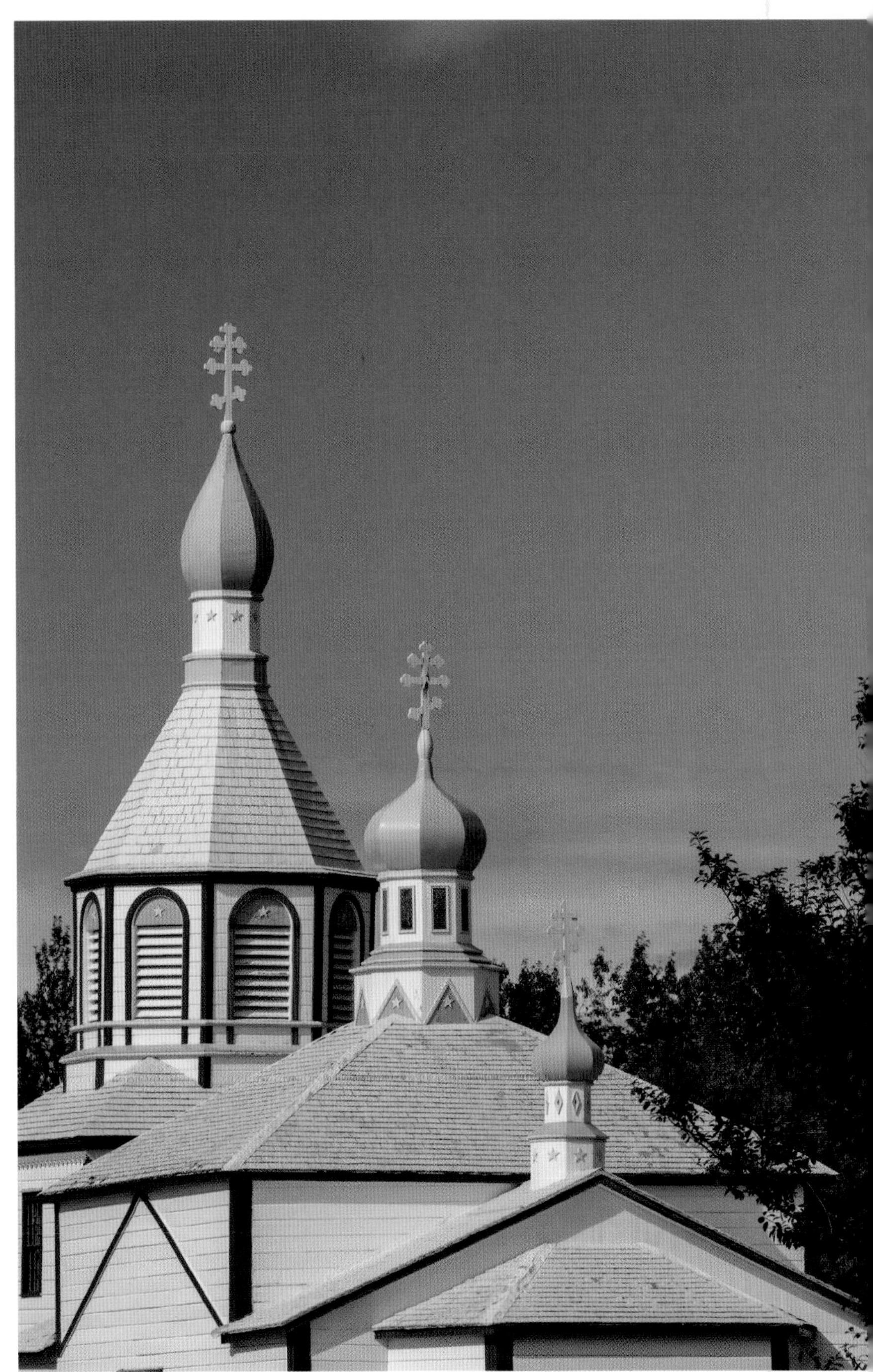

CHURCH OF THE HOLY ASSUMPTION OF THE VIRGIN MARY, KENAI

Kenai Peninsula

Alaska has been a diocese of the Russian Orthodox Church since 1840. Kenai's first church was constructed nine years later. The present white clapboard-covered church dates from the 1890s. The square nave, with its distinctive pyramidal roof, is entered via a little porch on one side. With the 25 m (81 ft) tower on the other side, crowned by an octagonal, arch-windowed belfry, a striking terraced effect is created. Three blue onion domes, each of them topped with bright, gold three-barred crosses, complete this attractive and historic building.

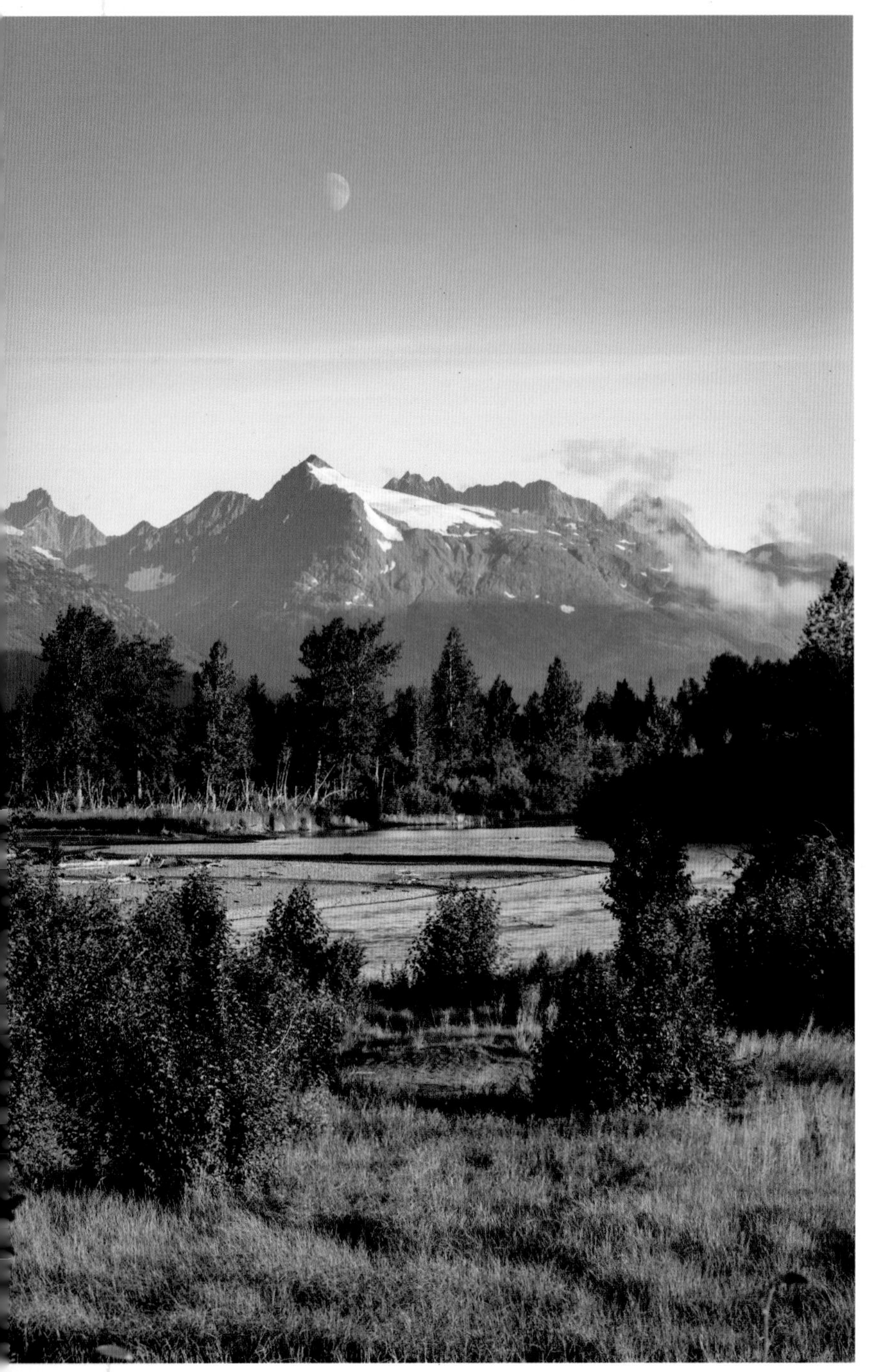

KENAI RIVER

Kenai Peninsula

It may lie only a short distance across the Turnagain Arm from Anchorage, but much of Kenai feels really remote. Kenai Lake, where this river starts, has an altitude of only 132 m (433 ft), but it is serried round by mountains rising up to 1,900 m (6,200 ft). Early on, the Kenai descends rapidly through rocky canyons and over whitewater rapids; here, in its middle reaches, its progress is more measured. By the time it completes its 132 km (82 mile) journey to the Cook Inlet, it has become a quiet, slow – and even a sluggish – river.

ENGINEER LAKE, KENAI NATIONAL WILDLIFE REFUGE

Kenai Peninsula

This lake lies a little way north of Lake Skilak in the Kenai foothills – but such facts seem superfluous, banal. The summer light is slowly softening in the stillness of a breezeless evening. The water surface is as smooth as glass. At a moment like this, there is a feeling of completeness about the Kenai scene; a feeling of self-containment.... What other beauty could we need? We are redundant here, our role to look on while the Alaskan landscape becomes its own Narcissus, admiring the surpassing beauty in itself.

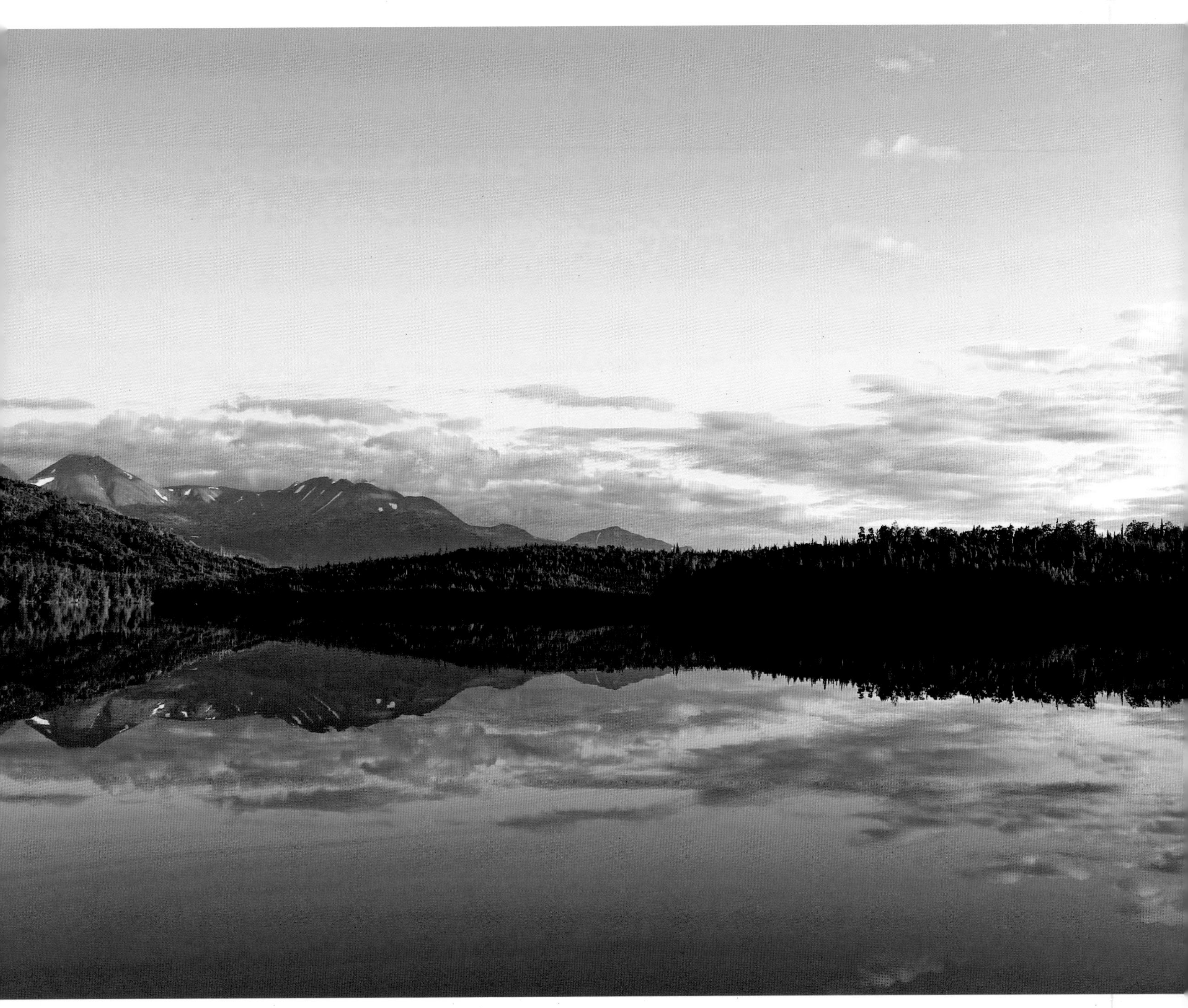

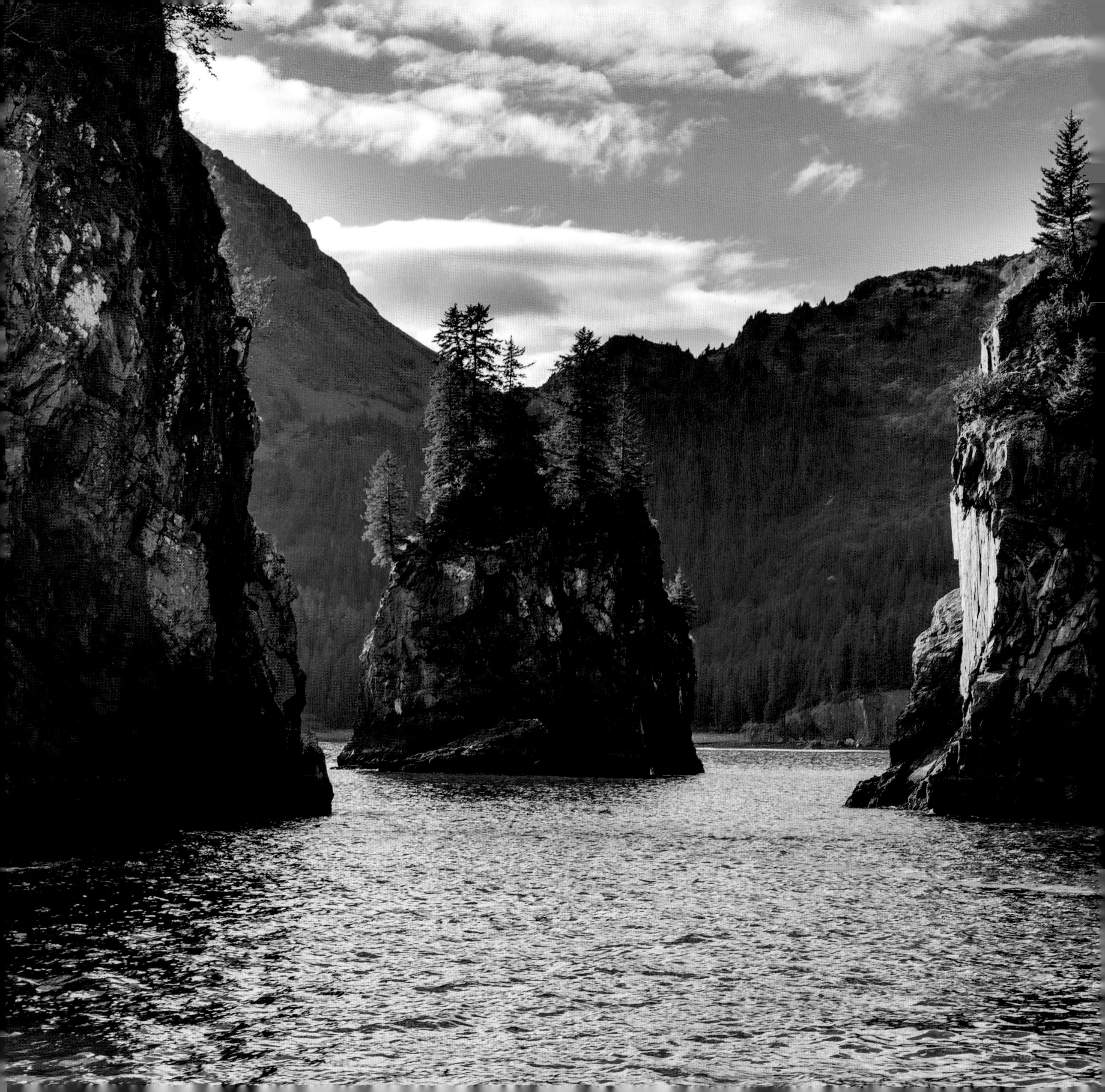

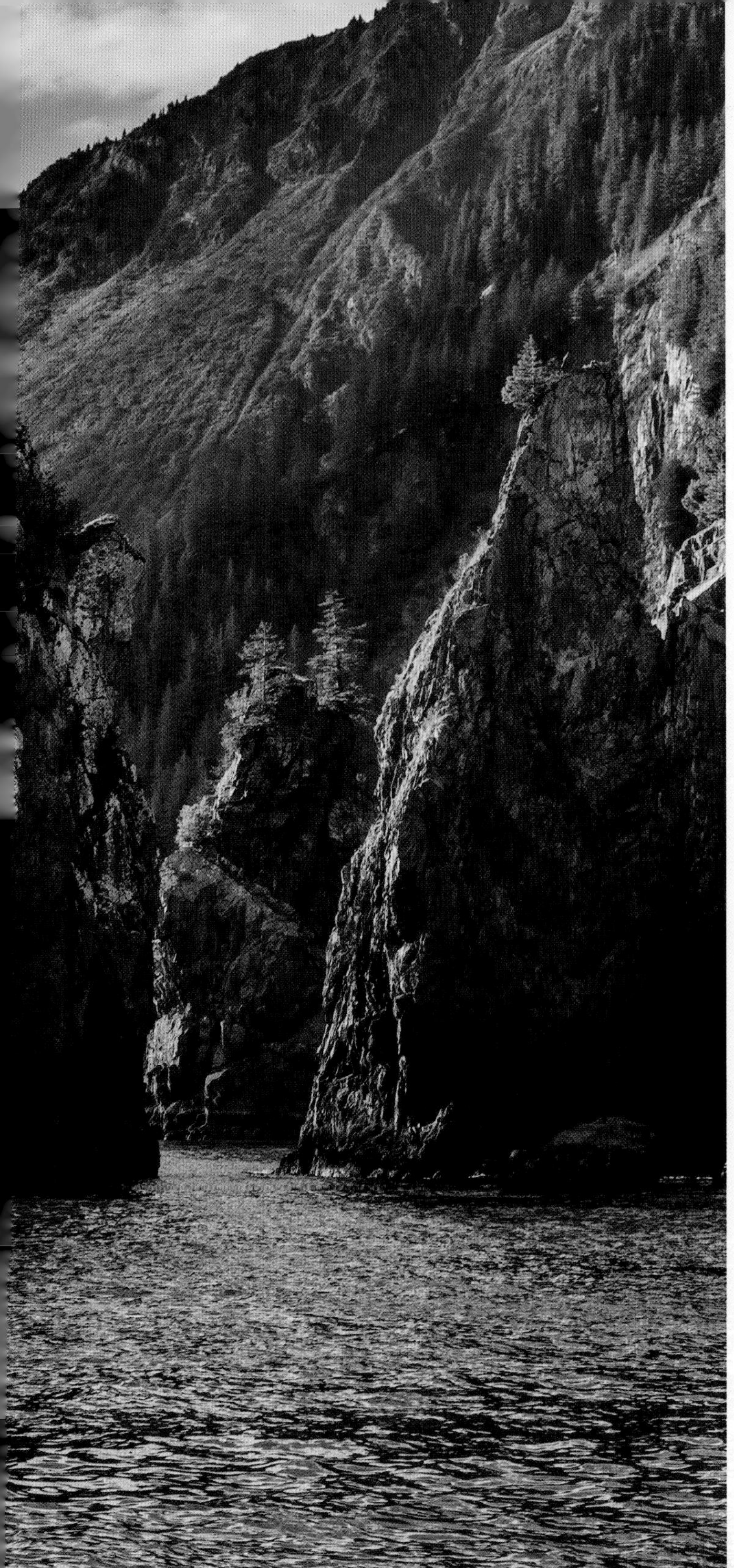

RESURRECTION BAY, SPIRE COVE, KENAI FJORDS NATIONAL PARK

Kenai Peninsula

During recent glaciations, much of the earth's water was 'locked up' in ice, meaning a dramatic rise in sea level when the warmth returned. In these more northerly regions, the broad, steep-sided valleys the glaciers had carved out for themselves were flooded with sea water, becoming fjords. No rock feature can expect to survive a full-on impact with an advancing glacier: along the edges, though, erosion is more erratic in its effects. Harder rocks, like the igneous granodiorite, can survive while others crumble away around them, leading to spectacular irregularities like these 'spires'.

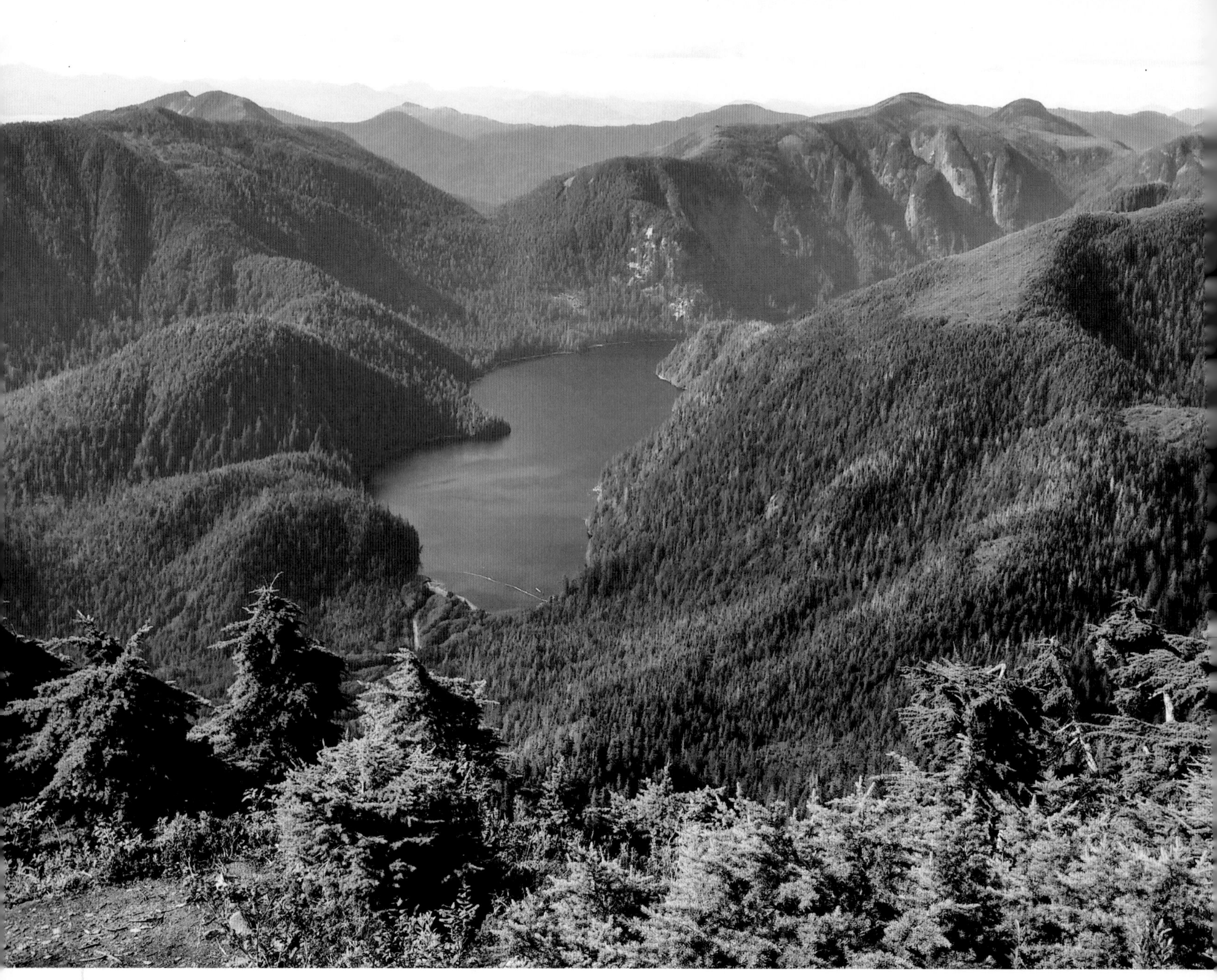

VIEW FROM MOUNT MARATHON TRAIL, SEWARD

Kenai Peninsula

Spare a thought, as you ramble up towards a 638 m (2,094 ft) summit, for those who run this course each 4 July. Their inspiration is, of course, the achievement of Pheidippides, who in 480 BC carried news of the victory over the Persians back to Athens, and the 26-mile (42-km) race that is run in his honour in modern times. Contestants can console themselves that, at 5 km (3 miles), their race is a great deal shorter, but it is a gruelling contest, none the less, in the summer's heat.

CHURCH OF ST NICHOLAS, NIKOLAEVSK

Kenai Peninsula

Alaska was, we know, a Russian territory for more than a century. But that history is irrelevant to us here. The community of 'Old Believers' who call Nikolaevsk home, set up here as recently as 1968. Till then they had lived peripatetically since going into exile in the seventeenth century, in objection to new rites being adopted by the Orthodox Church. Their generations-long journey here had taken them via Siberia, China, Brazil and Oregon. Through all that time, they have continued speaking Russian and living in line with their ancestral customs.

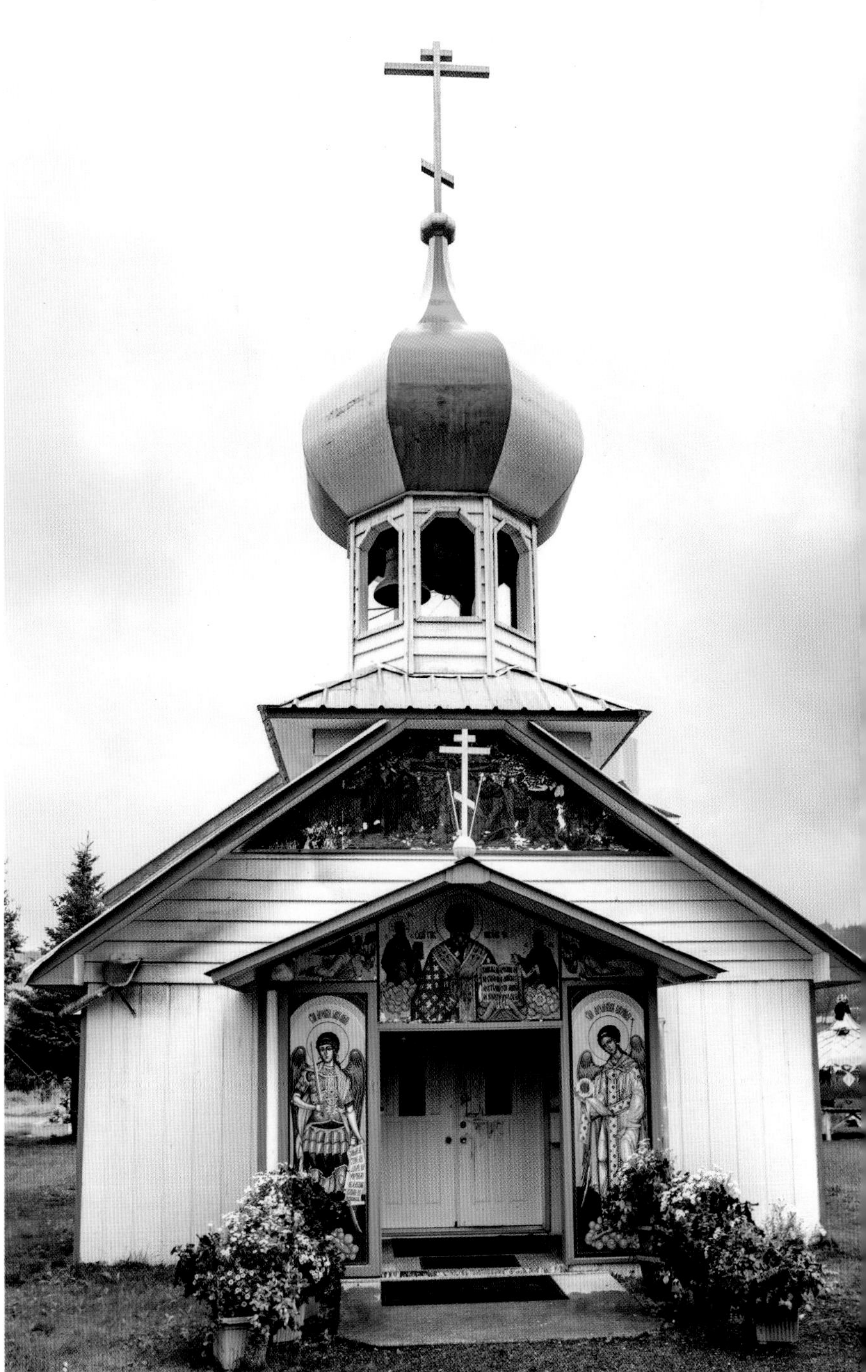

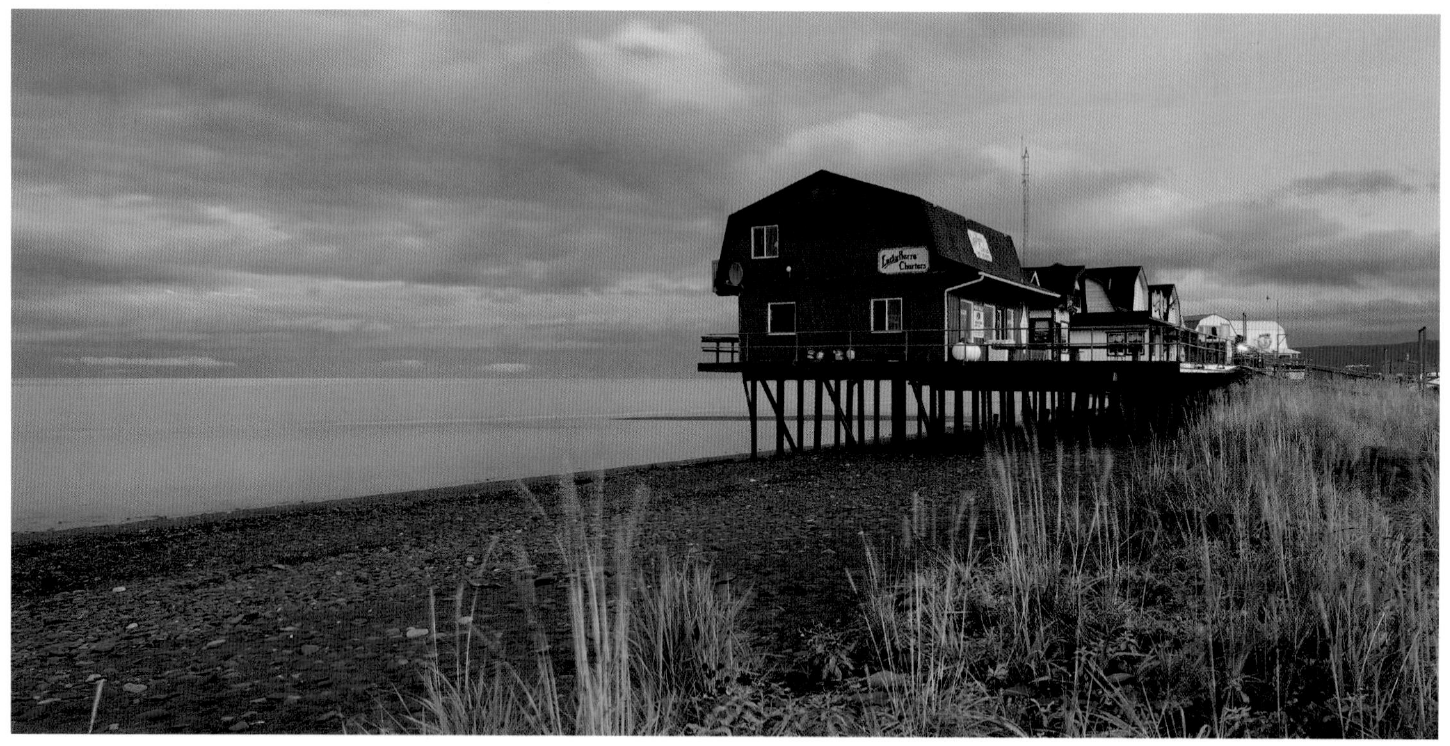

HOUSES, HOMER SPIT

Kenai Peninsula

Here at Homer a narrow sandbar stretches 7.2 km (4½ miles) out into Kachemak Bay, the result of wave-action over centuries, it is assumed. A natural breakwater, offering a sheltered area for sailing on its lee-side, it also serves as a sort of natural pier, of which these colourful shops and houses occupy the outer end. There is also a sizeable harbour, marina and ferry port, a couple of campsites, a heritage park and an artificial lagoon for fishing … a complete holiday experience in itself.

SUNRISE, HOMER SPIT

Kenai Peninsula

Bleached as bone against a dull grey beach, a gnarled and tortured driftwood stump sets off the ebullient colour of a clump of flowers. Given that the sands and gravels of Homer Spit are only here because they have slowly and surely been heaped up by the saltwater waves of the ocean, the miracle is that anything has grown at all. There is a heroism about this scene, but then Nature's determination to live and even flourish in the face of adversity is revealed in just about every sort of Alaskan environment.

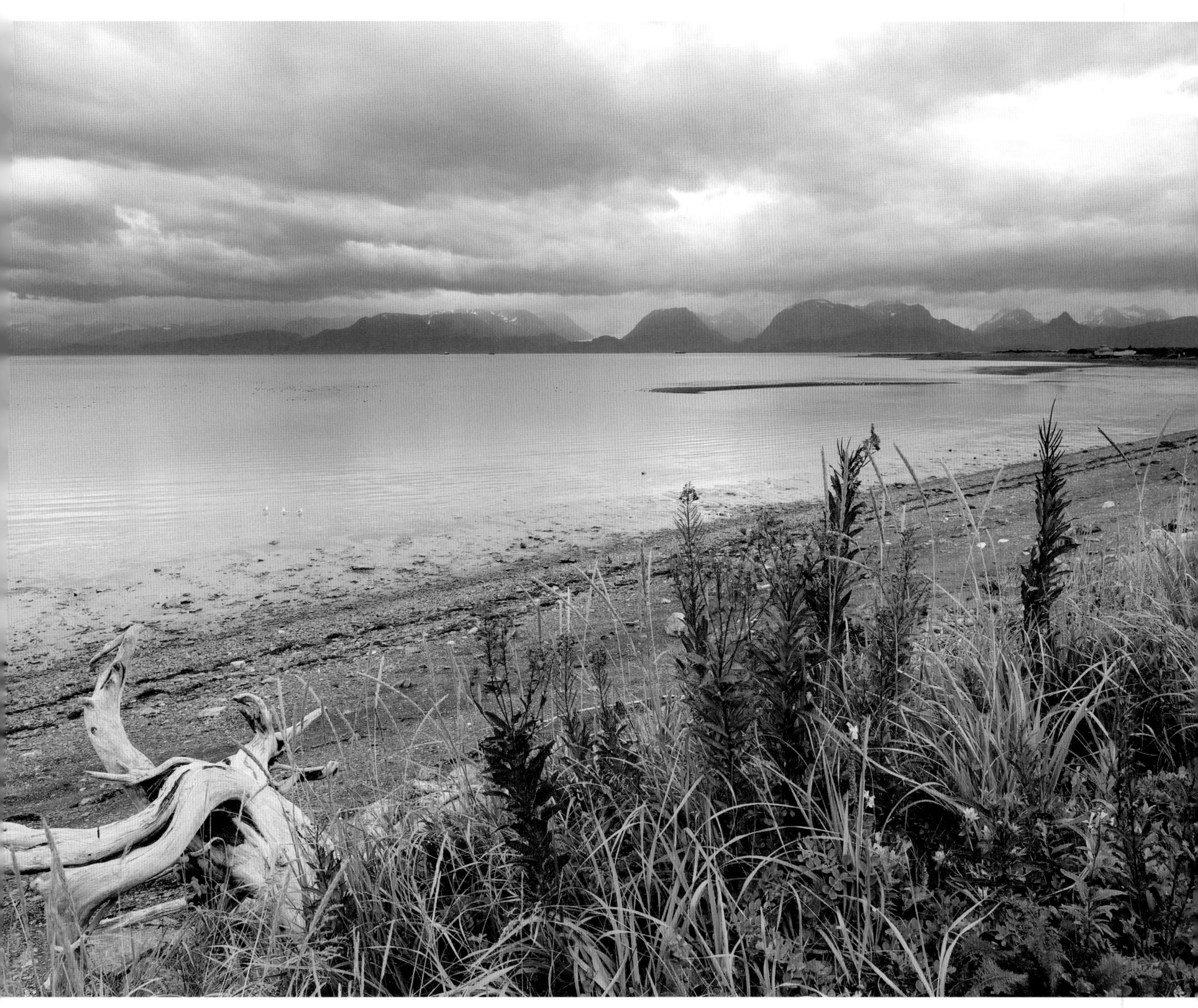

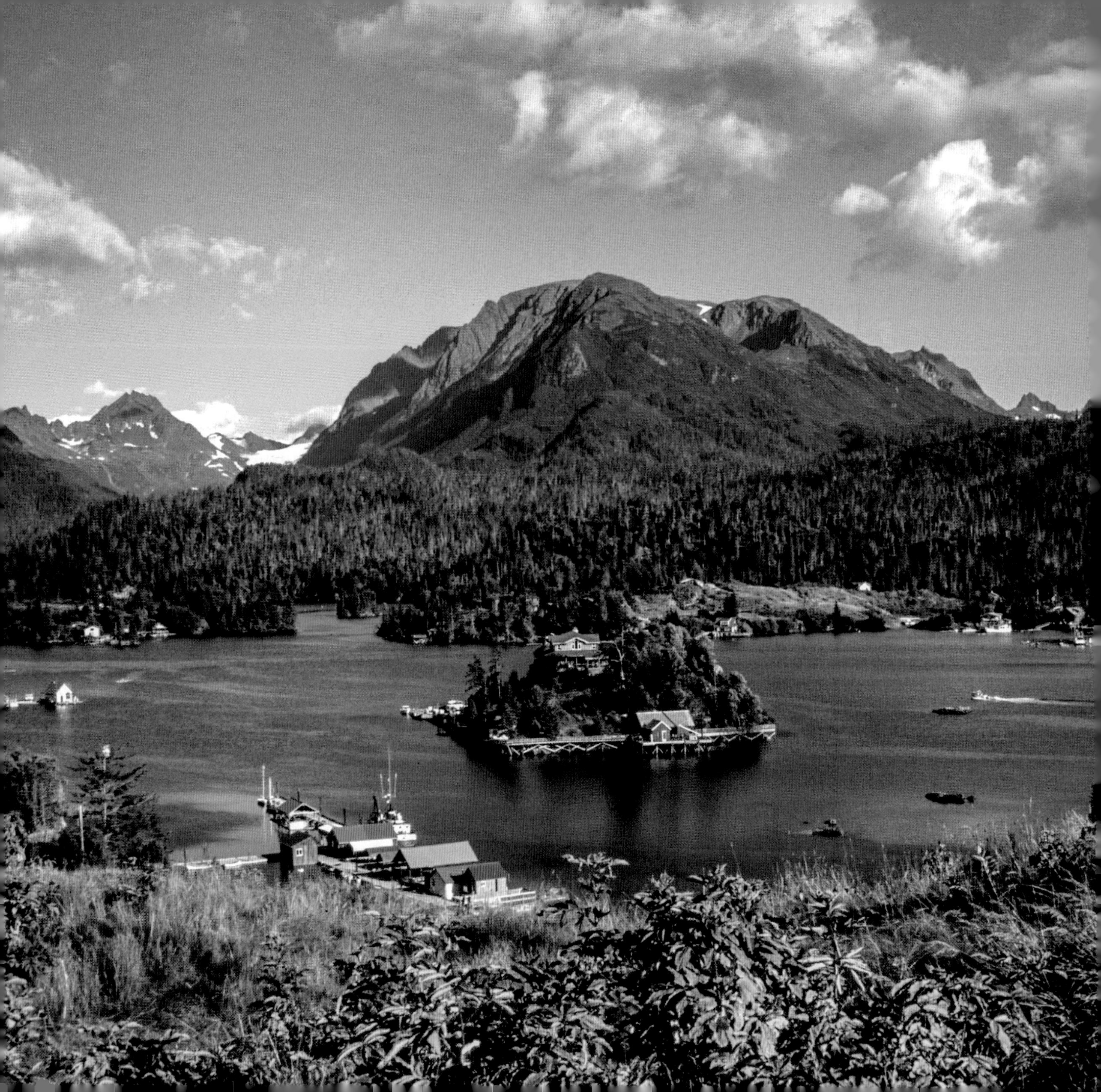

HALIBUT COVE, KACHEMAK BAY

Kenai Peninsula

Thickly forested at lower levels, rising sharply above to heights of 790 m (2,600 ft), the southern shore of Kachemak Bay is difficult to access. There are no roads, and even though there is a thriving community here at Halibut Cove, you can only realistically reach it by boat or seaplane. As discriminating tourists have been discovering, though, a visit is well worth the effort. Sheltered and secluded behind a wooded peninsula, this is its own little world – a bit arty, a bit bohemian, a bit exclusive.

KACHEMAK BAY STATE PARK, NEAR HOMER

Kenai Peninsula

Its own amenities apart, Halibut Cove (*see* opposite) is crucial in the access it provides to the Kachemak Bay State Park. Its 161,800 hectares (400,000 acres) are home to an extraordinary range of wildlife, with mammals from wolves and coyotes to moose, mountain goats and black bears. That is before you even get on to the marine species to be seen: everything from sea otters to whales, from porpoises to puffins. The pride of the park, however, is its own atmospheric ice field, high up in the mountains, the starting point for several glaciers.

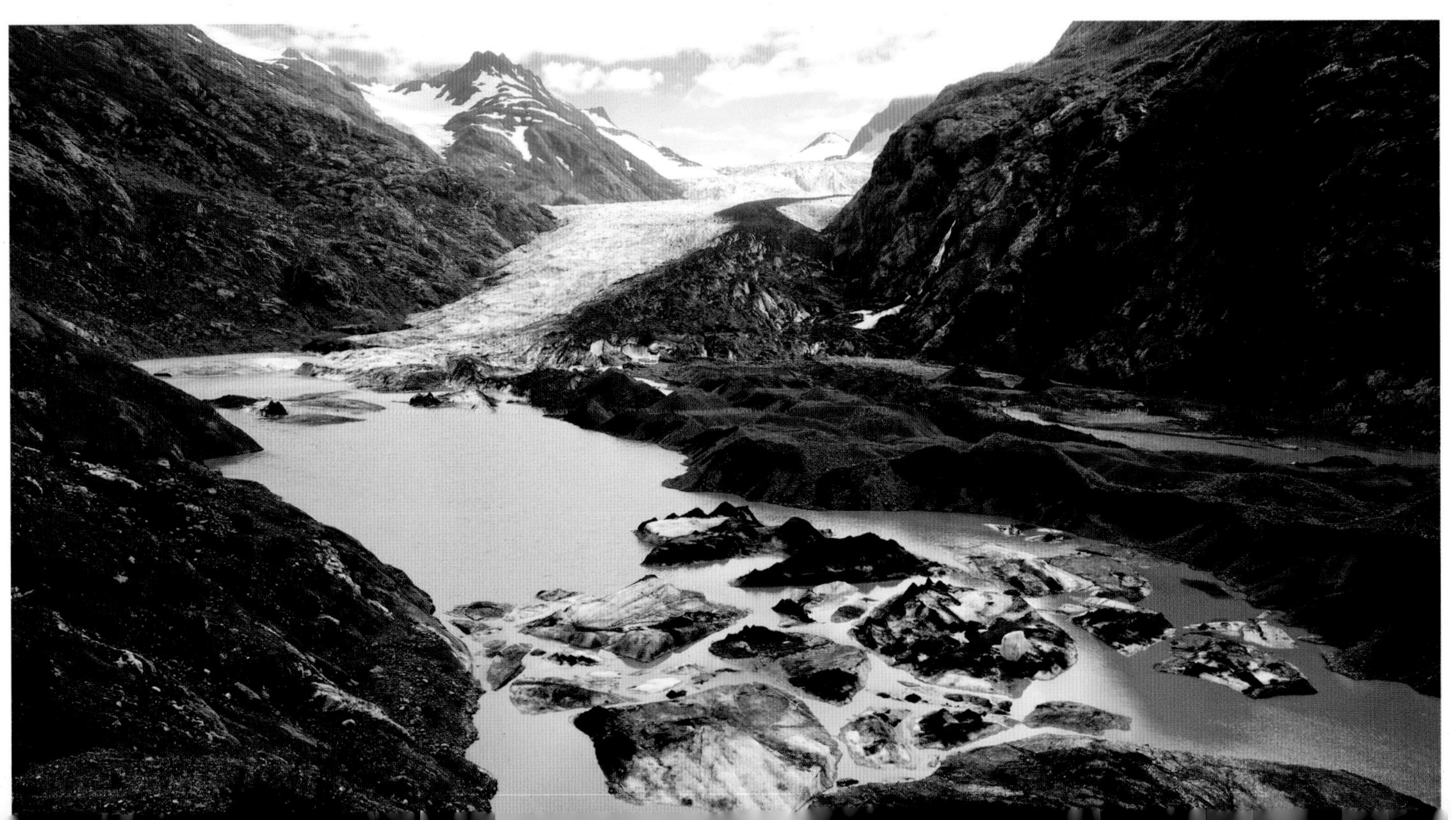

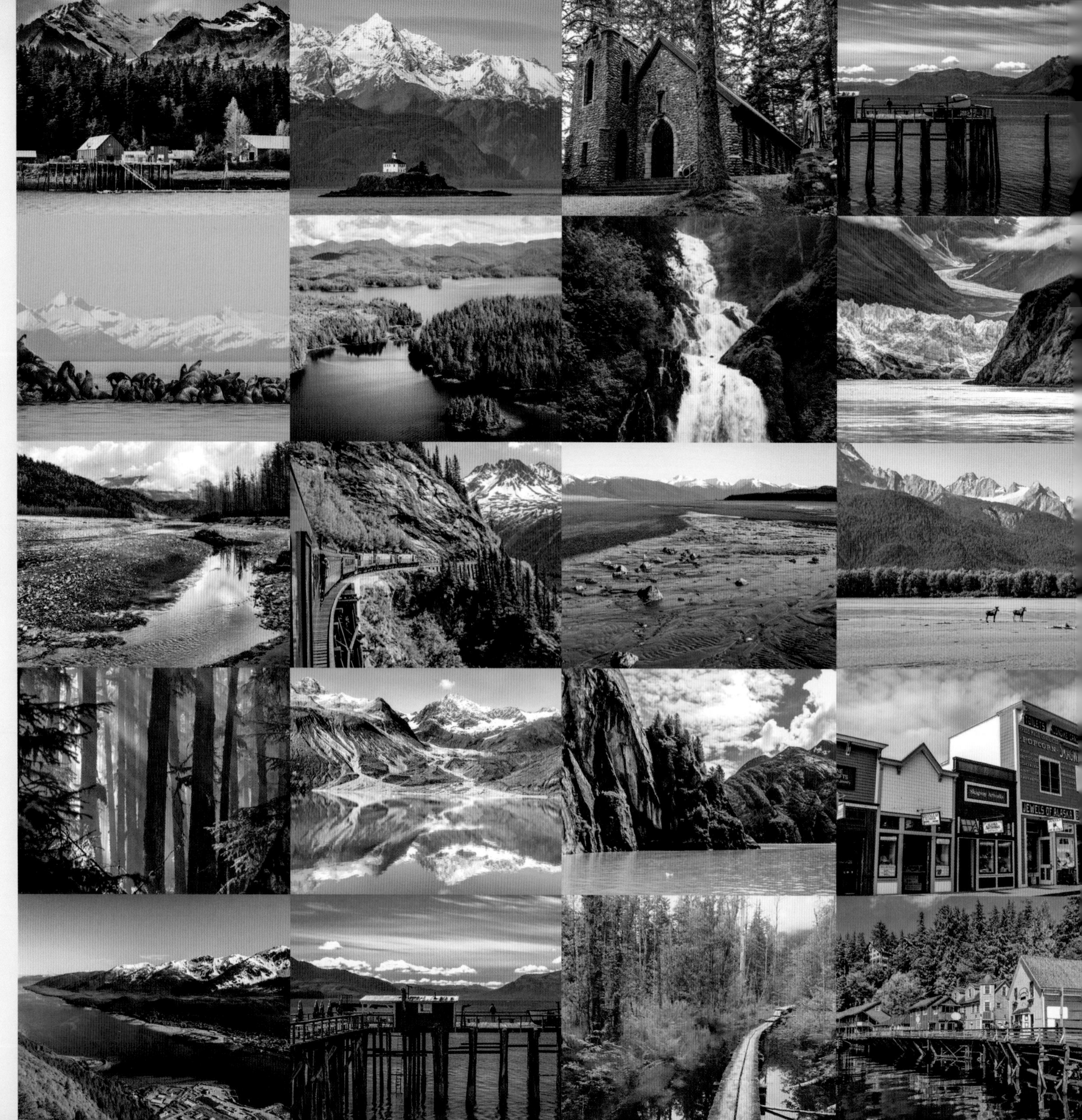
TOILETS
POPCORN
JEWELS OF ALASKA

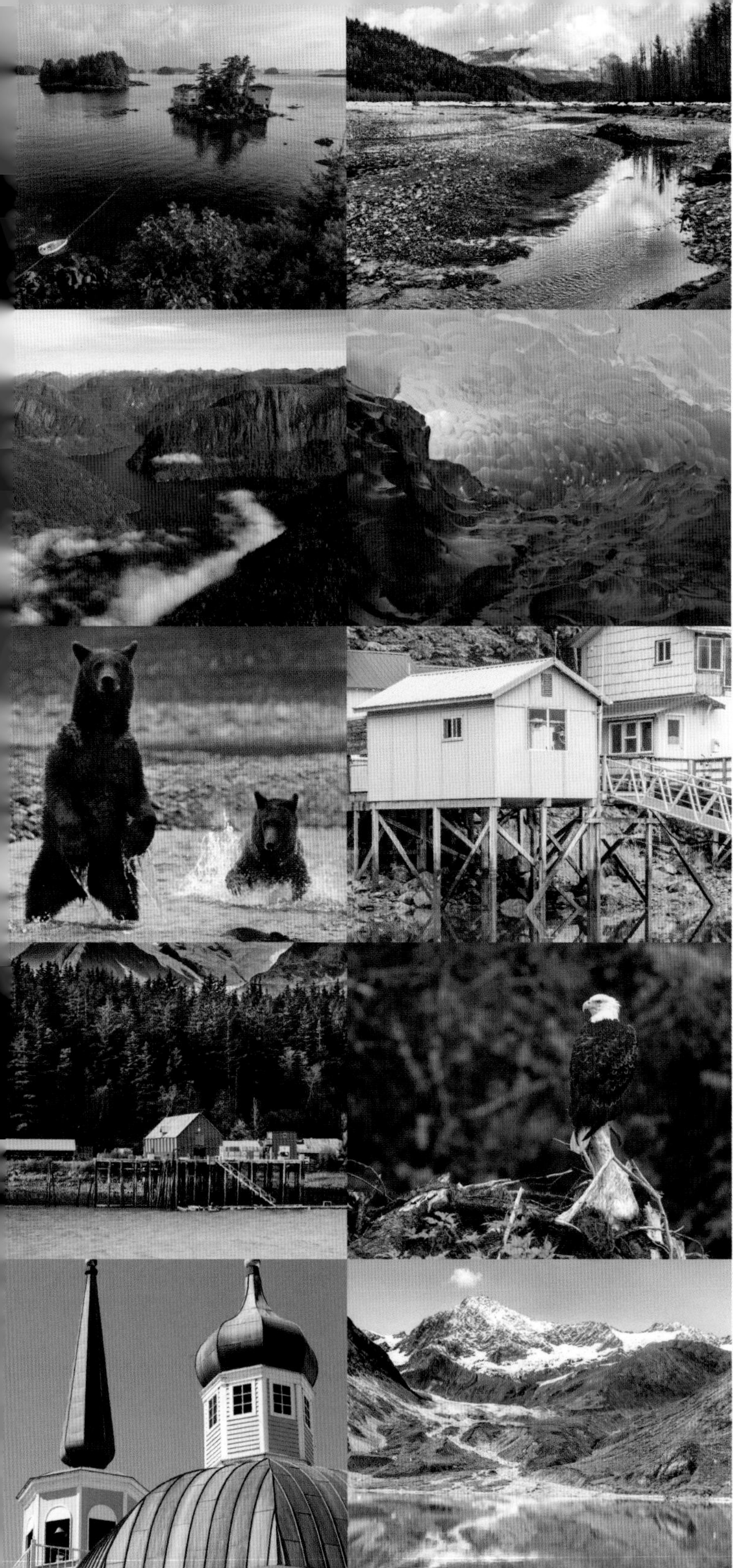

SOUTHEAST ALASKA

Alaska extends a long 'panhandle' from its far south eastern corner deep down into what we might have thought would be Canada; it is indeed bordered by British Columbia on its eastern side. The border's exact course had been disputed by the British and the Russians in colonial times, and the subject of ill-tempered exchanges between the United States, Canada and Britain after that.

But the principle of the 'panhandle' had not been at issue. Perverse as it may seem on the modern map, it had made perfect sense historically at a time when colonial interest was concentrated around the country's coasts. Russian merchants had been content to come to Alaska's estuaries to trade for furs and other items. The Natives could come down to the ocean and find them. Even further north, serious exploration of the interior was to come later, after the great gold finds. This coastal emphasis was only underlined by the existence here of the Inside Passage – a sea route stretching all the way up from Puget Sound, on the Canadian–US border, complicated but sheltered from the storms by innumerable islands. Long before the building of the Alaska Highway, its offshore equivalent already existed, making the Southeast still more crucial to Alaskan commerce and Alaskan life.

HUBBARD GLACIER, YAKUTAT BAY

Northern Region

The icebergs presently 'calving' – breaking away from the glacier's end and floating off – into Yakutat Bay consist of ice that formed before any of the disputes about the Alaskan Border had begun. It is estimated to take 400 years for any one crystal of ice to make the 122-km (76-mile) journey down from the Hubbard Glacier's start, 3,400 m (11,000 ft) up in the mountains. No respecter of boundaries in any case, the glacier's originating ice field extends into Canada's Yukon Territory to the north and east and into the St. Elias Mountains in the west.

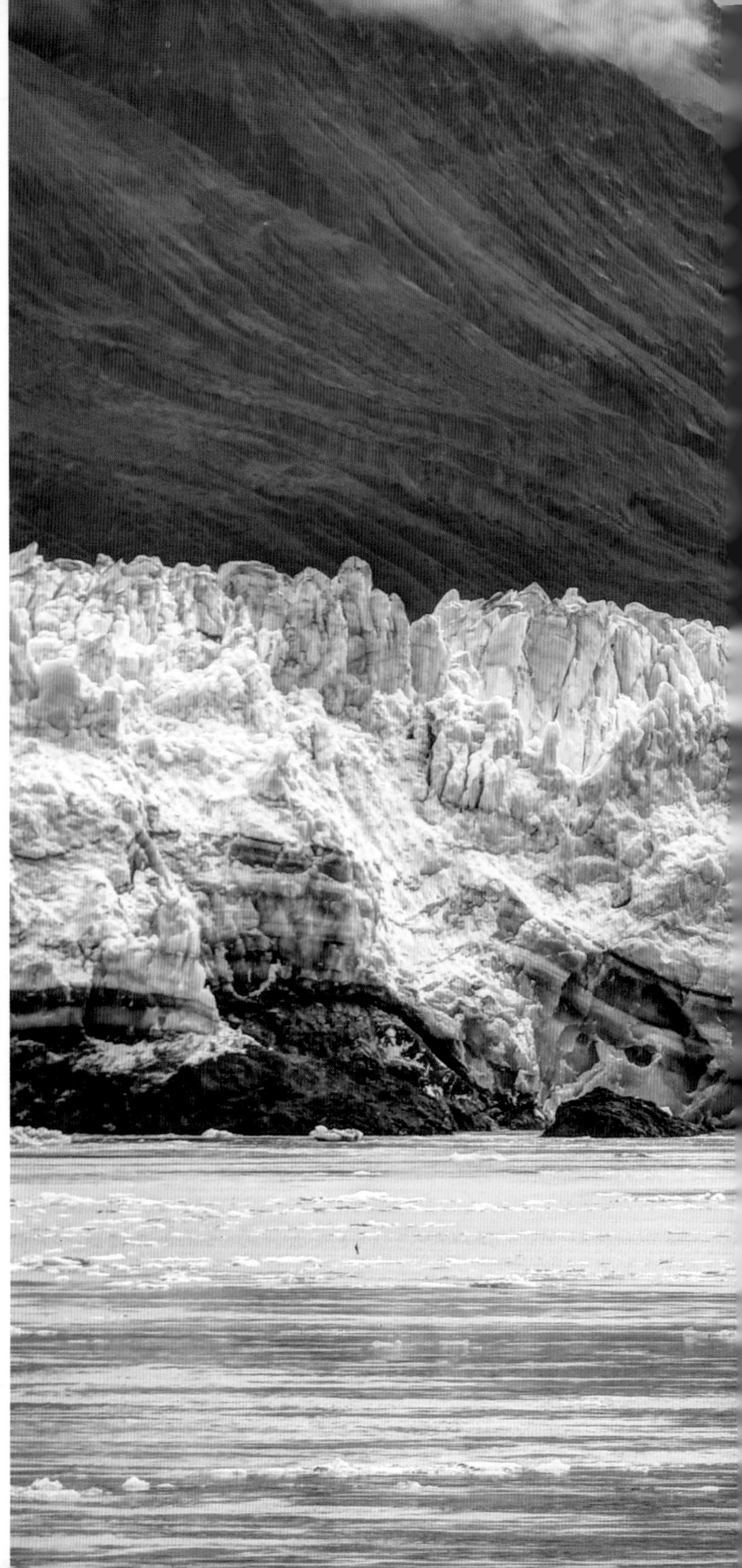

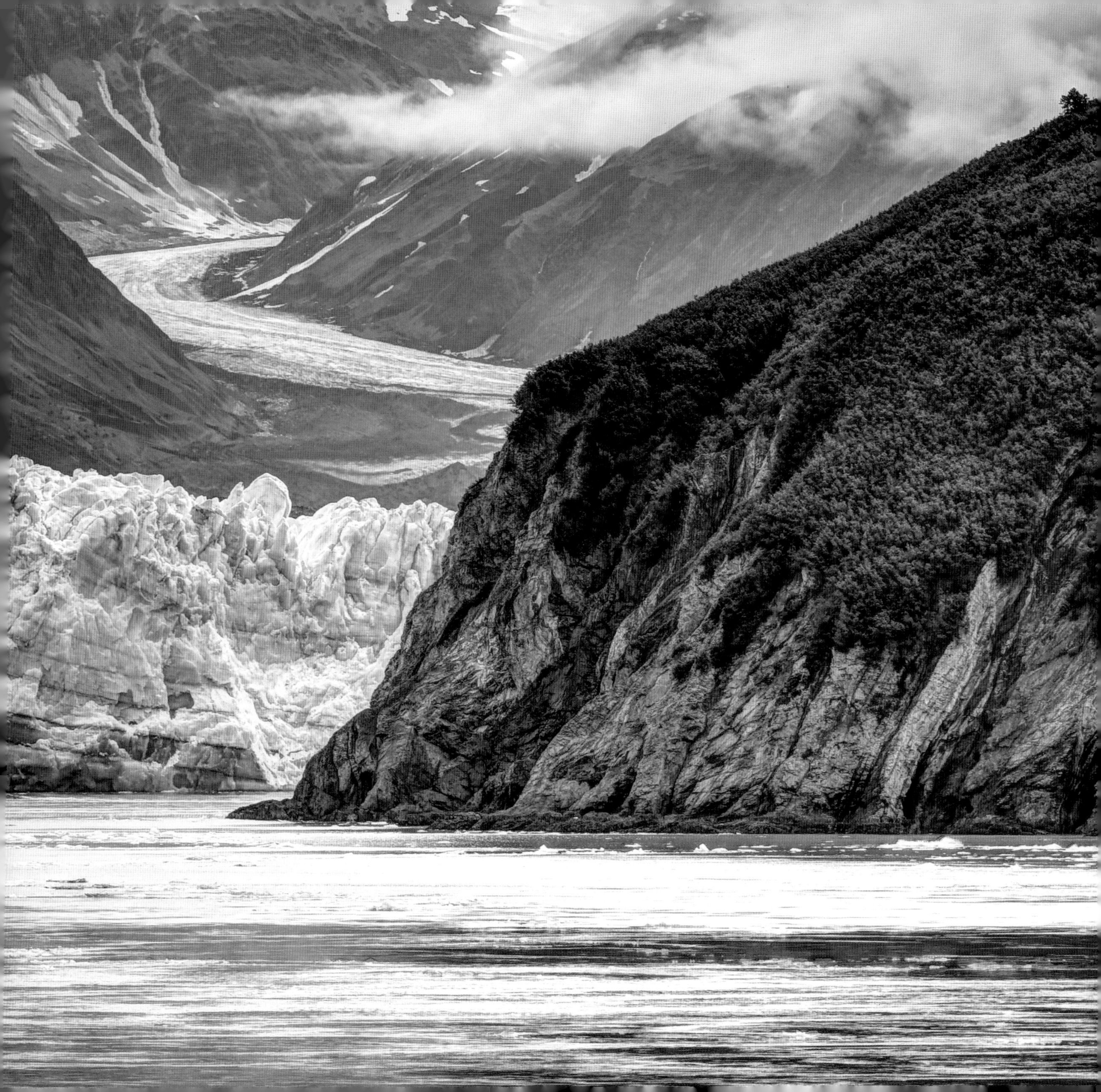

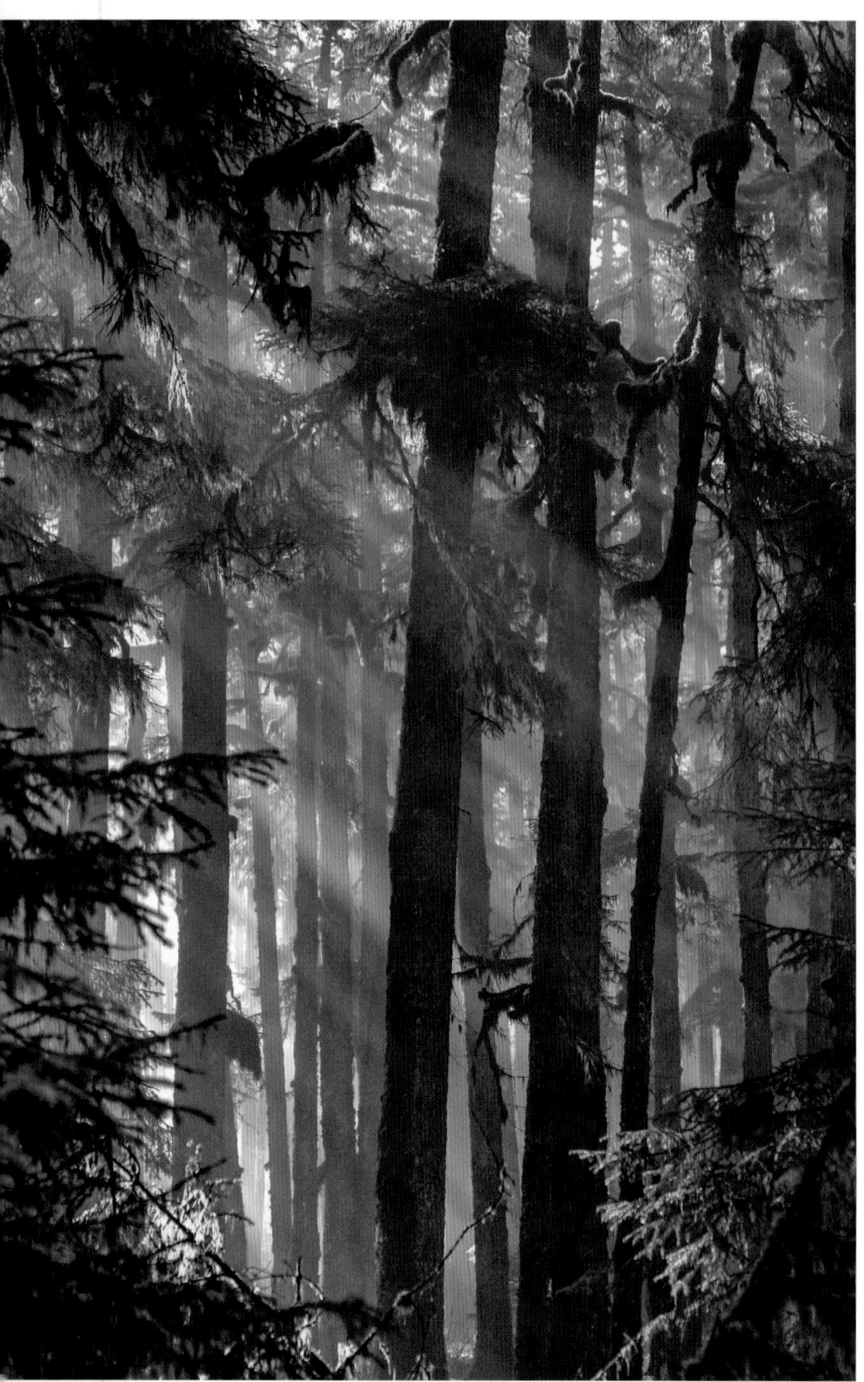

TONGASS NATIONAL FOREST

Northern Region

The United States' largest National Forest extends over 6,475,000 hectares (16.7 million acres), including hundreds of little offshore islands belonging to the enormous Alexander Archipelago. It is not Tongass' size that matters, though: it is the all but mystic sense of solitude and peace to be found in any square metre of its ancient woodland; the breathtaking beauty in every one of its majestic trees. Its security was hard won: Presidents Theodore Roosevelt and Coolidge (1872–1933) helped create the preserve, but the demands of developers and roadbuilders have been incessant and it has had to be defended in every generation since.

WHITE PASS & YUKON ROUTE RAILROAD

Northern Region

Bound for Skagway on Alaska's coast, this train weaves a vertiginous course through the mountains all the way from Whitehorse, capital of Canada's Yukon, in the north. This 172-km (107-mile) railway dates back to Gold-Rush days when it was built to offer easy access to the Klondike from the coast. Its narrow gauge of 914 mm (3 ft) allows it to negotiate twists and turns with which no ordinary train could cope – but not, of course, to link up with the wider railway network.

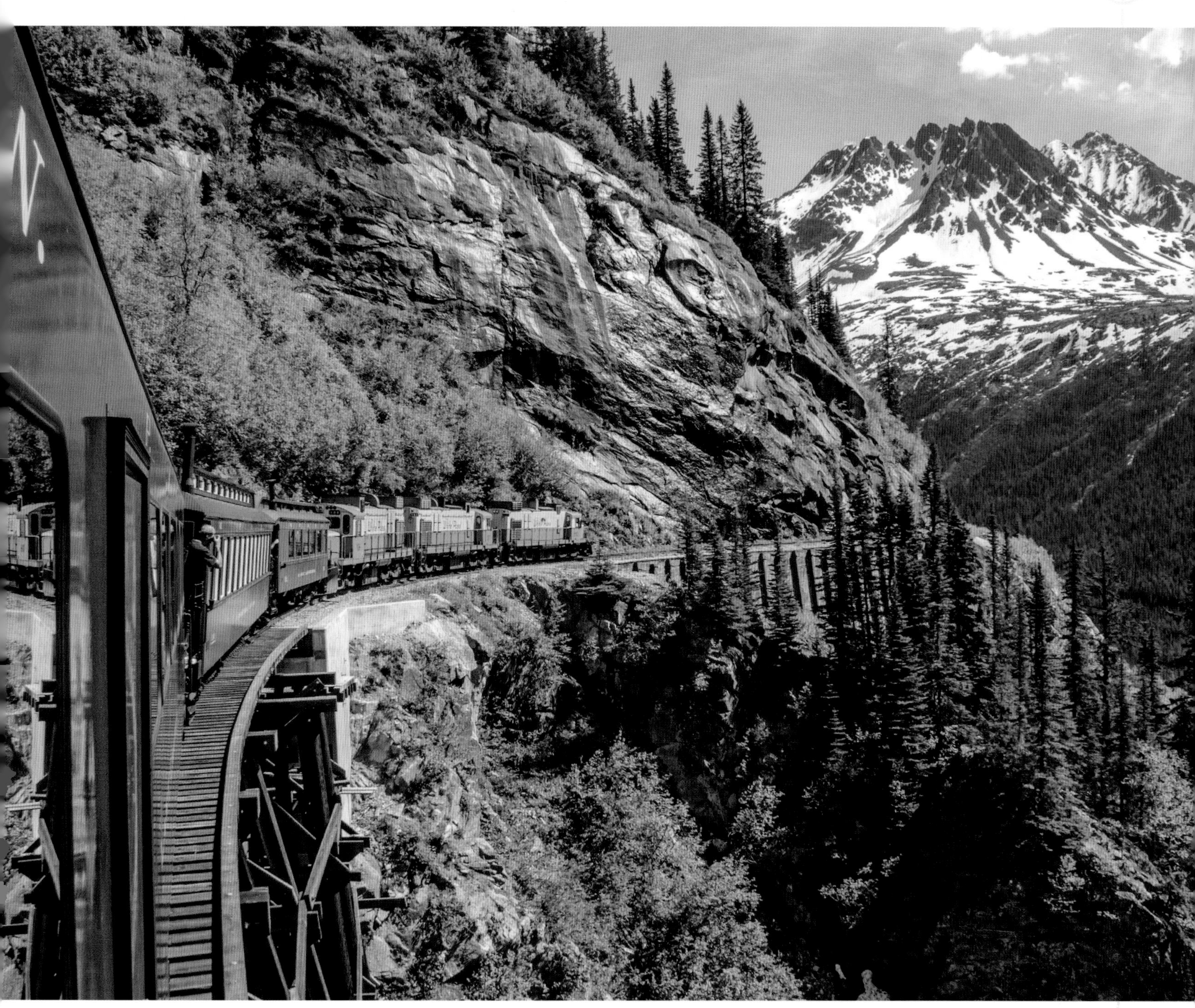

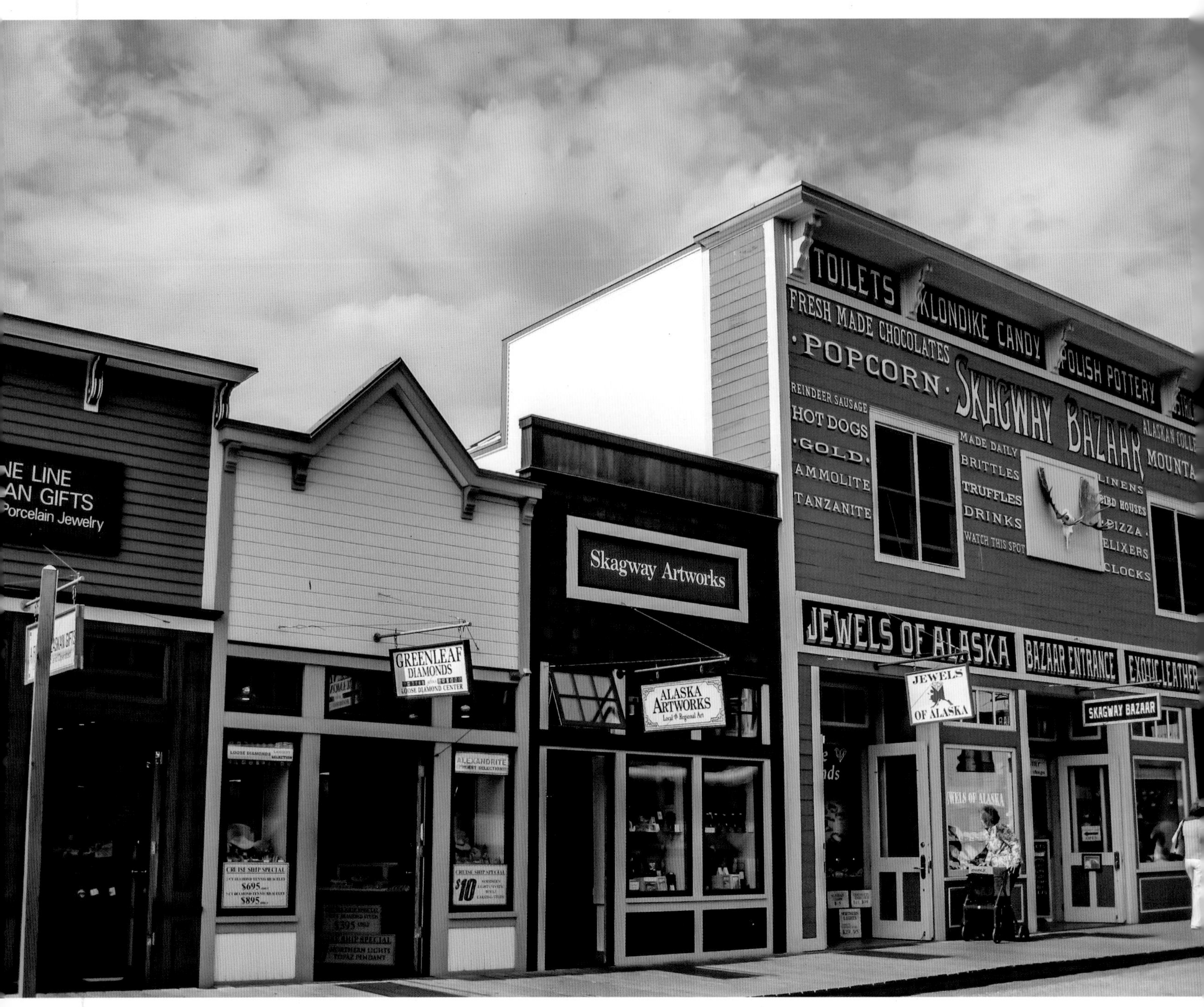
Porcelain Jewelry
GREENLEAF DIAMONDS
LOOSE DIAMOND CENTER
CRUISE SHIP SPECIAL
$695
$895
ALEXANDRITE
CRUISE SHIP SPECIAL
$10
NORTHERN LIGHTS TOPAZ PENDANT
Skagway Artworks
ALASKA ARTWORKS
Local & Regional Art
TOILETS
KLONDIKE CANDY
POLISH POTTERY
FRESH MADE CHOCOLATES
·POPCORN·
SKAGWAY BAZAAR
REINDEER SAUSAGE
HOT DOGS
·GOLD·
AMMOLITE
TANZANITE
MADE DAILY
BRITTLES
TRUFFLES
DRINKS
WATCH THIS SPOT
LINENS
BIRD HOUSES
·PIZZA·
ELIXERS
CLOCKS
JEWELS OF ALASKA
BAZAAR ENTRANCE
EXOTIC LEATHER
JEWELS OF ALASKA
SKAGWAY BAZAAR
JEWELS OF ALASKA

BROADWAY, SKAGWAY

Northern Region

Skagway was originally a Tlingit settlement. As a modern seaport, however, it came into its own in the 1890s. That was when a new generation of young men for whom the lessons of the California Gold Rush (1848–55) had not had a chance to register, headed north en masse by steamer. Many of the buildings from that fabled era have survived, under the protection of what is called the 'Klondike National Historical Park'. Klondike itself is, of course, quite some distance away and in another country, but the 'Park' has authority over much of downtown Skagway.

CHILKOOT TRAIL, KLONDIKE NATIONAL PARK

Northern Region

An old and moss-grown wooden walkway takes hikers across a forest glade flooded by a beaver dam along this historic gold prospector's trail. Connecting the coastal town of Dyea, a few kilometres north of Skagway, with Bennett, British Columbia, it had been in use by Native peoples for generations before the Gold Rush. From the 1890s, though, it became the main route for Americans and Europeans trying to get to the goldfields until the opening of the White Pass & Yukon Rote Railroad (*see* page 131) in 1900.

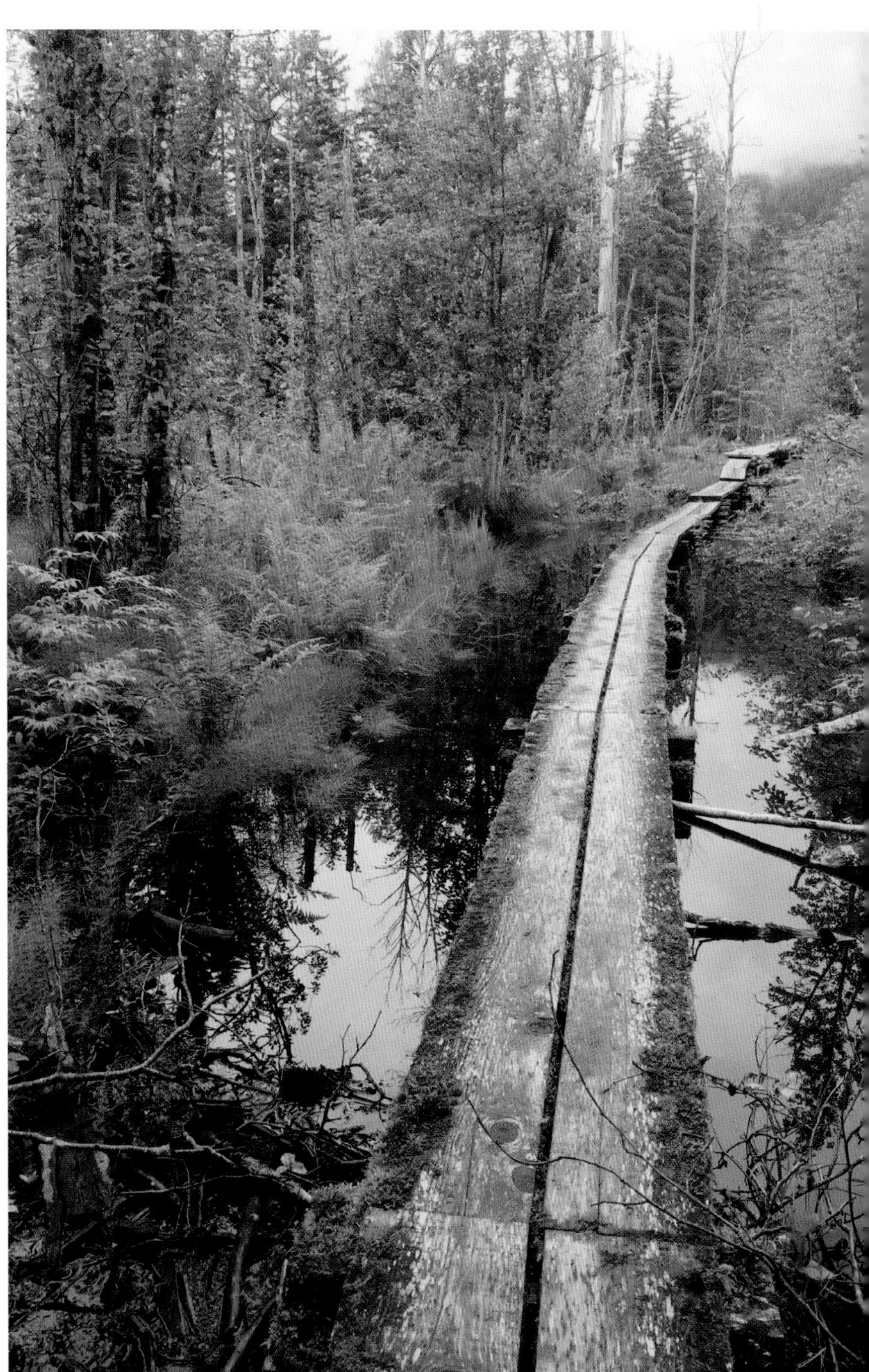

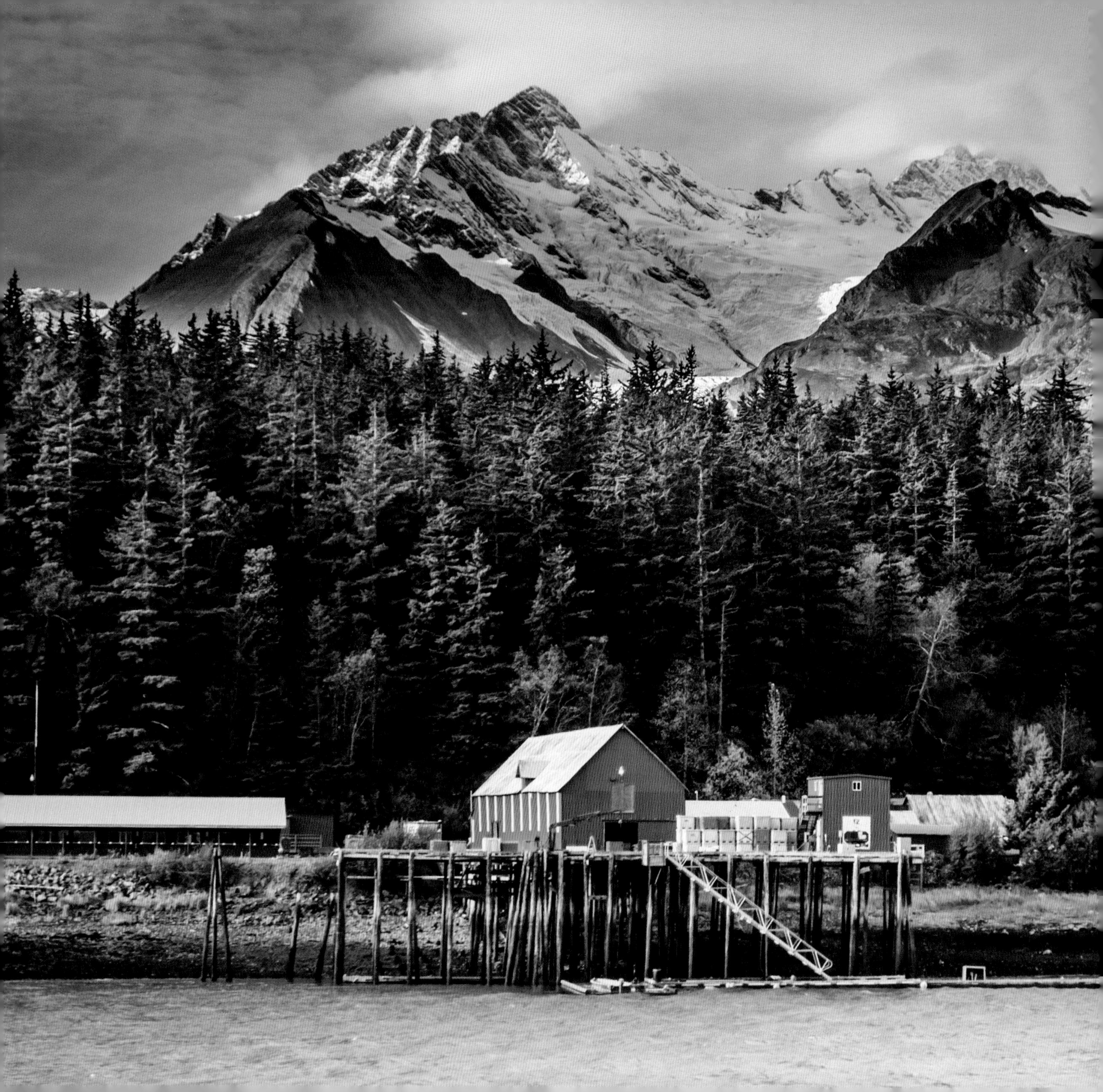

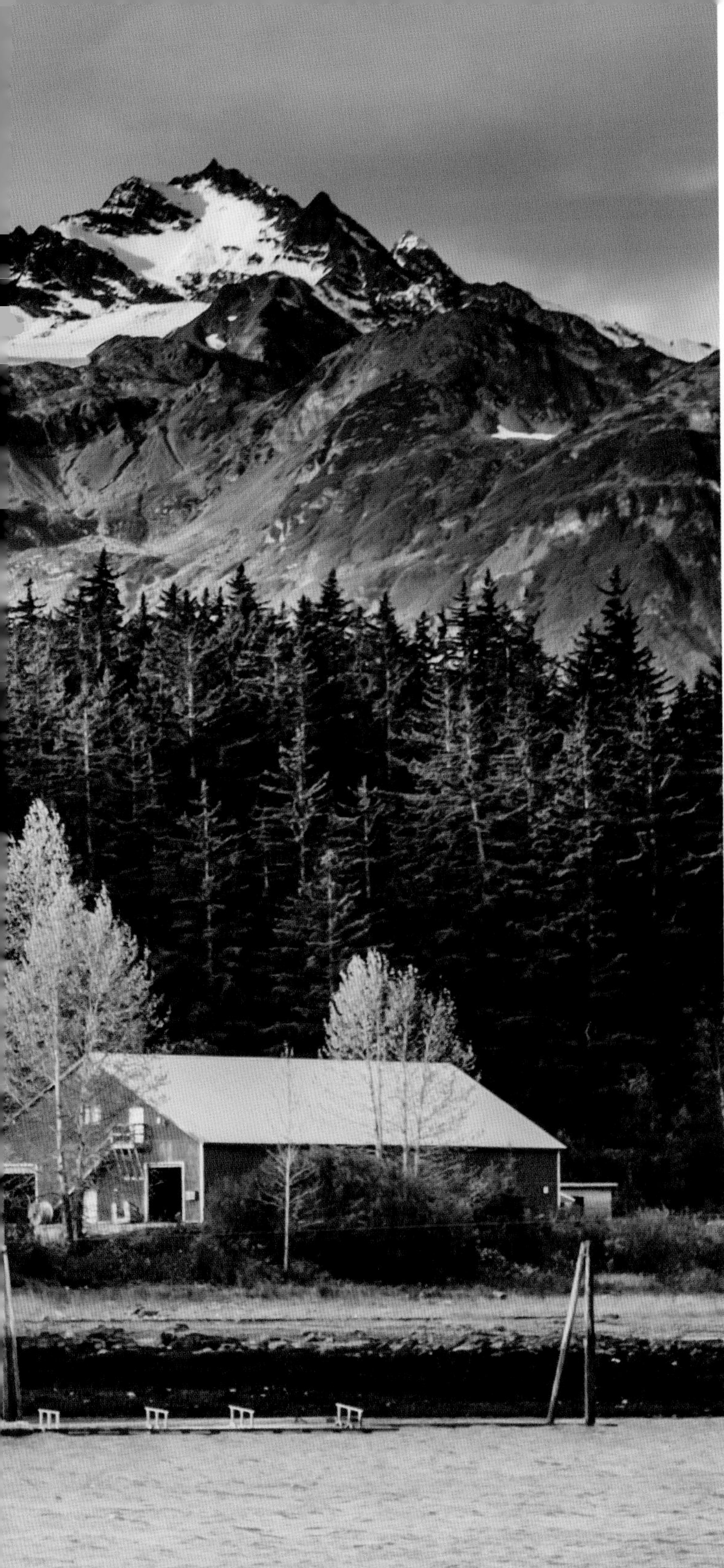

CANNERY, HAINES

Northern Region

Haines Packing Company has had a cannery at Leitnikof Cove, near Haines, since 1917, handling everything from halibut to crab and shrimp. But their most prestigious product has always been salmon, like all their other fish and seafood, locally caught. Once, this was one of a dozen canneries in the Chilkat Valley. (There were, of course, hundreds more down the Pacific coasts of Alaska, Canada and the United States.) Nowadays it is a rarity: at once a historical monument and a working industrial plant, it has become a popular visitor attraction.

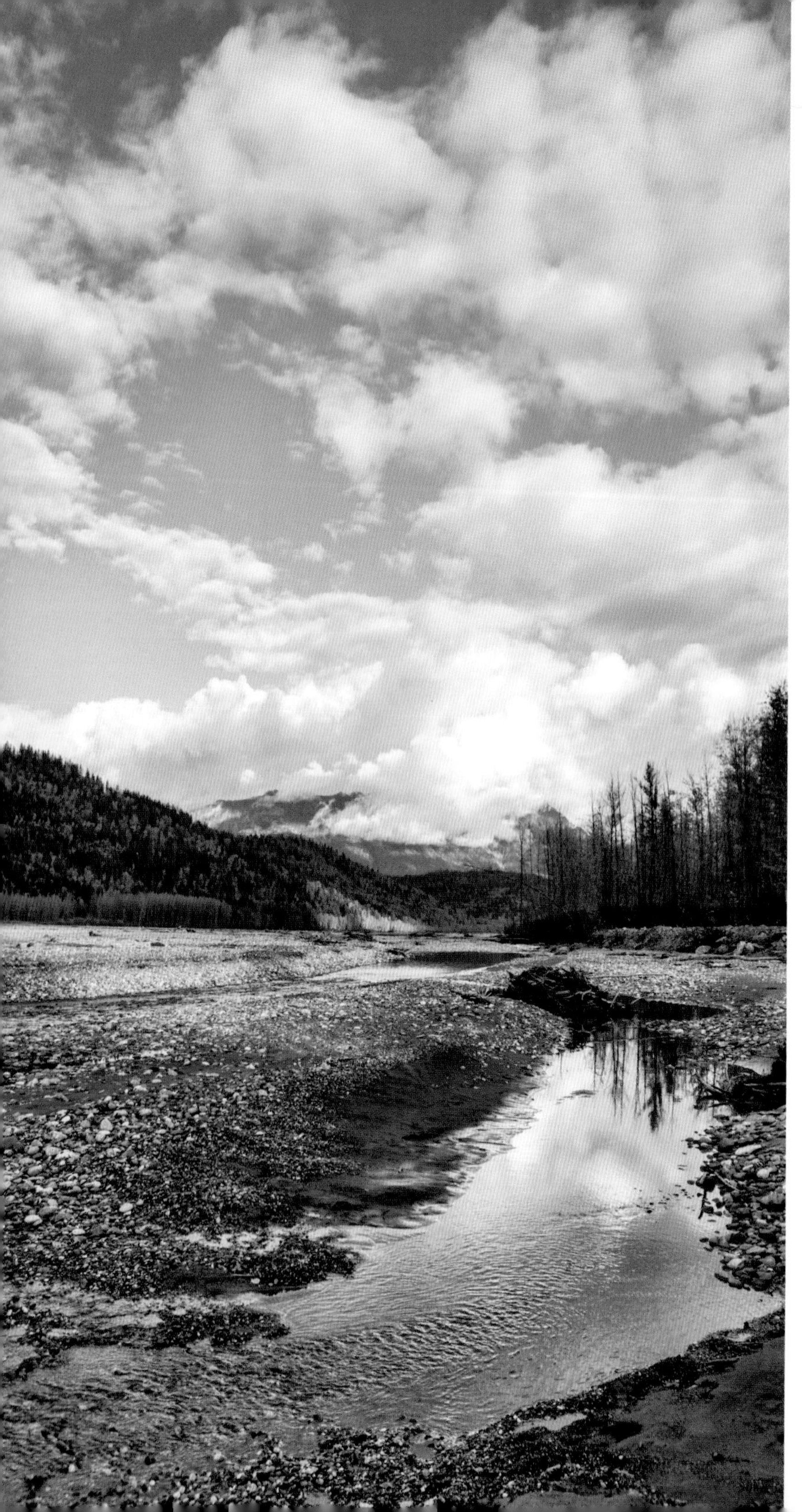

CHILKAT RIVER, HAINES

Northern Region

Though it begins life as a glacier in Alaska's eastern mountains, the Chilkat actually becomes a river in British Columbia, through which it runs for much of its 19 km (12 mile) length, before cutting across the panhandle as, together with the Taiya and Chilkoot Rivers, it approaches the sea through the Lynn Canal (despite its name, a natural inlet of the ocean – a fjord – *see* page 118). The Chilkat's name, in Tlingit, means 'salmon store' – appropriate enough, given that its fishery has indeed always been among the region's most important.

MOOSE, CHILKAT RIVER, HAINES

Northern Region

There is more to the Chilkat than salmon: bald eagles and ospreys soar across its skies, as do many other raptors. Smaller birds abound: there are half a dozen different woodpeckers alone, along with dozens of waterfowl species and every sort of finch and warbler. The wooded slopes along its valley are home to a wonderful range of wildlife, including wolverines, mountain goats, wolves, black and brown bears and many other mammals. The Chilkat Valley has in recent years become a focus for conservation efforts, aimed at securing the future of this extraordinary natural heritage.

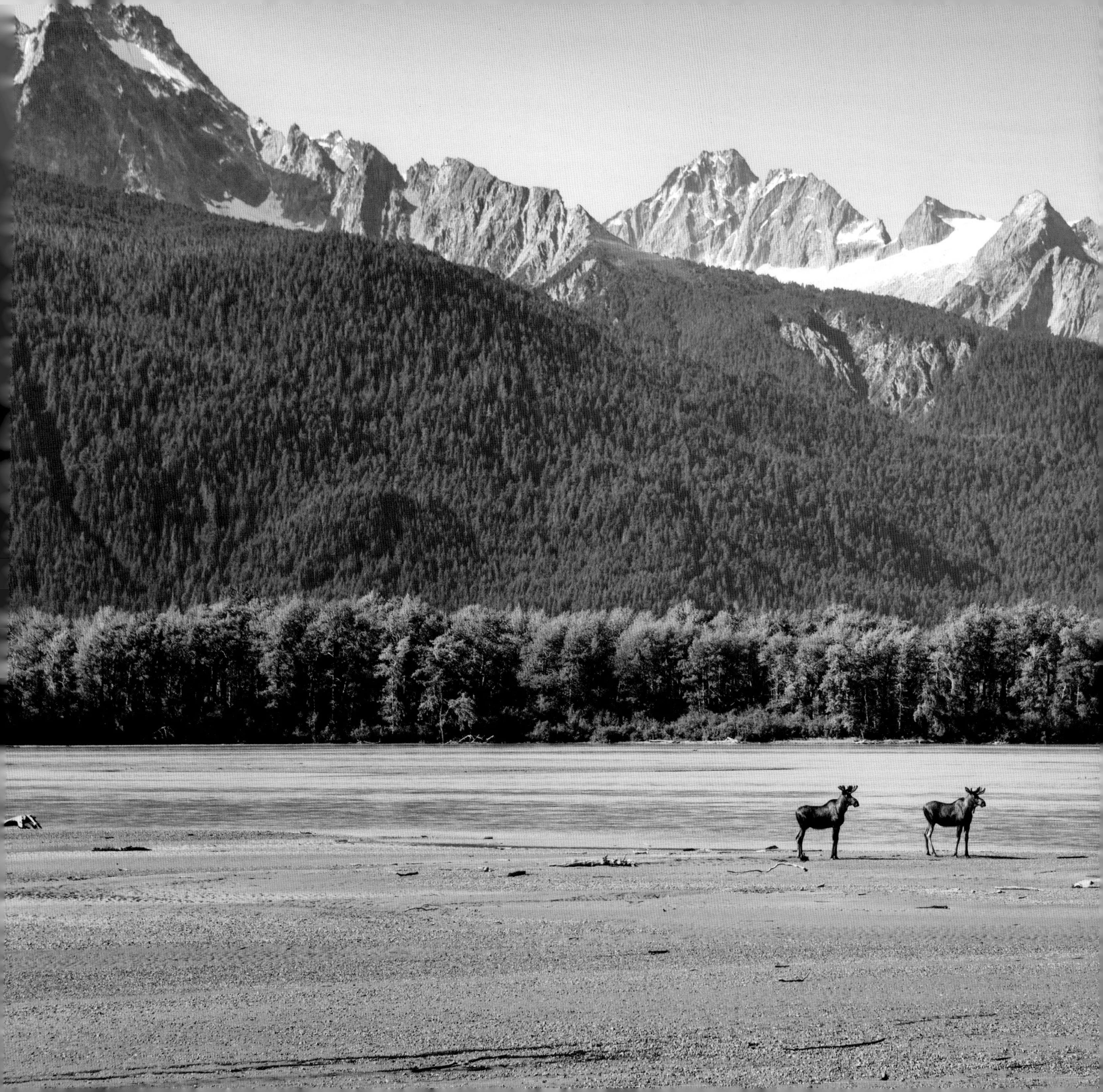

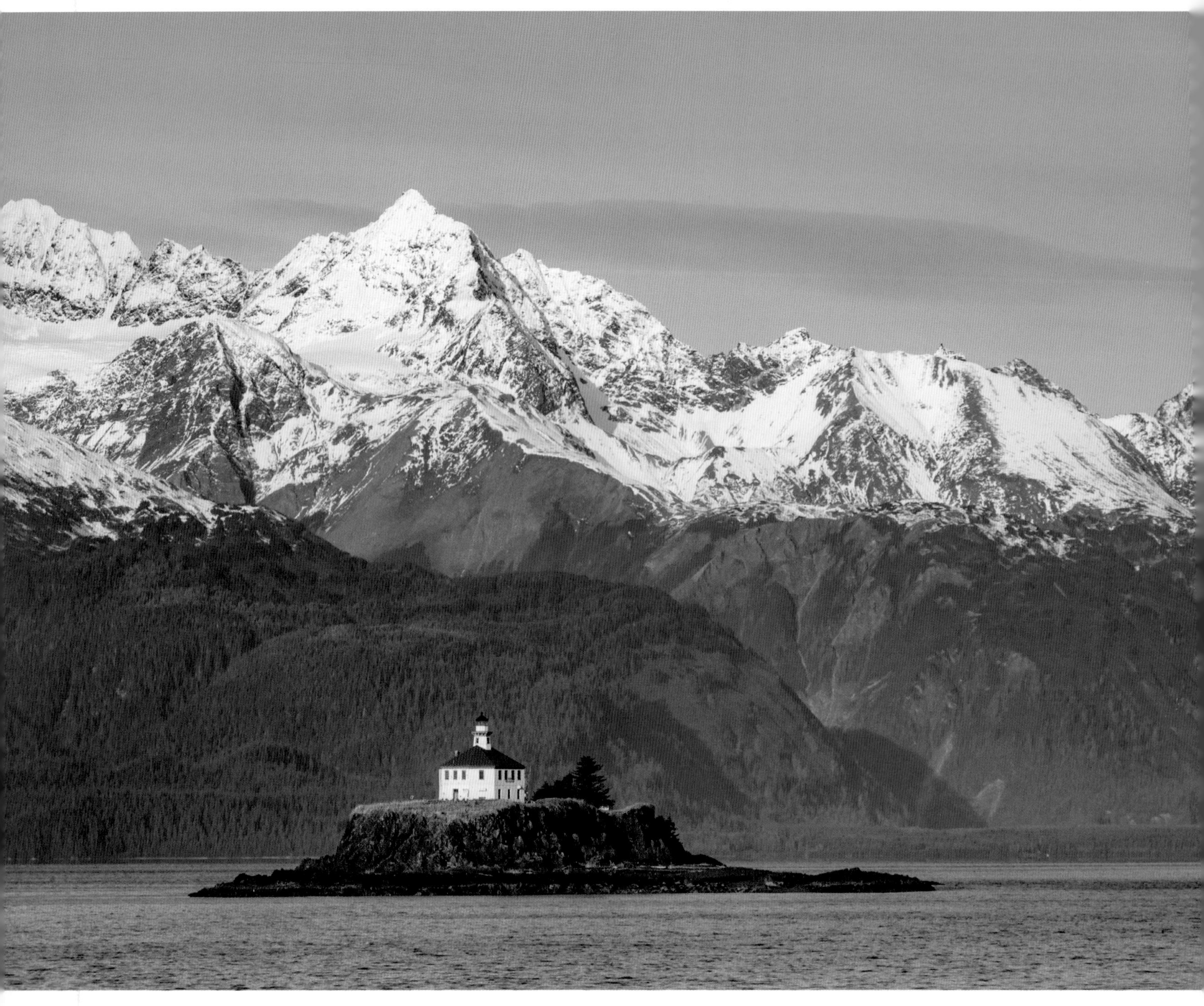

ELDRED ROCK LIGHTHOUSE, HAINES

Northern Region

Some 140 km (90 miles) long, with a depth of 610 m (2,000 ft), the Lynn Canal is deep enough to accommodate any sort of shipping, but it does have hazards – the odd sunken reef and the Eldred Rock. Several ships had been wrecked on this rocky islet when, in 1905–6, this handsome octagonal structure was installed by the United States Lighthouse Board. Though still in use, it was automated in 1973 and since then has been unmanned. It has officially been entered in the National Register of Historic Places.

ELFIN COVE, CHICAGOF ISLAND

Northern Region

This picturesque little fishing village has a year-round population of only around 20, but this is much augmented in the summer season. Though it is only reachable by boat or seaplane (*because* it is only reachable by boat or seaplane, perhaps), it has built a strong reputation as a resort. Fishing remains important, though for the most part it is guided sport-fishing now. Wildlife-watching is a big draw, too: people come to see the humpback whales disporting themselves offshore or the sea lions sunning themselves on nearby rocks.

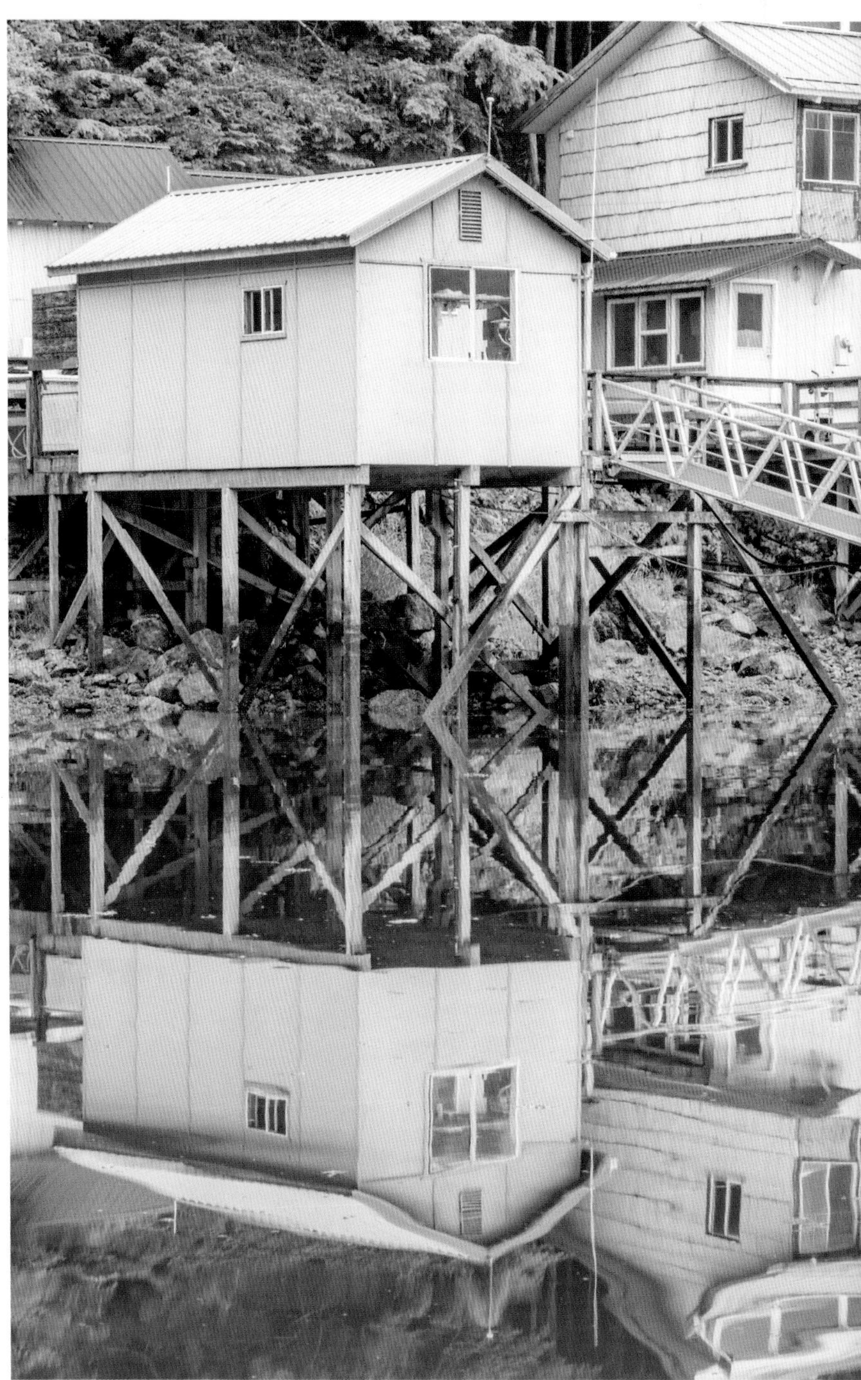

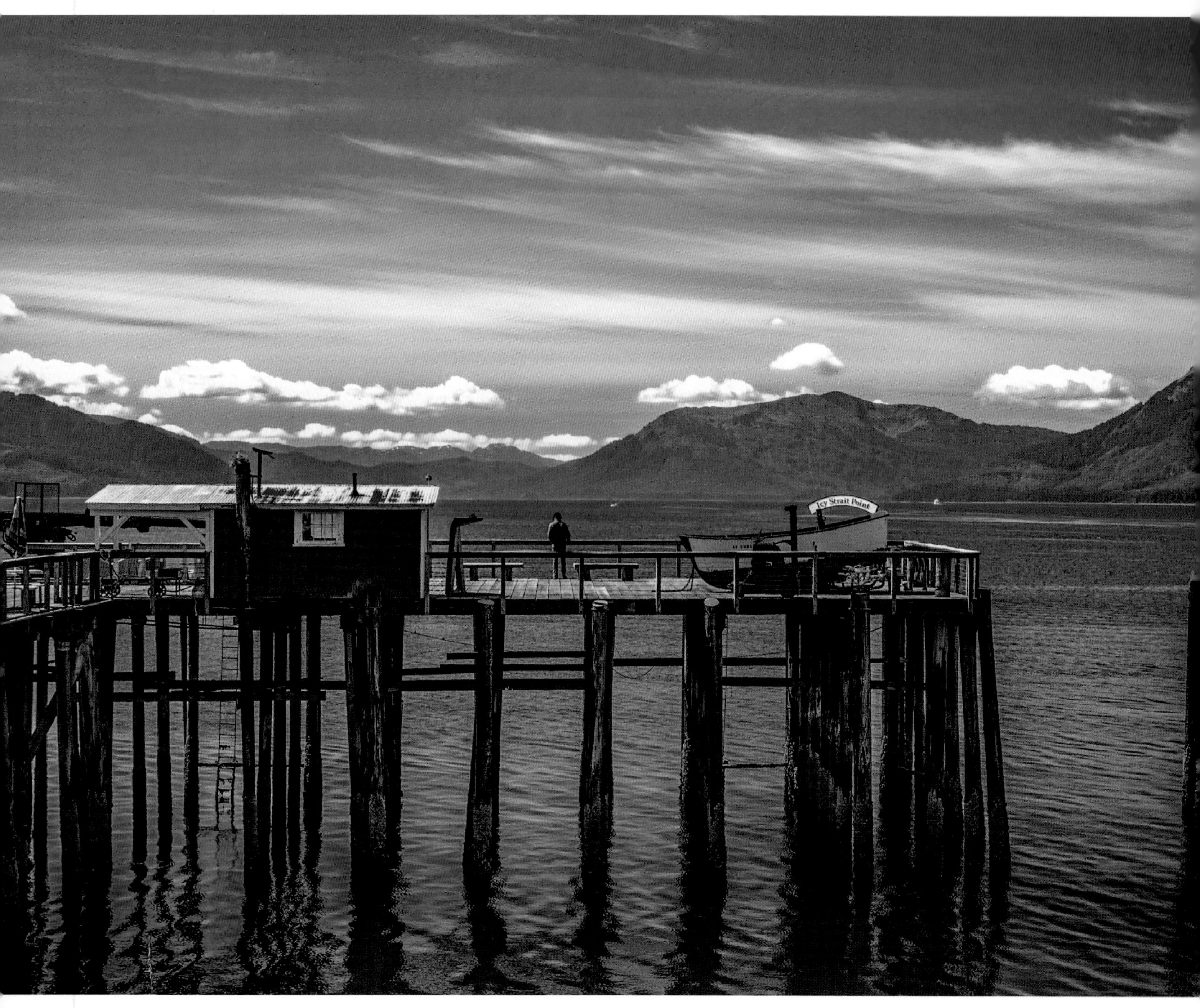
Icy Strait Point

ICY STRAIT POINT

Northern Region

A calling-point for cruise ships, Icy Strait Point is also a community project, owned and run by a group of over a thousand Native Alaskans from the region. It is much more than a docking-place in a beautiful location: visitors get to see how Tlingit locals live, making the short walk to their village, Hoonah, beside the strait; buying gifts in locally owned stores; watching the people working in their own cannery. The villagers organize whale watching and bear-spotting excursions, too.

PUMP HOUSE, TREADWELL MINE, DOUGLAS ISLAND

Northern Region

Over 2,000 people once worked here, at what in the 1880s was the biggest gold mine in the world. John Treadwell was one prospector who certainly made his pile. When he did find gold, he did not boast, but quietly set about buying up adjacent claims and lining up financial backing for the thoroughgoing industrialization of his mine. He introduced giant stamp machines, using them to crush the ore-bearing rocks: at its height, his mine had no fewer than 300 such machines running at once.

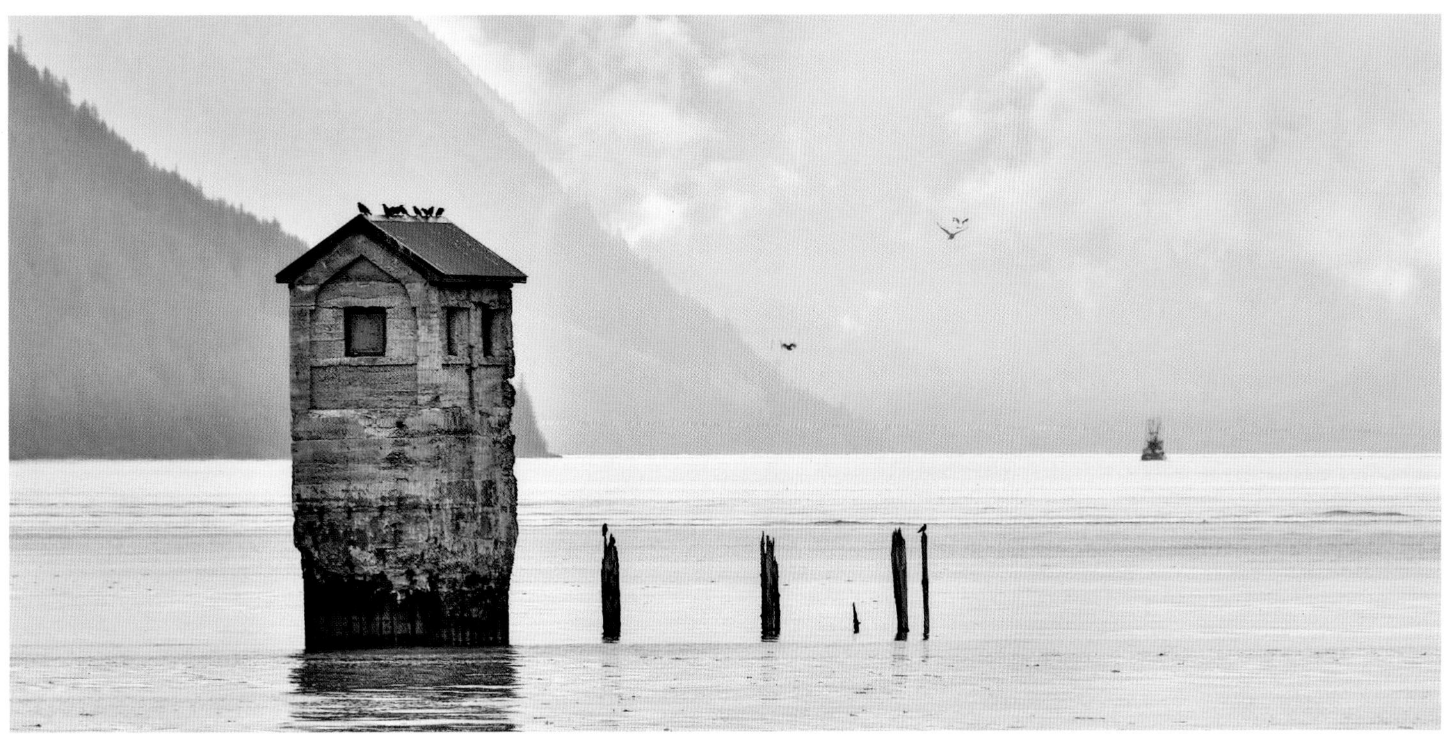

JUNEAU

Northern Region

Alaska's state capital is spectacularly situated. So rugged is its setting, indeed, that it cannot actually be reached by road, and must be approached by sea or air. Here, looking across the Gastineau Channel to the wooded eastern slopes of Douglas Island, we see the city framed by the rugged massif of Mount Juneau, 1090 m (3,570 ft). Beyond its summit the Juneau Icefield stretches away to the north-east. With a population of some 32,000, Juneau just edges out Fairbanks (*see* page 50) as Alaska's second most populous city, though both trail badly behind Anchorage (290,000).

SHRINE OF ST. THÉRÈSE, JUNEAU

Northern Region

It is hard now to recall the veneration Catholics felt for St. Thérèse of Lisieux (1873–97), the 'Little Flower', a generation or two ago. Not just veneration, indeed, but love. In her humility, in the simplicity of her 'little way of spiritual childhood' and her quiet acceptance of an agonizing illness (she died at 24), she represented a kind of piety for which all could strive. She had not even been canonized yet when, in 1919, the local bishop made her Alaska's patron saint. Volunteers built this shrine, bringing stones by hand from the nearby beach.

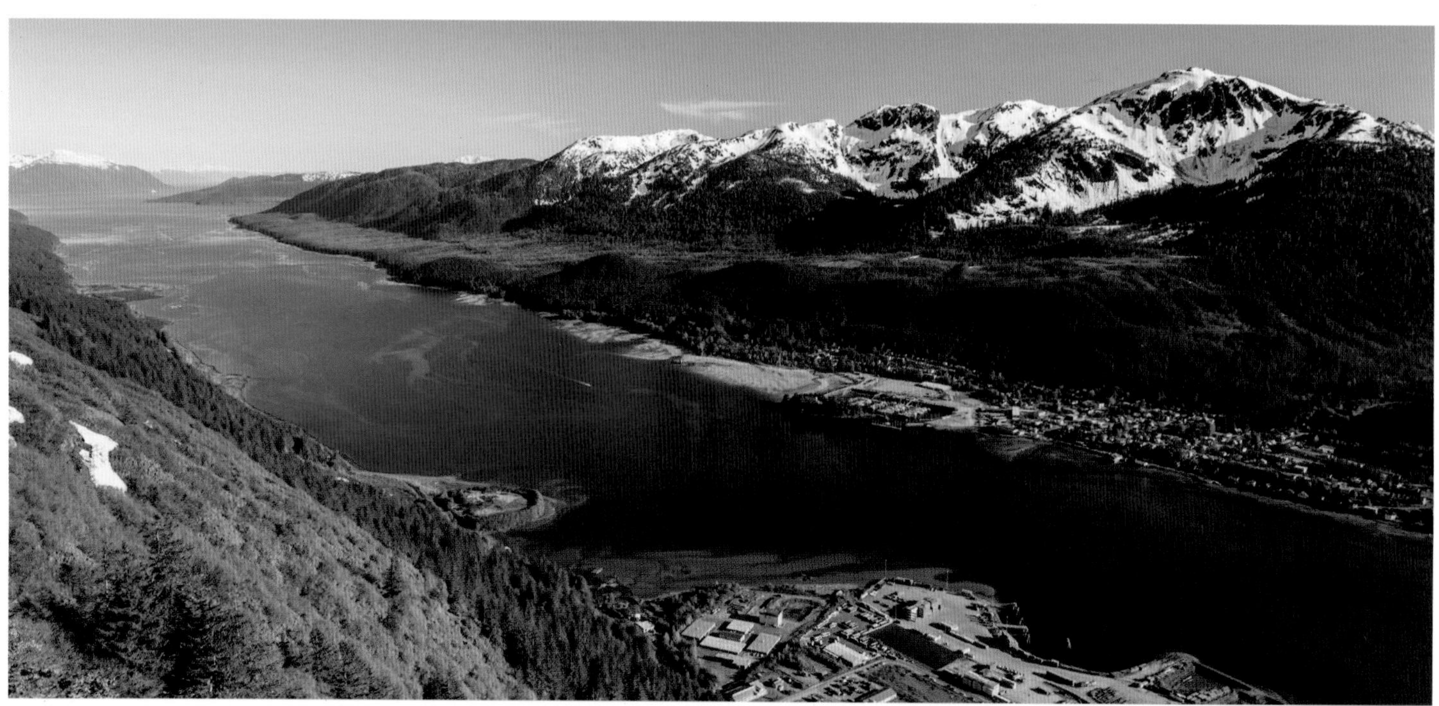

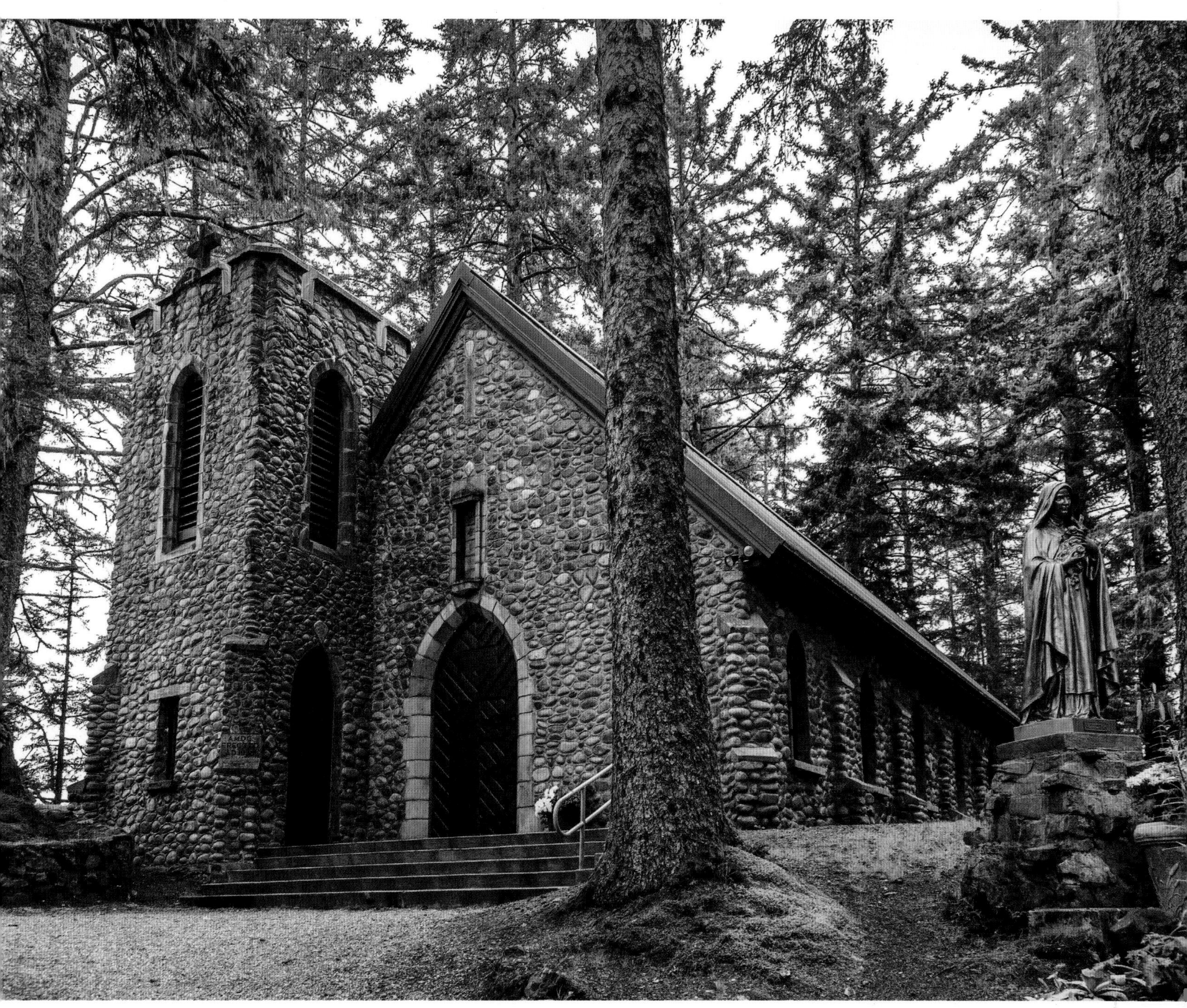

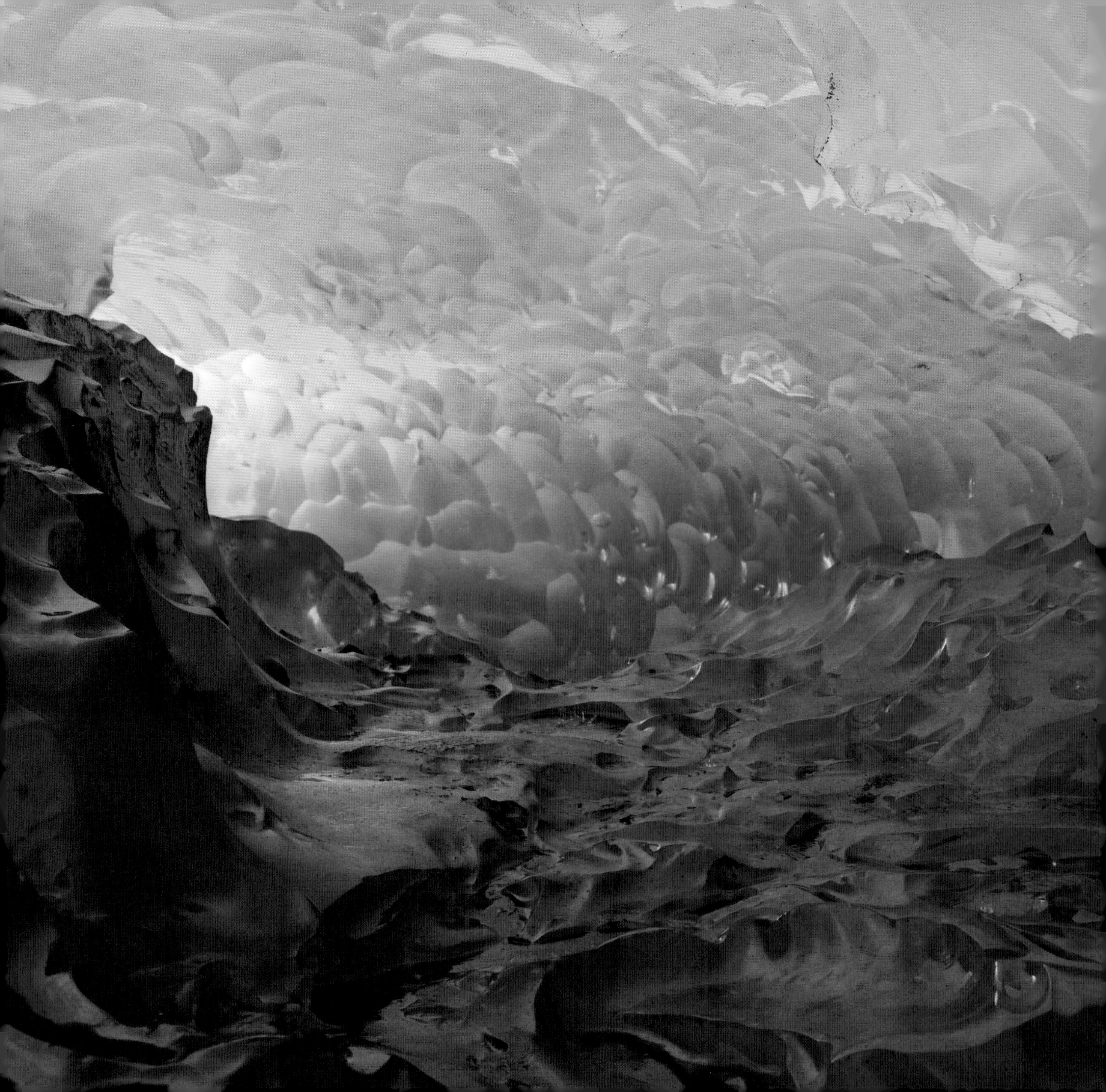

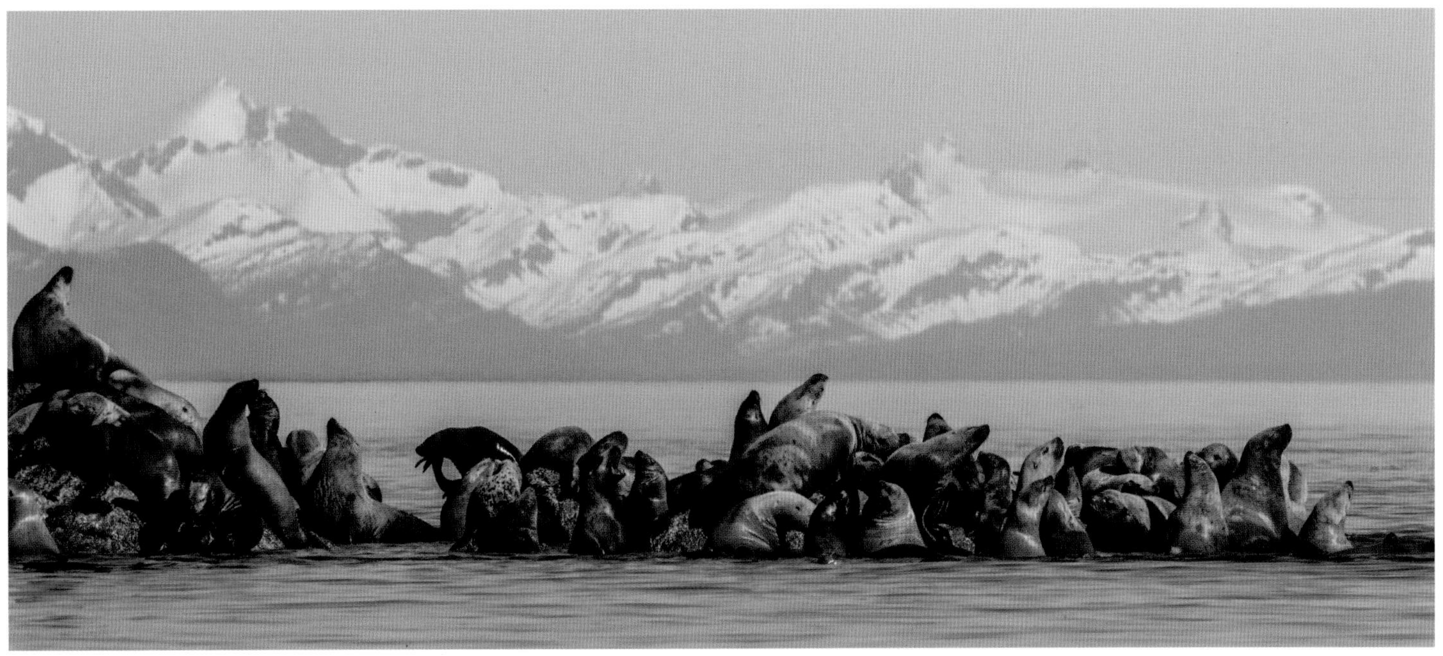

ICE CAVE, MENDENHALL GLACIER

Northern Region

An ice cave like this one forms when a glacier melts partially below the surface and the water carves out a pathway as it flows downhill; or, alternatively, when winds blow out a tunnel through drifts of not-yet-hardened surface snow. Rising in the Juneau Icefield, 19 km (12 miles) from the city and 1,580 m (5,100 ft) higher up, this glacier is some 22 km (13½ miles) long, but is very gradually retreating.

STELLER'S SEA LIONS, FREDERICK SOUND

Northern Region

An area of open water at the heart of the Alexander Archipelago, Frederick Sound lies between Kupreanof and Admiralty Islands. Though it is a favourite place for whale watching, it is home to other sea mammals like the sandy-coloured Steller's sea lions congregating here. This species used to breed all the way down the West Coast as far as southern California, but its range has diminished greatly over the last half-century. For reasons that are not entirely clear, it seems to be threatened even in Alaska. It is a real privilege to see this group.

TRACY ARM FJORD

Northern Region

The sheer sides of this broad, deep valley would be telltale evidence of its glacial origins (*see* pages 109 and 119) even if there were not a 'smoking gun' in the Sawyer and South Sawyer Glaciers. They are way upstream now – their 'snouts' or termini getting on for 50 km (30 miles) away in the mountains above the far end of the fjord. Just 20,000 years ago (the blink of an eye in geological terms), they were at work right here, carving away the virgin rock and pushing other detritus down before them.

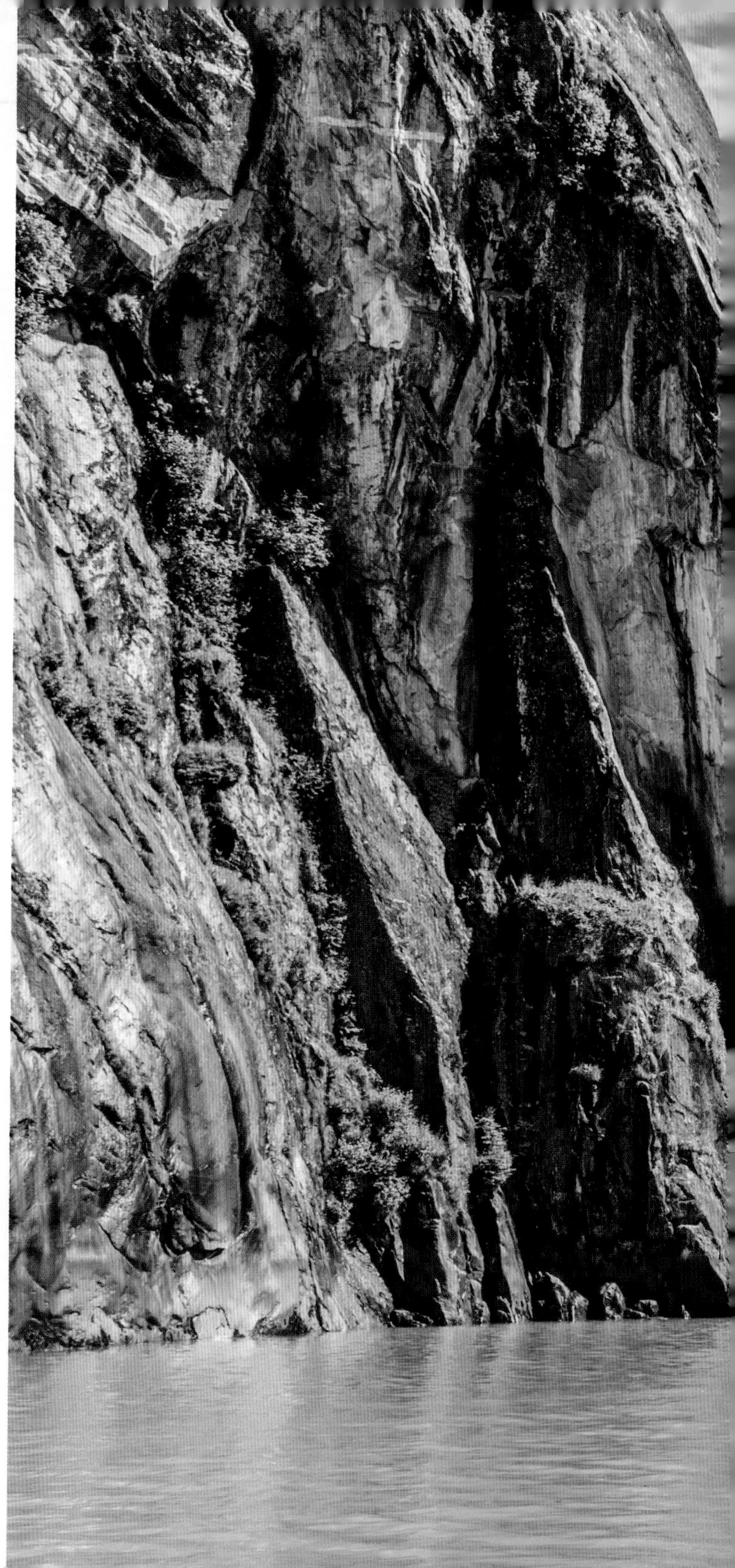

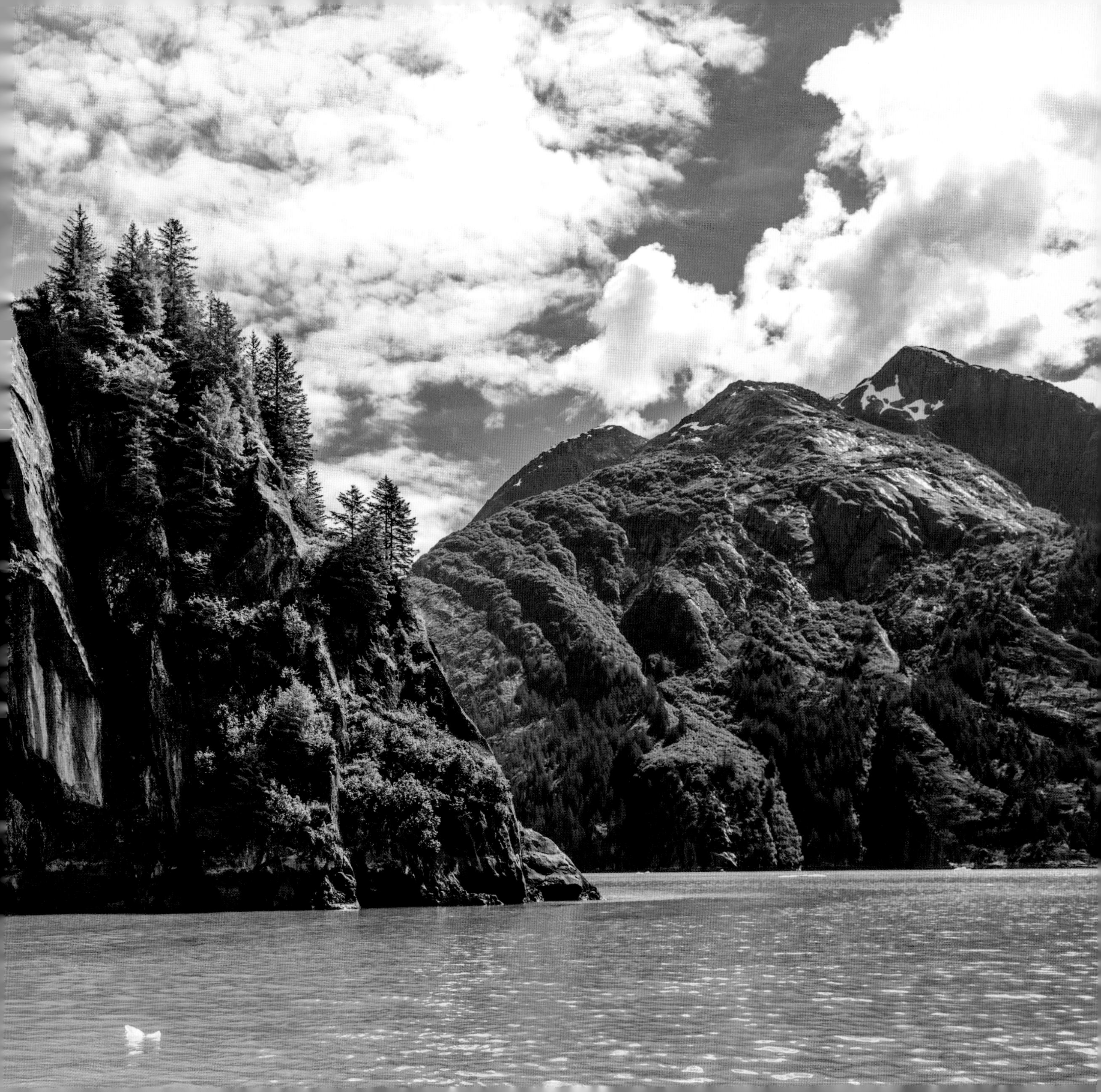

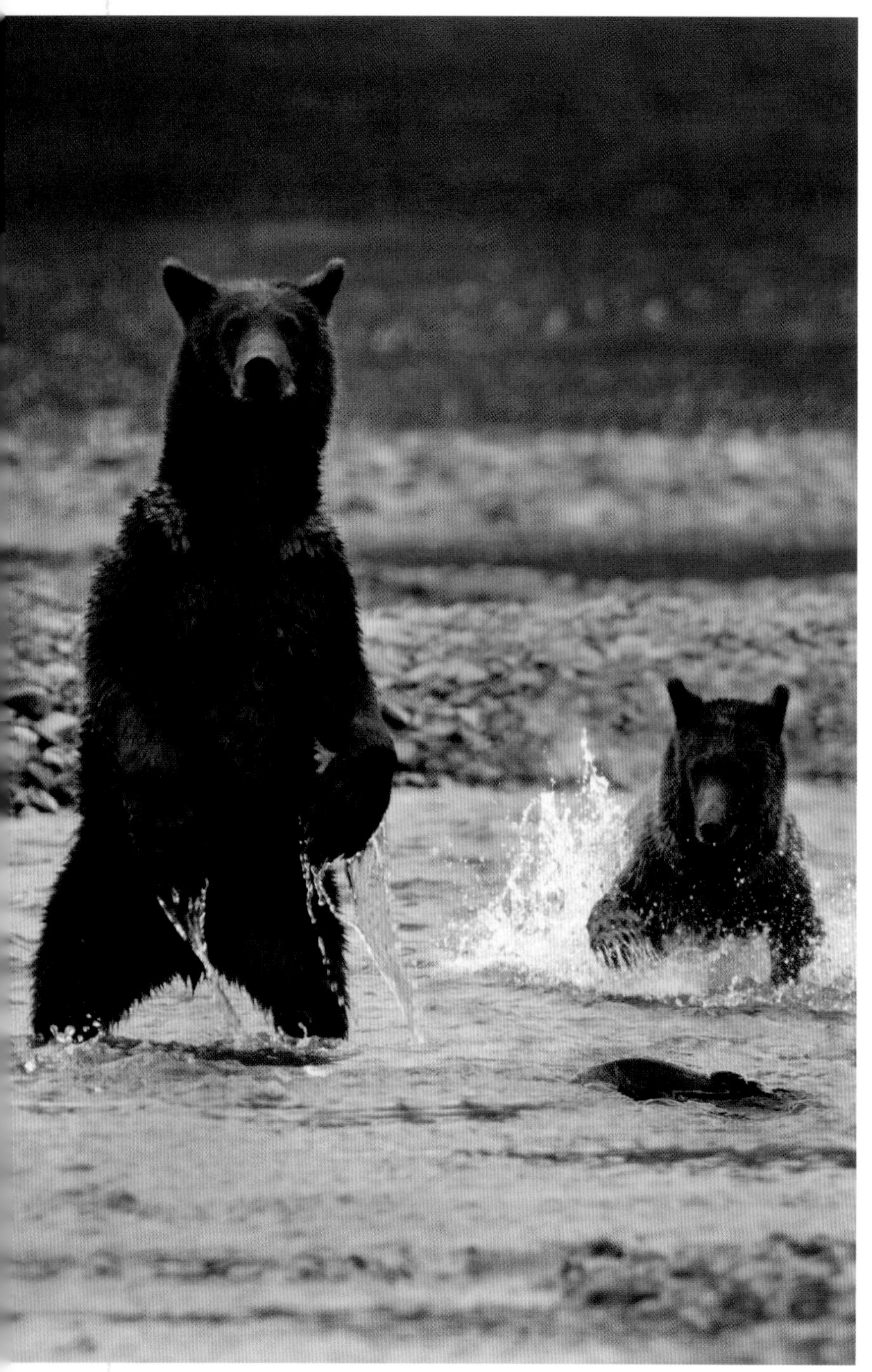

BEARS, ADMIRALTY ISLAND

Northern Region

Iconic and engaging, the sight of the brown bears (*Ursus arctos*) salmon fishing has become familiar to TV viewers around the world. In Alaska, though, you can see it live each summer in the salmon run. It is easy to forget, however, just how atypical this period is in the bear's seasonal subsistence cycle: it derives much of its eager, even festive, flavour from the fact that it comes after a winter that is both lean and long. It is not actually usual for brown bears to congregate like this: they are brought together by the prospect of a feast.

SITKA SOUND, BARANOF ISLAND

Northern Region

The Alexander Archipelago has in excess of a thousand islands, though some of these are little more than rocks. The largest, Prince of Wales Island, some way south of here (*see* page 159), extends over 6,670 sq km (2,577 sq miles), Chicagof over 5,305 sq km (2,050 sq miles), while Baranof itself covers 4,160 sq km (1,607 sq miles). There are also, however, hundreds of islets of the sort that we see here. Tiny little forested fortresses of solitude and peace, they offer an idyllic sanctuary from the stresses of the modern world.

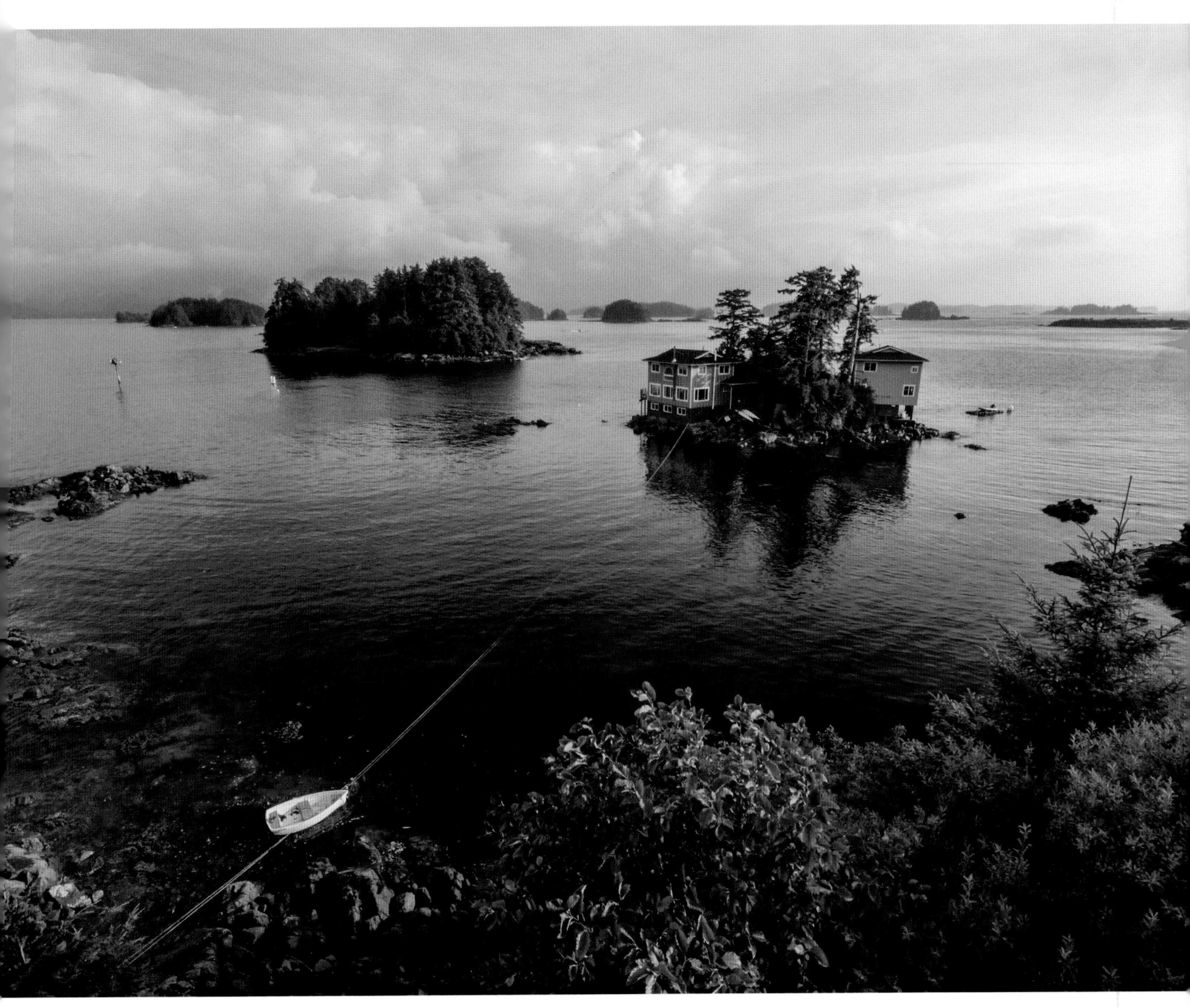

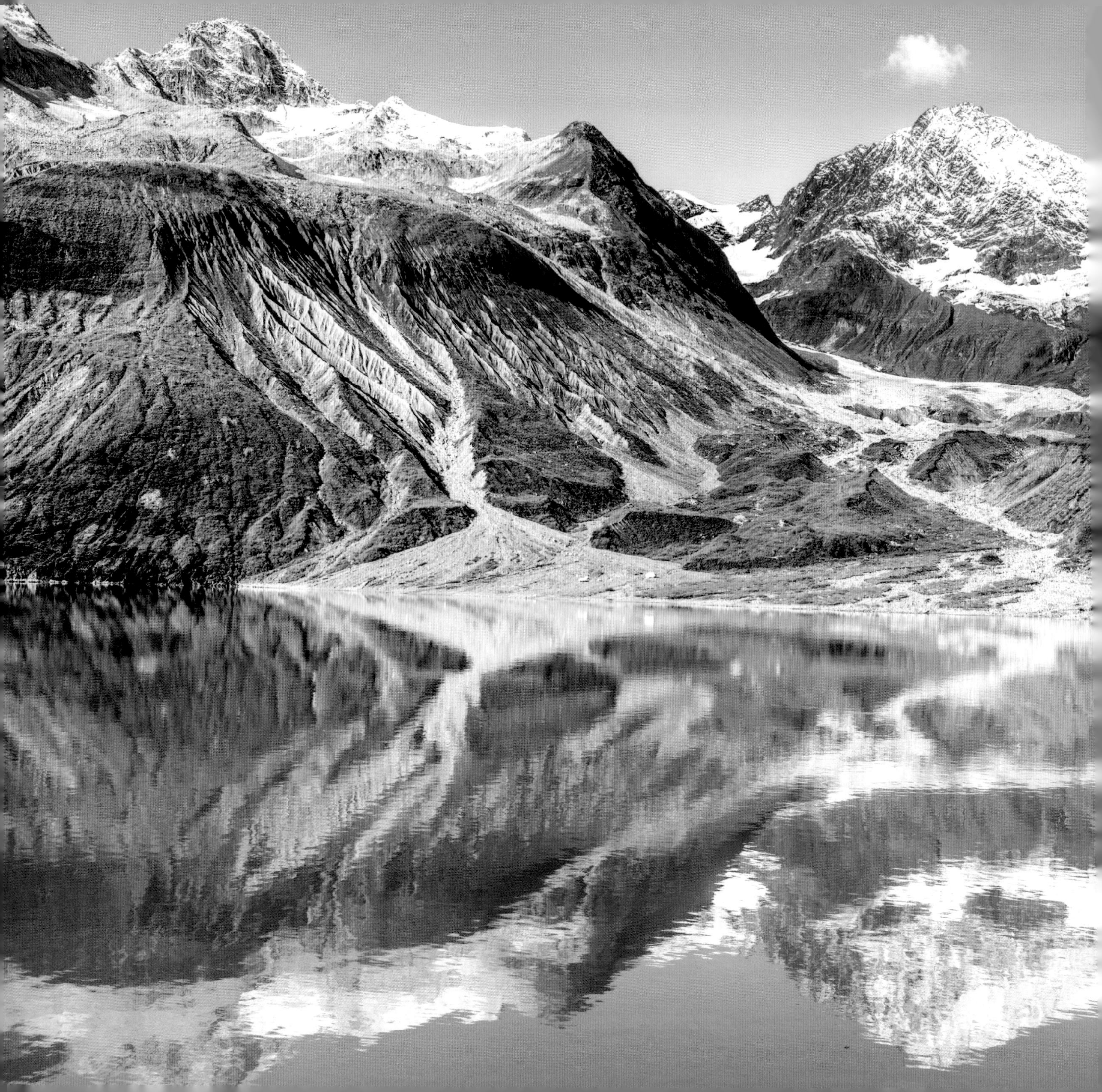

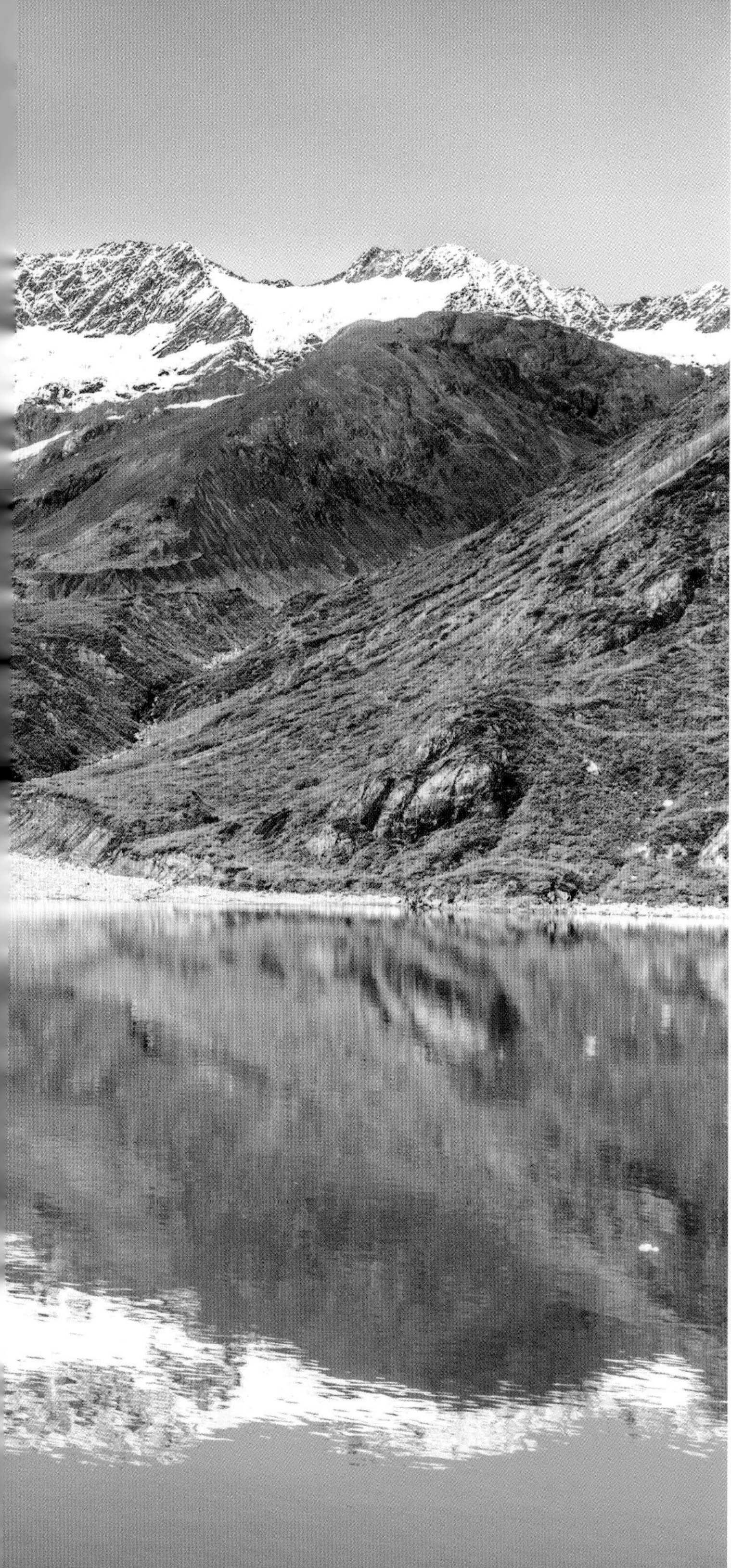

GLACIER BAY NATIONAL PARK

Glacier Bay

There are no prizes for guessing how Glacier Bay got its name. To this day, half a dozen glaciers reach the sea in its sheltered waters. A few more do not make it quite that far; but an extensive, 3,560-sq-km (1,375-sq-mile) ice field in the mountains above is the source for more than a thousand more. It is easy to see why UNESCO (the United Nations Educational, Scientific and Cultural Organization) designated this a protected biosphere – the biggest area so nominated in the world.

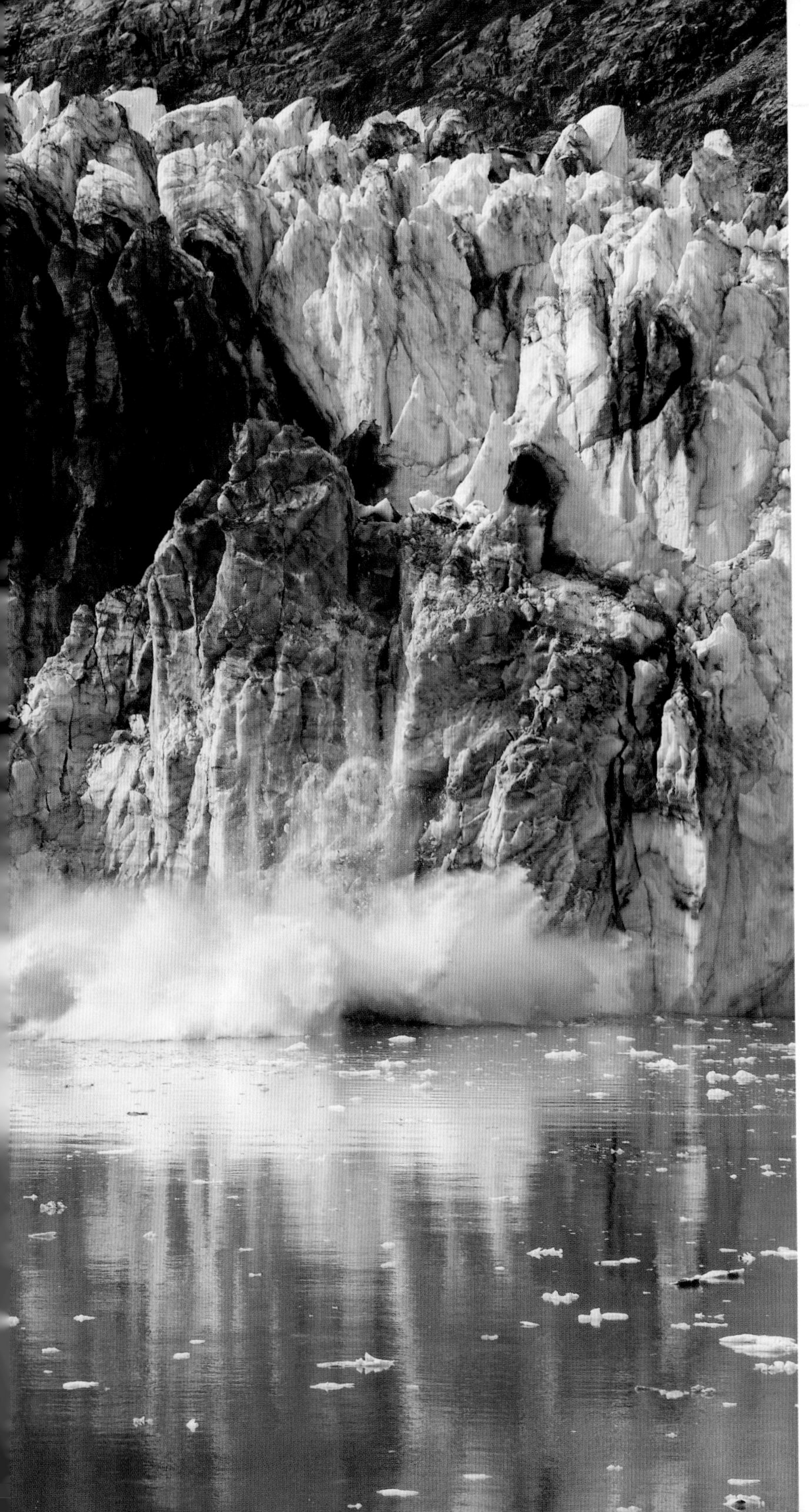

GLACIER CALVING, GLACIER BAY NATIONAL PARK

Glacier Bay

The conclusion, when it comes, is dramatically abrupt: after so many centuries inching down the mountainside, a fresh wall of ice breaks free and floats away. Not, of course, that it is really the end: icebergs melt only slowly, even under warm conditions, and can be carried long distances by winds and currents, at speeds of up to 14 km (8½ miles) a day. Given the confinement of these waters, though – crowded round by the islands of the Alexander Archipelago – that does not tend to be the case up here.

GUSTAVUS BEACH

Glacier Bay

Retreating glaciers left behind this vast wide beach: having razed the area flat through their centuries of inexorable advance, they then dumped enormous quantities of moraine (*see* page 108) as, slowly and imperceptibly, they then melted and withdrew. On a bright summer's day like this one, the snow-capped mountains on the far horizon look positively inviting, the cool ripples underfoot, refreshingly enticing. Tourism has indeed been becoming increasingly important economically to Gustavus, whose commercial fishery has been struggling for some years.

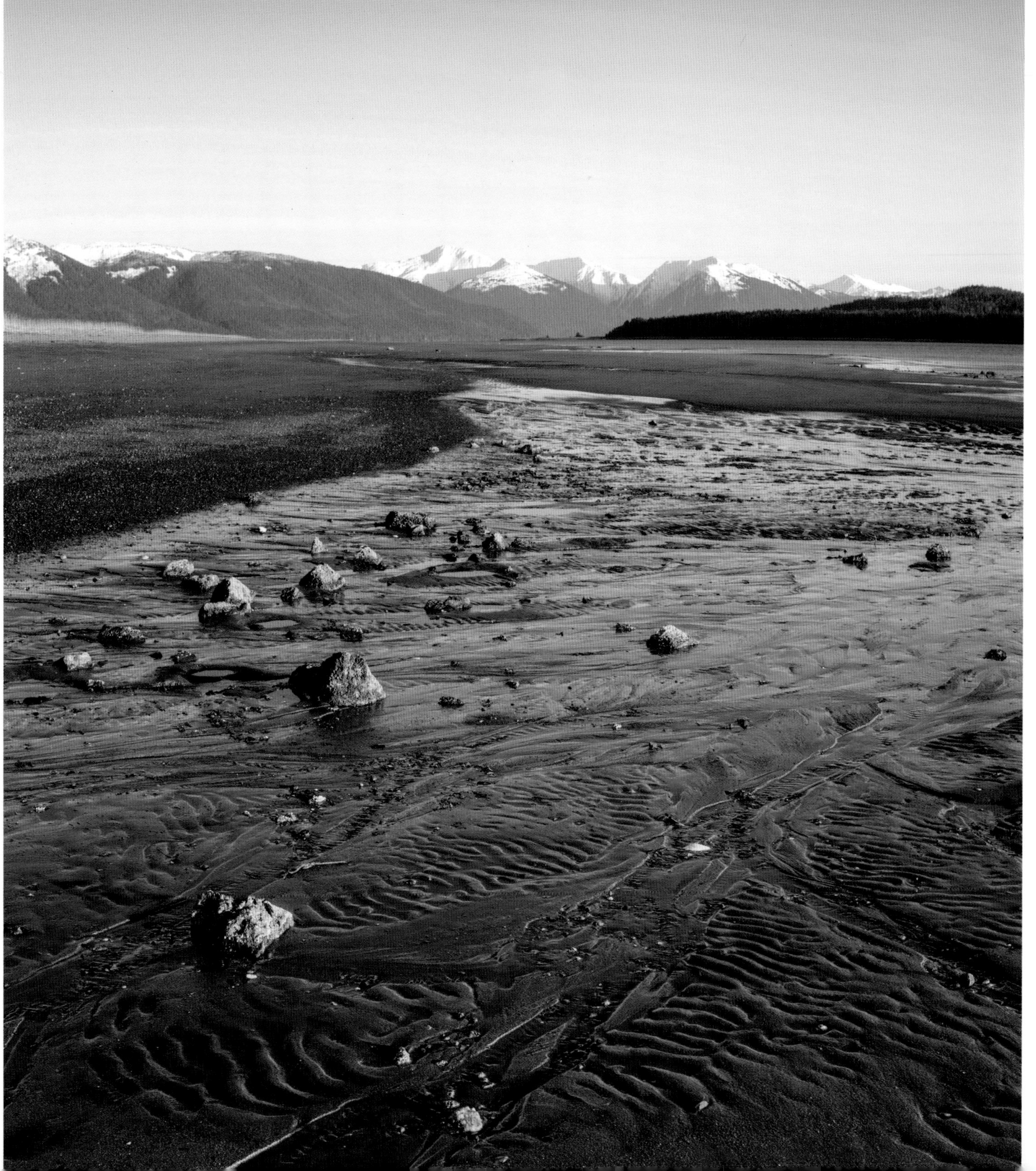

ALASKA MARINE HIGHWAY, INSIDE PASSAGE

Southern Region

The Alaska Marine Highway (AMH) is a state-run ferry line which, taking full advantage of the sheltered waters of the 'Inside Passage' (*see* page 127), plies up and down the entire North-Pacific coast. No fewer than 32 ports are visited, in Alaska, British Columbia and Washington. Most serve communities that, like this one, are not accessible by road: the AMH is vital to the economic functioning of the region as a whole. In addition to ferrying freight, it carries passengers – both local people and tourists.

TOTEM POLE, KAKE

Southern Region

Kake, on Kupreanof island, is home to the world's tallest totem pole. Standing 39 m (128 ft) tall, it was fashioned from a single tree to mark the 1967 centennial of the Alaska Purchase (*see* page 8). This Tlingit village's history has long brought the situation of Alaska's Native peoples into an unsettling focus: in 1869, three villages were destroyed by gunfire from the USS Saginaw. Now, however, the village works to strengthen tribal community and preserve their cultural traditions.

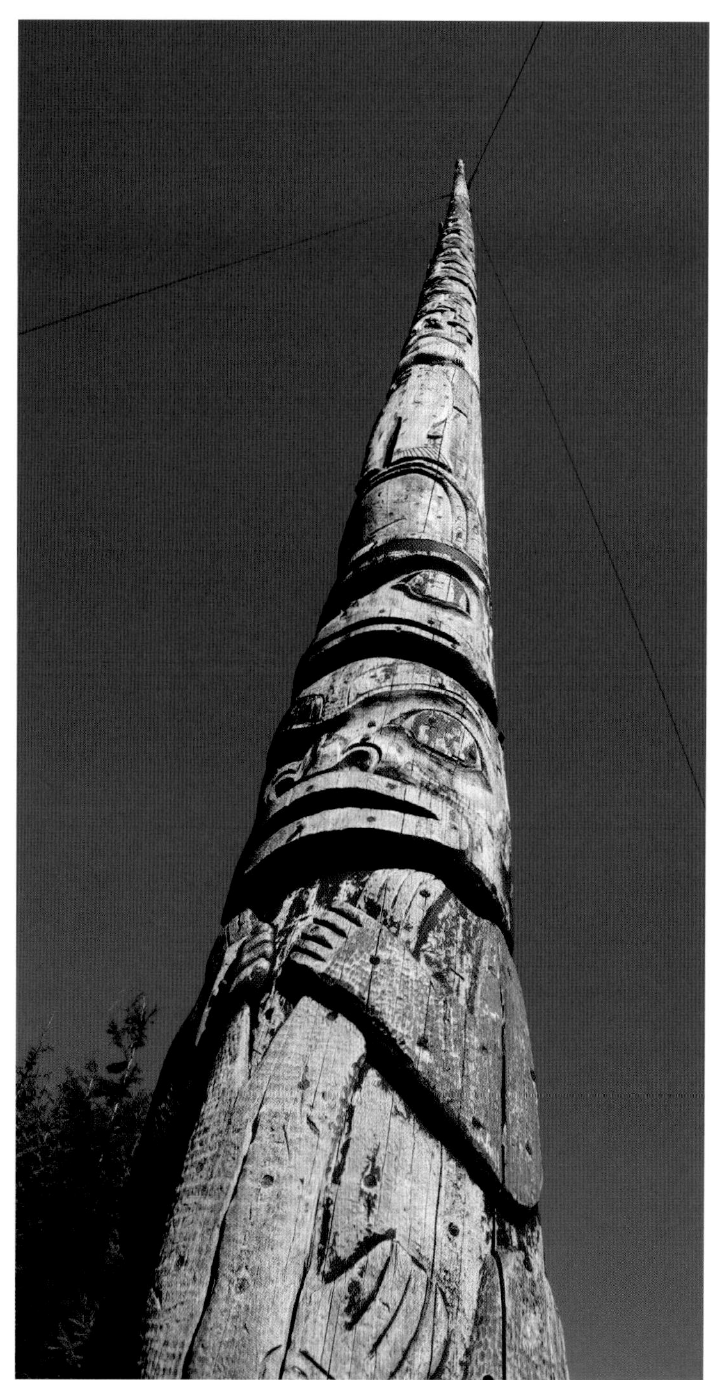

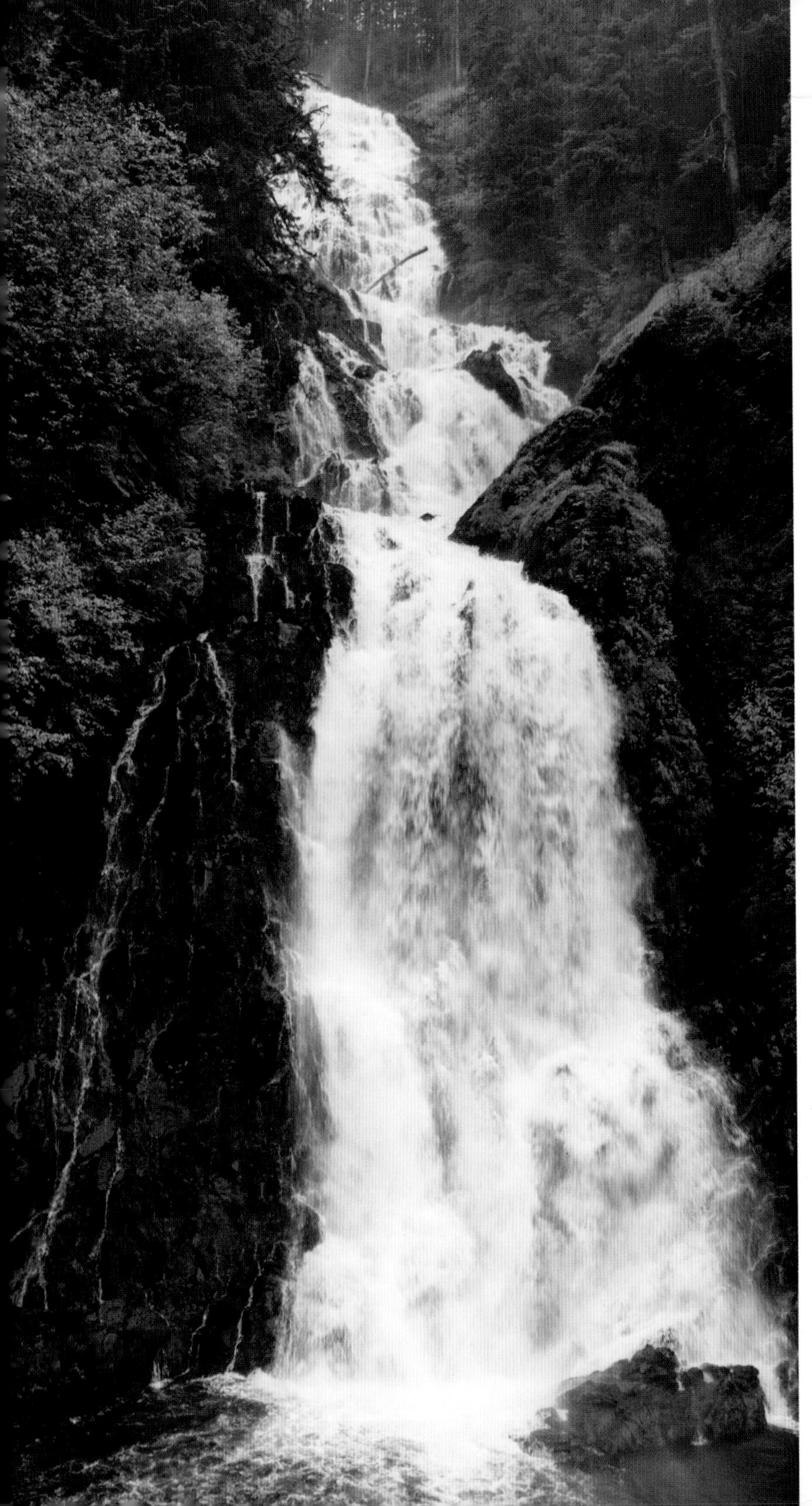

WATERFALL, RED BLUFF BAY

Southern Region

A deep fjord cutting into the eastern side of Baronof Island, Red Bluff Bay offers many scenes of sublime beauty, and large areas of unspoiled (and federally designated) wilderness in which to roam. Though nominally part of the Sitka urban area, it is actually a lengthy journey away – and one that must be done by foot and kayak or by seaplane. The 'steps' down which this waterfall plunges were left when glacial erosion undercut an earlier tributary river valley, leaving a sudden drop into empty space.

ST. MICHAEL'S ORTHODOX CATHEDRAL, SITKA

Southern Region

In the early nineteenth century, this city on the western coast of Baronof was 'New Archangel' and headquarters of the Russian-American Company. Bishop Ioann Veniaminov (1797–1879), 'St. Innocent of Alaska', founded this cathedral, whose construction began in 1844 and was completed four years later. Stylistically, its Russian inspiration is unmistakeable (inside there are also seventeenth-century icons from the Old Country). The original building burned down in 1966, but it was rebuilt in fire-resistant materials and remains one of the city's major landmarks.

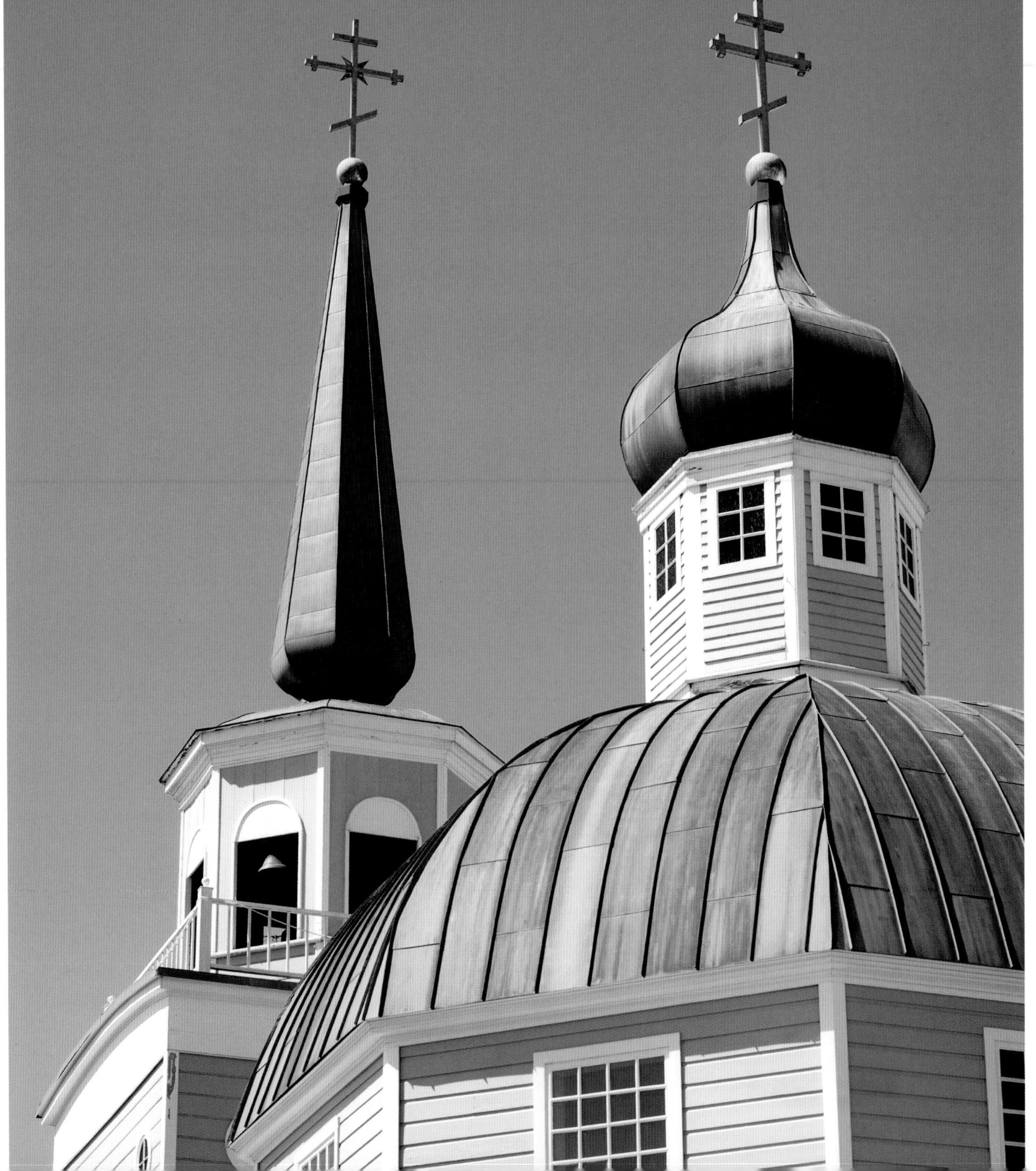

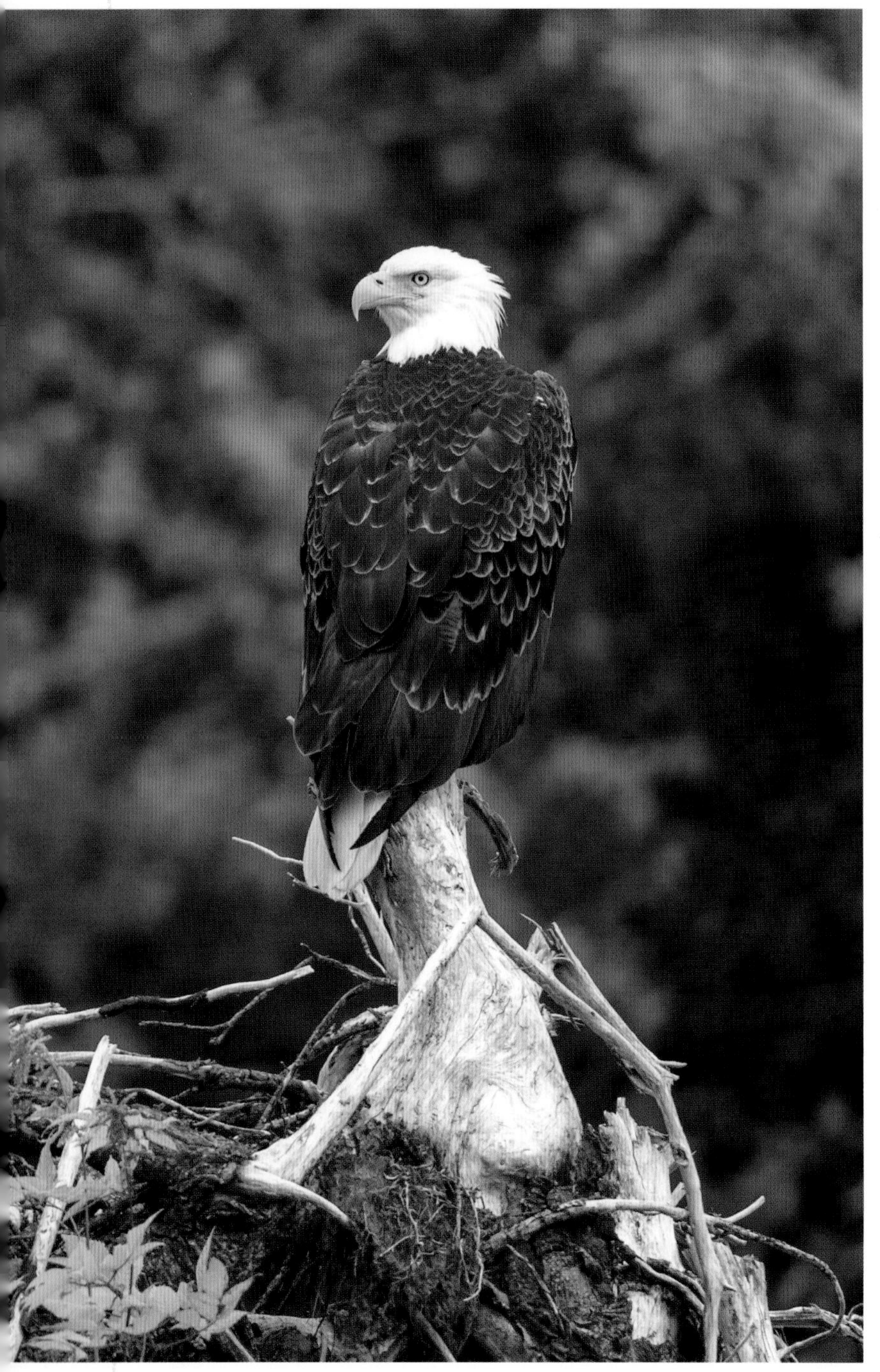

BALD EAGLE, STIKINE

Southern Region

The national bird of the United States is much more than an emblem to Alaskans. The Stikine River delta suits it perfectly. It is a sea eagle, so it lives on fish (over a hundred different species are known to be taken, but trout and salmon are the staple here). And then, of course, there are trees as well: the Bald Eagle's treetop nest of twigs, added to year by year, can grow cumulatively over generations to a gigantic size – 4 m (13 ft) in depth and a tonne in weight.

PRINCE OF WALES ISLAND

Southern Region

Lying towards the southern end of the Alexander Archipelago, this is the biggest in the group, and the United States' fourth largest island. It is very sparsely inhabited, though: the old saltery town of Craig accounts for almost half of its (approximately) 3,000 population; the fishing port of Klawock and the lumbering centre Hollis have just about all the rest. Hence an aerial view like this, showing nothing but mile after mile of clear blue water, lush green forests and an infinity of blessed emptiness.

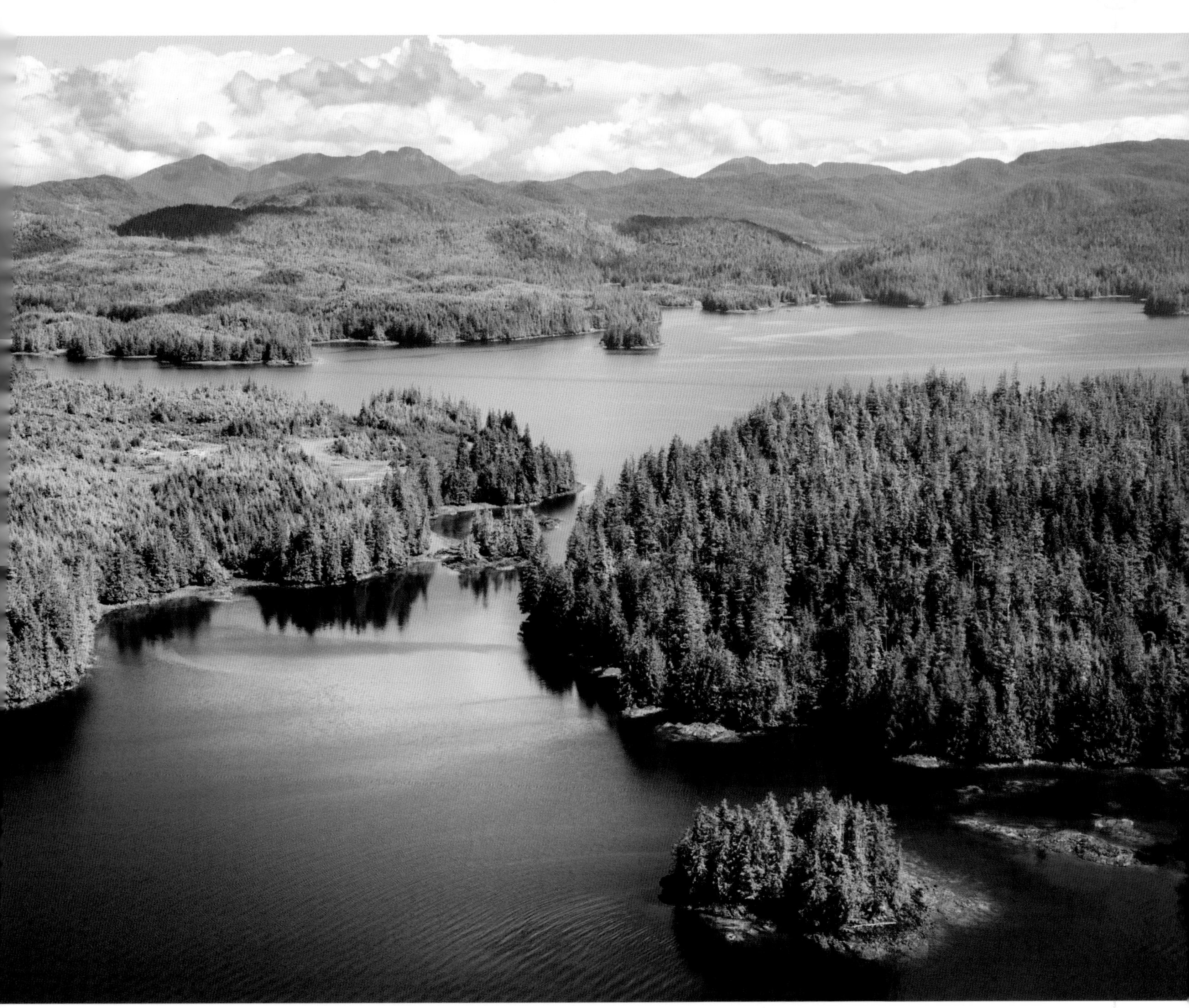

MISTY FJORDS NATIONAL MONUMENT, TONGASS NATIONAL PARK

Southern Region

With wispy clouds as advertised, despite bright summer sunshine, the Misty Fjords present a truly breathtaking sight. These deep inlets of the ocean are known locally as 'canals' (like the Lynn Canal, *see* page 138), despite being naturally formed fjords. They are particularly striking examples, though, their rock walls in places rising some 900 m (3,000 ft) above the water all but vertically. Mist and fine rain are not exactly scarce anywhere along North America's Pacific coast, but with over 3,810 mm (150 in) precipitation annually, this area does get rather more than its fair share.

CREEK STREET, KETCHIKAN

Southern Region

Brightly as it may be painted now, Ketchikan struggles to be as colourful as it was in its more raffish past, when this historic boardwalk was lined with brothels. There was something of a Wild West boomtown feel about the place, at a time when the salmon fishery was at its height and the town filled up regularly with fishermen and cannery workers – and, during prohibition, with smugglers bringing in whisky from Canada. Ketchikan is quieter now, no doubt for the best, but there is still a vibrancy about it, bustling as it is these days with summer tourists.

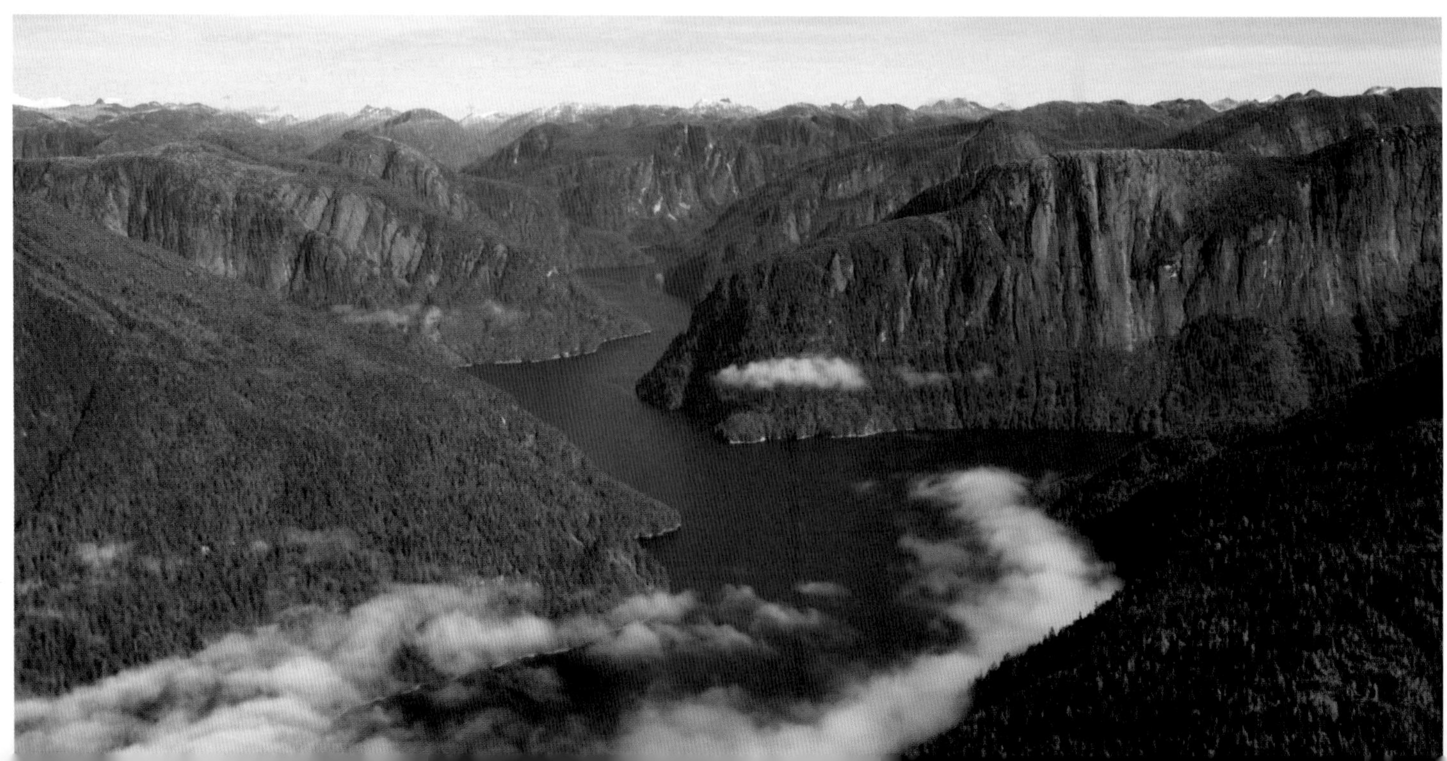

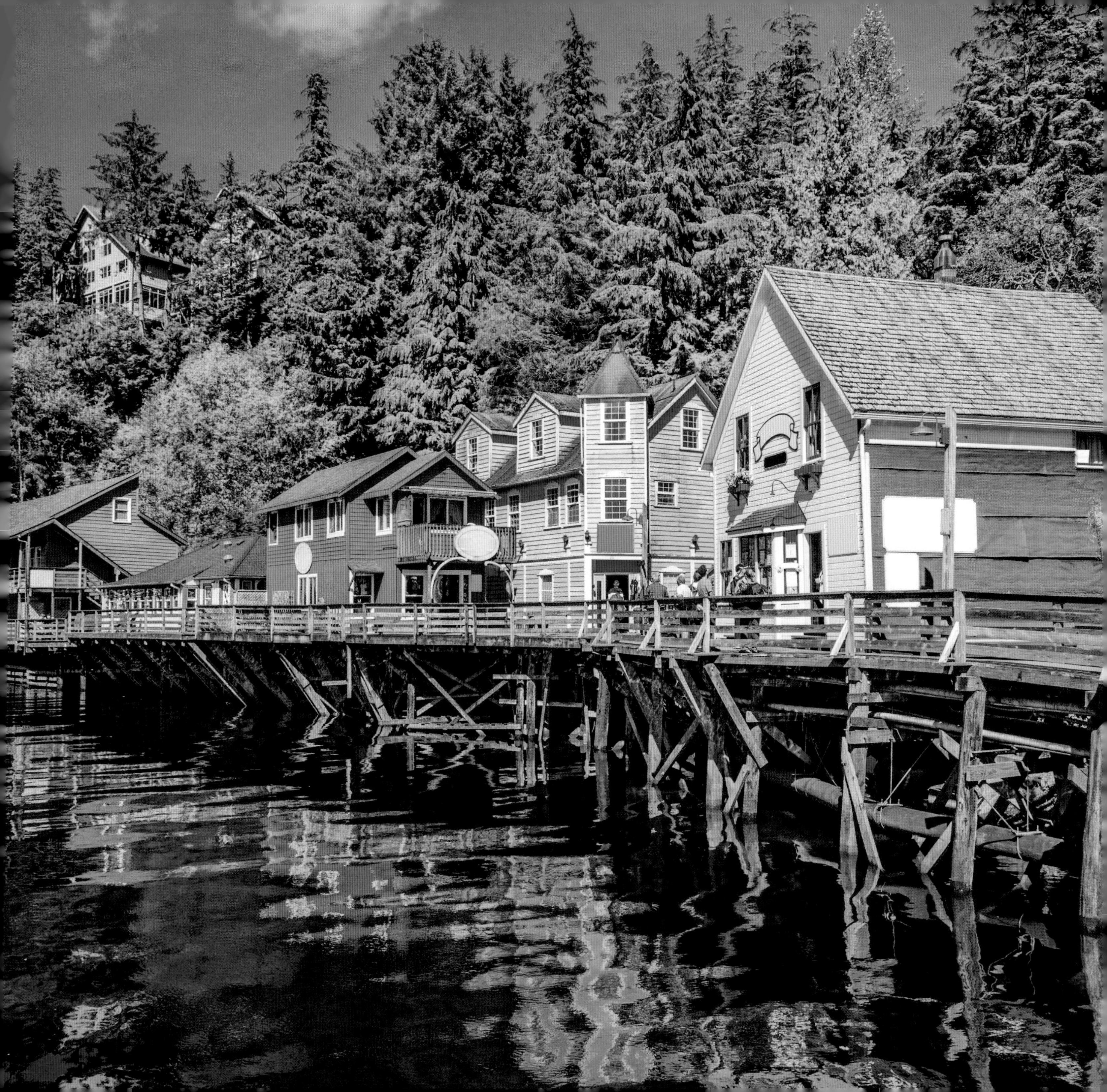

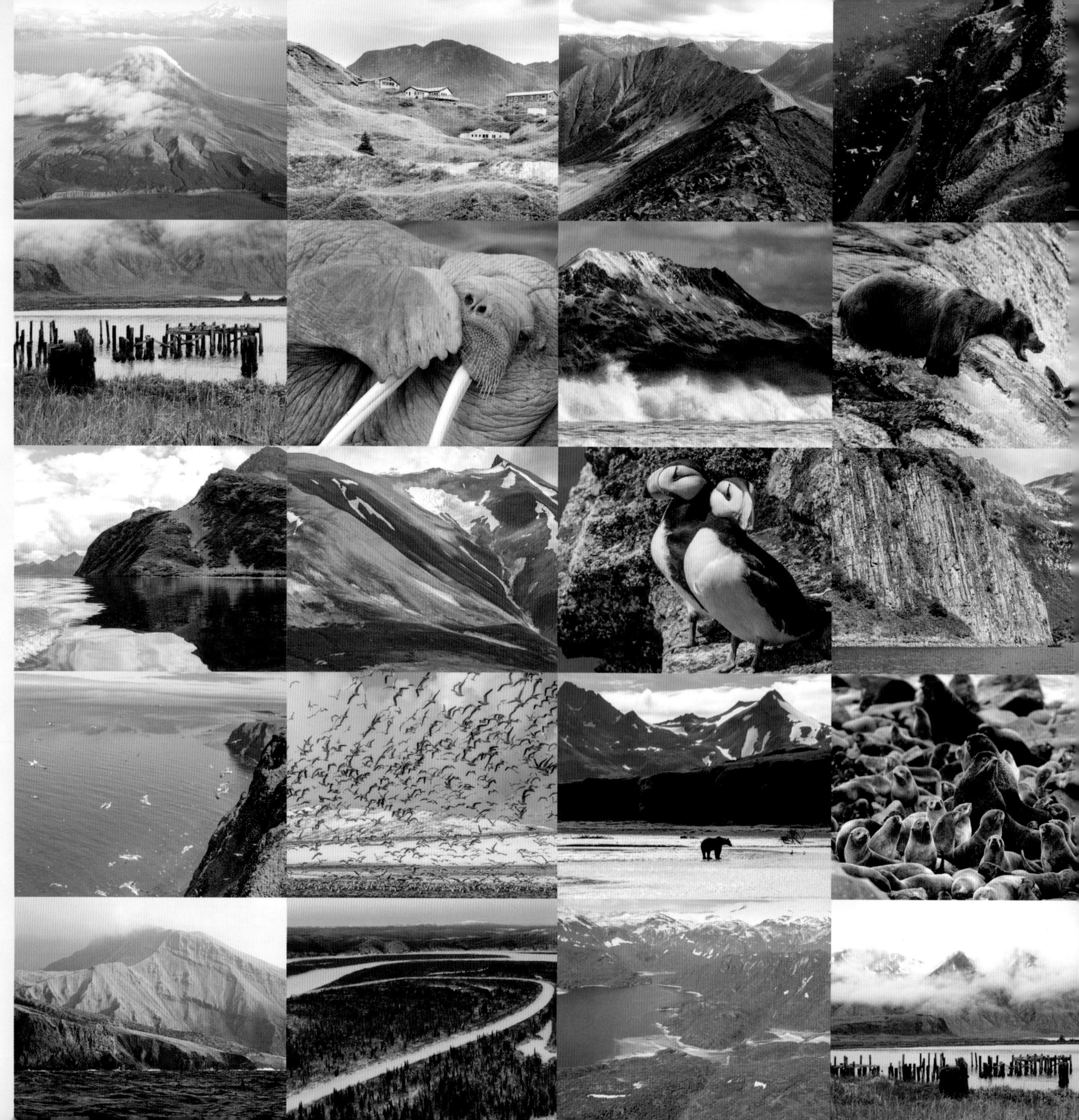

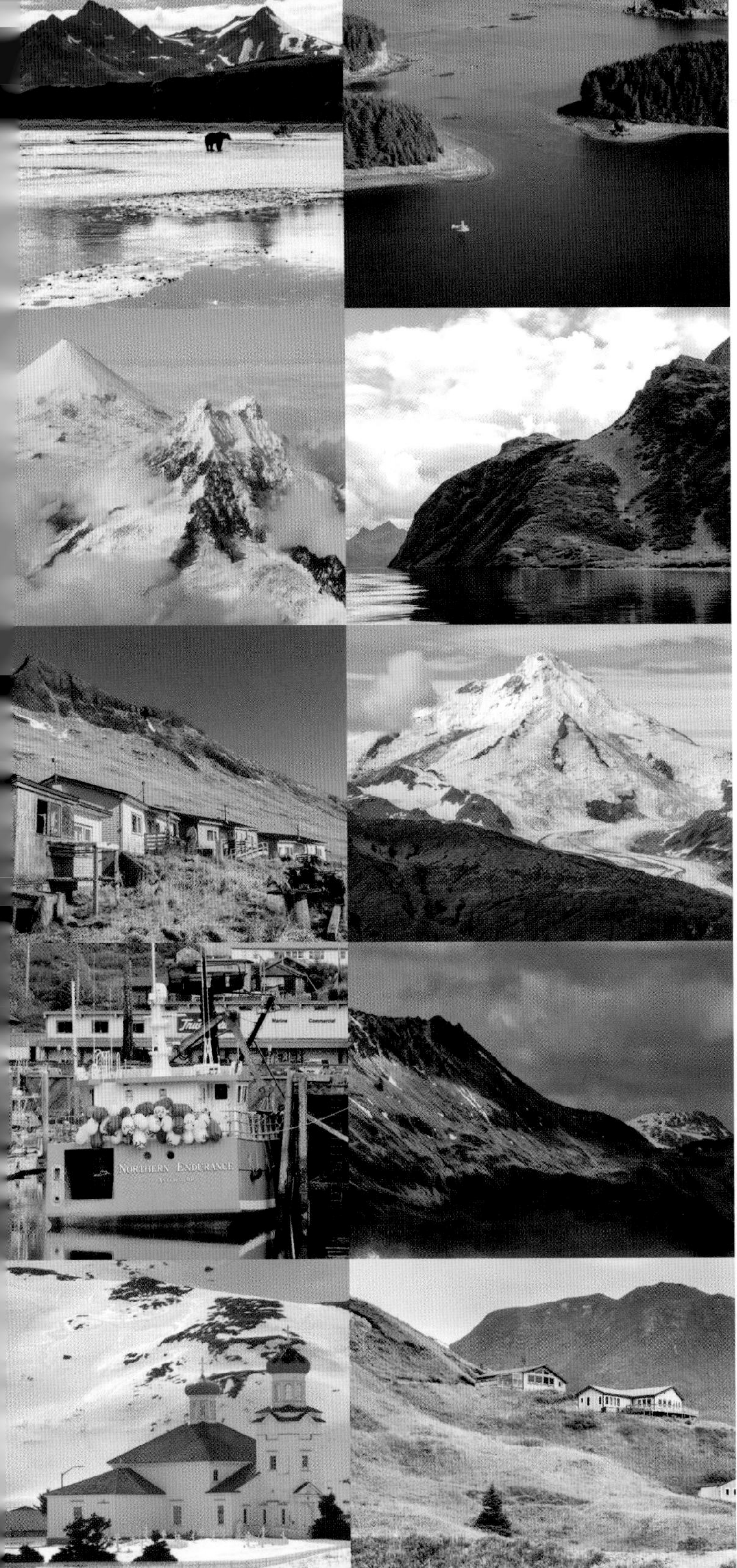

SOUTHWEST ALASKA

The Alaska Peninsula extends 800 km (500 miles) westward between the Bering Sea and the North Pacific. It is basically a lengthy chain of volcanic mountains, the Aleutian Range. Then, continuing its line (and clearly a continuation of the same mountain range, but partially submerged now), the Aleutian Islands extend a further 1,900 km (1,200 miles) west. There are over 300 islands in all, though only a dozen or so are of any size. Attu, the outermost, is 335 km (208 miles) from Russia's Commander Islands – far closer than it is to even the nearest point on the Alaskan mainland.

In these farthest flung of American islands, there is a real feeling of being in no-man's-land. And not just because of the immense austerity of the scene. Are we in the East or West, in Asia or North America? We are nearer Vladivostok than we are Seattle. We only know what day it is by special dispensation: the International Date Line has to make a detour to keep us on US time. If anything, yet more isolated are the Pribilof Islands, further to the north: a cluster of four volcanic peaks which a million years or so ago simply pushed their way up out of the middle of the Bering Sea.

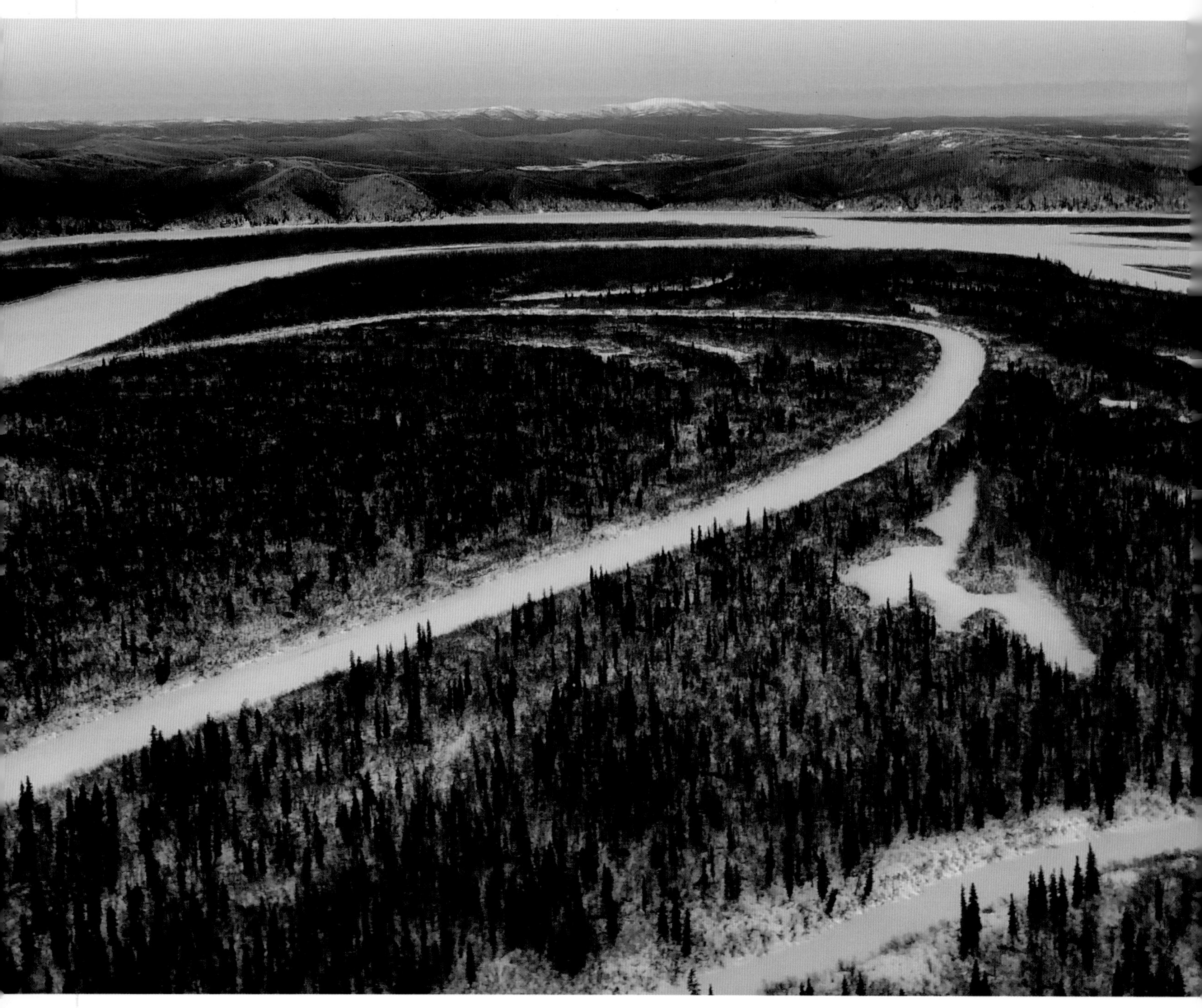

KUSKOKWIM RIVER

Yukon-Kuskokwim Delta

Like the Teklanika River (*see* page 70), the Kuskokwim is braided for much of its length, lacing a wide floodplain with extravagant loops and little ox-bow lakes. To see the effect to its fullest advantage, it is best to view it from the air, as here we do the section between Aniak and Kalskag. That it is a winter's day only enhances its entrancing beauty – as does the fact that we see it in the pinkish light of afternoon, when the river's icy swirls glisten most strongly in the setting sun.

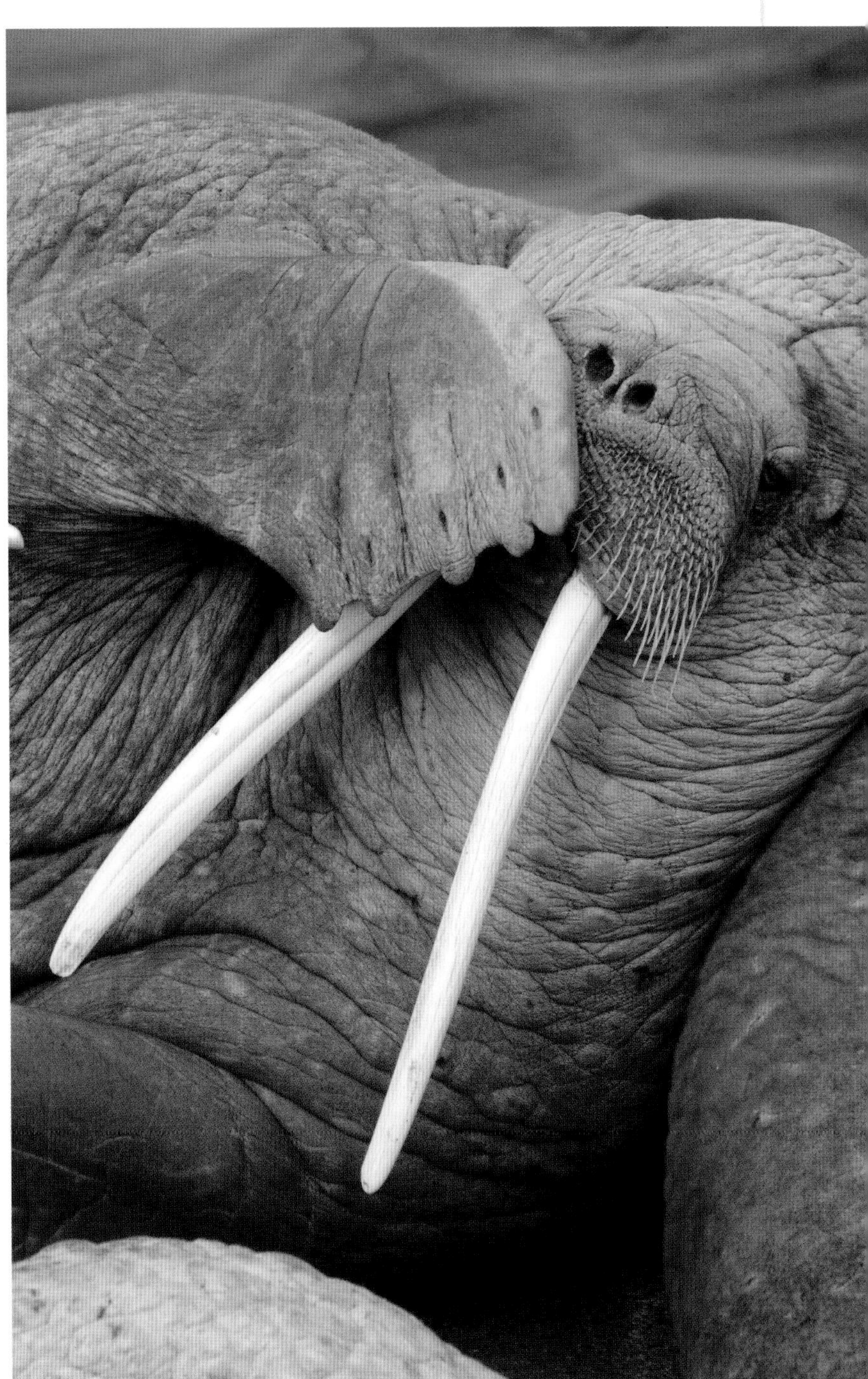

WALRUS, ROUND ISLAND, BRISTOL BAY

Bristol Bay

The Walrus Islands are in Bristol Bay, a little way north of the Alaskan Peninsula. As their name suggests, they are popular with walruses – and none more so than Round Island. This magnificent male is one of anything up to 14,000 which haul themselves ashore here on a typical summer's day. Every beach becomes a heaving, grunting mass of wobbly flesh as they recline here twitching. Their sharp white ivory tusks stand out, but they are mostly directed upwards out of harm's way, except when they are fighting, or posturing for dominance.

TANALIAN MOUNTAIN, LAKE CLARK NATIONAL PARK

Alaskan Peninsula

Though tantalizingly close to Anchorage (250 km/160 miles), the Lake Clark National Park is so remote it seems to belong to another world. It is another Alaskan wilderness that cannot be reached by road. Sublime as its scenery of lakes and mountains is, the climb up Tanalian Mountain (1,080 m/3570 ft) is something special. From its summit, there are spectacular views out over Lake Clark to the north and Lake Kontrashibuna to the south, and to the other mountains of the Aleutian Range.

WOOD-TIKCHIK STATE PARK

Bristol Bay

The United States' biggest state park extends over 6,500 square km (2,500 square miles) of mountains, tundra, lakes and forests. It is so remote, though, that you cannot get there by road. The result is a realm apart, a wild country that really seems to belong to its flora and fauna. All five species of Alaskan salmon (king, sockeye/red, pink, silver and chum) swim in its lakes alongside grayling, trout and Arctic char. There are caribou, moose and bears, along with beavers, wolverine and muskrat, together with a wide variety of birds.

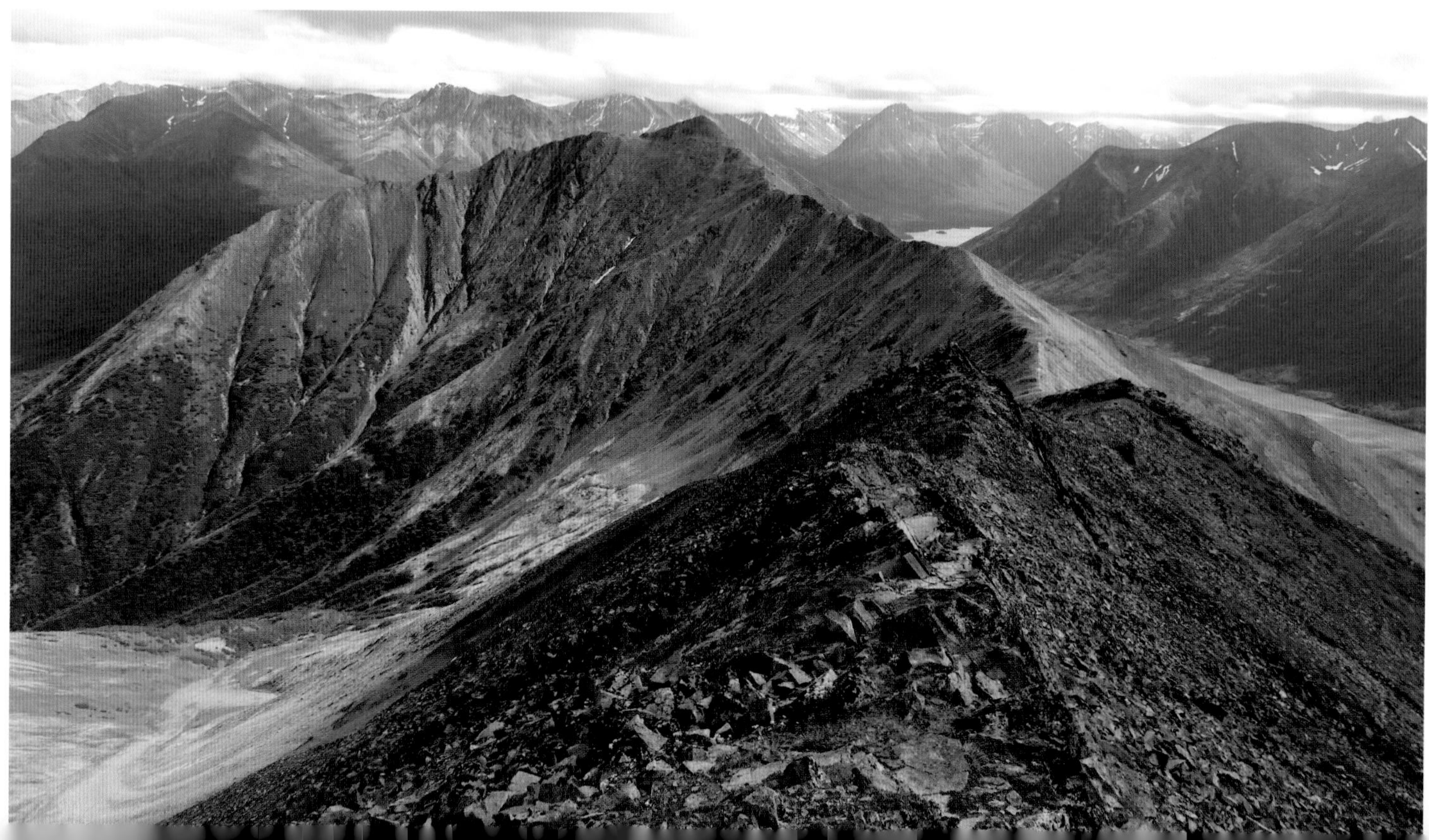

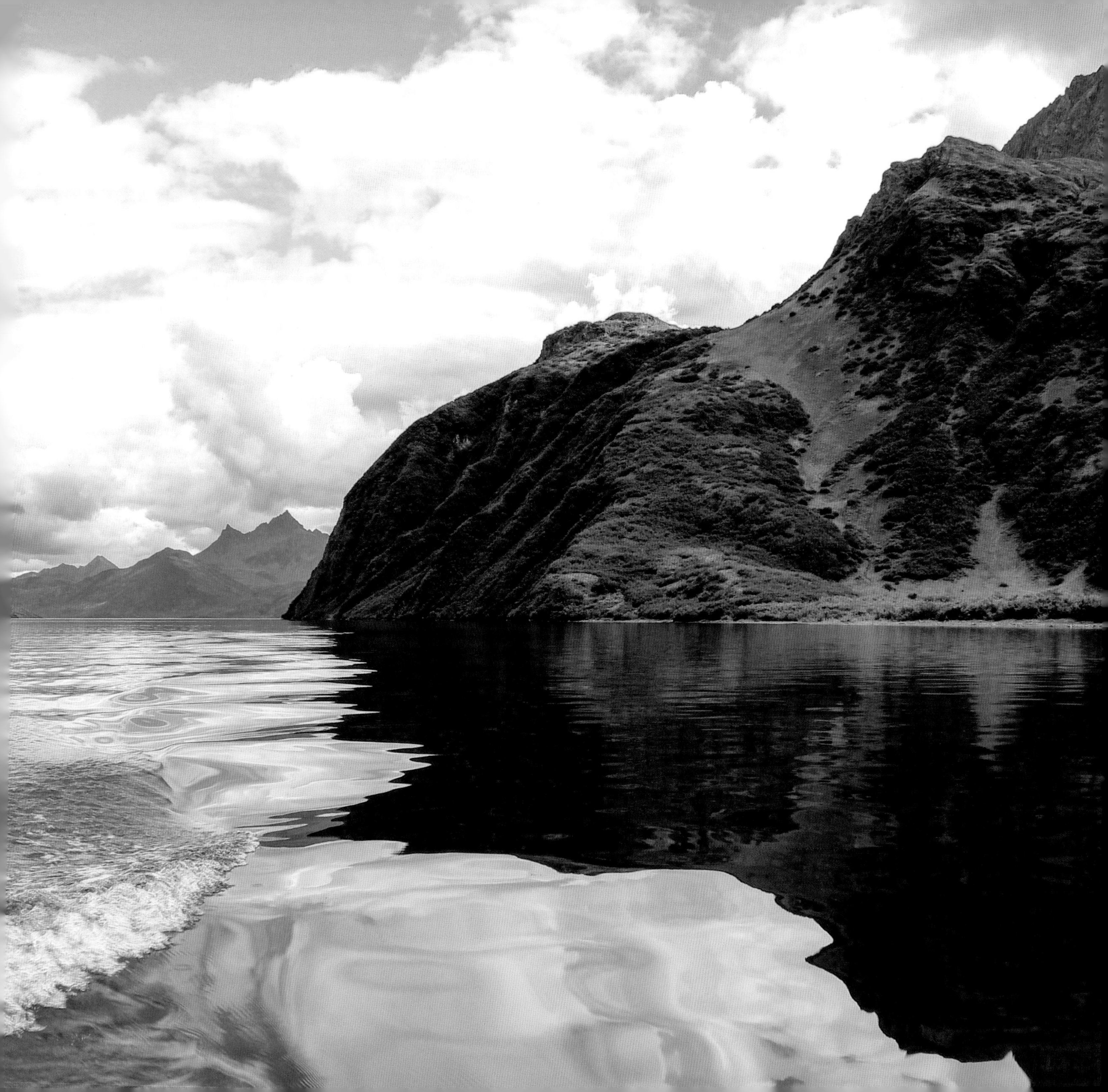

MOUNT ILIAMNA, LAKE CLARK NATIONAL PARK

Alaskan Peninsula

Fire and ice: the poetic opposition has long been seen as being too clichéd to be safely deployed, but nature has not read the writing guides. Not, at least, in Alaska, where in truth she never seems shy of seeming overstated in some of the most spectacular scenery in the world. Rising to a height of 3,053 m (10,016 ft), Iliamna is pretty much the perfect specimen of the snow-capped mountain (several glaciers start in its lower slopes). At the same time, though, it is very much an active volcano, perpetually emitting plumes of steam and gas.

MOUNT ST. AUGUSTINE AND THE COOK INLET

Alaskan Peninsula

This volcano is its own island, having forced its way up out of the seabed so emphatically that it now stands 1,260 m (4,134 ft) above the waters of the Cook Inlet. It was named by Captain Cook himself, the English navigator having first sighted it on St. Augustine's Day (26 May) in 1778. It has had several serious eruptions since, most recently in 2005, when it sent ash 13 km (8 miles) into the sky. Significant damage has, however, been confined to Mount St. Augustine itself: successive slides of debris have reshaped it several times.

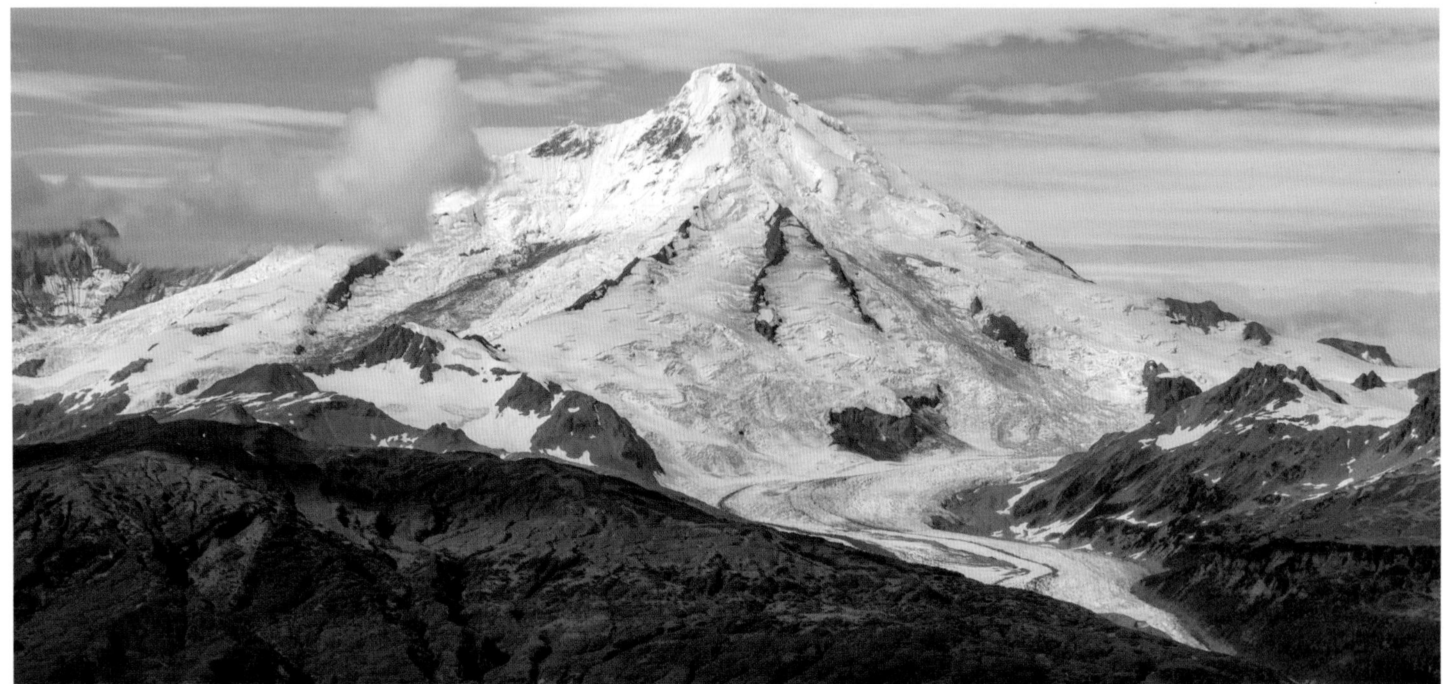

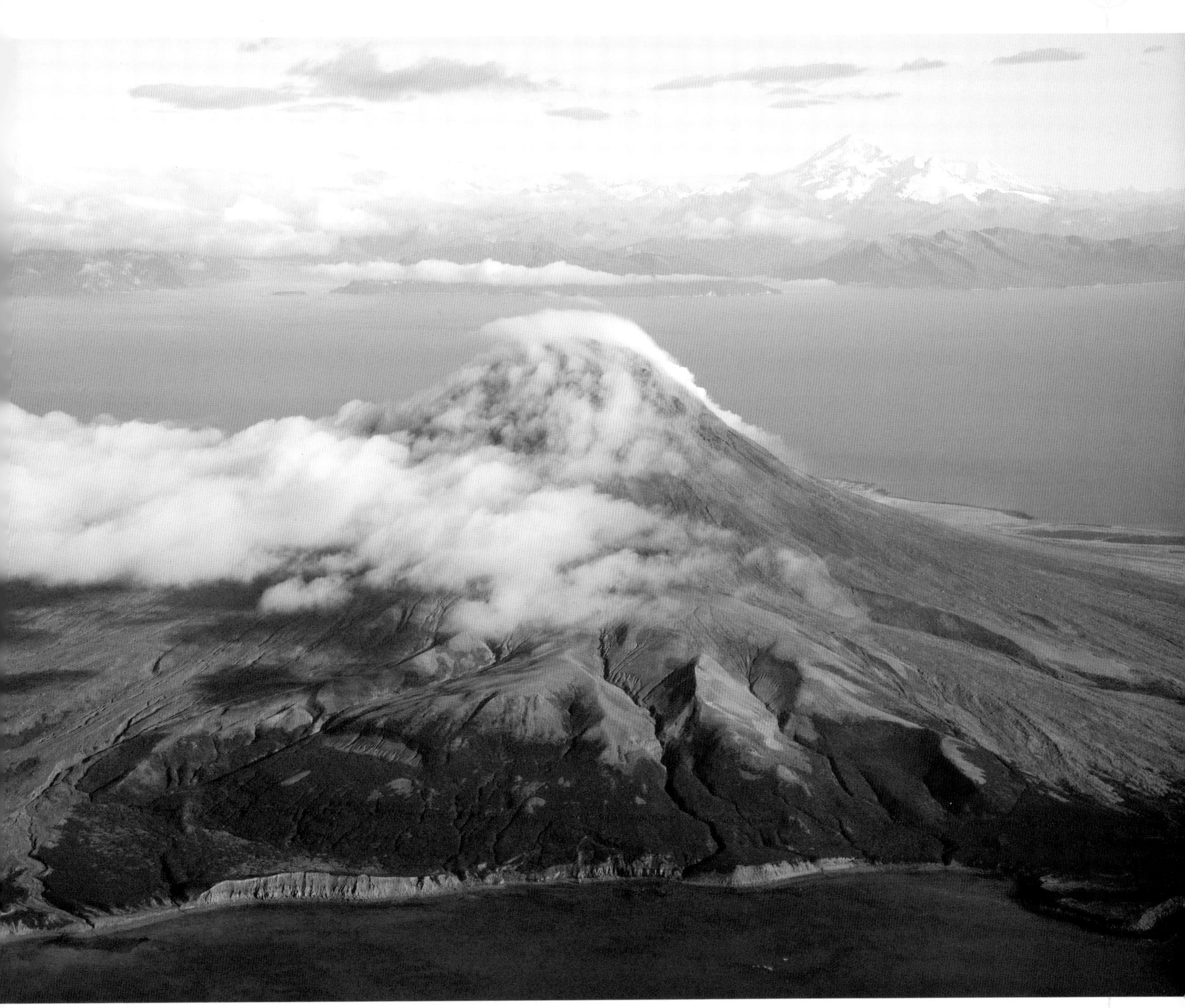

BASALT CLIFFS, KUKAK BAY, KATMAI NATIONAL PARK

Alaskan Peninsula

Lava flows from Mount Kukak (2,043 m/6,703 ft), cooling when it reaches the sea, solidifying into giant crystalline columns of basalt stone. Kukak is just one of eighteen volcanoes, including Katmai, after which the park is named, and Novarupta, in 1912 responsible for the biggest volcanic eruption of the twentieth century. Even so, life is mostly quiet here, the Katmai National Park being an important sanctuary for wildlife, and a great place for humans who like hiking, kayaking or fishing.

GRIZZLY BEAR, KATMAI NATIONAL PARK

Alaskan Peninsula

The river is wide but shallow here: not a bad place for a grizzly to try its luck. True, there are extensive areas of water on either side where the bear cannot possibly reach a passing fish, but if one *does* come close it will not be swimming very deep. Big and powerful as a bear may be, it is not equipped for catching fish. That is why the spectacle has such charm for us. While the quicksilver forms of the salmon slip by, it bounces and plunges, the picture of ineptitude – until, at last, it wins its lottery.

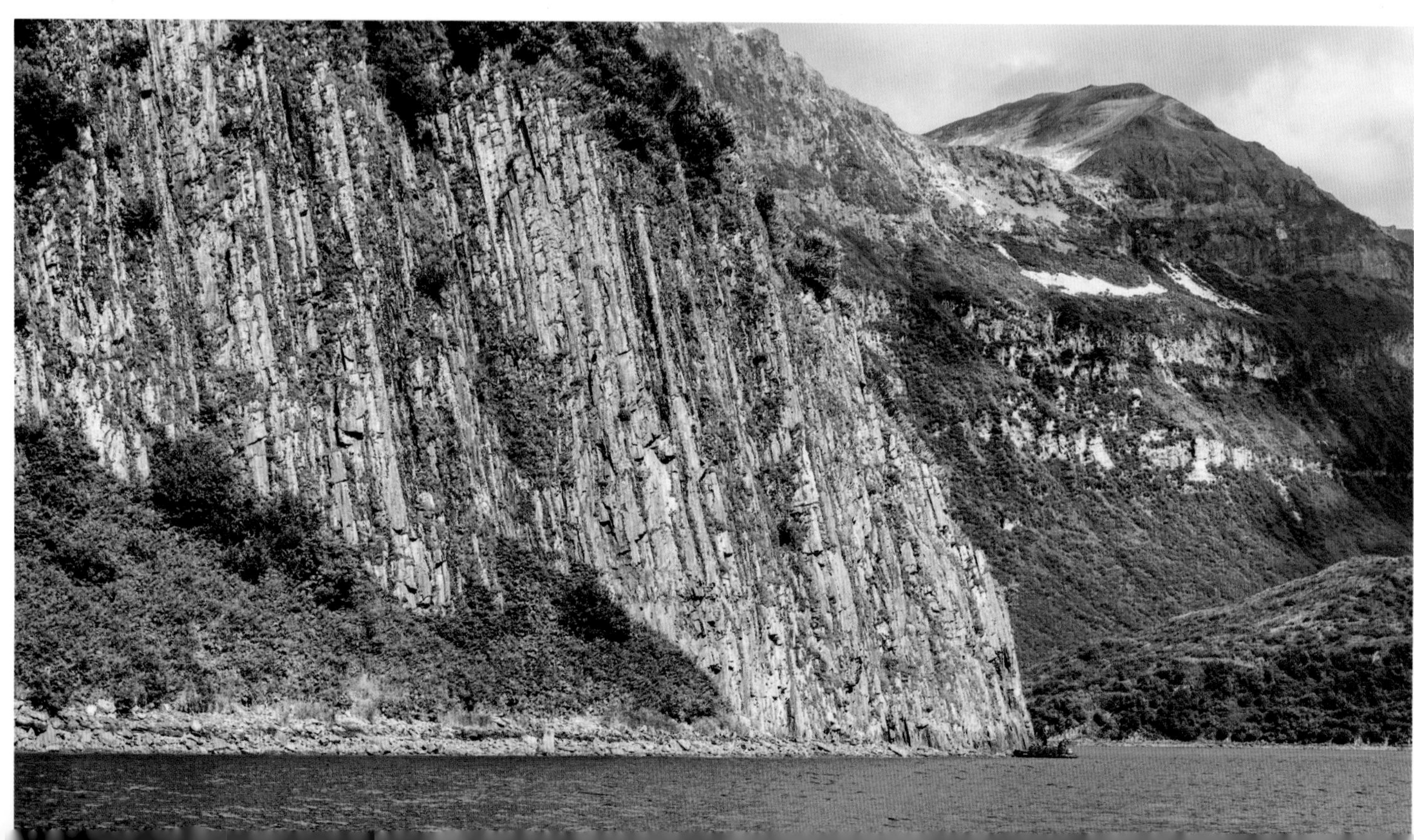

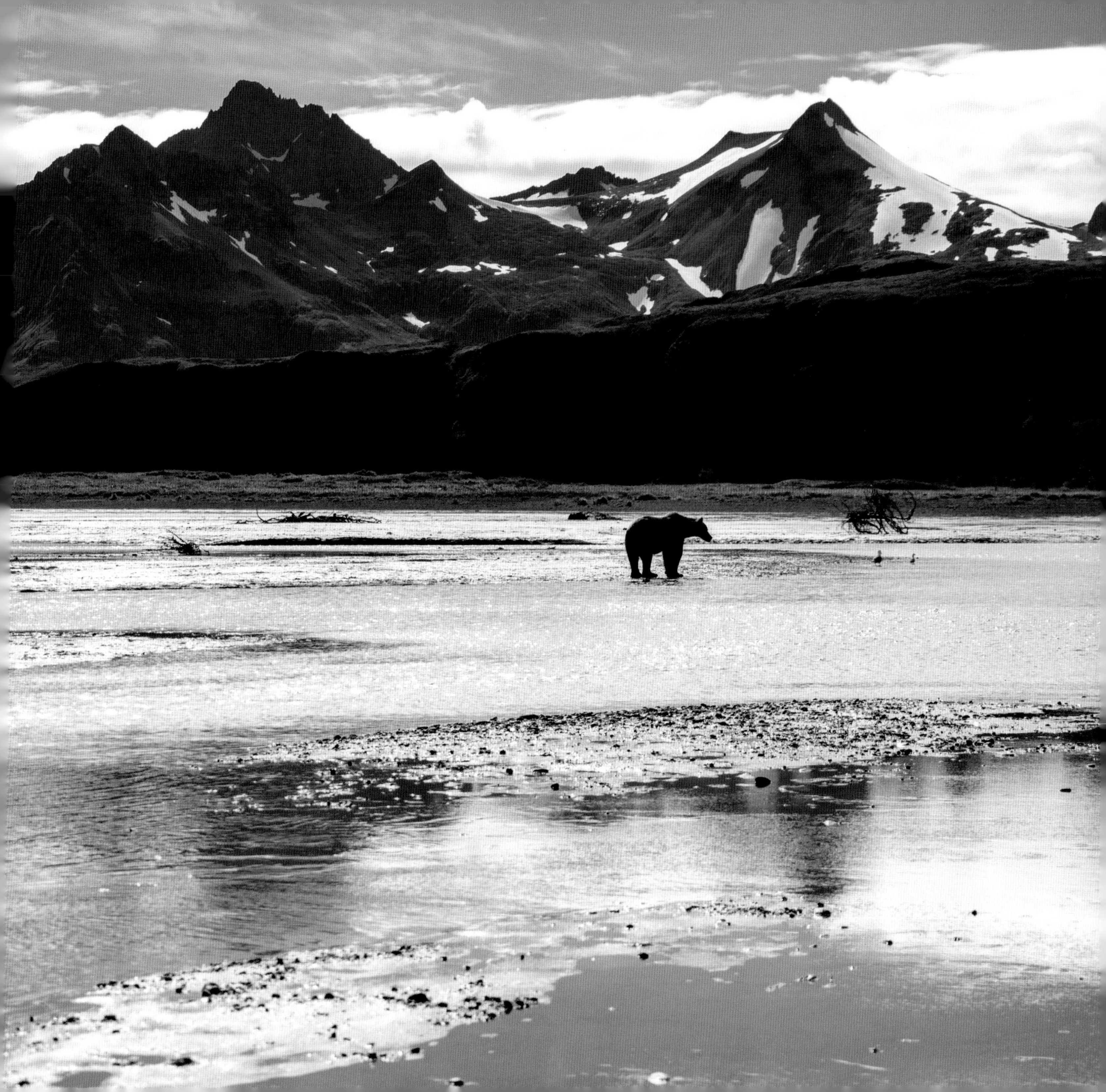

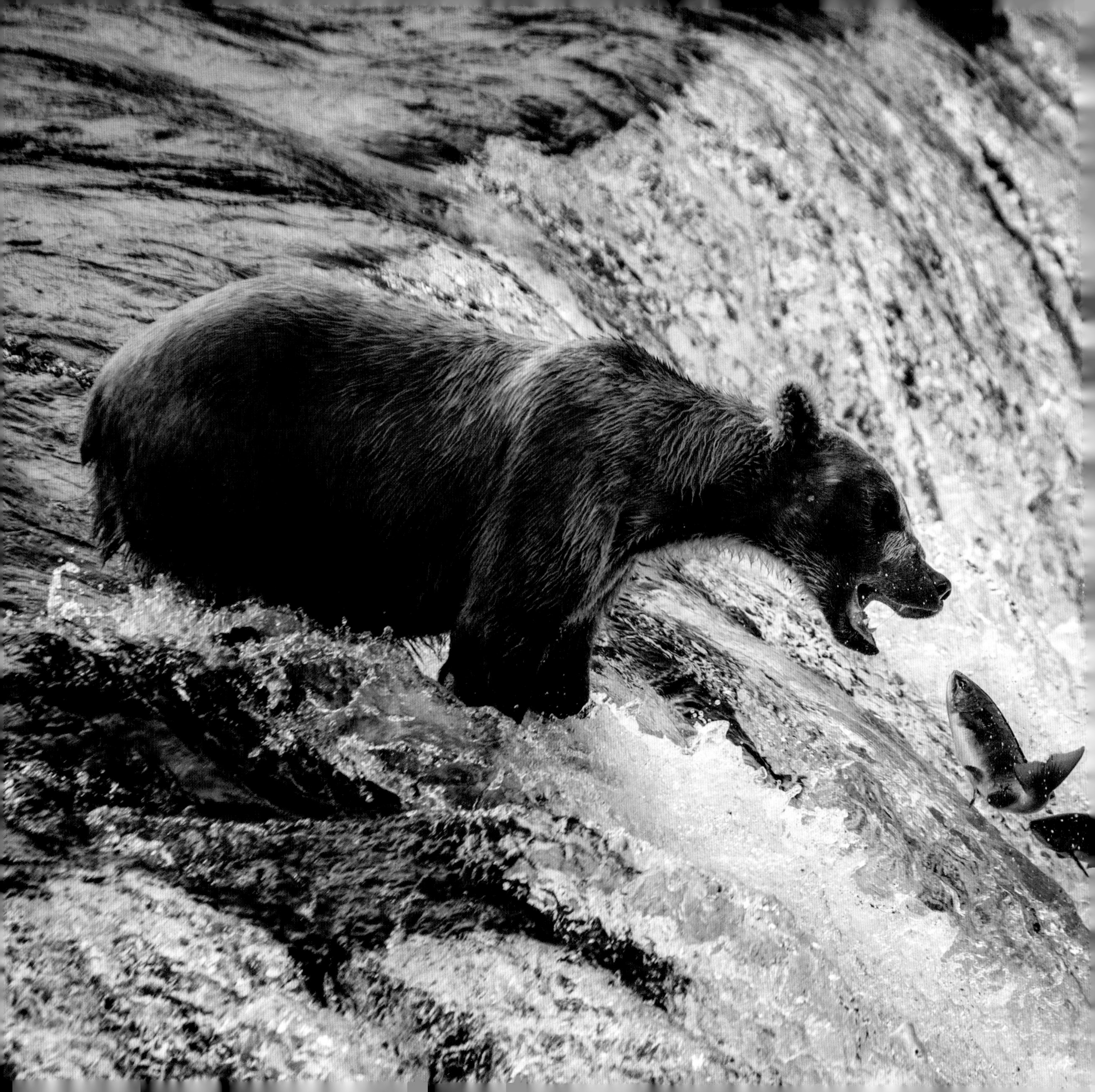

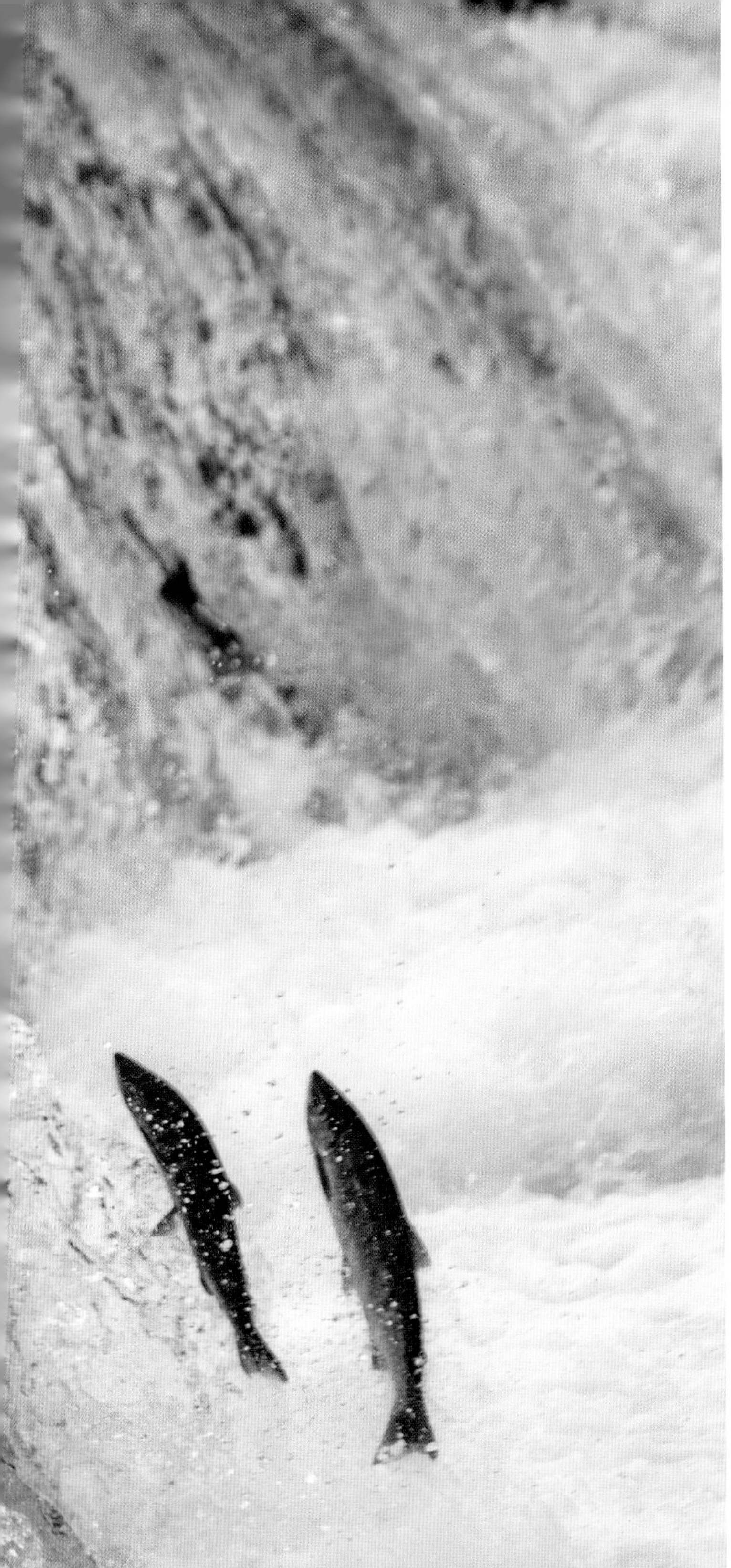

BROWN BEAR, BROOKS FALLS, KATMAI NATIONAL PARK

Alaskan Peninsula

If only it could always be this easy: a brown bear opens welcoming jaws to a leaping salmon. This sight is what makes the Brooks Falls famous. July is the best time to watch the salmon make the 1.8 m (6 ft) jump up the falls, with reports of up to 25 bears congregating here at a time during this month. The fish are driven by a powerful instinct to seek out the quiet pools of Brook Lake, 2.4 km (1½ miles) upriver, where they'll breed.

HIDDEN HARBOR, KATMAI NATIONAL PARK

Alaskan Peninsula

From the air, we can see clearly how, narrowing to what seems its innermost end, Kinan Bay opens out again to reveal what is literally a hidden harbour. It was 'discovered' in 1919 by Robert Fiske Griggs (1881–1962), who had made his life's work the study of the ecological impact of the great Novarupta eruption in Katmai. Griggs' work was not just important in itself: the regular bulletins he wrote for *National Geographic* magazine caught the public imagination, and kindled interest not just in Katmai, but also in the environment at large.

VALLEY OF 10,000 SMOKES, KATMAI NATIONAL PARK

Alaskan Peninsula

Robert F. Griggs (*see* left) gave this valley its arresting – if melodramatic – name. In the years following Novarupta's eruption, it does seem to have exuded steam from many hundreds of small fissures. That is no longer the case, though you would hardly describe this place as normal. Even so, life – and erosion – must go on. A stream has cut a little valley for itself through the crinkled, cooled remains of an ash flow here. Above are snow- and glacier-covered heights.

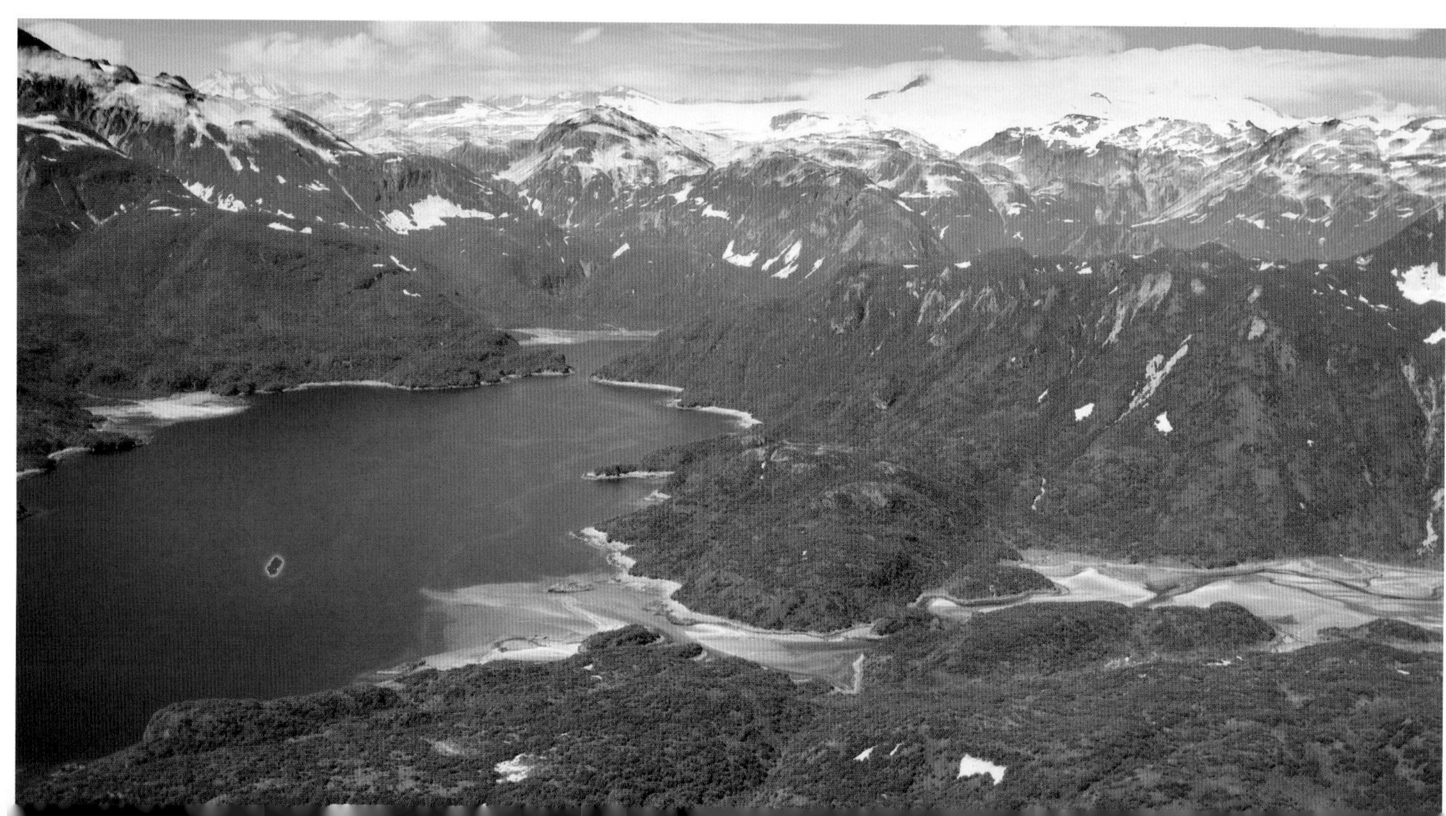

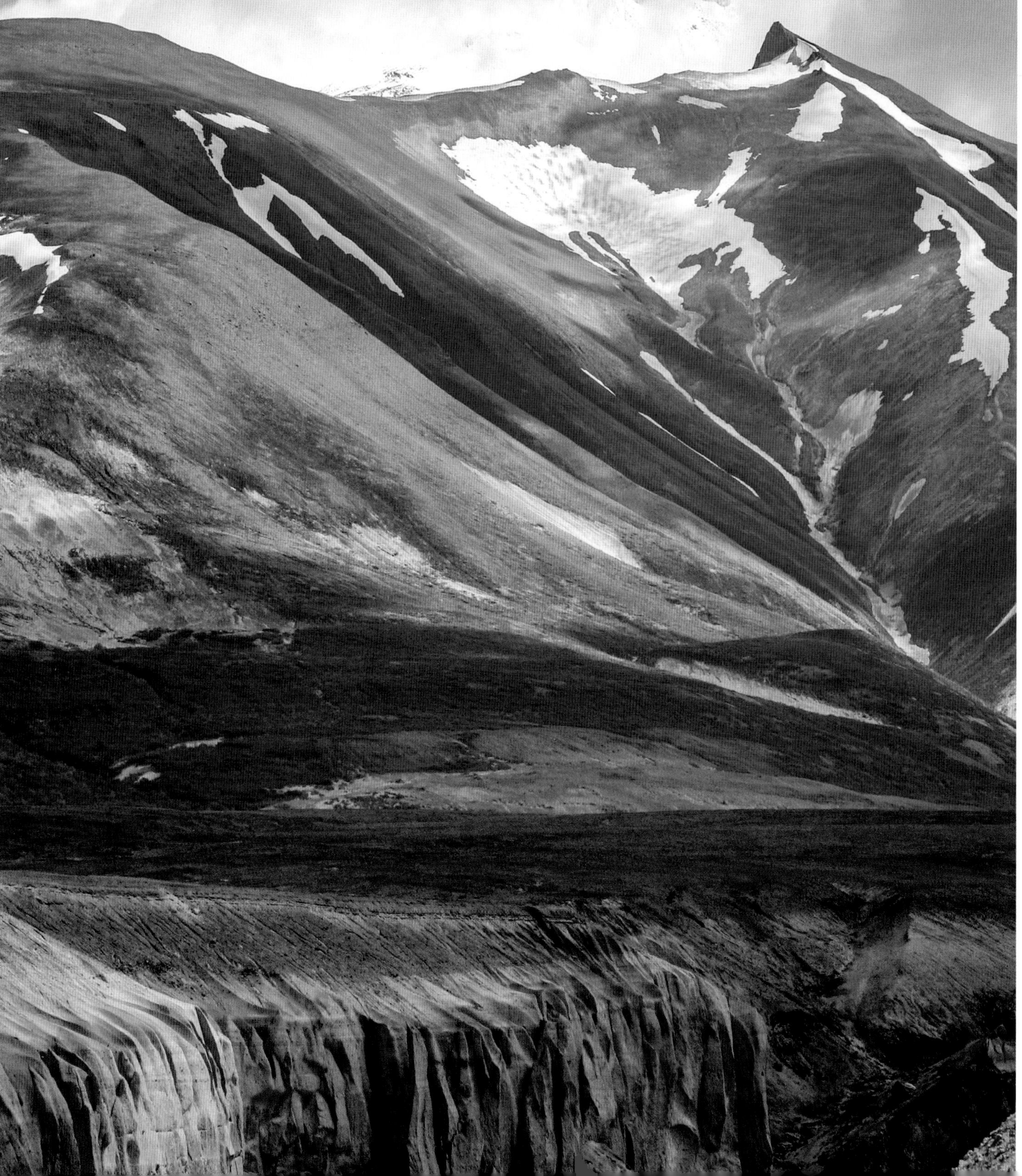

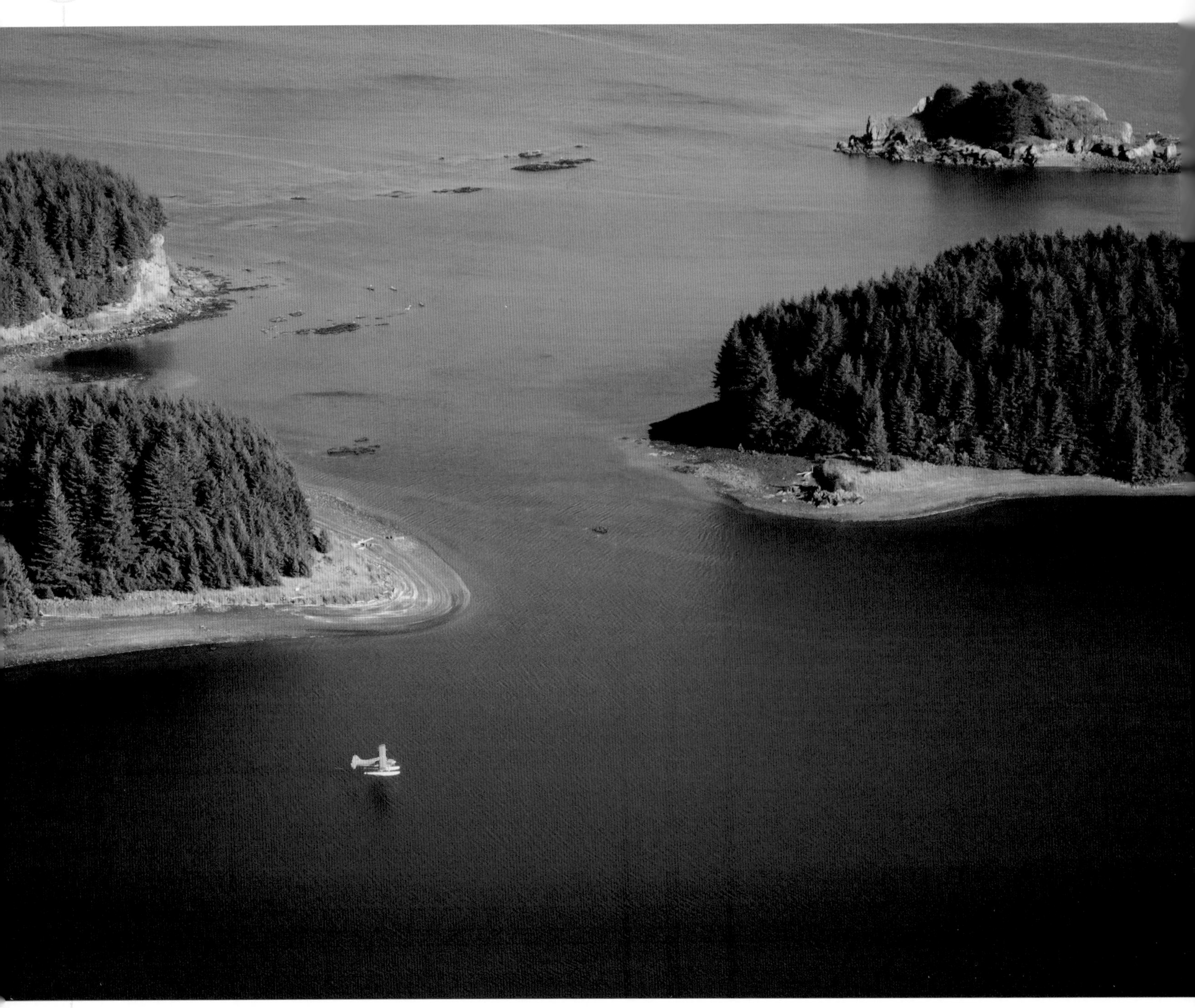

KODIAK BAY

Kodiak Archipelago

A floatplane begins its take-off run at the Trident Basin Seaplane Base, off Kodiak. Many thousands of passengers are served each year, whether with scheduled or with taxi-charter flights. Exotic as they might seem, seaplanes are very much part of the daily scene in Kodiak, where (as in much of Alaska) they are by far the most practicable way of getting around. It is really by no means unusual up here for homes or communities to be days away from their nearest roads. This is frequently the only means of transport that makes sense.

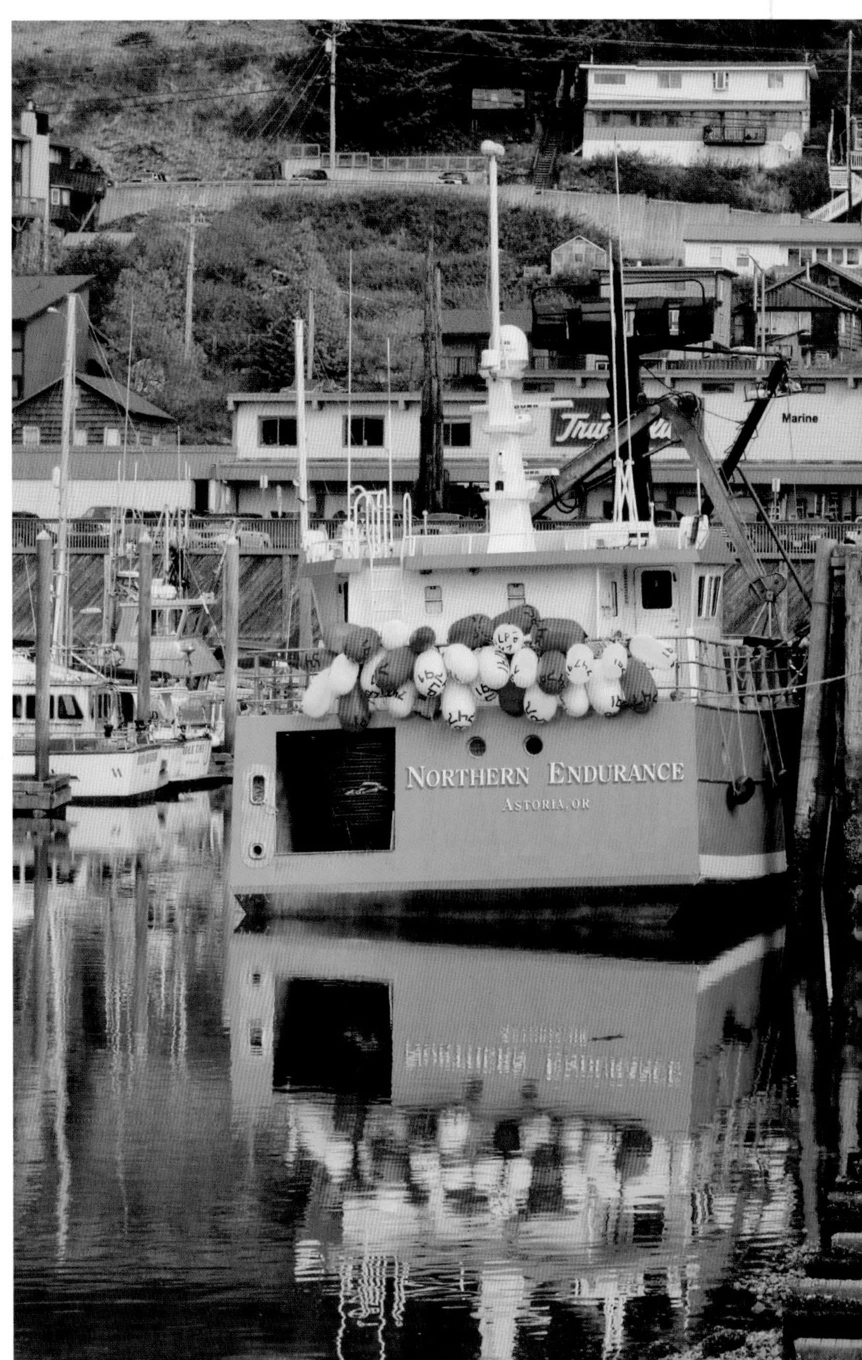

KODIAK HARBOR

Kodiak Archipelago

With tourism very much on the rise, you could not say that commercial fishing was Alaska's only major industry, but it is certainly an extremely important one. In recent years, the state's fishery has been the United States' largest, landing five times the volume and three times the value of its nearest rival. (The distinction matters: the most *profitable* US port remains New Bedford, Massachusetts.) The boats in this harbour may be small, but Kodiak is, by size of catch, among the biggest US fishing ports, second only to Dutch Harbor (*see* page 185).

KITTIWAKES, ST. GEORGE ISLAND

Pribilof Islands

St. George was the first of the Pribilof Islands to be discovered: Russian navigator Gavriil Pribylov (d. 1796) sighted it from his ship, the *St. George*, in 1786. He had come here in search of the valuable northern fur seal – and he found it (these were long referred to as the Northern Fur Seal Islands). Half the world's breeding population still live here. As, perhaps more visibly, do three quarters of its red-legged kittiwakes (*Rissa brevirostris*), alongside many thousands of the (much more common) black-legged kittiwake (*Rissa tridactyla*).

HORNED PUFFINS, ST. GEORGE ISLAND

Pribilof Islands

A little tag of dark flesh pointing upwards above each eye gives *Fratercula corniculata* its distinctive 'horned' appearance – and its faintly comic, fed-up air. Their peremptory manner is perhaps forgivable: St. George is bird world; people are emphatically outnumbered on an island with an estimated 2 million seabirds to around a hundred humans. In all, at one time or another, more than 300 different bird species have been recorded on the Pribilof Islands, many of them more closely associated with Asia than the Americas.

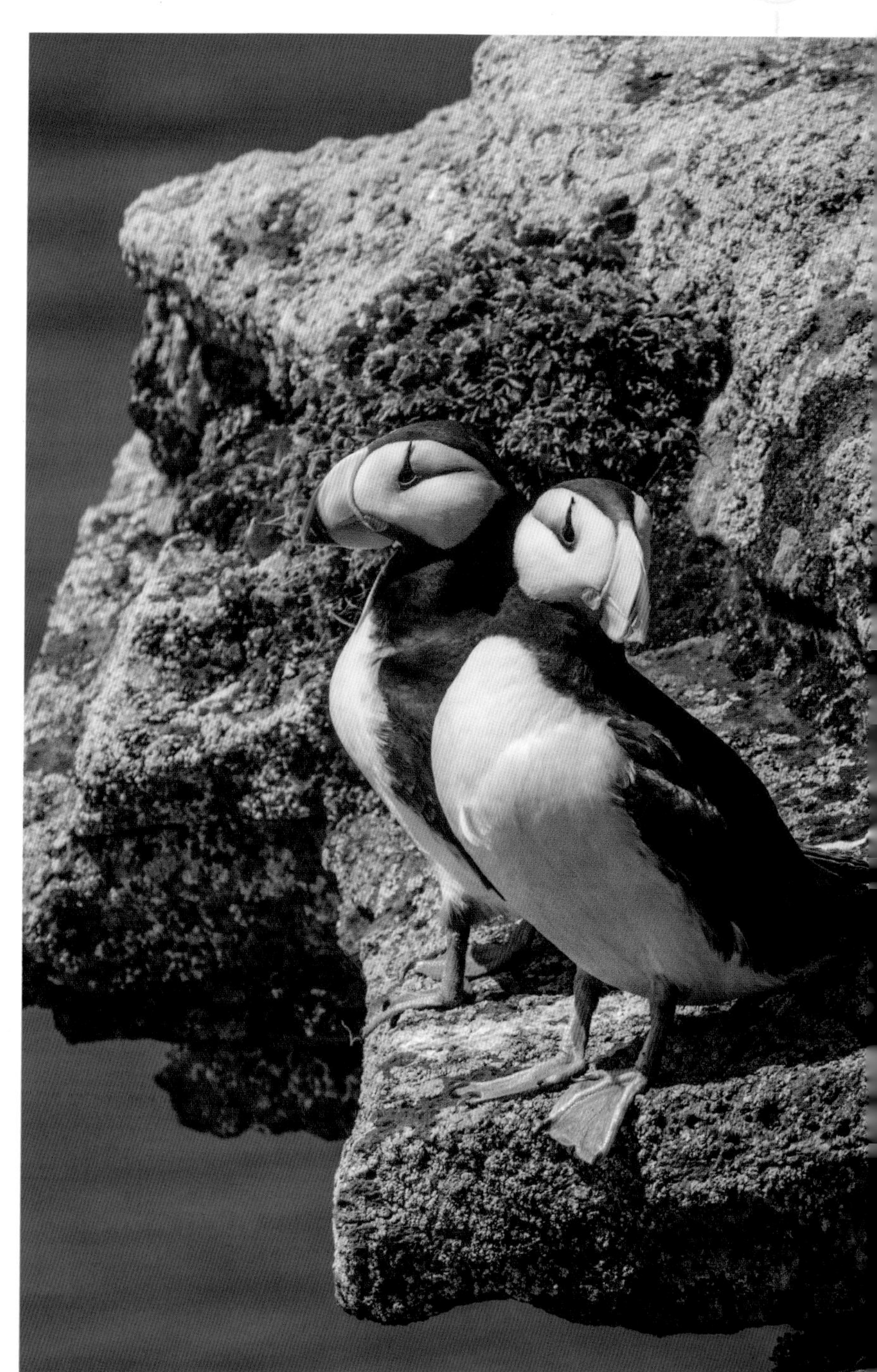

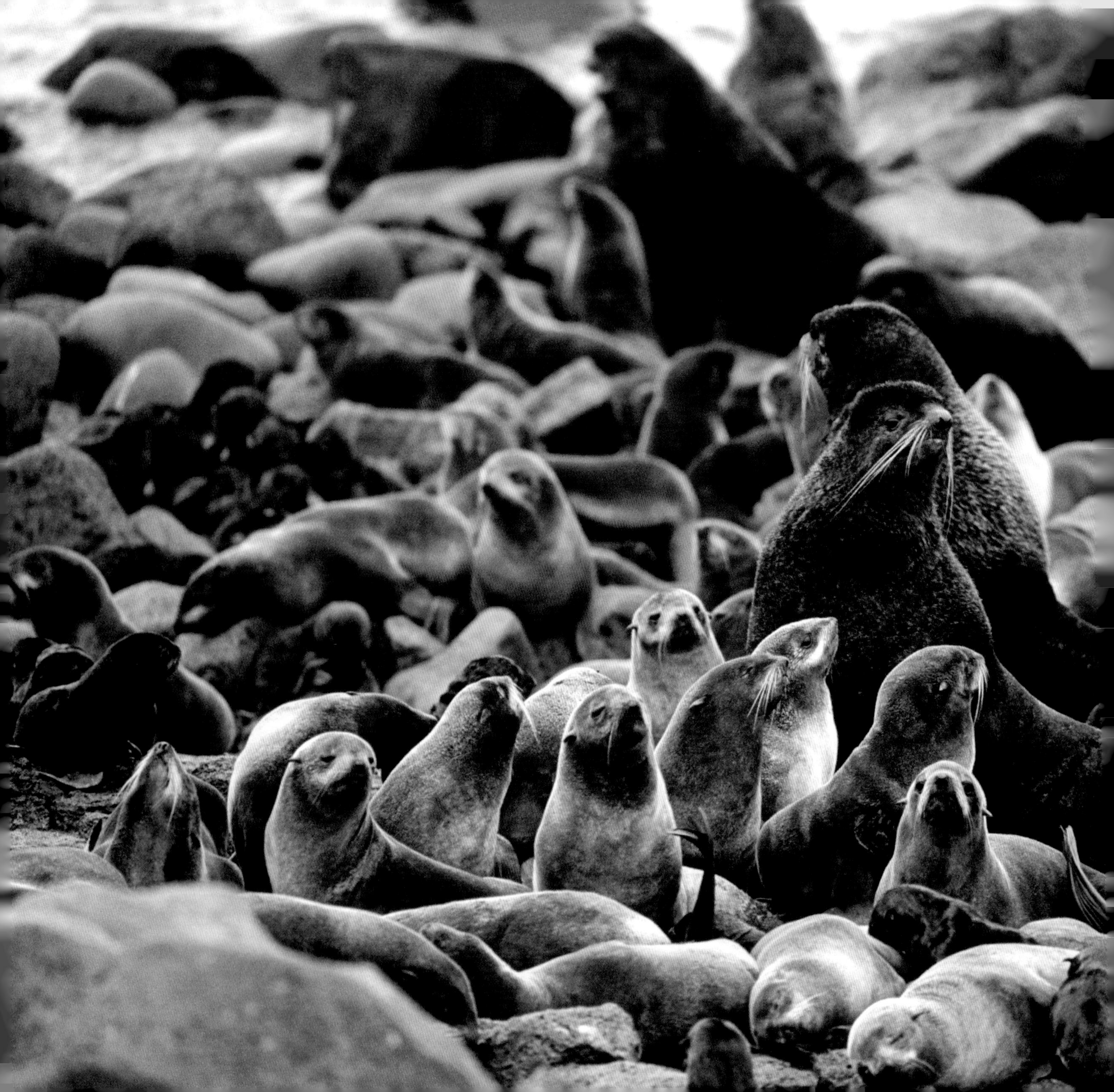

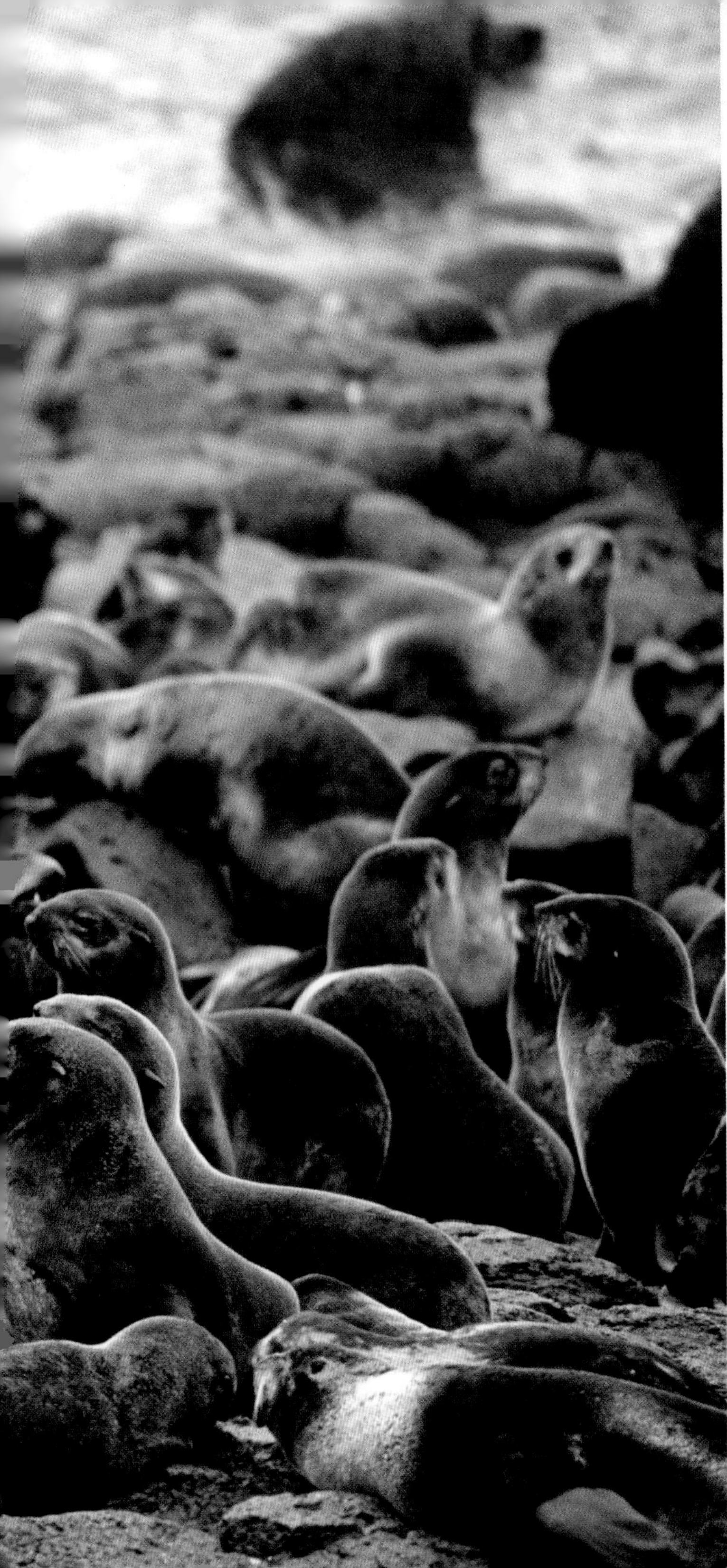

NORTHERN FUR SEALS, ST. PAUL ISLAND

Pribilof Islands

Their pelts a precious commodity, northern fur seals were an important prize for eighteenth-century Russian traders and trappers in the Aleutians. Since it had been noticed that the animals went off somewhere to the north each year and came back with young, the location of their breeding grounds became a holy grail. It was to be Pribylov who found it (*see* page 178). In those days there were some 4 million northern fur seals here. A century of slaughter saw these stocks catastrophically reduced, though they have stabilized under strict protection in recent decades.

COASTLINE

Aleutian Islands

Like a slowly fading memory of the United States, the Aleutians extend ever-westward out into the ocean, becoming more barren, less obviously Alaskan as they go. Tree-cover diminishes: the more exposed they are, the more immediately they bear the brunt of savage storms blowing in from the North Pacific and the Bering Sea. Yet archaeologists point to 10,000 years of human occupation, and to times when this was not quite the backwater it now seems. No great Romes or Babylons, but evidence that, linking Asian and American spheres, this was something of a commercial and cultural crossroads.

SHISHALDIN VOLCANO, UNIMAK ISLAND

Aleutian Islands

Like some Alaskan Fuji, Shishaldin rises 2,857 m (9,373 ft) high above Unimak. Strikingly symmetrical, its shapely summit is, if anything, even more perfect than the iconic Japanese mountain's: everyone's idea of what a volcanic peak should be. It does not, of course, have the advantage of being visible from one of the world's greatest cities: Unimak may be the biggest island of the Aleutian chain, but its population stands at around 60. By way of contrast, in the foreground here we see another of Unimak's volcanoes. Mount Isanotski is also known as 'Ragged Jack'.

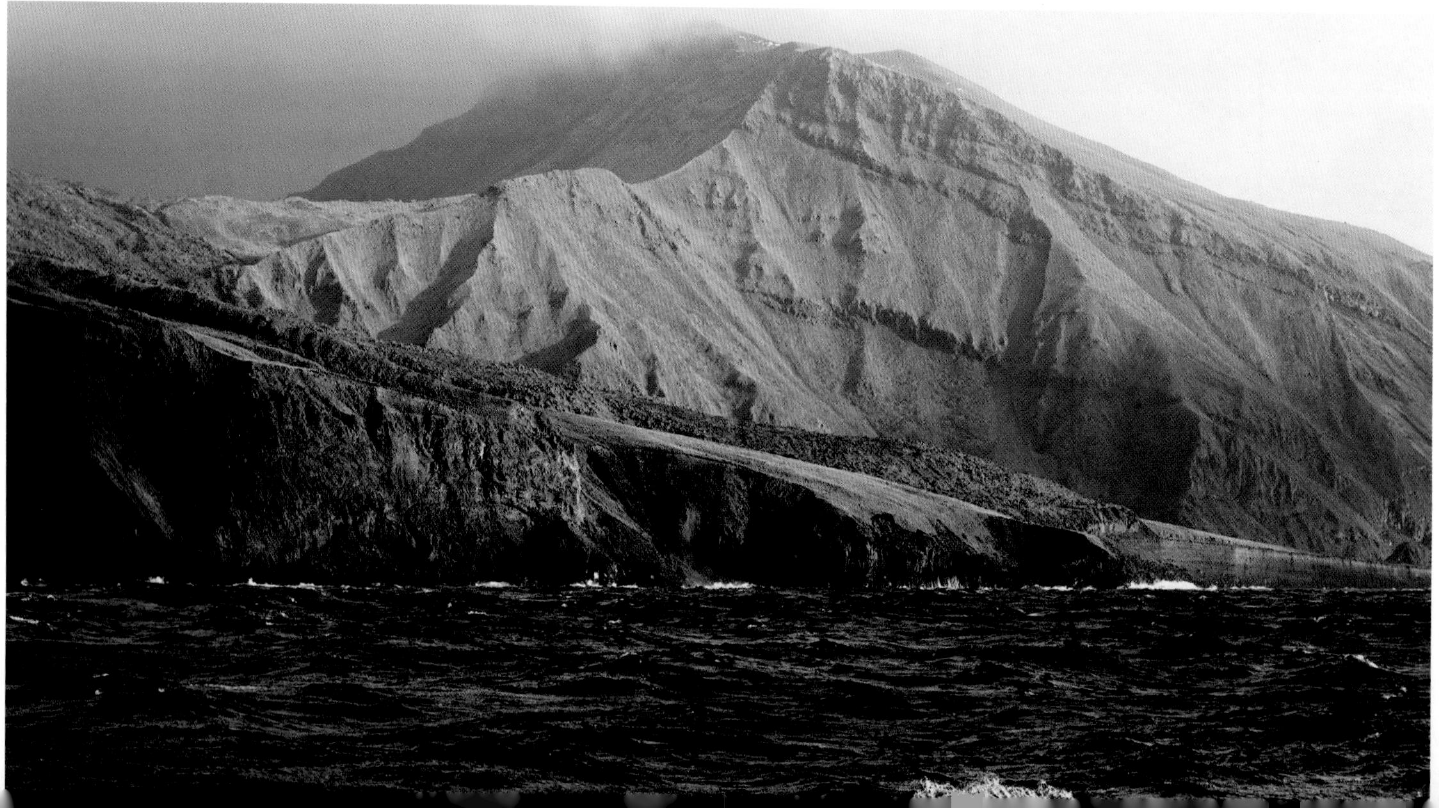

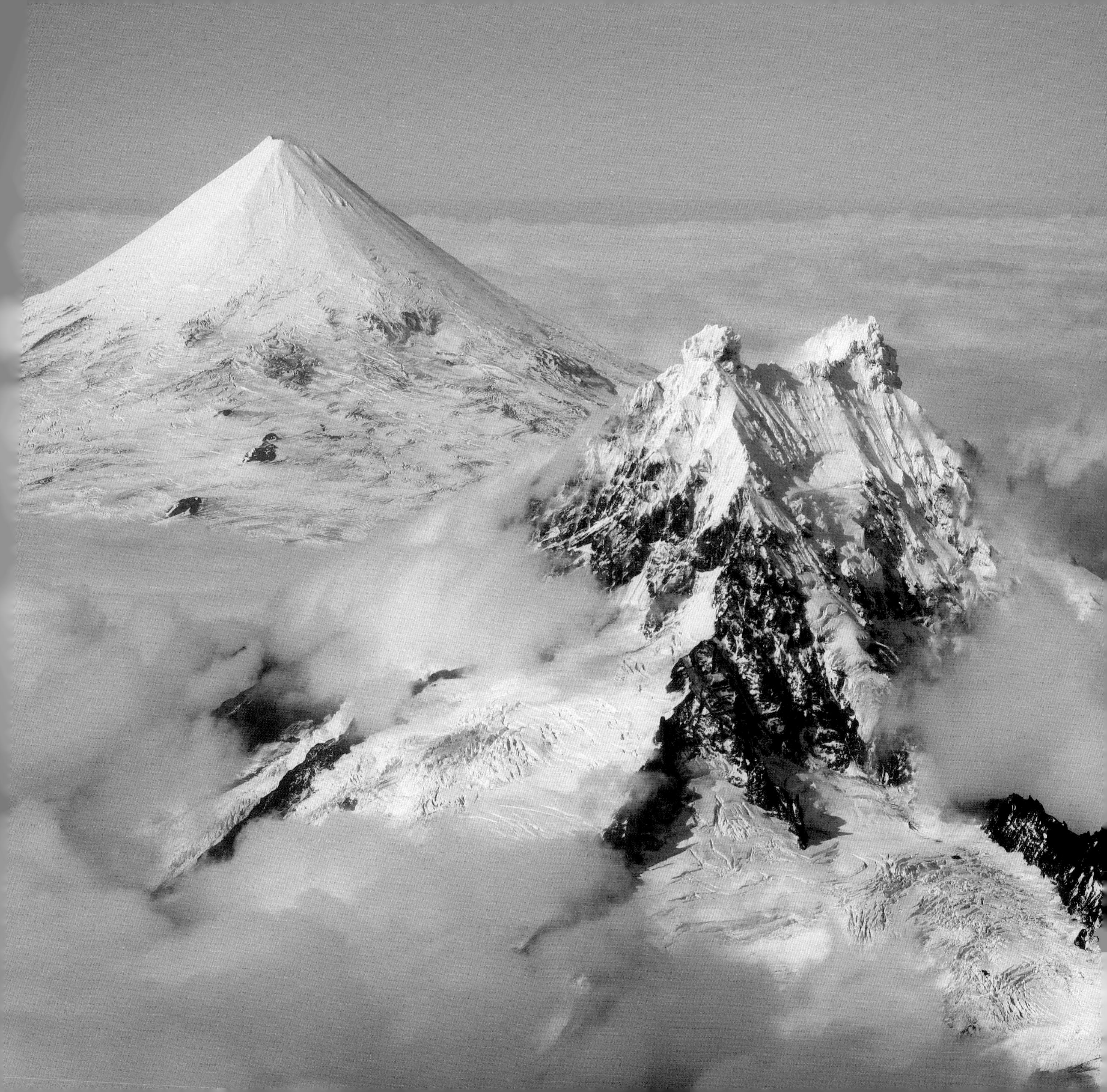

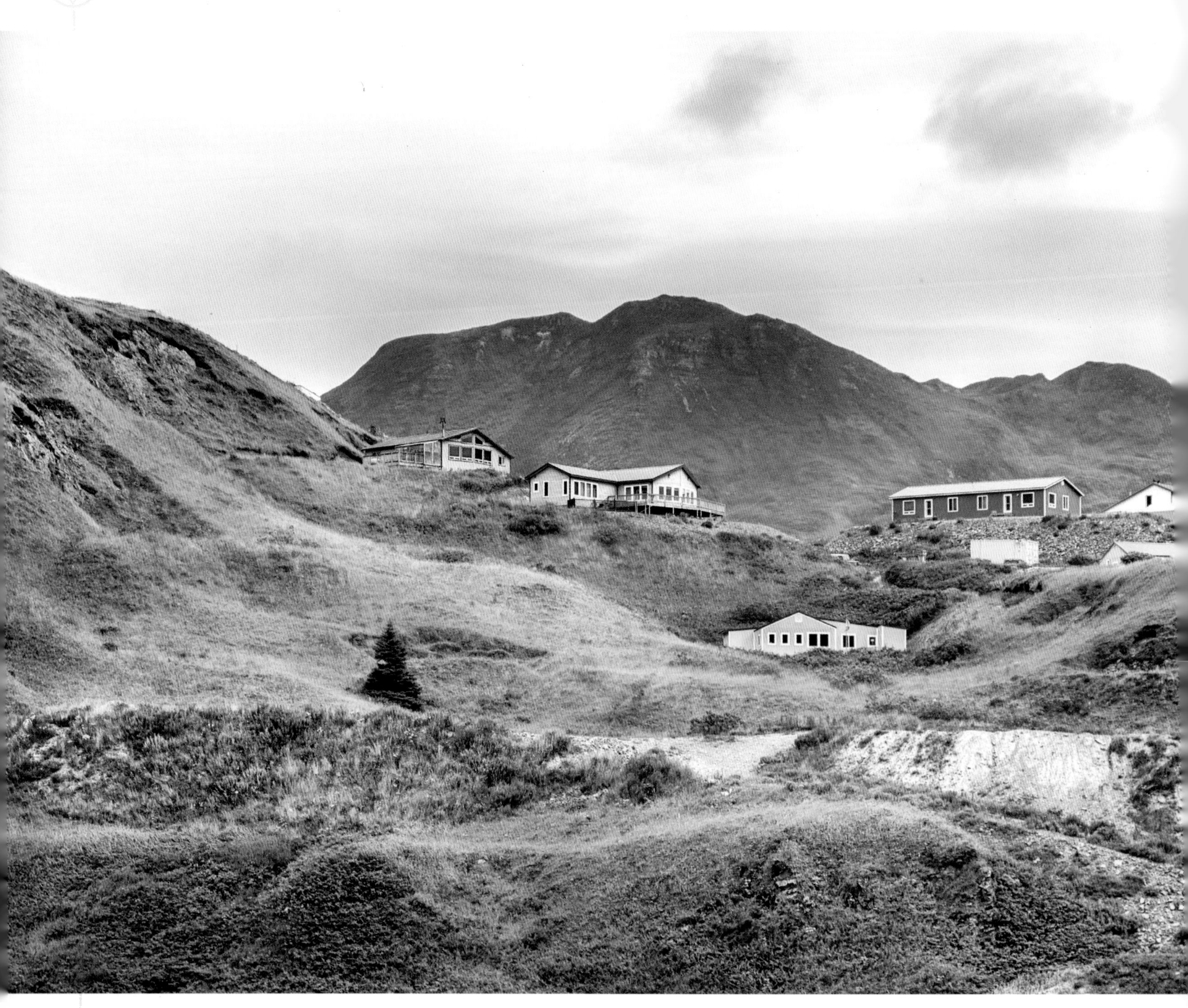

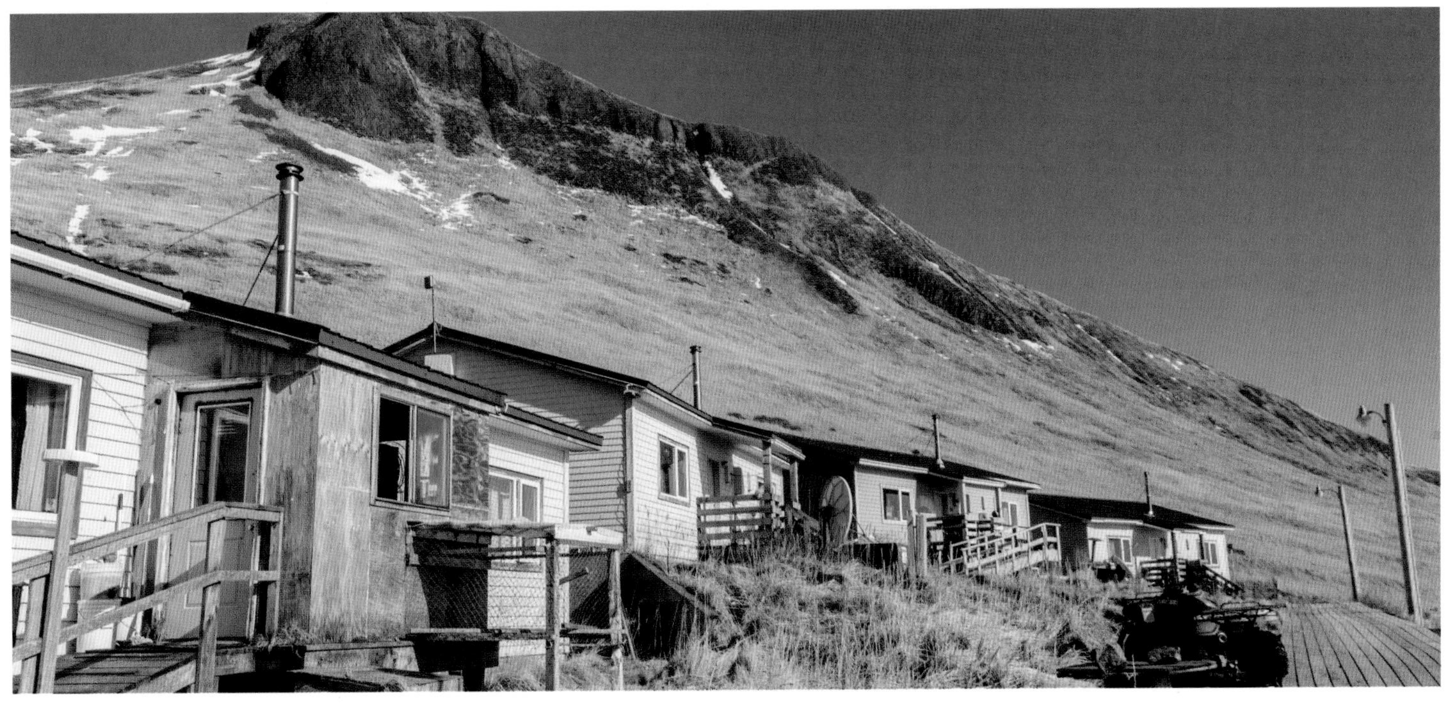

HOUSES, AKUTAN ISLAND

Aleutian Islands

Basic, functional housing for a basic, functional kind of place. This is not California or the Caribbean. The endless-seeming storms of winter do let up in spring, but only to usher in a summer of mist and rain. And yet you cannot contest the island's immense beauty. Akutan has a registered population of just over a thousand, though only a small proportion of these people live here year-round. Just about all are concentrated in Akutan town, a fishing village at the eastern end of this island, 30 km (18 miles) across.

HAYSTACK HILL, DUTCH HARBOR, UNALASKA

Aleutian Islands

In addition to being the United States' leading fishing port (*see* page 177), Dutch Harbor has the dubious distinction of having been the first US city to be bombed – by the Japanese in June 1942. Coming six months after the Pearl Harbor attack (and three weeks after supposedly secret Japanese communications had successfully been intercepted) this air raid did not come as a complete surprise. US Marines were dug in on hillsides all around. Today, the lower slopes of Haystack Hill have a peaceful, slightly suburban look.

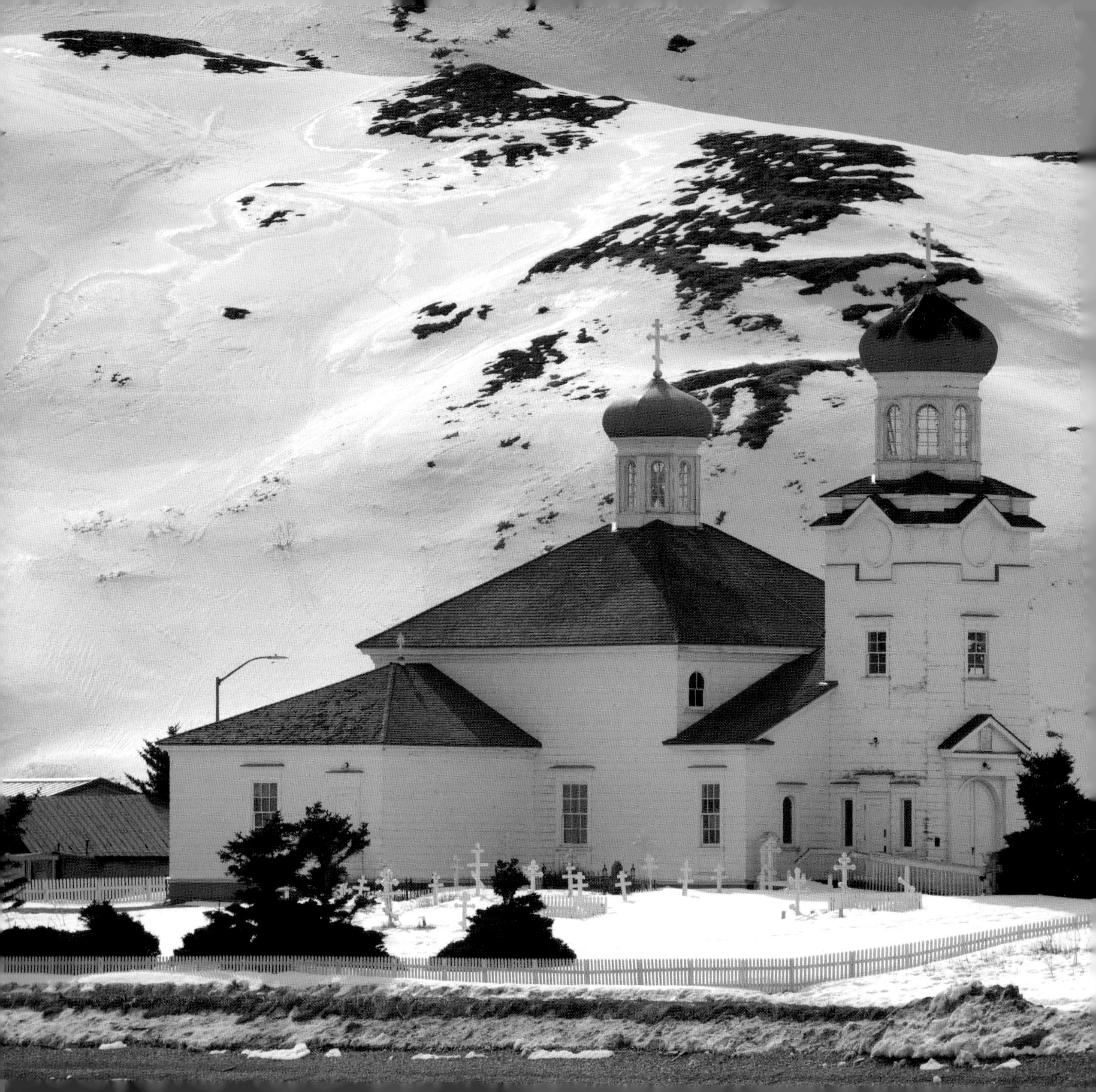

CHURCH OF THE HOLY ASCENSION, DUTCH HARBOR, UNALASKA

Aleutian Islands

There has been a Russian Orthodox church on this site for 200 years: the present building dates from 1898. An alien creed it may have been, but – as in Eklutna (*see* page 98), Kenai (*see* page 115) and elsewhere – this brand of Christianity established a strong spiritual hold over the Aleut population, becoming key to their cultural identity. During the Second World War, the church fell into disrepair. The bulk of Unalaska's population had to be evacuated – long a backwater, their home was now in the front line. It has been extensively refurbished since.

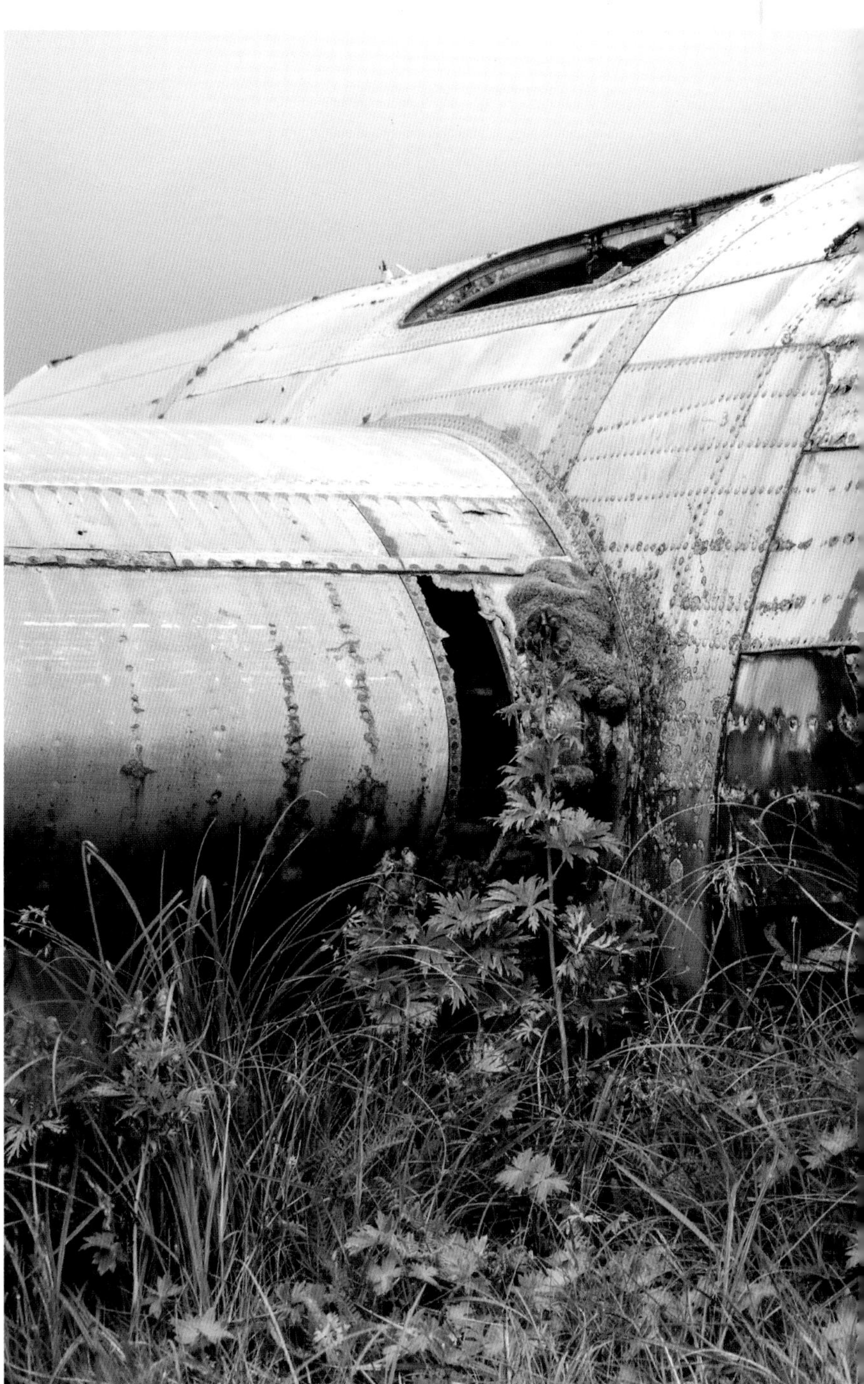

WRECK OF B-24, ATKA

Aleutian Islands

The B-24 came down on this open Atka hillside on 9 December 1942. It was ditched deliberately: so bad was the weather that this heavy bomber (ironically on weather reconnaissance) could not find an airstrip. Thanks to the skill and courage of its crew, no one was badly hurt. There it has remained, slowly rusting, since. In 2019, in association with selected sites in the Aleutians, Hawaii and California, the wreck was designated part of a new World War II Valor in the Pacific National Monument.

ADAK ISLAND

Aleutian Islands

Winds of up to 200 km/h (125 mph) have been recorded on this island. At Force-17-plus, that is literally off the Beaufort Scale. No tree could stand such treatment. Adak's predominant vegetation type is tundra, its beauty emphatically austere. And yet, that it *is* beautiful – exhilaratingly so – cannot be denied. While, as elsewhere in the Aleutians, an originally volcanic island was transformed by glaciation, the action of the waves has produced everything from sandy beaches to sheer 760 m (2,500 ft) cliffs.

MASSACRE BAY, ATTU

Aleutian Islands

The bleakness of this scene is perhaps exacerbated by the power of pathetic fallacy: no place with a name like this is going to seem enticing. In May 1943, US troops were landed here to retake the island from the Japanese: almost 2,500 of the defenders were killed (only 28 survived), as were over 549 American soldiers. But the bay had by this time already borne its dismal title for a couple of centuries: the name dates back to a 1745 attack on a Native village by Russian settlers.

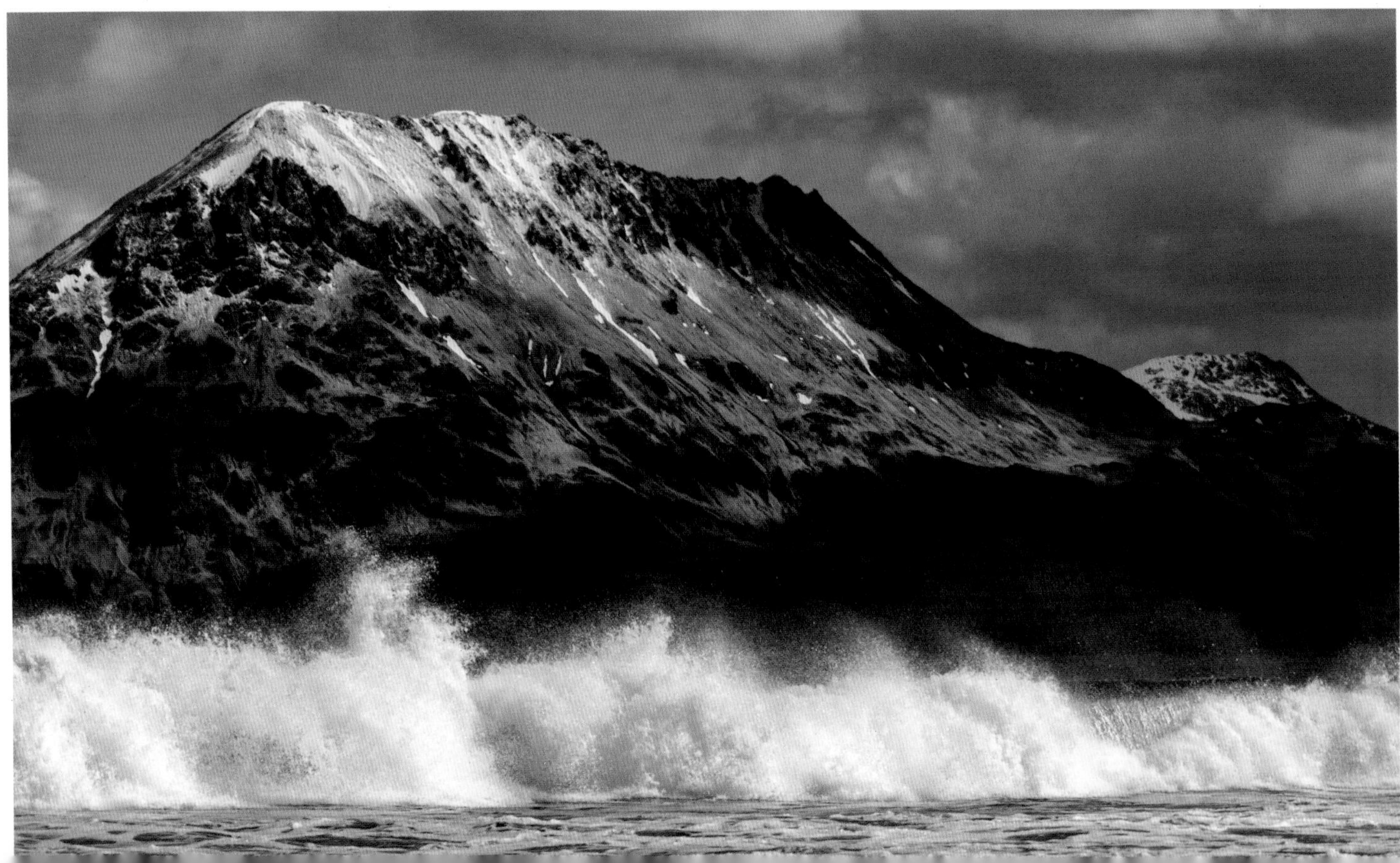

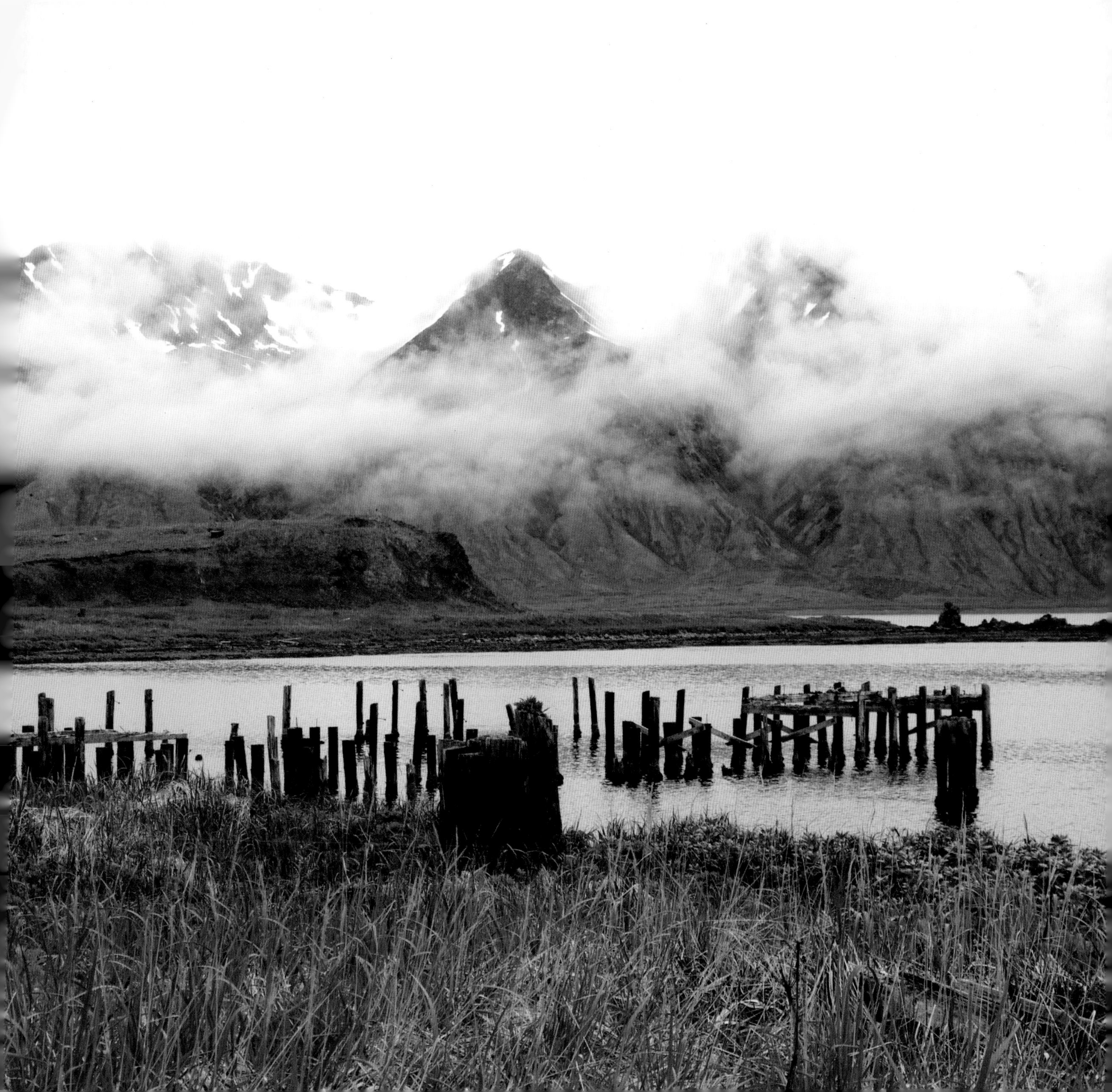

INDEX

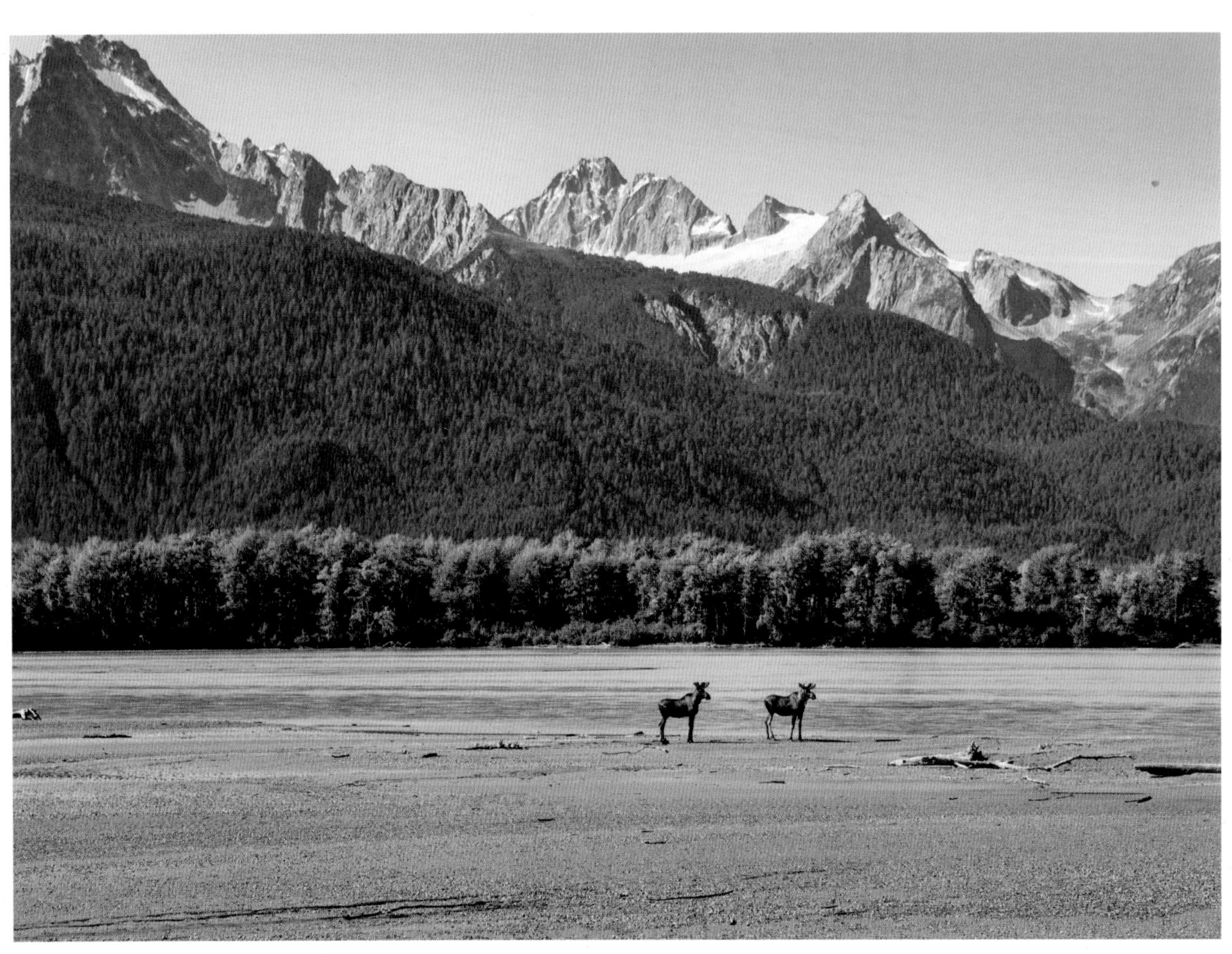